1987

The Drama Review
Thirty Years of Commentary on the Avant-Garde

Theater and Dramatic Studies, No. 35

Oscar G. Brockett, Series Editor

Leslie Waggener Professor of Fine Arts
and Professor of Drama
The University of Texas at Austin

Other Titles in This Series

The Drama Review
Thirty Years of Commentary on the Avant-Garde

Edited by
Brooks McNamara
and
Jill Dolan

UMI RESEARCH PRESS
Ann Arbor, Michigan

Chapter 26 reprinted from *The Drama Review*, Vol. 29, No. 1, Spring 1985 (T105), "The WOW Cafe" by Alisa Solomon, by permission of The MIT Press, Cambridge, Massachusetts. © 1985 by the Massachusetts Institute of Technology

Chapter 27 reprinted from *The Drama Review*, Vol. 29, No. 1, Spring 1985 (T105), "An Evening in the East Village: 30 November 1984," by permission of The MIT Press, Cambridge, Massachusetts. © 1985 by the Massachusetts Institute of Technology

Chapter 28 reprinted from *The Drama Review*, Vol. 29, No. 2, Summer 1985 (T106), "The Wooster Group's *L.S.D. (...Just the High Points...)*" by Arnold Aronson, by permission of The MIT Press, Cambridge, Massachusetts. © 1985 by the Massachusetts Institute of Technology

Produced and distributed by
UMI Research Press
an imprint of
University Microfilms, Inc.
Ann Arbor, Michigan 48106

Library of Congress Cataloging in Publication Data

The Drama review.

(Theater and dramatic studies ; no. 35)
1. Experimental theater. I. McNamara, Brooks.
II. Dolan, Jill, 1957- , III. Drama review. IV. Series.
PN2193.E86D73 1986   792'.022   86-11316
ISBN 0-8357-1746-1 (alk. paper)

Contents

Foreword

During the years covered by this volume, the American theatre developed a true and vital avant-garde. A theatre grew that began to partake of aesthetic concerns and formal strategies reflecting not only the exploratory theatrical thinking of the times, but also opening one art form most often "behind the times" to winds of change blowing from artistic disciplines other than the strictly theatrical.

The Drama Review has been, for the past thirty years, the primary documentary source and often the catalyst for that slow mutation. Under Richard Schechner and then Michael Kirby, the magazine has been a primary source of information, a goad to further exploratory effort, and a place from which to steal ideas, which all strong artists unabashedly do on occasion. For myself, *The Drama Review* has been a major source of contact with all that is most vital in the contemporary theatre.

And how the theatre has changed during that period! My own love/hate relation with the theatre might indeed have ended up on the hate side of the ledger had it not been for that "imaginary community" which *The Drama Review* brought into existence in the sixties and which continues until now as the peer group to which so many of us, relatively isolated in our work, turn for occasional regrounding and encouragement in the terribly important yet in fact marginal work of trying to keep some sort of alternative consciousness operating in the theatrical marketplace.

I cannot remember when I first encountered *The Drama Review,* but it must have been in the late fifties, during my college years. Like many of my generation, my first exposure to the notion that theatre could be anything but show business came through the work of Eric Bentley. Well—slight correction—I think my first whiff of something different came in the mid-fifties when, still in high school, I happened on a copy of Mordecai Gorelik's *New Theaters for Old* and for the first time in my life encountered the name of Brecht. I found the book in an art bookstore, which is significant in itself, since what developed in the experimental theatre in the later decades owed so much to its borrowing from the sensibilities of the art and dance world as opposed to an exclusively theatrical orientation. But after Gorelik's book had told me about a Brecht who based his theatre on something other than audience identification with actor, I was primed and ready for whatever exoticism I could lay my hands on.

Eric Bentley became my main source as I entered college. He spoke of a European art theatre of which I, and most Americans, had never heard, a non-naturalistic theatre that seemed informed by poetry and painting and music. Of course, he spoke of Brecht, but also of the aestheticism of a Barrault, a Visconti, and of plays by the great contemporary dramatists of Europe, few of which were ever produced in New York. The series of plays he published through Indiana University Press must have opened many young minds to the literary possibilities of theatre. As a young playwright at Yale, studying under John Gassner, I spent a year masquerading as Brecht, a next year as Giraudoux, six months as Grabbe, and time as Lorca, Cummings, Buchner— all owing to the hypnotic fascination of a world made available to young would-be theatrical creators exclusively by Eric Bentley in those quite dark years of the late fifties.

Then I became aware of *The Drama Review,* and it seemed like the logical, European-oriented extension of Bentley's playwright-oriented view of serious contemporary theatre. The issue seemed to be that "serious" and complex and challenging plays did not get written in America (because of the pressures of the marketplace) and hence, one had to turn for inspiration to Europe, where state support and a more viable intellectual (aristocratic?) tradition allowed the birth of texts for the theatre that operated more fully within the other high literary traditions of the culture. The theatre was not show business but rather one other voice in an ongoing literary dialogue in which poets, novelists, philosophers, and playwrights participated on an equal footing. In France, for instance, Jean-Paul Sartre himself chose to write plays. And such plays could then enter the arena of thought in a way that seemed quite impossible for the works of a Miller or Williams in the United States. Miller and Williams had to be produced on Broadway and had to speak to an audience that had never heard of most contemporary philosophers and did not read Rimbaud or William Carlos Williams. The French playwright could speak to a smaller coterie, which then, if fashion nodded in approval, might gain a sort of fifties "pop" status in a society that seemed to take its artists seriously as thinkers and not as mere entertainers.

So many of us dreamed of a European-style theatre, and some few wrote "intellectual" plays, which made no real aesthetic impact. But a viable alternative theatre at least existed as a kind of university dream (which is not to belittle that dream).

Then the sixties happened. It seems fashionable in some circles today to dismiss that decade as childish, irresponsible, and naive. So be it. As far as I'm concerned it's the decade that saved our culture—it certainly saved me. I don't think I could have gone on living and producing in the very repressive, provincial, and well—sad atmosphere I grew up in during the fifties. And the real heroes of American culture were those lonely men of the fifties—all the Beats, Cage, Cunningham, the early Living Theater—who prepared the ground for what was to come, who planted the seeds that later bloomed. And I say that even though, ironically, I had no patience with the performer-oriented, Grotowski-style theatres that surfaced in that epoch, which in its American manifestations, mixed with encounter group sensibility, so dominated the experimental theatre of the time. Indeed, I began to make theatre myself less in reaction to the commercial Broadway theatre, and more in rebellion against the "downtown" theatre—which of course was championed by *The Drama Review* in the sixties under the editorship of Richard Schechner, who was also a leading exponent of environmental and Grotowski-oriented performance.

Even though I didn't find myself on that particular wave-length, how important it was! For it did change the face of the theatre and opened the doors to undreamt-of possibilities. It freed all of us who yearned for a post–ego psychological-sociological theatre from the necessity of thinking that the alternative was by definition European.

Of course, Grotowski was Polish. And of course Artaud entered the stage, and Brecht was still there. But the adolescent messiness, the unmediated demand for happiness and wholeness and transcendence that are, I would maintain, undeniably central parts of the American character structure, made a strong and shocking appearance on our stages. And it was logical, I think, that Schechner, who was so much a part of that movement as creator and as editor of the magazine in that crucial period, soon developed his own intellectual extratheatrical interests along the lines of anthropological concerns. For indeed, until then we had had a theatrical tradition (O'Neill, Miller, Williams) that invariably lent itself to analysis along the lines either of sociology or of that particularly Americanized form of Freudianism that Lacan so objected to—ego psychology. Now, a new form and content demanded new intellectual tools, and today the Richard Schechner under whom *The Drama Review* came to prominence is about to return to the helm of the magazine with a strong anthropological orientation that can be viewed as growing not only from Schechner's intellectual concerns, but also from the very roots of his own particular lust for the particular sort of theatre he wants to see on stage.

The same could be said of Michael Kirby, who took over from Schechner and like Schechner was a creator in his own right. While Schechner championed and created a theatre oriented toward commitment and content, Kirby's formalist interests echoed and supported the so-called visual theatre that emerged in the seventies. Since I am a part of that movement, and since *The Drama Review* was supportive of my work and indeed probably contributed to my acceptance on a broader scale than even I know (doing the same, no doubt, for Meredith Monk, Bob Wilson, and other children of that particular seventies orientation), I can't deny that I strongly identify with the magazine as it was under Kirby's editorship. As the winds of intellectual re-orientation swept through the West, the concerns of structuralism and deconstruction entered *The Drama Review*'s pages. One felt one was truly participating in that international discourse—just as the theatre that the magazine focused on in those years was in fact an American theatre that was an international theatre (and vice versa), since most of the artists discussed spent as much time creating and performing in Europe as in the United States.

This book appears in the second half of the eighties, which feels to more than one observer like a rerun of the fifties. The American theatre has come a long way in thirty years. The preeminent change, it seems to me, is that with the existence of a sort of avant-garde tradition, the notion of style has entered the American theatre. Style not as just an icing on the "real stuff" of content, but style as a possible root content, style as the constituting element of a world, as the perceptual control mechanism that coagulates into a certain set of possible problems to handle, as opposed to other problems that no longer surface given a particular style, permitting certain social-psychological configurations, denying others. Style is the person? Style is also the message, more often than not. Style is also the constituting element, through which problems arise and fade in all their glorious transience. Under Kirby's editorship, *The Drama Review* has helped greatly in leading the American theatre into awareness of this fact of aesthetic life. Now that Richard Schechner has returned to head the magazine, I also look forward with delight to what I suspect will be a re-assertion of a more polemical stance. I know that Richard Schechner will build upon the achievements of that more formalistically oriented consciousness to show us, in the neoconservative eighties, how artistic forms not only manipulate the mechanisms of individual consciousness, but re-orient the social body itself, so that the future, as well as the past and the present, are visible in our theatre.

Richard Foreman

Acknowledgments

An anthology like this one, which covers 30 years of the most important period in contemporary theatre and performance, includes the direct and indirect contributions of people too numerous to name individually. We would like to thank each of the authors who allowed us to share their writing once again, and the artists and companies about whom they write. Without these artists, and their enduring spirit of innovation, there would be no need for this book. The staff of *The Drama Review* over the past 30 years was a proving ground for many people who have since gone on to stake their claims in other areas of publishing and performance. All of them, in one way or another, contributed to the ongoing preeminence of *The Drama Review*. We would like to thank personally the people who have served as editors of *TDR*—Robert Corrigan, Richard Schechner, Ted Hoffman, Erika Munk, and Michael Kirby have each been influential in directing the editorial philosophies represented by the selections in these pages.

The current publishers of *TDR*, Dean David Oppenheim, of Tisch School of the Arts at New York University, and Journals Manager Christine Lamb, at MIT Press, have maintained their faith in the journal through times when its editorial style was as controversial as the material it covered. We appreciate their support. We would also like to thank Mel Gordon and Kate Davy, former associate editors of *TDR*, for their input in shaping the selections in this anthology. And finally, editorial assistant Andrea Stulman has been invaluable to the success of this project.

Introduction

TDR: Memoirs of the Mouthpiece, 1955-83
(1983)

Brooks McNamara

> *We are proud that* TDR *is the "mouthpiece of its editors." Who else should it speak for? Of what use is an anonymous voice?... The real question is: who and what are the editors the mouthpiece for?*
> "*TDR* Comment," Summer 1964

In the fall of 1963 I arrived at Tulane University in New Orleans to begin work on a Ph.D. Like many other graduate students who came to Tulane's theatre department during the '60s, I was attracted in no small part by the fact that the *Tulane Drama Review* was there. Less than a decade after its founding, *TDR* had become the country's leading liberal theatre magazine, with a list of contributors that read like a *Who's Who* of the progressive theatrical and critical establishments, among them Eric Bentley, William Arrowsmith, Morris Carnovsky, Henry Popkin, Francis Fergusson and Harold Clurman. But things were changing. Although I was not aware of it at the time, *TDR* was just then embarking on an editorial voyage of exploration which, over the next two decades, would lead it in some very different and very controversial directions.

In 1955, Robert Corrigan, a young professor of English and Drama at Carleton College in Northfield, Minnesota, had begun to issue *The Carleton Drama Review,* a journal designed to act as a record of a lecture series at the college. The lectures were given in conjunction with productions presented by the Carleton Players, and featured Corrigan himself and such luminaries of the day as George Kernodle. In a recent interview, Corrigan described the magazine's early history. "When I got to Carleton," he said, "they had a kind of in-house record called 'The Carleton Bulletin' which contained lists of all the casts and crews, plus a lecture that was given for each production. It was strictly an internal document. I inherited $250 as a budget to produce the bulletin, and it occurred to me that we might use it to start a real magazine. I figured that we could get 100 subscribers outside the college, so I sent out a mimeographed announcement, asking people to buy a subscription to *The Carleton Drama Review*—three issues for two dollars a year. I believe we sold 30 subscriptions that year."

Corrigan added: "The third issue became the first important one historically because of a kind of fluke. A few people began to hear about *The Carleton Drama Review* and were supportive. Eric Bentley and John Gassner both gave me articles for the third issue. We were in page proofs in the spring of 1957—we even had 64 subscribers—but by that time I had resigned from Carleton and was going to Tulane. I had had a bad tiff with the head of the English Department, and when he learned I was leaving, he was adamant that the issue not be published. I said, 'Okay, but I'm damned if I'm going to write to the contributors and the subscribers—and, by the way, you owe each of our

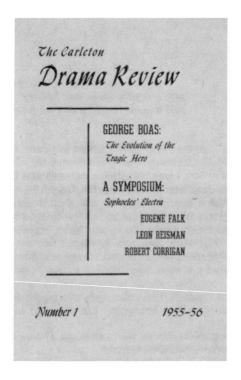

Robert Corrigan's first issue: "a journal devoted solely to the publication of articles on dramatic criticism..."

64 subscribers 66½ cents.' The business manager of the college had a fit, pointing out that it would cost $3.00 apiece to pay back 66½ cents, and besides, the magazine was already printed. Well, we hassled and haggled about it, until finally the president of the college stepped in. He told me that if Tulane would put its name on the magazine for just one issue, he would pay for it; 'Just change "Carleton" to "Tulane" on the cover,' he told me, 'and that would be that.' At that time there was absolutely no intention that the magazine would continue beyond Volume 1, Number 3."

The *Tulane Drama Review* did continue, of course, and it was no longer strictly a vehicle for reproducing lectures, although reprinted material figured prominently in the early issues. Corrigan chose a distinguished but hardly radical board of advisory editors, including critic Eric Bentley and several prominent university professors. The articles that appeared during the five years of Corrigan's editorship at Tulane were, for the most part, also by prominent academics. There was a script series and a theatre documents project. The latter, edited by theatre historian Barnard Hewitt, frequently reprinted historical material about theatrical production. But the overwhelming emphasis of the journal, as its name implied, was on drama, especially the classics and the liberal wing of 20th-century playwriting— Shaw, Pirandello, Brecht, Sartre, Ghelderode, Durrenmatt.

There were, Corrigan says, several important factors in the magazine's

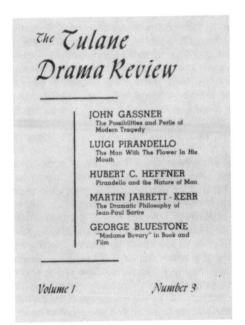

The *Tulane Drama Review*

JOHN GASSNER
The Possibilities and Perils of
Modern Tragedy

LUIGI PIRANDELLO
The Man With The Flower In His
Mouth

HUBERT C. HEFFNER
Pirandello and the Nature of Man

MARTIN JARRETT-KERR
The Dramatic Philosophy of
Jean-Paul Sartre

GEORGE BLUESTONE
"Madame Bovary" in Book and
Film

Volume 1   *Number 3*

First issue of the *Tulane Drama Review*, edited by Robert Corrigan, included Eric Bentley and Monroe Lippman as advisory editors early growth at Tulane: "Eric Bentley's support was crucial. He was constantly sending us new material and making us look at it seriously. And it was he who really came up with the idea that we ought to become a national, even an international, magazine. Eric was an advisor to Hill and Wang's Drama Book series. Because of him, Hill and Wang decided that they would become distributors for the magazine, sell it in bookstores and feature it in their advertising. They completely redesigned *TDR* at their own expense, and as of Volume 3, Number 3, we had national distribution.[1] But I don't think we had an esthetic that we were trying to fulfill in those days. I don't think we had any vision of what theatre ought to be. The prevailing attitude was reflected in my own attempt to relate what was happening in the new theatre to what had happened in the past."

By the end of the '50s, *TDR* had begun to take up the cause of Ionesco, Beckett, Adamov and the other so-called Absurdist writers. Commenting on Adamov's play *Ping-Pong,* Corrigan wrote that the author was "opening up new territories which other playwrights (and audiences) must explore if the theatre is ever to go beyond the narrow and mechanical limits of naturalism." He expanded this idea in his 1961 article, "The Theatre in Search of a Fix." In it Corrigan wrote that "for all their seeming unintelligibility and simplicity," the Absurdist plays "possess a vitality we have missed, and more important, in their boldly experimental nature they are symptomatic of the unrest which prevails in the contemporary theatre." Increasingly, glimmers of that unrest were finding their way into the pages of the *Tulane Drama Review.*

Corrigan published an article by Richard Schechner about Greek drama in the June 1961 issue [T12]. "At the heart of Euripides' masterpiece, *The Bacchae,*" Schechner wrote, "is a communal sacrifice." It was, for the time, an unusual starting point for a piece of dramatic criticism and a clear foreshadowing of one of Schechner's later preoccupations as both editor and theatre practitioner—the relationship between ritual and performance. Schechner, a graduate of Cornell with an M.A. in English from the University of Iowa, had enrolled in the Tulane Ph.D. program in 1960. He turned out to be a kind of academic *wunderkind,* with an equal capacity to intrigue and annoy the more conventional faculty and students in the department. An immensely creative if unorthodox theoretician and a matchless debater, he was also jokey, irreverent, and often impossibly contentious. In spite of the aura of controversy that surrounded him—or perhaps because of it—he had the respect and support of department chairman Monroe Lippman and several other faculty members, and he joined the theatre faculty in September of 1962. Corrigan had left Tulane for a position at Carnegie Tech (now Carnegie-Mellon University), and Schechner ultimately became the second editor of *TDR.*

"When I began as editor," Schechner recalls, "I had no clear idea how I wanted to change *TDR,* except that I wanted it to be more theatrical. I knew literature pretty well and I felt that the theatre should be something different. And I also thought that the magazine ought to be involved politically and socially and that it also ought to have a kind of journalistic relevance; people had to pick it up and read it because it meant something to them at the moment, because it was immediate. Also, being something of a strategist, I felt that if a young guy was going to take over, he had to make his own mark or be submerged. No matter how much I respected them, I couldn't allow those people who already had established reputations—Fergusson, Brustein, Bentley, and so on—to tell me what to do. The only way I could establish my own style was not to meet them on their own ground, but to shift ground."

Schechner's impact on the magazine was not immediately apparent. There was a backlog of previously-commissioned articles that had to be published, and Schechner's first few issues seemed to reflect an editorial policy not very different from Corrigan's. But by 1963 there were clear signs of a shift in direction. In the summer issue [T20] he initiated the first "*TDR* Comment," in which he laid out for readers his own most pressing loyalties—and by extension those of the magazine he now edited. "You choose Broadway," Schechner wrote, "and I'll choose an experimental theatre. There are many roads to truth. But neither of us can choose both Broadway and the experimental theatre. That's a contradiction in intention." If this did not apparently represent a radical change of direction, it was only because the experimental theatre that interested Schechner was in the air but not yet on the table. Soon *TDR* would help to put it there, much to the distress of some editorial board members and a number of conservative critics, academics, and theatre practitioners.

Joining Schechner as associate editor was Theodore Hoffman. Referred to in a *Time* article on *TDR* as the *"homme terrible"* to Schechner's *"enfant terrible,"* Hoffman already had a considerable reputation as an academic iconoclast. He recalled for me his early connection with Corrigan, Schechner and *TDR.* "I think Corrigan looked me up; he had read something of mine. We hit it off, as one usually does with Corrigan, and very quickly the two of us were dreaming vast dreams about the future of the theatre. He asked me to write an article for *TDR,* which I did. It made a big impression so he asked me to become an advisory editor, which I also did, helping him to find material and that sort of thing. Then Bob came as a visiting professor to Carnegie, where I was head of the theatre department, and the musical chairs began. I decided to leave for Stanford, and Bob was offered my job at Carnegie, which he took. There was the question of what to do with *TDR.* Tulane said, logically enough, that Bob couldn't run their magazine from Carnegie. So Bob and I began talking about the possibility of putting out our own magazine. At that moment Schechner was introduced. Monroe Lippman had appointed this mad young man as the new editor of *TDR*. Bob was frankly perplexed."

Schechner recalls the situation vividly. "I heard that Corrigan was going to start a magazine at Carnegie which would replace *TDR*, and that Ted was going to be the new magazine's co-editor. I respected Ted's journalistic ability and his pungency—and I also felt that if Corrigan did start a new magazine, it would go hard with me. So I called Ted and told him that he could either join Corrigan on a new magazine which didn't exist yet, or he could join me as associate editor of *TDR*. I told him that he had three or four days to think it over. If he accepted my offer, he had to agree not to do any editorial work for Corrigan; if not, I was going to get out as many issues of *TDR* as I could before the two of them had a chance to get their magazine in place. Well, Ted decided to go with *TDR*, and that torpedoed Bob's idea for a new journal."

Hoffman remembers the details somewhat differently. "All of a sudden Richard popped up in my kitchen in Pittsburgh. We had a long session, a sort of Stanislavski-Danchenko evening. We just sat there and drank and talked for hours. Richard wanted me to stay with *TDR* in some capacity and advise him. I can't recall the sequence, but shortly after that I became associate editor. It was all very hectic and very exciting. I used to feel that he was wild, crazy. Then I would read over a back issue and wonder what was so wild about it. It wasn't always the content. Maybe it was the tone—a kind of wonderful defiance. He certainly espoused the polemical in those days. We both did."

Hoffman's enthusiasm for the regional theatres then springing up around the country was virtually boundless. "I felt," he said, "that they would be more active than any American theatre had ever been before. *They* were to be the future of the theatre, not Broadway." His particular *bête noire* was the low state of training offered by American college and university theatres. "The educational community theatre," he wrote in his first *TDR* Comment, "is rapidly becoming a fossil. Whether it will choose to become something else or die in a battle of attrition is its problem. What is needed is university support of resident professional theatre, which, after all, embodies in theatre the principles on which universities allegedly are built."

It is clear that Hoffman's concerns and his enthusiasms strongly influenced Schechner's early editorial policy. A *TDR* Comment in the Winter 1963 issue [T22] contained a manifesto signed by both men, laying out what they felt to be the redefined mission of the magazine. They pledged *Tulane Drama Review* to promote a framework of seven points: "An absolute commitment to professional standards. The decentralization of the professional theatre. A deep and continuing interest in both practical and theoretical experimentation. A committed employment of the open stage. The reintroduction of the playwright into the theatre. A recognition that the best contemporary theatre is international. The redirection of educational theatre into the mainstream of American theatre." One or two of these points were to remain important to Schechner's later editorial policy. However, he told me recently that, "as I moved on through the years, my attention shifted away from thinking about the regional and professional theatres as touchstones, as I had been influenced to do by Hoffman, and in the direction of experimental theatre and the anthropological aspects of performance."

Much of Schechner's editorial flamboyance surfaced in the Spring 1964 issue [T23]. Titled "The Living Theatre and Larger Issues," it featured Kenneth Brown's abstract and violently anti-military play *The Brig*, set in a marine prison barracks, as well as an unorthodox interview with one of the play's very unorthodox producers, Judith Malina of The Living Theatre. Malina and her husband Julian Beck had been locked out of their theatre on 14th Street in New York City by the IRS because of their failure to pay taxes as a statement of protest against the war in Vietnam. They had managed to get back into the building and were barricaded inside at the time that Schechner conducted his interview. Malina described the scene this way: "This interview is being conducted from the street to the third floor, which is the office of The Living Theatre. Richard Schechner is down on the street with an improvised megaphone. It is 1:30 a.m., Friday, October 19. My name is Judith Malina. I'm standing in the window of The Living Theatre, where we are now captives, or free-will captives, since we do not want to leave."

On the heels of the somewhat startling Living Theatre interview came an issue [T24] containing a piece by Jerzy Grotowski, the Polish director, whose distinctive and highly unusual theatre work was then virtually unknown in the United States. The article was made up essentially of the program notes for Grotowski's Theatre Laboratory production of Marlowe's *Doctor Faustus*. In it "the text was reordered into a 'montage,'... drawing on all the Quartos and rearranging the sequence of scenes, creating new ones and eliminating some others." The piece presented readers with a production concept of the most radical sort. It also had a significant effect on Schechner's own vision of performance, both as editor and as theatre practitioner. His introduction to the article notes that two more pieces about Grotowski would appear shortly in the magazine; in fact, more than a dozen have found their way into the pages of *TDR* over the years, mirroring Schechner's developing interest in Grotowski's work.

Schechner recalls a gradual shift on his part over the next few years from "the writings and thoughts of Brustein and Fergusson, who are the best of their kind, to the writings and thoughts of Grotowski. It was a shift in focus and a rationalization—not an attempt at justification, but an attempt to bring things into logical coherence for myself. The shift ran something like this: If the theatre is to be about the theatre and not about the literature of the theatre, then it has to find its own language, as Artaud would say. That language, I felt, had to be the language of action, and action would be more likely to be found in those experimental performance arts that derive from non-literary sources—dance and painting and music—than from those that are enslaved to literature. Given that shift, one could reinvigorate literature through a new scenography, and through new forms of actor training that would make the performer and the director primary creators rather than interpreters."

In the Summer 1964 issue [T24], Corrigan responded with a certain irritation to Schechner and Hoffman's recent manifesto. He claimed not to see the editorial move "from academic theatre, from history to living theatre, from the eclectic to the particular," that its editors had claimed was in progress. And he added that manifestos "are a useless appendage to a quarterly magazine. What a magazine stands for is always found in its table of contents." The same issue contained instant, largely unenthusiastic responses to Corrigan's statement by several contributing editors, among them Paul Gray of Bennington College, who dismissed the former editor as "twenty years behind."

The internal controversy continued. By the winter of 1964 [T26], theatre critic and contributing editor Gordon Rogoff was implying that Schechner and Hoffman were "anti-critical." Hoffman, in the meantime, had resigned as associate editor. "It was becoming more and more Richard's magazine," Hoffman says. "We had no fundamental quarrels about it, although I think one of my functions as associate editor had been to keep him from doing really wild things. And of course he did lots of them; his strength has always consisted of gathering in everything that comes within range of his antennae. In any case, during this period we hit it off beautifully because both of us were sensing where everything was moving and constantly adjusting to that movement." Schechner recalls it somewhat differently: "Finally, I think, Ted felt that he ought to be co-editor, or maybe senior editor. After all, he had a big reputation and I didn't. But I'm not very good at sharing power when power is mine. I enjoy using it. I think I'm graceful enough about letting somebody else have it when I don't. But I don't like to have it and yet not have it. If he was going to be associate editor, then he was going to be associate editor, not co-editor. I was very careful about those terms, and I think that disappointed him."

For some time there were reverberations from two Stanislavski issues [T25 and T26] that generated both partisans and violent detractors. Throughout the two issues, the American home of the so-called Stanislavski system, the Actors Studio in New York City, came off badly. Its director, Lee Strasberg, was castigated for lack of credibility and for the tenuous relationship of his approach to the actual teachings of the great Russian director. Strasberg bided his time. More than 15 months later, after brooding

TDR's *hommes terribles*, June 1967: (left to right) Theodore Hoffman, Richard Schechner, Jerzy Grotowski, and Paul Gray

at length on the charges against him, he wrote a letter to the editor, excoriating the pieces by Rogoff and Gray. "Gray's endeavor to suggest my ignorance only serves to reveal his own," wrote Strasberg. He dismissed Rogoff's article as "completely personal, based on hearsay, rumor, and insinuations." In the same issue Rogoff coolly referred to the "mediated fact" that "Mr. Strasberg has been less than an auspicious force in American theatre," while Gray righteously insisted that "Nobody, not even Lee Strasberg, can control or adjust the criticism of his contemporaries to suit himself."

Meanwhile, Schechner attempted to clarify his personal vision of the critic's function and to respond to Rogoff's suggestion that he was anti-critical. As Schechner stated it in the spring of 1965 [T27], the vision was an off-center one, much more closely related to the European concept of the *Dramaturg* (then virtually unheard of in America) than to the conventional wisdom of the day about the task of the drama critic. "Properly understood," he wrote, "the theatre critic's intent is to mediate between the play and those who produce it, not between the play and the audience. His work is rewarded by more informed productions, not by more enlightened audiences. The audience should learn from the plays they see." Variations on this vision were to reappear in several later issues and probably helped to establish dramaturgy as a legitimate and important part of the non-profit theatre in America.

Another of his points in the piece was to loom very large in *TDR*'s later editorial policy. "The modern theatre critic, as I see him," Schechner wrote, "should take as his major occupation the elucidation of the play's structure. Interpretation and thematic studies are valid and valuable appendices to theatre criticism (and good fun, too); but they are no more than that. . . . The structural critic, like the others, uses all the primary and auxiliary information available to him; but he does not stop when he has related that material to his play. His definitive step is to focus all the information on the play's structure; his modest goal is descriptive. The only judgment he makes in the body of his work is implicity; if he has chosen to examine a play, he has declared it worthy." (This position interested Schechner greatly but it was hardly an editorial article of faith with him. Later, however, a similar point of view was to become one of the editorial canons of Michael Kirby, who was to assume the editorship of *TDR* several years after Schechner.)

In the 1966 tenth anniversary issue [T32], Schechner would offer readers an essay that, at the same time, capped his thinking about the problem of theatre criticism and suggested his own personal attempt to define the nature of theatre. In "Approaches to Theory/Criticism" he presented the then radical position that ritual, play, games and sports are all activities related to theatre—and hence relevant to our understanding of the theatre. "Methods of analysis of one may be useful in the analysis of others," he wrote, and went on to stress the need for "theorist, critic and practitioner to learn the language of other disciplines." Among the new tools that Schechner saw as important were transactional analysis and model building. With such tools, he believed, the "possibility exists that a unified set of approaches will be developed that can handle all theatrical phenomena, classical and modern, textual and non-textual, dramatic and theatrical." In effect, Schechner had now shifted his own interest from *theatre* to *performance* in its broadest definition. It was a shift that was to color much of the magazine's later editorial policy.

Schechner took on the cultural Establishment in the Fall 1965 issue [T29], called "Dollars and Drama." Featuring a banknote-green cover emblazoned with the famous Thomas Nast caricature of Boss Tweed, the issue centered around his less than rapturous conclusions about the work of major American foundations in support of the performing arts. Along the way he advocated the formation of what he called "island theatre institutions." This concept forecast the sort of theatre that Schechner himself was later to found in New York at the Performing Garage, a theatre that eventually was to draw him away from editorial work and from *TDR*.

The same issue contained a *TDR* Comment by Bennington College professor Paul Gray that, in essence, applied the island theatre institution idea to an academic setting. As in the Hoffman days, the magazine took a notably dim view of the sort of training provided by college and university theatre departments. Gray's "Bennington Blueprint" pointed out what he considered to be the failings of such institutions, including a lack of commitment to new plays and to experimental staging. Gray laid out an alternative approach, that he was initiating at Bennington and that included, among other innovations, a faculty member whose function was essentially that of a dramaturg. A similar distaste for the conventions of academic theatre was illustrated in the next issue, in which Hoffman announced the formation of a new school of the performing arts at New York University. The cast of characters was familiar to *TDR* readers. Hoffman himself was to be head of the theatre program and the dean of the new school was Robert Corrigan. The NYU School of the Arts, according to Hoffman, would be unique in that it would not be "a bastardized paradigm of the liberal arts."

The Winter 1965 issue [T30] in which Hoffman's comments appeared, perhaps more than any other from this period, presented readers with a concentrated body of radical material about the performance process. The guest editor of the issue was Michael Kirby, a Princeton graduate, and a sculptor with a background in theatre, who did occasional performances. Kirby had immersed himself in the New York avant-garde art world of the '50s and '60s, and had become especially interested in the Happenings movement, which he recorded in a classic book on the form. T30 was titled "New Theatre" but came to be known as the "Happenings Issue." It featured articles and descriptions of performances by such avant-garde luminaries as John Cage, Claes Oldenburg, Robert Whitman, Ann Halprin and Yvonne Rainer.

Kirby recalled some of the background of the issue for me in a recent interview. "Nothing like this had appeared in the *Tulane Drama Review* before that time, and my feeling was that Richard knew next to nothing about the subject. But I believe the issue was his idea. He was learning. In a sense, it wasn't a hard issue for me to put together, since I knew most of the people who were involved in that sort of performance. But the introduction was more difficult, because it was not easy to find background information in those days. Now there is much more material available on all of that sort of work. The reaction to the issue was interesting. A lot of traditional theatre people were very offended and very upset. They thought we were attacking traditional theatre. We weren't, although an attack of a sort may be implicit in certain kinds of avant-garde performance. But we certainly weren't saying that they couldn't do their kind of theatre—only that we were presenting something different."

The information in Kirby's issue was not generally known to the theatre community, and its impact was considerable. As he suggests, its relationship to theatre was hotly contested by a number of readers, who saw it as pretentious and faddish. But many others began to envision possible crossovers between contemporary theatre and Happenings, Environments and the other forms of performance art discussed in the issue. Writing in the magazine's tenth anniversary issue [T32], Corrigan found the Kirby issue controversial but of considerable importance. "A new theatre is aborning," he wrote, "and the Happenings (and all the other intermedia experiments) are the harbingers of the shape of things to come. Just what this shape will be, no one knows for certain; but that it will be different seems incontestable to me, and those who cannot accept this fact are making the most noise. They include both the Broadway establishment and the regional repertory establishment."

At the same time that the Kirby issue was in preparation, Schechner held a public "*TDR* Conference" at the Carnegie International Center in New York. Called—perhaps unfortunately—"The New Establishment," the meeting featured a number of *TDR* regulars on the platform, along with major figures from Off-Broadway and the regional theatre. Among the observers was actress Peggy Wood, who was incensed at the intellectual drift of the discussion and stormed out of the meeting, later recording her reactions in an irate letter to *The New York Times*. In the next several issues of *TDR*, Schechner laid out his second thoughts about the Peggy Wood incident and the conference, describing it as, in a sense, a failure since the topics under consideration could not be "reduced to systematic speech." The panelists themselves, he admitted, "split on whether the session had value." But he noted prophetically that the meeting had made clear that "a new avant-garde" was in the air and that "the intellectual sponsors of these new activities have been the Movements—freedom, student, peace."

Schechner's recollections today are less critical. "From my vantage point now," he told me, "it was a success of a kind because the magazine took off quite a bit after that. In part, it was probably a fortunate accident. To tell you the truth, when it happened, I didn't even know who Peggy Wood was; and the huffing and puffing in the press surprised me. But if Peggy Wood had been happy with what happened there, we wouldn't have had all that publicity. And there wouldn't have been so much attention paid to some of the concepts we were promoting, such as new types of actor training and the environmental theatre."

The seeds of the concept of environmental theatre had been sown in Kirby's special issue. In the spring of 1967 [T35], Schechner cast these new concepts in a more tangible form in a *TDR* Comment called "The Journal of Environmental Theatre." In it he wrote that "scripted theatre, traditionally produced, is dull. . . . We are in a transition between proscenium-thrust-open-arena (any kind of) *staged* theatre and environmental theatre; between a theatre where things *come from* words and a theatre in which words are *part* of the event. . . . Perhaps we should stop publishing *TDR* and begin *The Journal of Environmental Theatre*." The change never happened, but the concept interested Schechner greatly and led directly to an issue on radical theatre architecture and performance environments in the spring of 1968 [T39]. The issue, with contributions from such major avant-garde figures as R. Buckminster Fuller, Allan Kaprow and Jacques Polieri, also contained Schechner's attempt to clarify his own particular environmental philosophy, an essay called "Six Axioms for Environmental Theatre."

In the essay Schechner postulated a set of radical principles of environmental theatre performance: "The theatrical event is a series of related transactions. All the space is used for performance; all the space is used for audience. The theatrical event can take place either in a totally transformed space or in 'found space.' Focus is flexible and variable. All production elements speak in their own language. The text need be neither the starting point nor the goal of a production. There may be no text at all." Many of the illustrations came from a production of Ionesco's *Victims of Duty*, which had been presented by the New Orleans Group, an experimental theatre company in which Schechner had participated. In a way the article was a kind of theoretical rehearsal for his *Dionysus in 69*, which would open in June of 1968 at the Performing Garage.

The Kirby issue had also led to another important change. In the fall of 1966 [T33], *TDR* adopted a new, larger format that moved it farther away in appearance from the standard academic journal. Schechner believes that "Michael Kirby's issue really burst the magazine's seams; it was filled with foldouts and that sort of thing. And after his issue, we knew that we couldn't deal with a new kind of performance which was highly visual using the old format. So Frank Adams, a New Orleans artist, and I, and Erika Munk, who had been managing editor of the magazine since the early '60s, developed a new look for *TDR*."

In the summer of the following year Schechner announced that the magazine would move to New York City. Behind the move lay a complex political situation at Tulane. As a result of irreconcilable differences between the Tulane theatre department and the central administration, a number of the best-known theatre faculty quit and headed for other institutions. Among them were Schechner and Monroe Lippman, the department chairman, both of whom accepted positions in Robert Corrigan's newly formed NYU School of the Arts. *TDR* came with them, to be based in the Graduate Drama Department (now called the Department of Performance Studies), which was headed by Lippman. After some discussion, it was decided to keep the magazine's old initials and change the name to *The Drama Review,* even though drama was scarcely the focus of the magazine's attention in this period. I had recently been offered a position at Tulane; instead, in the fall of 1968, I joined Lippman and Schechner on the NYU faculty.

Schechner believes that *TDR* "obviously became more of a New York journal. We had always been interested in European developments and

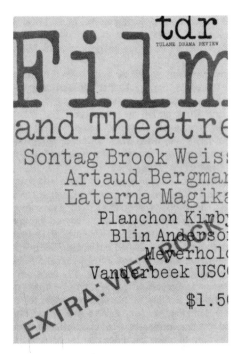

Kirby's "Happenings" issue inspired the new, larger format established with T33.

regional theatre. But the magazine had become more and more involved with experimental theatre, and after we moved to New York we began to concentrate on people who were doing their work here. There were exceptions, of course, but to a certain degree the New York avant-garde *was* the American avant-garde of the late '60s. Without being a chauvinist, I think it is possible to say that almost all of the important experimental theatre performance either originated in New York or at least soon played there. We did a group of articles on the Ridiculous Theatre movement, for example, as well as pieces on Joe Chaikin, and on the Living Theatre's *Paradise Now* at the Brooklyn Academy of Music. Of course, we tried to keep in contact with the important west coast groups, and with the early populist groups in the South like the Free Southern Theatre."

A certain number of articles about political theatre groups had appeared in the magazine from time to time, but up to this point Schechner's chief concerns as editor had been artistic and theoretical, not political. In fact, in a 1969 article about him in the *Sunday Times Magazine,* Schechner was to express a rather mild social vision: "I'm not even sure I'm a leftist," he told interviewer Eleanor Lester, "but I do want some absolutely basic changes in the social structure—an end to exploitation and authoritarianism—and if that's being a leftist, well, maybe I am." The unsettled political situation of the day, however, disturbed Schechner greatly during the middle and late '60s, and managing editor Erika Munk, whose star was rising at the magazine, had always been politically active. Munk became guest editor for the two issues of *TDR* devoted to Bertolt Brecht that appeared in Fall 1967 [T37] and Winter 1968 [T38]. With these issues came an intensification of *TDR*'s concern with politics.

The first Brecht issue contained an advertisement signed by more than a hundred "contributors, editors and staff from the last five years," urging "swift withdrawal of troops from Vietnam." Schechner wrote a *TDR* Comment warning the artist in such times to "ignore current events at his own peril," and Munk added an introduction that linked Brecht's work and the current American political situation. A good deal more political material was to surface several years later when Munk replaced Schechner as editor. For a time, in fact, the magazine's balance was to shift distinctly to the left and toward the concerns of the radical political theatre.

In the summer of 1968, Schechner turned the magazine over to guest editor Ed Bullins. Bullins organized a black theatre issue [T40], totally free from the usual editorial control Schechner exercised in such cases. Schechner relinquished veto power over Bullins, he said, because too often "'white media' present black ideas as filtered through white consciousness." The same issue contained an advertisement for Radical Theatre Repertory, a leftist political theatre group which for a time operated out of the *TDR* office.

"Because of Radical Theatre Repertory," Schechner says, "we had Jerry Rubin and Abby Hoffman and the Living Theatre people coming in and out of our office. We became a base for certain of the peace and radical movements that had an interest in media freaking, performances in the street, and guerilla theatre." Schechner himself was soon to be involved in guerilla theatre, as director and performer. In fact, theatre production had become Schechner's consuming interest, and after the controversial but successful opening of his *Dionysus in 69,* he decided that it was time to leave the magazine for work in the theatre.

Schechner's official farewell in the Summer 1969 issue [T44] noted that he was resigning "to spend more time writing and directing—and also because editing has lost its push for me." In November of 1968, he recalled for me, he had begun the workshops that were to lead to the formation of his theatre company, The Performance Group. "By June of 1969, *Dionysus* was in production, and I was working on another play, *Makbeth.* I just had to decide at last whether I was going to be an absentee editor. Later I sometimes thought that I had made the wrong decision, because nobody asked me to resign, and in my position I didn't really have to. In Erika I had a person who was loyal to my basic point of view and who was a very good managing editor, and all in all things were running well. But part of the radical tone of the day was bound up with the fact that you couldn't be an absentee anything. I believed it—I still do. And I reasoned that if I couldn't give my full energy to the magazine, I shouldn't allow my name to be on it. My full energy, in fact, was going to The Performance Group. So I quit.

"Erika had been running the magazine for a year or more, not making editorial decisions, but running it all the same. She wanted the job, and I thought it was logical that she have it. She turned out to be much more overtly political than I had been, and much more interested in political theatre. And she was less academic than I was. I think of myself to a certain degree as a scholar and a teacher, and I think that side of me was in the magazine when I ran it. Erika was a journalist and a magazine person; her background before *The Drama Review* was with *Partisan Review.* Now, of course, she is theatre editor of the *Village Voice.* Then, too, she didn't have a practical theatre background, so she wasn't much interested in training or the problems of making a performance. She cared more about the relationship of theatre to an audience, its social and political effects. But in fact she was only editor for a half a dozen issues, so she wasn't really with *TDR* long enough to put her stamp on it very clearly. A short-lived magazine called *Performance,* which she later edited for Joe Papp, was more clearly hers, although it bore a subtle relationship to *TDR,* both in terms of appearance and content."

In the introduction to her first issue as editor, Munk pointed out that "there is no editorial line about either politics or performance, though some basic sympathies are manifest on the next two pages." Those pages contained a Provo manifesto, together with a montage of related photographs and poems. The manifesto includes the lines, "Provo regards anarchy as the inspirational source of resistance. Provo wants to revive anarchy and teach it to the young." The next issue [T45], however, was not notably anarchistic, and seemed to be made up largely of Schechner-commissioned material: an article by critic Jan Kott; another, on stage fright, by psychologist Donald Kaplan; an interview with Eugenio Barba and a group of pieces on Grotowski and the Polish Laboratory Theatre. In fact, throughout the next several issues, it became clear that Schechner's hand was still very much in evidence.

Munk's issue on Latin American performance [T46] was clearly political in orientation. In many ways, however, it featured Schechner more than the new editor since it was built around a tour he and Theatre of Latin America director Joanne Pottlitzer had taken to several Latin American countries. He wrote that he had found Latin American plays basically "19th-century" in their approach and that he longed to see something more challenging. "A really experimental play in Brazil," he wrote, "would have to begin with Macumba and the rites of the dead, something indigenous." The comment catches quite clearly the interest in the anthropological aspects of performance that had begun to absorb him more and more during the last several years of his editorship. "My work," Schechner said recently, "gradually drove me step by step toward considering rites and those forms of human action in which action itself is the core and the heart of the meaning. I guess that my struggle with the current experimental theatres is that as they became more and more involved with action, they left out meaning. What interests me about rituals and traditional performance forms is that action and meaning are conjoined in them."

At the same time, questions were being asked about late issues and other administrative matters. Some NYU people came to feel that Munk had perhaps been the wrong choice. And yet, in a sense, she was clearly starting to hit her stride as an editor. Her next issue [T49] contained a piece of what, in later years, would be called investigative journalism. In it she traced the complex web of connections between the military and the American Educational Theatre Association, a group made up of representatives from the nation's college and university theatre departments. Another similar piece by William Oliver dealt in detail with censorship in university theatres. Along with these came substantial articles on Peter Handke and the Grand Magic Circus, as well as an article on Futurist performance by Michael Kirby. Soon he was to become the new editor of *TDR*.

Munk edited only one more issue of *The Drama Review,* a double issue devoted to Asian performance [T50] and guest-edited by Sri Lankan scholar A. J. Gunawardana. The impulse behind the issue, once again, was almost certainly Schechner, who had begun to be enthusiastic about Asian theatre and ritual some years before, probably in part as a result of Grotowski's interest in Indian actor training techniques. With the issue that followed Kirby took over the magazine's editorship, although not without considerable controversy. It is hard today to determine the exact turn of events. Kirby, by now a long-time contributing editor of *TDR,* had recently received his Ph.D. from NYU and taught for one year at City College in New York. Now he was about to become the chairman of NYU's Graduate Drama Department. He recalled the situation for me this way: "The dean was going to drop the magazine because of a huge deficit and because there was a problem getting issues out on time. It had become too much of a burden to him. He had given Erika a deadline for taking it to some other school, because he really didn't want to see the magazine end. So she was negotiating, trying to find some other university that would take it. Then I got the idea of becoming editor myself. I suddenly realized that I wanted to reach the people who were doing theatre, to influence ideas and productions. Then, too, as the new chairman, I wanted to keep *The Drama Review* in my department. I thought I could find a way to produce the magazine much more cheaply and keep it at NYU. I discussed my idea with Erika, and she was pretty upset about it. But finally I was able to convince the dean to keep *The Drama Review* here."

"I felt that I had a lot to offer *TDR,*" Munk told me recently. "Both in terms of continuity with Richard's editorship and on my own. I was more interested in politics and I was more interested in writing per se—meaning quality of mind and quality of prose as those two things come together on paper. I think people were more serious about the theatre then, too, and the result was a lot of passion, and a lot of commitment, a lot of trendiness, and a lot of phoniness. But it all had vitality.

"Still, it turned out to be a hard time to take over *The Drama Review.* There was a great deal of conflict between NYU and *TDR,* some of which had started when Richard was the editor. The magazine had published too much radical stuff to be safe—sexually radical, esthetically radical, politically radical. When I took it over and continued all that, I was in a much worse position than Richard because I didn't have a contract and I had no academic standing. I was just this souped-up clerical person who had taken over *TDR.* I'm astonished as I look back that I never questioned, except privately, the extraordinary amount of anti-woman prejudice in those days. I don't think it was unique to *The Drama Review,* but I was a managing editor who was still fetching coffee.

"In any case," Munk continued, "here's the story I heard—it may be half true, three quarters true, or not true at all, I really don't know. Supposedly, the dean at NYU wanted Michael to become the head of the Graduate Drama Department. Michael said he wouldn't do it unless he could also have the editorship of *TDR*. That was the deal. At that point my relations with Richard had become very bad. I think it was just a personal thing; I doubt that there was any major intellectual issue. But that didn't help things much, and soon it all became very complex."

"As you recall," Kirby told me, "there was a big flap about everything in the *Sunday Times.*" A letter, published in the February 21, 1971 issue, was headed "End of *The Drama Review?*" In it were claims that censorship as well as financial issues were involved in the *TDR* matter, and that the NYU administration had behaved high-handedly in relation to Munk and her staff. The letter also claimed that Kirby proposed to "reduce *TDR*'s size, its scope, and its contentiousness—by obvious extension, removing *TDR*'s radical thrust, its libertarian imagination, and its willingness to make spectacularly healthy mistakes." The letter was signed by some 20 important theatrical figures, from John Arden to Irving Wardle, including several who had been prominent contributors.

Kirby responded on the following Sunday with a letter in which he called the charges against him a "deliberate lie" and pointed out that he hoped to increase, not decrease, the scope of the magazine. He wrote, "And the articles that interest me the most will be those that challenge orthodox concepts, theories and 'facts.' As an artist and teacher, I am not ashamed that contentiousness is part of my intellectual nature."

Kirby's contentiousness is of quite a different sort from either Schechner's or Munk's, but it was apparent from his first issue, which appeared in the summer of 1971. In the introduction to that issue, he advanced an editorial approach from which he has scarcely deviated in a dozen years and 50 issues of *The Drama Review.* Unlike Schechner, whose policies were constantly evolving during his editorship, Kirby seems to have known precisely what he wanted on his first day as editor. And it is precisely what he still wants today. "It was all very clear," Kirby told me. "I was taking over *TDR* and I wanted to keep whatever I liked about it. The magazine had been exciting and tremendously important to me; I was proud to be associated with it. On the other hand, I did have my own interests, and they were not necessarily Richard's. I was perhaps more historical, and strangely enough, more oriented toward the avant-garde than he was—or at least toward the historical avant-garde and a kind of art theatre. But I'm always interested in new ideas in theatre, wherever and however they appear."

In his introduction [T51] Kirby stated firmly that the magazine had not been limited to the consideration of "drama" for some time. Recalling his 1965 Happenings issue, Kirby said that *TDR* had demonstrated "an interest in the wider scope of performance in general, rather than dealing exclusively with types of performance involving characterization and narrative. The interest in other forms of presentation as well as drama will be continued." Perhaps the most distinctive aspect of Kirby's policy, however, was—and continues to be—his antipathy toward "reviewing." The magazine, he announced, "will no longer be involved in 'reviewing' productions."

It is worth hearing Kirby out on this matter: "'Reviewing' a performance means evaluating it. We are not interested in opinions and value judgments about what is 'good' and what is 'bad'. We feel that the detailed and accurate documentation of performances is preferable and gives sufficient grounds for a reader to make his own value judgments. Of course we realize that implicit value judgments on our part are involved in the selection process itself, but these can be intellectual rather than emotional, and they should not be involved in the presentation of the material. 'Reviewing' usually, although not necessarily, involves interpretation. We are not interested in interpretation, in the explication of 'meaning,' in the explanation of one thing in terms of another. These processes are subjective and personal; although they may make interesting reading, there is no need for documentation or theory to be impressionistic."

Over the years, Kirby's concept of documentation and the allied idea of reconstruction have become a kind of critical mass at the center of the magazine. Today he explains them this way: "Documentation of current performance is the same thing as reconstruction of a historical one. In both cases I think the important thing is to make the material available. I trust the personal taste of the people who read the documentations and reconstructions. It's the same as seeing a performance; some may like it, some not. In any case, I feel strongly about not saying anything negative about theatre. I dislike a lot of the theatre I see, but on the whole I like the theatre and want to help it, and I would never publish anything negative about it. But, on the other hand, I try not to add positive values to anything either. I publish articles about productions that I don't like, that aren't to my own taste. But I do it because people are talking about those productions, because people are interested in them, because they find something important in them. I may not, but when I hear about the interest, I'm willing to publish something. Criticism is not involved: we don't push anything. I try to be objective. When I publish an article about a production I suppose, in a sense, that amounts to pushing it. But *The Drama Review* doesn't push it in terms of explaining values. There may be certain values in a work, but *The Drama Review* doesn't assign them there."

Some find the approach rather arid. In December of 1975 [T68] Peter Lackner, a former contributor, wrote an irate letter to *TDR*. "Formalism," he said, "is a recurring emphasis in all the arts, but all theatre events should not be given only formalistic analysis. . . . It is ironic that in a time when theatre is one of the few holdouts of humanistic endeavor, the main theatre magazine of America employs a system of values that is technocratic, isolational,

The Kirby staff, March 1973: (left to right) Kate Davy, Ronald
Argelander, Michael Kirby, Paul Ryder Ryan, and Mel Gordon
(Photo: Peter Moore)

abstractional." In his response, Kirby pointed out, with characteristic directness, that he would continue to "prevent our readers from being told what to feel and think about theatre.... If they know the form, the content does not need to be explained to them and interpreted for them."

Lackner is not alone. Even Schechner has quarreled with what he once called Kirby's need "to live in a positivist world, where meaning is clear, and human behavior is stripped of its problematical elements." Yet Schechner readily admits that he finds a special significance in Kirby's measured approach to editorship. As he sees it today, "Michael is the most conservative of the editors in the sense that he conserves his resources: he detaches himself and the magazine from the hurly-burly of the day, and he edits only special issues, organized around some sort of central theme, instead of letting the chips fall where they may in broadly based general issues. For these reasons, I find his *TDR* very valuable as a teaching tool, as a research resource, and, because of his interest in documentation, as a historical record. What I miss is the sense of overt polemics. There are lots of polemics in Michael's magazine, but they are not overt."

Schechner makes several interesting points about Kirby's editorship. Unlike Kirby, he has always sought out controversy. "I want public discussions," Schechner once wrote, "manifestos, coffeehouse debates, publications; I think art flourishes in a soup of opinionated disagreements and fiercely defended value judgments." To Schechner's frequent frustration, Kirby has never thrived on controversy and polemic, but rather on virtually unshakable convictions about art that were already formed when he first took up his editorship. In areas that do not involve his strong anti-critical feelings or his convictions about documentation and reconstruction, on the other hand, he is in fact quite liberal and eclectic as an editor—probably considerably more so than Schechner.

The special issue did not originate with Kirby. Schechner was using it early in his editorship, although not exclusively. Kirby, on the other hand, almost never departs from the special issue format and considers it essential to his editorial approach. *"The Drama Review,"* he wrote in September of 1979 [T83], "feels that by grouping articles dealing with a particular subject area and/or with related ideas, one article—merely because of its context and in addition to its particular inherent content—reflects upon, compliments, sets off, and elucidates another. This factor of implicit cross-reference would not be possible in a general issue that juxtaposed unrelated articles."

Typically—although not invariably—one of his issues contains a block of articles on the theme being explored and a second, smaller block devoted to historical aspects of the same theme, often featuring early plays or documents. Kirby's own particular interest is and always has been the avant-garde. He seems to have a special affinity for the work of such figures as Richard

Foreman, Robert Wilson, Memè Perlini (whom he calls, with uncharacteristic subjectivity, "perhaps the most significant of the 'new' artists"). Considerable space has been given over to what is sometimes called "Performance Art," and to the activities of such "post-modern" dancers as Joan Jonas, Trisha Brown, Laura Dean and Lucinda Childs. Like Schechner, Kirby is a director, and his own particular brand of "structuralist" performance has also received a certain amount of attention over the years.

Schechner had relatively little interest in historical material, although a certain amount continued to appear in *TDR* throughout his editorship. Kirby, on the other hand, has a passionate interest in the early 20th-century European avant-garde, and the magazine has become an important source on Expressionism, Italian Futurism, Meyerhold, and the entire Russian avant-garde tradition. But Kirby's *TDR* is by no means strictly an avant-garde magazine. In his response to Peter Lackner's 1975 criticism of his editorial approach, Kirby could write quite accurately: "Lackner seems to feel that *The Drama Review* is concerned only with experimental theatre and that we 'ignore everything that is happening on "traditional" or "commercial" stages around the world.' Yet we have published, among others, issues devoted to popular entertainments, indigenous theatre, and political theatre. Experimentation is not our only interest."

Increasingly, over the last decade, a broader range of forms has been examined in the magazine. In part this has probably come about because of what many see as a decline in the quantity and quality of experimental performances in the last few years. There is simply not as much interesting avant-garde performance to document and discuss. No less important, however, is Kirby's increased awareness of potentially fruitful areas for exploitation. Kirby himself is probably most interested in *theatre* of a particular sort; but the magazine's mission, he believes, is to study the entire range of *performance*. It was an idea that had developed initially in the '60s during Schechner's editorship, yet it is one to which Kirby maintains increasing allegiance.

In a number of cases Kirby has edited or asked one of his contributing editors to edit issues that are not strongly connected with experimental theatre or that have absolutely no connection with it at all. Several have dealt with aspects of traditional performance. Among them are my own issue on popular entertainment [T61], co-edited with circus historian and clown John Towsen, as well as issues on puppets, masks [T96], African performance [T92], and folk performance (what Kirby calls "indigenous theatre") [T64]. Featured in several of these issues have been articles by E. T. Kirby, Michael's brother and a pioneer writer about the relationship between anthropology and performance. A number of issues focused on the connections between the performing arts and some other area (theatre and therapy [T69], women and performance [T86]), on national theatres (Germany [T85], Scandinavia [T95]), or on the craft aspects of performance (acting [T71, 91], directing [T54, 91], rehearsal procedures [T62]). Many of these issues have drawn heavily on experimental productions, but relatively few have been entirely dependent on experimental material.

Schechner has been the guest editor of three issues, in which he has continued to present his distinctive point of view about performance. In a 1973 issue on social science and the theatre [T59] Schechner defined performance theory and studied the application of social science techniques to the theatre; and in a 1979 Southeast Asian issue [T82] he examined the impact of Asian performance on the European theatrical tradition. A 1982 issue [T94] focused on what Schechner has called "intercultural performance," an approach that he defines as "the attempt to join together certain of the techniques of experimental performance with certain of the social concerns of an emerging globalism." In many ways, Schechner's concerns and enthusiasms are quite removed from those of Kirby. Often the two are vigorously at odds. And yet it is clear that there are certain intellectual crossovers between them that are still important in the magazine's continuing existence.

How long *TDR* will continue to exist is anybody's guess. As little magazines go it is positively antediluvian; but, like all other little magazines, it has always been short of funds and always in danger of closing down. It has been pulled back from the brink any number of times, most recently through a co-publishing venture between NYU and the Massachusetts Institute of Technology Press. Kirby recalls something of the magazine's business history: "When I took over *The Drama Review* it was losing a lot of money. It always had; there was never a year when it broke even. The university was just subsidizing it and writing it off. In the '60s there was a lot of grant money around, but expenses were still always higher than income. Then grant funds began to decline and we lost even more. A publisher wanted to buy the magazine about three years ago. They said they would publish it and continue to let us edit *The Drama Review* from NYU. The dean was interested in the possibility since it meant that the publisher would pick up the loss. I went down to talk to them and we had a number of meetings. But I didn't like the work they were doing and they thought I was an eccentric—I wore my cowboy hat.

"Just then Annette Michaelson, one of the editors of *October,* called me up. *October* is published by the MIT Press, and she told me that they were looking for another quality journal in the humanities. Through Annette's good offices we made contact and eventually worked things out. Because they publish a number of journals and have everything computerized, they are actually running *The Drama Review* at a profit. I hope they keep it up for many years to come. I will continue to edit *The Drama Review* as long as I feel I can. But I hope that there will be other editors in the future. I don't think of it as *my* magazine. *The Drama Review* serves the theatre, and I serve *The Drama Review*."

Schechner is a great one for the last word, and perhaps he should have it here. "*TDR* was never a popular magazine," he told me, "its circulation never got above 12,000. But it was and is a place where ideas are first presented. For that reason, it has been very important to the American theatre—both as a place where experimentation is reported and as a place where the theatre is linked to things outside itself, among them politics and anthropology. *TDR* has also been a major pipeline, bringing Europe to America and America to Europe. Recently, it has helped to connect Asia and America. A contemporary African connection is still to come. Beyond that, I think that a number of experimenters in theatre—the Becks, Chaikin, the post-modern dancers, and many, many others—learned about each others' ideas through *TDR*. Certainly Grotowski got to America first because of it. The magazine's ripple effect is bigger than one might at first expect. There has been a change in the American theatre—even in the mainstream—in directions that were first discussed in *TDR*. The magazine has not been the cause, but an important part of a network of change.

"Each editor of *TDR*," Schechner told me, "was trying to define himself or herself in relation to what had gone on before. That's the nature of editorship. I was moving toward theatricalism and anthropology, and that set me apart from Corrigan and the early *Tulane Drama Review*. Erika was moving toward social action, and that set her apart from me and what she perhaps felt were my bourgeois tendencies. Michael was moving toward formalist art and set himself apart from Erika's involvement in a kind of political street theatre that ignored many of the qualities of art. And all that was as it should be. If *TDR* has been a mouthpiece, it has been a mouthpiece for the editor and for the writers whom the editor has selected—and for the ideas of those people, not for any institution. I think that great magazines— and probably *TDR* is one—are at base *both* personal and conceptual. It is in the joining of the two that their great strength lies."

1986: An Epilogue

It appears that Schechner gets not only the last word, but the last, last word as well. During the winter of 1985, after 14 years, Kirby edited his final issue of *TDR*. The new editor was the old editor, Richard Schechner, who sees his second period of leadership as a very different proposition from his first. For one thing, Schechner says, the nature of the theatre about which *TDR* reports has drastically altered. "Looking both near and far," he writes in the introduction to T109, "I don't see anything coming comparable to the upheavals of the 1930s or 1960s—changes in the very perceptions of what performance is, what it can do, who its audiences are, and what its basic techniques might be."

Yet, being Schechner, he is at no loss for a handle on *TDR*'s editorship. He sees significant "movement" on "two non-art performance fronts: the intercultural and the theoretical." That "movement" reflects Schechner's own developing concern with what he views as a world-wide awakening of interest in integration—both in the theory and practice of performance. "The performance genres are converging, overlapping, and infecting each other," he writes. "It is a plague whose spread I will encourage. Performance scholars are beginning to realize that they need to know about neurology, ethology, anthropology—a whole bunch of '-ologies.' And scholars of the '-ologies' are learning more about performance.... The expanding view of what performance is demands that people both in their art and in their thinking deal with politics, economics, and ritual."

As a result of his concern, Schechner is actively seeking a new breed of writer for *TDR*, "authors whose home bases are or used to be linguistics, feminism, literary theory, deconstruction, philosophy, politics, psychology, history, semiotics...." At the same time, he calls for a different kind of readership. The new readers of *TDR* "will be artists, scholars, and 'undefinables' who are generalists, comparativists, and interculturalists: those who hinge two or more disciplines, moving each." The new *TDR*, Schechner believes, "will be indispensable to those people whose work, thought and play can no longer be boundaried." These propositions will no doubt seem inspired to some—to others, Messianic or hare-brained or irrelevant. But the wheel turns, and many of the propositions fervently expounded by *TDR* in the mid-'60s are now commonplace in our theatres and universities. Which is perhaps part of the very reason that Schechner has kept his old address, but moved to a new neighborhood.

Note

1. They also had a new and unusual numbering system. Dean Earle Gister of Yale, who was Managing Editor of *TDR* in the early days, wrote to me recently: "And finally, as I'm sure you know, T100 will not be a centennial issue. The use of the T started when Hill and Wang took over distribution in 1958. But actually the first issue to have a 'T' number was T3, which was Vol. 3, No. 3 [March, 1959]. The issue to be called T100 will actually be T109." So much for the centennial.

1

When Is a Play Not a Play?
(1960)

George Hauger

Nowadays, what is more often than not meant by *theatre* is the theatrical realization of plays, yet any view of theatre that excludes opera and ballet is obviously incomplete. A careful examination of the natures of these three theatrical forms ought to reveal clearly the limitations and potentialities of each, and to indicate the desirability, or even possibility, of mixing the forms in order to make available new theatrical experiences. Naturally, such an examination cannot be accomplished within the space of a short article, and in any case a thorough examination will have to await the attention of some theatrical Leonardo da Vinci with vast knowledge, sensitivity, and experience. Yet the rushing of the fool into an unknown region has its value. If it results in disaster, wiser men are warned of things they would have had to establish by cautious experiment; but it is not unknown for an uncalculated risk to make clear to the angels that in fearing to tread they are being unnecessarily hesitant. Thus, the present expedition may hope to serve some useful purpose. Like many expeditions, its goal is a land long dreamed of, and its departure has been made under an immediate stimulus—in this case, the chance reading of three pieces in *The Tulane Drama Review* (September, 1959) immediately after looking through Mary Caroline Richards' translations from Artaud.[1]

In the Artaud volume, in Ionesco's "Discovering the Theatre," in Theodore Hoffman's "The Lost Art of Seeing Plays," in Meyerhold's "Farce," we learn the ideas of men who are dissatisfied with the theatre as it is, and who suggest approaches to theatrical art different from those currently in general favor. All four are disturbed about language in the theatre. Artaud wants to make the theatre express thoughts "beyond the reach of the spoken language," and Ionesco wants to make language "almost explode, or destroy itself." Meyerhold and Hoffman want to free the theatre from the bugbear of literature. Few thinking people will dispute the claim that the theatre is not a branch of literature; but if a theatrical work is not based on the use of language (allowing *language* its normal common-sense meaning), then that work surely cannot be a play. A crude but effective way of demonstrating this is to try to discover which parts of a play can be removed without the work's losing its essential nature. *Hamlet* played in daylight, in a bare room, with the actors in their everyday clothes (as distinct from a modern dress *Hamlet*), is still *Hamlet*. In so far as the theatre depends on the performer and his relationship with the audience, some of *Hamlet* will be lost if the characters are not allowed to move—some of *Hamlet*, but not the essence of the play, for the carefully spoken words will remain. If, on the other hand, one tries to present *Hamlet* in no matter what theatrical style, without restrictions on costume, décor, lighting or movement, but with the elimination of speech, then the play will not come into being. And as well as the play's not existing without the words, the words give dramatic significance to all the other elements. It is the words that give the dramatic significance to costume, for example: it is not the costume that gives significance to the words. A character who appears in elegant formal dress may be a diplomat come to tea, a habitual crook come to blackmail, or the man come for the garbage. The words now being spoken, or already spoken, or to be spoken later, will define the costume as neutrally naturalistic, sinisterly deceptive or laughably incongruous. Similarly, the words give the dramatic significance to sunrises, sunsets, rainfall, and other stage effects: otherwise they remain more or less approximate imitations of natural phenomena which can at most be taken to indicate the time of day, the state of the atmosphere, and so on. Even the movements of the characters and their exits and entrances are implied by what is said. In *The Art of the Theatre (The First Dialogue)*, Gordon Craig makes his stage director claim, "Whatever picture the dramatist may wish us to know of, he will describe his scene during the progress of the conversation between the characters," and he goes on to quote the beginning of *Hamlet*. If we hold Craig to the exact meaning of his words, his statement is either innocent or inexact. It is more satisfactory to maintain that whatever nonverbal theatrical elements the playwright may wish us to be aware of will be implied by the dialogue, which may not contain a description of the scene or of any of the other elements: and it is wiser not to quote *Hamlet* or any play that could arouse argument about verbal scene painting and the special conditions of the Elizabethan theatre. *Rosmersholm* would be an effective enough example.

It is not suggested that the nonverbal elements of a play are theatrically superfluous. The contention is that they are not the seat of life. Although he is not as he ought to be, a man who has lost all of his limbs is still essentially a man, in the same way that a play invested of all of its nonverbal elements is still essentially a play. A creature in human shape and possessing limbs, but without certain ratiocinative and imaginative powers (part of whose function is to give significance to the limbs) would not be a man. Similarly, there cannot be a play that is not wholly dependent on language.

The essential element in opera is music. It is not for nothing that we talk of Mozart's *Don Giovanni* and Verdi's *Otello*. We do not talk of Da Ponte's *Don Giovanni* or of Boito's *Otello:* we do not even talk of *Don Giovanni* by Mozart and Da Ponte, or of *Otello* by Verdi and Boito. If one strips an opera in the way it was suggested that a play can be stripped, all can be removed except the music. Remove the music and, no matter what is left, the opera ceases to be. Egon Wellesz has observed: "It is well known that the best music cannot save an opera if the libretto is nonsensical and leaves the public dissatisfied."[2] It would have been wiser to have commented, "...if the libretto leaves the public dissatisfied," since there are several fine operas, such as *Die Zauberflöte,* that leave one wondering how far a libretto has to go before Wellesz considers it nonsensical. In any case, to accept the statement one must attribute to it the very strict—but not very illuminating—meaning that the best music cannot save an opera if the libretto does not satisfy as a libretto, and it is the nature of a libretto to be of no very great significance in itself. If a script is capable of successful theatrical realization without a musical setting, then that script is a play and not an opera libretto. To quote Wellesz again, "Through the music the action is raised into a sphere in which the composer gives finality to the words."[3] In a play the words already have their finality.

In opera, the music provides an aesthetic experience appropriate to the situation indicated by the words. In a play, the words must themselves provide the aesthetic experience appropriate to whatever they indicate. It is because the aesthetic element in opera resides in the music, and because the aesthetic element in any human creation is the factor that distinguishes it as a work of art, that the music of an opera is that part of the work that cannot be eliminated without the work losing its essential nature. It is not sheer snobbery that causes people to attend performances of operas in languages of which they are completely ignorant. One does not need to know the words of an opera: to know about them is sufficient. But it is not sufficient only to know about the music. Eric Bentley has written about Verdi's *Otello:* "The performer sings, so it seems, *about* Othello; he cannot *be* Othello."[4] He has further observed:

> The death of an operatic hero—a Tristan, an Otello, a Boris Godunov—may be impressive in many ways but it is not a supreme event. It is the decoration of an event. We appreciate very openly the skill with which the event is circumvented, and when the actor pretends to fall dead we applaud.[5]

This is surely because in opera it is the music that does the dying, in the important aesthetic sense, not the words. Again, the only occasions on which we obscure the words in a play by having several characters speak at once, are occasions on which we wish to create an effect of confusion, whereas in opera we are content to have extended passages—duets, ensembles, choruses—in which the words, no matter how clearly sung, cannot be distinguished because of the musical texture. We even accept solo arias in which the musical contribution of the voice to the vocal-orchestral ensemble is effective, but in which the total musical effect precludes the hearing of the words. And frequently we accept the repetition of words in operatic numbers because the music demands such a repetition, not because the language as such requires it.[6]

One need hardly labor the point that movement is to ballet what speech is to the play, what music is to opera. In ballet there are no words to provoke argument over their significance. Leave Giselle's cottage and Loys' hut on the vine-clad stage with its distant castle, let the orchestra play Adam's score, allow the costumed dancers to be seen, but forbid them to move—and the ballet does not exist. Let the dancers perform their appointed dances, though in silence and in a bare room, and *Giselle* is essentially there.

Each of these elements which may be made fundamental in a theatrical work—speech, music, movement—has its own essential characteristics which must inevitably be fully acknowledged. These characteristics may be wrestled with, exalted, glorified; but they cannot be denied. In particular, music must stand alone and must obey its inherent laws. Music may acquire associations—hymn tunes are associated with religion, they are not inherently religious—but it has no representational qualities. The "stories" attached to symphonic poems need to be already known to the listener, who will, at best, find the music not inconsistent with them; and the "story" suggested by the composer is never the only satisfactory narrative accompaniment. A symphonic poem or "descriptive music" is only valuable to the extent that it is worthy music. It can never be important as narrative or description. If Richard Strauss' *Till Eulenspiegels Lustige Streiche* is a work of art, this is because the composer has taken certain musical material and has realized some of its musically significant implications. He has used musical means to realize musical implications in musical material. The story of Eulenspiegel has been told by Charles de Coster, and by many anonymous authors, much more unequivocally and much more effectively than Strauss "tells it." It may be insisted that there are musical works whose narrative or descriptive qualities are not equivocal. Beethoven's opus 91, *Wellingtons Sieg oder die Schlacht bei Vittoria,* perhaps leaves one in no doubt that here we have the story of the defeat of the French at the hands of the British, although no one but a clairvoyant could receive an impression of Wellington or Vittoria; but the work accomplishes its description by extra-musical means, by relying on the associations of particular tunes. This *Battle Symphony* is much more accurately descriptive than the *Pastoral Symphony;* but it is much less valuable, and the whole reason for this is that it is musically inferior. Music cannot indicate anything. When it appears to describe accurately, it relies on associations or reproduces, as nearly as it can, the thing itself, as in the call of the cuckoo, the chiming of bells, and so on.

Like the plastic and the graphic arts, theatrical movement may be of either of two kinds. It may be nonrepresentational, as in abstract ballet, or representational, as in mime. Speech has not the versatility of movement, and is at the opposite pole from music. It is always representational and must always refer to something outside itself: a word must have a meaning. It is from the discovery that speech has neither the nature of music nor that of movement that much unjustifiable dissatisfaction with the play arises. There is a tendency to assume that the nonrepresentational is the noumenal, and thus to want to make words nonrepresentational; but this would be to destroy words. There is a tendency to believe that the dignity of words would be raised if they could be made to manifest an organic form dependent on utterly internal laws. Colors and shapes may or may not be used as indicators, but in a work of art they must be satisfactorily organized as colors and shapes. The sounds and rhythms of words may be organized, but only in deference to the meaning of the words. Also, there is a tendency to underestimate the worth of words because they are a man-made material, whereas colors, shapes, sounds, and movements exist independently of man, and it has been held that to use words is to work with a fiction, but to use these other materials is to handle reality.

Artaud declares:

> I say that the stage is a concrete physical place which asks to be filled, and to be given its own concrete language to speak.
> I say that this concrete language, intended for the senses and independent of speech, has first to satisfy the senses, that there is a poetry of the senses as there is a poetry of language, and that this concrete physical language to which I refer is truly theatrical only to the degree that the thoughts it expresses are beyond the reach of the spoken language.[7]

It is not difficult to agree that the stage must be given its own language to speak; but if it is to express thoughts "beyond the reach of the spoken language," then the stage's concern is not with plays, which accomplish all that is possible when spoken language is used in a highly specialized context. Again, although there is "a poetry of the senses" to the extent that aesthetic pleasure arises from appropriate satisfaction of the senses, and although this kind of "poetry" may be made available by the effect on hearing caused by music, on seeing by abstract painting and abstract ballet, on feeling by abstract sculpture (and perhaps it may be possible to similarly affect the senses of smell and taste), nevertheless, this kind of "poetry" cannot occur in any art created in a medium that is, or is used as, an indicator; for example, representational painting, mime, ballet d'action. Above all, it cannot occur in the play, which is created in a medium that is inevitably an indicator. The play, the representational picture or movement, whatever its aesthetic content, refers to thoughts and ideas which are within the reach of spoken language. When Artaud says that "even light can have a precise intellectual meaning,"[8] he is surely mistaken. Light may have associations, but this is not the same as having an intellectual meaning. The particular lighting of a certain scene on the stage may give that scene a different meaning from that it would have under a different kind of lighting; but it is the lit scene that has meaning, not the lighting. Similarly, a black cloud in a picture may cause that picture to have a meaning different from that it would have if the cloud were white; but the colors black and white have in themselves no meanings—although they may have powerful associations. Of course, it may be held that Artaud is hinting at a completely new language based on light. In this case, in the absence of satisfactory concrete examples and in view of man's experience so far, it would not be uncharitable to regard the matter as a cranky idea.

Since Artaud claims precise intellectual meaning for light and since he is concerned about a language that is "truly theatrical only to the degree that the thoughts it expresses are beyond the reach of the spoken language," one may well wonder what place, if any, he reserves for spoken language in the theatre.

> It is not a matter of suppressing speech in the theater but of changing its role, and especially of reducing its position, of considering it as something else than a means of conducting human characters to their external ends, since the theater is concerned only with the way feelings and passions conflict with one another, and man with man, in life.[9]

One does not quarrel with the idea of considering speech as something other than a means of conducting human characters to their external ends (although in opera it is largely used as such a means); but considering it as something more does not reduce its position in the play: on the contrary, it exalts it. If Artaud wants a theatrical form in which the spoken words have any position other than that of the fundamental element, he does not want the play.

Ionesco would hold that "If one believes that the theatre is only a theatre of words, it is difficult to admit that it can have its own language. It can only be dependent upon other forms of thought which are expressed by words: philosophy or ethics."[10] The use of "words" is either so vague or so special, according to the way you look at it, that this observation on the nature of the theatre is hardly illuminating, and Ionesco's next four sentences must strike all who have a serious interest in the theatre as naïve:

> Things are different if one considers that words constitute only one of the elements of theatrical shock. In the first place, the theatre has a special way of using words: dialogue, words of combat, of conflict. If dialogue is nothing but discussion in the plays of some

authors, that is a great fault of theirs. There are other ways of making words theatrical: by using them with ferocious exaggeration in order to give the theatre its true measure, which is lack of measure, the Word itself should be strained to its limits, language should almost explode, or destroy itself, in its impossibility to contain meanings.

The theatre's true measure is lack of measure because the true measure of all art is lack of measure. The Word should be strained to its limits because one aspect of all art is the realization and exploitation of the ultimate potentialities of chosen media. Language should only *almost* explode, because if it were actually to disintegrate, the medium in which the play is created would not exist at all. None of this is essentially new, as Ionesco himself suspects: "It may be said that I have expressed nothing new here. I may even be accused of presenting only the most elementary truths." One certainly can accuse him of presenting these—and not in the most lucid way; but such an accusation is a kind of compliment, for he rightly notes that "nothing is more difficult than returning to elementary truths, fundamental principles, certitudes."[11] In any case, his ideas are all consistent with language's being the fundamental element in the play, even though "words constitute only one of the elements of theatrical shock." Any uneasiness he has is due to the ways in which language is being and has been used in certain plays.

In another part of his article, Ionesco insists, "Theatre language can never be anything but theatre language."[12] If by this he meant that theatre language is language used in a very special way because of the particular demands of theatrical representation, and that used in any other circumstances it would be inappropriate, one would at once agree; but this is not his meaning. He points out that music is music and painting is painting, and contends that to deny that theatre language can never be anything other than theatre language is as wrong as to "claim that music should be archaeology, or painting, physics and mathematics."[13] So long as Ionesco refers to music and abstract painting, he is right; but representational painting may be physics and mathematics, or many other things, and language can never be other than an indicator. Like representational painting, theatre language may be physics or mathematics or other things: in any case, it must be something other than "theatre language" in Ionesco's sense, or else it will have no validity as language for anyone other than theatrical characters. It will be like two straight lines in an abstract painting that are one inch apart at one extreme and two inches apart at the other, as against two similarly disposed lines in a representational painting. In the first instance we have merely two lines which have an effect on the viewer, but which have no meaning for him. In the second instance we have lines with an effect on the viewer and with such meaning for him as is conveyed by linear perspective. Linear perspective may be held to be a mere convention—but so may language.

If it may be said that a theatrical work can only be a play when its fundamental element is language, it may further be said that the play in its most embracing form is the greatest of the theatre's manifestations. Joseph Chiari has written:

> The only realism which has meaning is that of Rembrandt, Dante or Shakespeare, and of the few great artists who can suggest beyond the phenomenon—whether it be a wrinkle, the crease of a dress or the emotional surface of words—the perennial force which informs all these appearances. [14]

Abstract ballet suggests the perennial force, but it has no place for the wrinkles and creases. Opera suggests the perennial force, and it indicates the wrinkles and creases, although very sketchily; but the force and the wrinkles exist separately in opera, or, one may say, the wrinkles are a costume put on for the occasion by the force. The force is not inevitably suggested by the wrinkles. The same applies to representational ballet. In opera the fundamental element is music, in ballet it is movement; and this music exists in terms that are musically significant, this movement in terms that are significant in self-justifying dynamic design. These fundamental elements are not concerned with wrinkles or creases or anything else beyond themselves. In mime, movement's attempt to assert its self-sufficiency in the face of its use as an indicator is constantly apparent, and its limitations as an indicator are equally obvious. In his everyday life man has to deal with the immediately apprehensible world of wrinkles and creases, and the use of words gives him his most effective way of dealing with it. It is inconceivable that the use of either representational movement or song should not have replaced spoken language by the present stage of man's evolution, had either of these been a better indicator than the word, or that they should not exist as wholly satisfactory alternatives to spoken language, were they as good indicators as the word. In having spoken language as its fundamental element, the play is bound to concern itself with wrinkles and creases, for the language must inevitably refer to something beyond the sound of its words. The informing perennial force will be suggested to the extent that the play is a work of art. The important fact is that this force will be suggested by the very words that indicate the wrinkles and creases. There is no parallel of force and appearance, but an identification.

It was stated above that the greatest of the theatre's manifestations was not the play, but the play in its most embracing form, and by this was meant the play that presents us most unequivocally with an apprehension of the immediate and suggests the force informing this immediate. This unequivocal presentation must not offer us the thing itself, as the worst naturalistic plays try to do. When man is able adequately to perceive the informing force in the immediately apprehensible world, he will have no need of art, naturalistic or otherwise. The play must bear the same inevitable relationship to the immediately apprehensible as the word bears to the object it indicates. From this it follows that expressionistic plays, fantastic plays, and the like, are necessarily not the most valuable of plays. They emphasize the informing force at the expense of the appearances it informs. They are the plays that make great use of music, dance, lighting, the plays that grudge the word its fundamental role. These works do not completely destroy appearances, for then they would cease to be plays; but they present appearances from such angles that the identification of the appearances becomes difficult for the audience. This is very different from presenting a new and revealing view of immediately observable reality, for that is most successfully done when the identification of the immediate is still easily accomplished by the audience.

Most of Artaud's comments on the theatre arise from a dissatisfaction with the play as it is today, and proceed to the conclusion that since this theatrical form which is based on language is not what it ought to be, it cannot be what it ought to be. When he writes of considering speech "as something else than a means of conducting human characters to their external ends," he passes strictures on no one but bad playwrights. When he asks, "who ever said the theater was created to analyze a character, to resolve the conflicts of love and duty, to wrestle with all the problems of a topical and psychological nature that monopolize our contemporary stage,"[15] one must answer that many people have said this, or something similar; and whilst one agrees that such people are mistaken if they take these objectives to be the exclusive ends of the play, nevertheless such matters belong to the play since they are the necessary wrinkles and creases whose informing force will be suggested. Artaud's suggestions of creating a theatrical form based on music, movement, light, and so on, and admitting speech in a new way, are most dubious. There can be no theatrical form resulting from the fusion of opera, ballet, and the play, since each of these depends on a different supremely dominant element, and one can have only one supremely dominant element in any given context. There can be no use of music and movement and speech on anything like equal terms throughout a theatrical work. To add aesthetically satisfying music to words that are adequately indicative and that carry with them their own aesthetic satisfaction would be incongruous. One does not add to that which is already complete. If something less than aesthetically satisfying music is used with words that are less than adequately indicative and less than aesthetically satisfying, an utterly inferior work will result. There can be no form which is a successful mixture of opera, ballet, and the play, since the three contain immiscible elements. At best there can be a form that embodies a pattern of sections that are differently dominated by speech, by music, and by movement; and such a form has been used long ago in the masque. It may be that our present day theatre would been enriched by the revival of the masque as a theatrical form; but it should be noticed that the tendency of the masque is—and historically has shown itself to be—to move away from speech and the play and to arrive at opera or ballet or sheer visual spectacle.

Artaud complains: "In the theater as we conceive it, the text is everything. It is understood and definitely admitted, and has passed into our habits and thinking, it is an established spiritual value that the language of words is *the* major language."[16] Can one doubt that for man's purposes, the language of words is the major language? As far as the play is concerned, can the text, in its capacity as indicator of which words are to be spoken, be other than everything? To continue, as Artaud does, "But it must be admitted even from the Occidental point of view that speech becomes ossified and that words, all words, are frozen and cramped in their meanings, in a restricted schematic terminology," is merely to complain that speech cannot accomplish all that even those who believe it to be the major language would like it to accomplish; and to complain of that constant necessity to revitalize language which is acknowledged by all who attempt to use words significantly, of that task which is accomplished by those who create art based on language—notably the creators of great plays.

Notes

1. Antonin Artaud, *The Theater and Its Double,* trans. Mary Caroline Richards (New York: Evergreen Books, 1958)—from which all of the Artaud quotations in the present article are taken.

2. Egon Wellesz, *Essays on Opera,* trans. Patricia Kean (London, 1950), p. 90.

3. Wellesz, p. 7.

4. Eric Bentley, *The Modern Theatre* (London, 1948)—being the English edition of *The Playwright as Thinker*—p. 52.

5. Bentley, p. 53.

6. Interesting comments on the nature of music and the nature of the theatre are to be found in several articles in *Polyphonie,* Premier Cahier (Paris, 1947–48), especially in Boris de Schloezer, *Le Temps du drame et le temps de la musique.*

7. Artaud, p. 37.

8. Artaud, p. 95.

9. Artaud, p. 72.

10. Eugène Ionesco, "Discovering the Theatre," trans. Leonard C. Pronko, *The Tulane Drama Review,* IV, 1 (September, 1959), p. 12.

11. Ionesco, p. 16.

12. Ionesco, p. 15.

13. Ionesco, p. 16.

14. Joseph Chiari, *The Contemporary French Theatre* (London, 1958), p.1.

15. Artaud, p. 41.

16. Artaud, p. 117. Artaud's italics.

2

TDR: 1963–?
(1963)

Richard Schechner and Theodore Hoffman

TDR began as a journal designed to bring the same order of scholarly and critical responsibility to drama that other university publications have brought to more academic disciplines. It has forged an existence out of old ambitions by avoiding old habits, and must now probe and create its identity. Our commitments have revealed themselves. Where they will take us is a matter of action born through achievement, not theory. A majority of our readers work in theatre production. Their interest, like ours, has been directed towards whatever in theatre is most imaginative, complex, and experimental. *TDR* has become increasingly committed to the most ambitious standards and artistically perilous ventures of the professional theatre. Although the kind of professional theatre we subscribe to may exist nowhere in the world today as an established cultural institution, there does exist an informal league of persons working to perfect the crafts of the theatre and apply them to the most profound plays of the past, present, and future. *TDR* intends to be of service to these people.

There will always be a commodity theatre, but the real work gets done elsewhere. At this moment, a movement towards resident professional theatre is on the verge of engaging the core of America's theatrical imagination. The American theatre *is* the San Francisco Actors' Workshop, the Washington Arena Stage, the Houston Alley, the Minneapolis Guthrie, the Stratford, Ontario Shakespeare Festival, the reborn Stratford, Connecticut Shakespeare Festival, the UCLA Theatre Group, Michigan's APA, Chicago's Second City, the Actors' Studio Theatre, the Lincoln Center Company, The Living Theatre, and their increasingly numerous colleagues across America and Canada. An approach which has placed traditional American pragmatism at the service of an age-old vision is indeed creating a new theatre.

Despite the entropy of any large-scale organization, these theatres represent the long-awaited realization of old, good hopes. We do not propose to become the house-organ for these emerging theatres. They are hardy enough to survive, supple enough to absorb the kind of criticism we shall direct at them.

The new theatres, with rare exceptions, have been founded without overt ideology. There are no manifestos to collect and dissect, no stylistic innovations to brag about. But new theatres ask for new ideas, and if we are to have a real theatre on this continent, one which readily translates art and theory, ideas will necessarily emerge that recognize the particular historical, political, and social facts of American life as well as the unique aesthetics of our own theatre practice. If it seems distressing that the people we *rightly* admire most are Europeans, we may soon encounter, without chauvinistic compulsion, American figures to admire.

Right now our task is to explore the implicit framework that binds the new theatres into a fertile conspiracy (if not a "movement"), despite their admirable diversity. If this framework seems shamefully basic, we can only plead that a decade ago its very appearance would have seemed utterly improbable. The editors of *TDR* feel obliged to spell out this framework of commitment, the source of those standards and goals we mean to serve, to encourage, and to help formulate.

1. An absolute commitment to professional standards: Theatre demands a lifetime's application; nothing less will do. A living theatre needs professional playwrights, directors, actors, designers, technicians, managers, dramaturgs, and critics. To do without professional competence is to settle for a half-baked half-loaf.

2. The decentralization of the professional theatre: A genuinely regional theatre assimilates what is happening elsewhere in order to develop the talent and satisfy the cultural needs of its own area. Only resident professional companies can realize the hope of a decentralized American theatre.

3. A deep and continuing interest in both practical and theoretical experimentation: A theatre, or a thinker, without the audacity to explore new ideas and new ways of doing things practices self-mutilation.

4. A committed employment of the open stage: We welcome the open stage not for its budgetary economics, nor without an awareness that it may wrench many plays out of their inherent shape, but because it offers the most appropriate spatial metaphor for the public and aesthetic questions of our day, and because it provides an actor-audience relationship that stimulates the imagination of our best theatre talent, including those designers who do not feel deprived of their identity outside of the opera houses and auditoriums that have stultified our production techniques.

5. The reintroduction of the playwright into the theatre: Honored in words, the writer is the ultimate whore of our theatre. Until he is actively involved in the life and craft of the theatre, our stock of worthwhile plays will remain depressingly low. The new work of young writers must be produced before these writers adjust to the perversions of the commodity theatre. The relationship between the writer and the director has yet to be acceptably defined.

6. *A recognition that the best contemporary theatre is international:* There is no major theatre artist alive today who has not been influenced by colleagues in other countries. In an age which is learning to dissolve the fear of miscegenation, mastery of one's own theatre means enthusiastic exposure to that of other countries.

7. *The redirection of educational theatre into the mainstream of American theatre:* The universities must support resident professional companies, provide fully trained personnel to the professional theatre, become the proving ground for new playwrights, encourage experimentation, and produce viable scholarship. The truth is that these are all interdependent and the universities had better buy the package or shop in some other store.

What is a role of a magazine within this framework? Certainly its very form removes it from the creative heart of the theatre. But it can, like a political pamphlet or scientific paper, record, assess, and influence the work that is being done. Each point of the basic framework demands clarifying discussion and serious debate. There is altogether too little experimentation in our theatres. Even the professional theatres, which have fostered much of what sporadic experimentation there is, have become increasingly burdened with box-office imperatives and the energy-consuming business of holding a company together. If the universities wish to become the experimental laboratories of the theatre, they need "only" to renovate their methods and faculties, to start testing the discoveries of the last quarter-century (which still frighten most of us), and to embark on an earnest confrontation of the present. But educational theatre, unlike the new theatres, is already entrenched, and it has dug in at precisely the wrong places. Clearly, the necessary concentration of resources and policy would equal that of the sciences, but obviously even in a cultural millennium theatre will not elicit the need, talent, support, and market that have fostered the sciences. Only a very few schools can manage full theatre programs. Whether there is any real hope for theatre as an academic discipline remains debatable. At best, most schools will become a transit point for talent, the place where students discover their commitment to theatre and their need for professional training. If such schools act on their alleged love for the liberal arts, they will at least stop trying to provide commodity theatre to the community and properly subsidize a theatre where the great plays that deserve serious study are presented and where playwrights can see new plays staged for what they and the productions are worth. Only if real theatre is brought to the university is the work of its scholars likely to be brought to the theatre. The proliferation of useless drama scholarship and criticism within universities has been as scandalous as the intellectual vacuity of the commodity theatre. If the theatre has taken to educating itself, there is no reason why scholarship cannot do likewise.

No problems are solved by merely listing goals. We have all provoked an arduous debate that may be as productive as it is difficult.

TDR takes it as a primary duty to print plays that need printing for good reasons: not the forgotten ephemera of established playwrights which contribute only to historical scholarship, not the well-intentioned conventional play the commodity theatre narrowly rejected, but the unknown play of the past that deserves production and enlightens our understanding of a playwright or an age of drama, the new play that unveils talent, the play that opens unexplored territory. The *TDR* Play Series will continue (as will the Document Series). With the current issue we begin the John Golden Play Series, which we hope will make available the most venturesome work of young American writers—not to fall dead on the page, but to find life on some stage.

We find it impossible to separate dramatic literature from theatre, and although we shall continue to publish close textual studies of drama, our standards of selection will emphasize theatrical applicability and thematic importance. We also believe that the isolated remarks of genuine artists about their own and others' work, whether found in essays, notes, letters, diaries, or interviews, are often worth more than formal criticism. We intend to print a good deal of theatre theory, both that which has not appeared in English and that which is now being written here and abroad. The time-lapse between work done and work known about must be shortened. We shall continue to review productions on all the continents to which we can afford to send out reviewers. *TDR* Comment will continue to harass and encourage our friends, and to open controversies to view. We shall become increasingly unaware of the useless work of the commodity theatre. There are better things to argue about.

Many future issues will center on themes the editors believe important to the American theatre. We plan these special issues: "Italian Theatre since the War," "Christopher Marlowe," "Stanislavski and America," "Communist Theatre Theory," "New German Theatre," "Pirandello," "The Theatre Art," "Latin American Theatre," and "Film Theory and Theatre Practice." In some of our general issues, there will be special features on "The Economics of the American Theatre," "The Methodology of Drama Criticism," and other topics.

TDR has shifted its loyalty from the academic to the professional theatre, from history to living theatre, from the eclectic to the particular. These tendencies have been present from the beginning. If we are activists, it is because we rejoice that there is more to fight for than against.

3

Corrigan on *TDR* and *TDR* on Corrigan
(1964)

Corrigan on *TDR*

I read the *TDR* Comment of Volume 8, Number 2 (T22), "*TDR*: 1963–?" with no little surprise and disappointment, and was prompted to write a replying comment immediately. However, I resisted this impulse because I have never believed in getting involved in a controversy just for the sake of controversy, and furthermore, such a reply might have been interpreted as a lack of grace or even as defensive "sour grapes," and thus lose whatever force or meaning it might have had. So, I said to myself, why dispute such noble aims and sentiments? And I was content to let my reactions rest dormant. But soon, and with increasing frequency and vehemence, I received or heard so many reactions from *TDR* readers concerning your statement of new aims that I decided to send you my own comment in the belief that it reflects the attitude of a good many of *TDR*'s readers.

To begin with, to openly proclaim that "*TDR* has become increasingly committed to the most ambitious standards and artistically perilous ventures of the professional theatre" is like being for Mother, God, and Country. Such statements are too easy and a bit pretentious; and, more important, in their inflated rhetoric they tend to alienate a large number of those who are actively engaged in the professional theatre. The reaction, quite honestly, is "those guys at *TDR* making all this fuss couldn't make it in the professional theatre if they tried." In your tendency to dismiss most of the theatre in New York as commodity theatre, I believe you are making a serious mistake, for you are cutting yourselves off from the people whom you can help and influence the most. As I compare even this year's poor New York season with the fall programs of those theatres which you say *are* the American theatre, I cannot help but notice that New York seems to be committed to more ambitious standards, greater daring, and more artistically (not to mention financially) perilous ventures than the TCG theatres which you believe are "on the verge of engaging the core of America's theatrical imagination." Where are the new plays—be they bad or good—being produced? Where are the experiments in directing techniques, new concepts of design, imaginative lighting? Where do we see the best acting? I'd say in New York. What's so daring about the repertoires of most of our decentralized professional theatres? I'm delighted that the Guthrie Theatre, for instance, did Shakespeare, Molière, Chekhov, and Miller last year, but is America's living theatre to be only a museum of the classics? I am convinced new plays are not generated by the production of great old ones, no matter how well they may be produced, but only by a commitment to the continuous production of new scripts. And of the theatres you mention as the heart of the new American theatre, only one—The Living Theatre, and even they are now homeless—has such a commitment and only they have consistently encouraged and produced at least interesting new writers. The one great advantage of a commodity theatre is that it must constantly produce new goods to be consumed. While I'll be the first to admit that much of what such a theatre produces is lacking in nourishment, I would also have to insist that when important new plays (either American or continental) are produced they are usually produced first in New York. To argue otherwise, as you appear to do, is to prompt people in the professional theatre to the belief that *TDR* has gone more academic than it ever was in the past.

I also think you are blind to another important fact. As excited as I am personally about the decentralization of the professional theatre, I don't believe the young talent now in training for professional careers in the theatre shares our enthusiasm for these new companies. As the head of a large drama department which is unabashedly training young students for careers in the professional theatre, I know that almost 100% of our students are aiming for a career in New York and they look on the new professional companies either with cynicism or with the pragmatic view that they are good places to get some more training, or a place to get a job with a good possibility of being seen by someone who will want to bring them to New York. For most of them, to plan a career in one of these companies is to choose from the beginning to be a loser. This attitude may change, but it won't until the leaders of the theatre— the top directors, the best actors, the imaginative designers, and the great playwrights—stop treating the decentralized theatre as an interesting busman's holiday or a happy hunting ground for one who is fatigued by having constantly to meet the stiff competition of the New York theatre. But why should they change? In spite of the bad conditions of the commodity theatres, the conditions there are usually better than anywhere else; and if you do get a job there the pay is better.

Until I became directly involved with the training of young talent for careers in the professional theatre, I believe I would have agreed with your position. But now I question it, and I am afraid that *TDR* has its money on the wrong horse. And, I might add, that for a magazine which is going to take its stand for professionalism in the theatre, there is a glaring paucity of genuine professional theatre people on its editorial staff or board. Don't get me wrong; it is an able and distinguished board, but it is obviously not one which can be strongly identified with the professional theatre.

Finally, before closing, one question: What do the editors mean when they write, "*TDR* has shifted its loyalty from the academic to the professional theatre, from history to living theatre, from the eclectic to the particular"? What has the magazine published in recent issues or what has it announced for the future that is so radically different from the past? What indications are there that *TDR* will be taking new directions, except a change of format and the fact that the editors tell us things will be new and different? The recent Artaud issue is a case in point: the essays are fine, but *The Theatre and Its Double* has been available for some time now, the *Evergreen Review* publishes Artaud items fairly regularly, and the editors seem to have forgotten that excerpts from *The Theatre of Cruelty* were published in *TDR* in 1958 before any of Artaud's work had ever been published in English in this country. Certainly the magazine is making more good material on Genet, Artaud, Ghelderode, Betti, and Brecht available to us, and it is being presented in a handsome and tasty manner, but this is not new for *TDR,* and it isn't even very new for the theatre any more.

I believe *TDR* will serve the American theatre most effectively if it avoids particularity in its aims. An artist may need definite goals and objectives; he certainly needs to know what he stands for. But if a magazine of the arts is only a mouthpiece for its editors' beliefs, or if it stands for too definite aims, it will risk being blind to new ideas and different, but valuable, attitudes. I believe the greatest contribution *TDR* can make to the theatre is to serve its artists by providing a forum for all the ideas and cross-currents of attitude that exist in the theatre both here and in the rest of the world; it should pioneer and take a few far-out risks; it should publish more pieces on the theatre which conservative journals wouldn't touch; and it can only succeed in doing this if it stays open enough to be receptive to all ideas—even those that the editors may personally think are crazy, wrong-headed, or detrimental.

I am happy with *TDR* and as a member of its advisory board I commend the fine job the editors are doing. But as a conservative former editor, I am a little leery of such high-flown statements as "action born through achievement" and "we are activists." Manifestoes are an absolute necessity for politicians and certain of our public institutions, and sometimes even for daily papers, but they are a useless appendage to a quarterly magazine. What a magazine stands for is finally always to be found in its table of contents.

Robert W. Corrigan

TDR on Corrigan

We sent Mr. Corrigan's Comment to our editors, and they have replied:

Theodore Hoffman: We hope Mr. Corrigan will find time to visit resident professional theatres, or read the programs straight. Has he seen this year, on or off Broadway, *The Caucasian Chalk Circle, The Queen and the Rebels, The Dream Play,* Pirandello's *Henry IV,* Whiting's *The Devils*—to name a few of the plays from this season's resident programs? Where in New York will he see such plays from the classic repertory as *The Birds, Tartuffe, Scapin, Volpone, The Country Wife*—to say nothing of Shakespeare? He can, of course, see APA and National Repertory productions originally staged for non-Broadway audiences. Good theatre demands producer commitment, responsive audiences, and artistic proficiency. Whether it grows best out of the single-shot, jerry-built, flossy-fronted Broadway construction firm work or out of the long-term organic persistence of resident companies is a question currently the subject of a great American experiment. We happen to believe that only audiences that respond to the great drama of the past are going to respond to the real drama of the present. And while no one claims that resident theatres have the resources of Broadway, which has been almost totally committed to new plays for half a century, the resident theatres are doing what the commodity theatre has not tried to do and are winning audiences Broadway has ignored. Either the new theatres are filled with daring, or Broadway is filled with cowardice.

If Mr. Corrigan's drama department (Carnegie Tech, which he is leaving for a chair in Dramatic Literature at NYU) is what it is because its students want Broadway, let him talk both to its unemployed recent alumni in New York and its recent alumni employed in resident theatres. Let him also note what percentage of the Carnegie generation of the last ten years or so which is making a name for itself (William Ball, Lester Rawlins, Nancy Wickwire, Ellis Rabb, Nan Marchand, Ann Roth, Claud Woolman) developed its talent in resident theatre. Let him examine the history of only one resident theatre, the Washington Arena, to learn what Carnegie alumni have contributed to it and what it has contributed to them.

Charles L. Mee, Jr.: I don't believe the New York theatre will ever die. Any place that has a concentration of eight million people is bound to have a theatre, and much of it is destined to prosper aesthetically and financially. Having said this, I must add that as it is now the theatre in New York is a corpse. The European theatre is decentralized and regional. I think that is a substantial part of the reason Europeans are now doing such exciting work:

the European theatre feeds from human beings who populate its countries. Broadway, and much of Off-Broadway, feeds from an artificial world that has nothing to do with the roots of American life. It is bound to lose its vitality. I see nothing wrong with *TDR*'s policy of junking the romanticism of the status quo in New York and attempting to prepare the way for—and shape—the theatre that is growing, nothing wrong with *TDR* identifying itself with an organic, developing theatre.

I'm sorry Mr. Corrigan is perpetuating the myth that there will be jobs in New York for his students. All he need do is ask Equity for statistics and he would discover that the unemployment ratio is higher in the New York theatre than in any other business in America. Furthermore, he would know that of those who do work only the smallest proportion make a wage that permits them to live off their earnings as actors. It's a pity Mr. Corrigan lets his romanticism about Broadway interfere with his duties as counselor to those aspiring actors. He has been too long in academia. Instead of teaching his students, he asks his students to teach him—and he informs us that his students (paragons of experience that they are) are better informed about the life of the New York theatre than he is, so he documents his case with their evidence. My only question: once Mr. Corrigan finishes with these students, who tests whom? Who gets the degree?

As for *TDR* not taking a new tack, I would like to agree that what *TDR* is now doing is not revolutionary. I would like to agree, but in the next paragraph—in which Mr. Corrigan criticizes the aim of particularity and definite point of view in *TDR* as it is now—he disputes his own argument. Apparently he does feel something is new. Point of view a bad thing? What notable magazine has not had one? Mr. Corrigan's plea for blandness is the plea of academia.

Manifestoes are for politicians, newspapers, public institutions? Why not for quarterlies? I think we've embarrassed Mr. Corrigan with our manifesto. He would be more shy with his point of view, more conservative and subtle, well-mannered. He would not take a chance. And there's the crux—that is what makes *TDR* less academic now than before, closer in temperament to the dynamics of good theatre: the academic approach is to open everything up to everyone so that it is not necessary to take chances, make choices, dare to be delightfully right or stupidly embarrassingly wrong. The gamble of making choices is closer to what the theatre is really, or should be, all about.

Paul Gray: It's alarming to notice how fast things change. Five years ago Mr. Corrigan's mind might have been looking ahead and making a contribution, but now, suddenly, he seems twenty years behind the sources of creative energy necessary to establish a theatre. In my opinion, he did not have enough insight into the problems behind the *TDR* Comment in T22 to explode the argument. By publishing Mr. Corrigan's criticism we dramatize the tremendous energy that has changed the shape of the magazine. Also, it is important that the editors have the courage to present a manifesto and that they also have the courage to change it as they learn more about the theatre. The editors, contrary to Corrigan's statement, are indeed professional. Instead of "unabashedly training young students" for careers in New York theatre, they are engaged in the crucial issues facing the American theatre, and you can tell Mr. Corrigan the old Greek adage that "through suffering comes wisdom" (and our readers will suffer with us) and through this all of us, editors and readers alike, will gain insight into the problems besetting our theatre. Even if we have a new manifesto every day, there can be no more creative a magazine than one which admits to growing pains in the search for a new theatre.

Gordon Rogoff: Mr. Corrigan's letter reveals an ear well attuned to the voices of nameless others and almost completely separated from himself: which is to say that, while many of his arguments might find most of us in at least partial agreement, they rest so firmly on the premise that the audience ("a good many of *TDR*'s readers") and the young actors (who want to make it in New York) are always right, that whatever else he has to say falls aimlessly into the background. Why, in 1964, must we seriously reconsider Mr. Corrigan's market-place premise? The audience is not always right. Dreaming youth is almost always heading for screaming disillusion. And people who are making it in our theatre, whether on or off Broadway, in or out of New York, are not by definition and defensive fiat automatic professionals.

That the profit motive often brings important new plays to Broadway cannot be denied. That it also brings them belatedly and badly to Broadway, however, is the parallel fact unmentioned by Mr. Corrigan. The unacademic fact is that even the profit motive doesn't serve to bring many of the most important plays to New York first. Edward Albee was "discovered" in Berlin. England's best young dramatist, John Arden, has had only one play produced in America, and that one in San Francisco. Max Frisch is getting better representation in the Seattle production of *The Firebugs* than he ever received in New York. Meanwhile, some of the most promising young Americans are getting their first full productions away from New York: Conrad Bromberg and Maria Irene Fornes in San Francisco, Herbert Boland in Washington, D.C., and Terence McNally in Minneapolis.

Mr. Corrigan's fear of "too definite aims" and his concern that *TDR* risks an unreceptivity to new ideas is really the vocabulary of new euphemisms covering fear, a comfortable sense of purposelessness, abdication, and conformity.

Richard Schechner: What more is there to say? During the eight issues since Mr. Corrigan gave up the editorship of *TDR*, our renewal rate has risen to 80%, subscriptions have gone from 1,100 to 2,800, and total sales from 3,500 to 9,000 per issue. If our readers are "vehement" about our policies, they have not chosen to ignore us.

Certainly there is no lack of professionals, young and old, contributing regularly to *TDR*. Furthermore, we consider ourselves professionals because we edit a magazine and that, too, is a profession, and one which we feel is essential to the theatre. *TDR* is designed to help get the theatre moving again, and there is no doubt in our minds that it is moving. We have said a great deal about the resident professional theatre (and we must include the Lincoln Center Repertory and the Actor's Studio Theatre in our list), but there are good new plays being written as well, and new writers whose names we hope will become more familiar to us all very soon: Robert Head, James Lineberger, Kenneth Brown, Dennis Jasudowicz—to add just a few to Gordon Rogoff's list. The new theatres need not be bereft of playwrights.

Certainly all is not sweetness and light—but the hope of the American theatre is the resident professional movement, the ensemble company, the new socially-aware writers.

Finally, we are proud that *TDR* is the "mouthpiece of its editors." Who else should it speak for? Of what use is an anonymous voice? Who can quarrel with blandness? We welcome divergent opinions in our pages, but certainly we are not about to print what we feel is worthless or destructive. That kind of eclecticism is cowardly and suicidal. Mr. Corrigan's criticism of our editorial approach is hard to understand, since we must apparently espouse Broadway while printing stuff Broadway doesn't care about, be conservative and way out simultaneously, and serve everybody by being all things to all men. The real question is: who and what are the editors the mouthpiece for?

The Editors

4

Doctor Faustus in Poland
(1964)

Jerzy Grotowski

In 1963, Jerzy Grotowski's Theatre Laboratory in Opole, Poland—an industrial town of 50,000 some sixty miles from Auschwitz—produced Marlowe's Doctor Faustus. *Not one word was changed in the script, but the text was reordered into a "montage," as Grotowski calls it, drawing on all the Quartos and rearranging the sequence of scenes, creating new ones and eliminating some others. We are printing the program notes to this production, including the sequence of scenes as Grotowski conceived them. Although the play was performed in Polish, Grotowski wrote the program in French. The Theatre Laboratory is small, seating only sixty, and productions are mounted only when they are ready. For* Faustus *the long, low theatre room—about forty by fifteen feet—was painted black, and the set consisted of two long tables running the length of the room and one smaller table at one end of the room. In a future issue, we shall have an article about the Theatre Laboratory's work and an interview with Grotowski by Eugenio Barba, who spent some months in Poland with Grotowski's company. We would like to thank Mr. Barba for sending us the program and photographs printed below.*
—The Editors

The mise-en-scène and the reordered text. Faustus has one hour to live before his martyrdom of hell and eternal damnation. He invites his friends to a last supper, a public confession where he offers them episodes from his life as Christ offered his body and blood. Faustus welcomes his guests—the audience—as they arrive and asks them to sit at two long tables on the sides of the room. Faustus takes his place at a third, smaller table like the prior in a refectory. The feeling is that of a medieval monastery, and the story apparently concerns only monks and their guests. This is the underlying

The set for *Doctor Faustus* at the Theatre Laboratory in Opole. Faustus awaits the arrival of his "guests."

archetype of the text. Faustus and the other characters are dressed in the habits of different orders. Faustus is in white; Mephistophilis is in black, played simultaneously by a man and a woman; other characters are dressed as Franciscans. There are also two actors seated at the table with the audience, dressed in everyday clothes. More about them later.

Faustus: saint against God. This is a play based on a religious theme. God and the Devil intrigue with the protagonists—that is why the play is set in a monastery. There is a dialectic between mockery and apotheosis. Faustus is a saint and his saintliness shows itself as an absolute desire for pure truth. If the saint is to become one with his sainthood, he must rebel against God, Creator of the world, because the laws of the world are traps contradicting morality and truth.

> *Stipendium peccati mors est.* Ha! *Stipendium, etc.*
> The reward of sin is death. That's hard.
> *Si peccasse negamus, fallimur*
> *Et nulla est in nobis veritas.*
> If we say we have no sin,
> We deceive ourselves, and there's no truth in us.
> Why then belike we must sin,
> And so consequently die.
> Ay, we must die an everlasting death.
>
> (I,i,39–47)

Whatever we do—good or bad—we are damned. The saint is not able to accept as his model this God who ambushes man. God's laws are lies, He spies on the dishonor in our souls the better to damn us. Therefore, if one wants sainthood, one must be against God.

But what must the saint care for? His soul, of course. To use a modern expression, his own self-consciousness. Faustus, then, is not interested in philosophy or theology. He must reject this kind of knowledge and look for something else. His research begins precisely in his rebellion against God. But how does he rebel? By signing his pact with the Devil. In fact, Faustus is not only a saint but a martyr—even more so than the Christian saints and martyrs, because Faustus expects no reward. On the contrary, he knows that his due will be eternal damnation.

Here we have the archetype of the saint. The role is played by an actor who looks young and innocent—his psycho-physical characteristics resemble St. Sebastian's. But this St. Sebastian is anti-religious, fighting God.

The dialectic of mockery and apotheosis consists then of a conflict between lay sainthood and religious sainthood, deriding our usual ideas of a saint. But at the same time this struggle appeals to our contemporary "spiritual" commitment, and in this we have the apotheosis. In the production, Faustus' actions are a grotesque paraphrase of a saint's acts; and yet, he reveals at the same time the poignant pathos of a martyr.

Montage and interpretation of the text. The text is rearranged in such a way that Act V, scene two of Marlowe's script—where Faustus argues with the three scholars—opens the production. Faustus, full of humility, his eyes empty, lost in the imminence of his martyrdom, greets his guests while seated at his small table, his arms open as on the Cross. Then he begins his confession. What we usually call virtues, he calls sin—his theological and scientific studies; and what we call sin; he calls virtue—his pact with the Devil. During his confession, Faustus' face glows with an inner light.

When Faustus begins to talk about the Devil and his first magic tricks, he enters into the second reality (flashbacks). The action then shifts to the two tables where Faustus evokes the episodes of his life, a kind of biographical travelogue.

Scene 1. Faustus greets his guests.

Scene 2. Wagner announces that his master is soon to die.

Scene 3. A monologue in which Faustus publicly confesses as sins his studies and exalts as a virtue his pact with the Devil.

Scene 4. In a flashback, Faustus begins to tell the story of his life. First there is a monologue in his study recalling the moment when he decided to renounce theology and take up magic. This interior struggle is represented by a conflict between an owl, who symbolizes the erudite personality, and a donkey, whose stubborn inertia is opposed to the owl's learning.

Scene 5. Faustus talks to Cornelius and Valdes, who come to initiate him in magic. Cornelius turns a table into a confessional booth. As he confesses, Faustus, granting him absolution, begins his new life. The spoken text often contradicts its interpretation; for example, these lines describe the pleasures of magic. Then Cornelius reveals the magic ceremonies to Faustus and teaches him an occult formula—which is nothing other than a well-known Polish hymn.

Scene 6. Faustus in the forest. By imitating a gust of wind, the tumbling of leaves, the noises of night, the cries of nocturnal animals, Faustus finds himself singing a religious hymn invoking Mephistophilis.

Scene 7. The appearance of Mephistophilis (the Annunciation). Faustus is on his knees in a humble pose. Mephistophilis, on one leg, a soaring angel, sings his lines accompanied by an angelic choir. Faustus tells him that he is ready to give his soul to the Devil in exchange for twenty-four years of life against God.

Scene 8. The mortification of Faustus. A masochistic scene provoked by the arguments of the Good and Bad Angels. Faustus rubs his own spit in his face, knocks his head against his knees, rips at his genitals—all while reciting his lines in a calm voice.

Scene 9. During a walk Faustus tells Mephistophilis of his decision to give him his soul.

Scene 10. Faustus' baptism. Before signing the contract, Faustus is almost drowned in a river (the space between the tables). Thus he is purified and ready for his new life. Then the female Mephistophilis promises to grant all his wishes. She comforts Faustus by rocking him in her lap (the Pietá).

Scene 11. Signing the pact. Faustus reads his contract with Mephistophilis in a commercial tone. But his gestures reveal a struggle to suppress the anguish which torments him. Finally, overcoming his hesitation, he tears his clothes off in a kind of self-rape.

Scene 12. The double Mephistophilis, using liturgical gestures, shows Faustus his new vestments.

Scene 13. Scene with his "devil-wife." Faustus treats her as if she were a book which held all the secrets of nature.

> Now would I have a book where I might see all
> Characters and planets of the heavens, that I might know
> Their motions and dispositions.
>
> . . . .
> Wherein I might see all the plants, herbs, and trees that
> Grow upon the earth
>
> (1604 Quarto I,v,618–620, 623–24)

The saint examines the slut as if he were carefully reading a book. He touches all the parts of her body and reads them as "planets," "plants," etc.

Scene 14. Mephistophilis tempts Faustus. In Scene 13 the young saint has begun to suspect that the Devil is also in God's service. Scene 14 corresponds to a real break in reality. Mephistophilis, at this point in the production, is like a police informer. He takes three roles: Mephistophilis himself, the Good Angel, and the Bad Angel. It is not by accident that the double Mephistophilis is dressed as a Jesuit who tempts Faustus to act sinfully. But when Faustus begins to understand the consequences, he calmly evaluates the Good Angel's words. In this scene, Mephistophilis, as the Good Angel, offers Faustus a meeting with God. They act as if it were late at night in a monastery, and two dissatisfied monks were talking quietly out of everyone's hearing. But Faustus refuses to repent anything.

Scene 15. Astrological discussions. Mephistophilis plays the role of a loyal servant exalting the harmony and perfection of his master's creation in duplicating the sound of the celestial spheres. The conversation is interrupted by two guests who talk of beer and whores. These are the two actors who have been sitting for the whole performance among the spectators. They have played all the farce roles (Robin, Vintner, Dick, Carter, Scholars, Old Man, etc.). In their scenes they represent the banality that marks our everyday life. One of these comic scenes (with the Horse-Courser) is acted right after Faustus asks Mephistophilis, "Now tell me who made the world?" Our daily platitudes are themselves arguments against God. Our saint demands to know who is responsible for the creation of such a world. Mephistophilis, servant of God's evil urge, falls into a real panic and refuses to answer: "I will not." Naturally, in this scene, as in others, the text contradicts the gestures.

Scene 16. One by one Lucifer shows the Seven Deadly Sins to Faustus. Faustus absolves them as Christ absolved Mary Magdalene. The Seven Deadly Sins are played by the same persons: the double Mephistophilis.

Scene 17. Faustus is transported to the Vatican by two dragons, the double Mephistophilis.

Scene 18. Faustus, invisible at the feet of the Pope, is present at a banquet in St. Peter's. The banquet table is made of the bodies of the double Mephistophilis, who recites the Ten Commandments. Faustus slaps the Pope, breaking him of his pride and vanity. He transforms the Pope into a humble man—this is Faustus' miracle.

Scene 19. At the palace of the Emperor Charles V, Faustus performs miracles in the tradition of the popular legends. He splits the earth and brings forth Alexander the Great. Then Faustus outwits Benvolio, a courtier who wants to kill him: Benvolio's rage is directed against the tables—he actually dismantles the table-tops, and turns sections of the tables over, all the while thinking he is dismembering Faustus. Then Faustus turns Benvolio into a little child.

Scene 20. Return to the present—Faustus' last supper. Faustus picks up his conversation with his guests. Upon the urging of a friend he conjures up Helen of Troy, unmasking by comic allusions the female biological functions. Helen begins to make love to him—immediately she gives birth to a baby. Then, while in this erotic position, she becomes the wailing infant. Finally she is transformed into a greedy baby at suck.

Scene 21. The double Mephistophilis shows Paradise to Faustus. This would have been his had he followed God's precepts: a good, calm, and pious death. Then they show him the Hell that awaits him: a convulsive and violent death.

Scene 22. The final scene. Faustus has but one minute to live. A long monologue which represents his last, and most outrageous, provocation of God.

Benvolio, thinking he has killed Faustus, has destroyed the set in a fury.

> Ah Faustus,
> Now hast thou but one bare hour to live,
> And then thou must be damned perpetually!
> (V,ii,130–131)

In the original text, this monologue expresses Faustus' regret for having sold his soul to the Devil; he offers to return to God. In our production, this is an open struggle, the great encounter between the saint and God. Faustus, using gestures to argue with Heaven, and invoking the audience as his witness, makes suggestions that would save his soul, if God willed it, if He were truly merciful and all-powerful enough to rescue a soul at the instant of its damnation. First Faustus proposes that God stop the celestial spheres—time—but in vain.

> Stand still, you ever-moving spheres of heaven,
> That time may cease and midnight never come.
> (V,ii,133–134)

He addresses God, but answers himself, "O, I'll leap up to my God! Who pulls me down?" (V,ii,142). Faustus observes an interesting phenomenon: the sky is covered with the blood of Christ, and just one half drop would save him. He demands salvation:

> See, see, where Christ's blood streams in the firmament!
> One drop would save my soul, half a drop!...
> (V,ii,143–144)

But Christ vanishes, even as Faustus implores him, and this prompts Faustus to say to his guests, "Where is it now? 'Tis gone." (V,ii,147). Then God's angry face appears, and Faustus is frightened:

> ... And see where God
> Stretcheth out his arm and bends his ireful brows!
> (V,ii,147–148)

Faustus wants the earth to open and swallow him, and he throws himself to the ground.

> Mountains and hills, come, come, and fall on me,
> And hide me from the heavy wrath of God.
> (V,ii,149–150)

But the earth is deaf to his prayers and he rises crying, "O no, it will not harbor me!" (V,ii,153). The sky then resonates with the Word and in all the corners of the room the hidden actors, reciting like monks, chant prayers like the Ave Maria and the Pater Noster. Midnight sounds. Faustus' ecstasy is transformed into his Passion. The moment has come when the saint—after having shown his guests the guilty indifference, yes, even the sin of God—is ready for his martyrdom: eternal damnation. He is in a rapture, his body is shaken by spasms. The ecstatic failure of his voice becomes at the moment of his passion a series of inarticulate cries—the piercing, pitiable shrieks of an animal caught in a trap. His body shudders, and then all is silence. The double Mephistophilis, dressed as two priests, enters and takes Faustus to Hell.

Mephistophilis lugs Faustus away on his back, holding him by the feet, the saint's head down near the ground, his hands trailing on the floor. Thus he goes to his eternal damnation, as a sacrificial animal is carried, as one is dragged to the Cross.

The female Mephistophilis begins to hum a sad march which becomes a melancholy religious song (The Mother of Sorrows following her son to Calvary?). From the saint's mouth come raucous cries; these inarticulate sounds are not human. Faustus is no longer a man, but a panting animal, an unclaimed, once-human wreck moaning without dignity. The saint against God has attained his "summit," he has lived God's cruelty. He is the victor— morally. But he has paid the full price of that victory: eternal martyrdom in Hell where all is taken from him, even his dignity.

Translated by Richard Schechner

5

The New Theatre
(1965)

Michael Kirby

Since the turn of the century, most art forms have vastly expanded their materials and scope. Totally abstract or nonobjective painting and sculpture, unheard of in 1900, is practiced by many major artists today. Composers tend to discard traditional Western scales and harmonies, and atonal music is relatively common. Poetry has abandoned rhyme, meter, and syntax. Almost alone among the arts, theatre has lagged. But during the last few years there have been a number of performances that begin to bring theatre into some relation with the other arts. These works, as well as productions in other performance-oriented fields, force us to examine theatre in a new light and raise questions about the meaning of the word "theatre" itself.

In discussing this new theatre, new terms are needed. A few have already been provided by public usage, although they need clarification and standardization. Others will have to be created. Accurate nomenclature is important—not for the sake of limitation but to facilitate easy, accurate, and creative exchange among those concerned with the work and its concepts. If my own approach seems too serious, it may be justified as a reaction against those who take the new theatre very lightly and thus dismiss, without seeing them, theatrical developments of real importance.

It is clear, however, that perfect definitions are almost impossible to derive from actual recent theatrical productions. Just as no *formal* distinctions between poetry and prose can be made in some cases, and passages of prose are published in anthologies of poetry, and as traditional categories of painting and sculpture grow less and less applicable to much modern work, so theatre exists not as an entity but as a continuum blending into other arts. Each name and term refers only to a significant point on this continuum. Definitions apply to *central tendency,* but cannot set precise limits.

For example, we find that theatre blends at one extreme into painting and sculpture. Traditionally these arts did not structure the time dimension as theatre does, but in recent years paintings and sculptures have begun to move and give off sound. They have become performers. Some of the works of Rauschenberg and Tinguely are obvious examples, and pieces of kinetic sculpture by Len Lye have been exhibited to an audience from the stage in New York's Museum of Modern Art. Art displays, such as the large surrealist exhibitions and the recent "labyrinths" of the Groupe de Recherche d'Art Visuel de Paris, are turned into environmental mazes through which the spectator wanders, creating a loose time structure. The Environment which completely surrounds the viewer has become an accepted art form.

Although almost all Environments have made use of light, sound, and movement, *Eat* by Allan Kaprow went one step further by employing human beings as the mechanized elements. The people involved functioned within narrow and well-defined limits of behavior. Their tasks, which had no development or progression, were repeated without variation. They responded only to particular actions on the part of the spectators—only when their "switch was turned on." It may be easy to keep "performing" paintings and sculptures within the categories of those arts, but does Kaprow's use of the human performer make his *Eat* "theatre"? Certainly *Eat* is at the dividing line between forms. My own opinion is that the very strong emphasis upon static environmental elements outweighs the performance elements. *Eat* is not quite theatre. It is just this kind of weighing, this evaluation guided by dominant characteristics and central tendency, which must be used in assigning works of the New Theatre to a category.

The most convenient beginning for a discussion of the New Theatre is John Cage. Cage's thought, in his teaching, writing, lectures, and works, is the backbone of the New Theatre. In the first place, Cage refuses as a composer to accept any limits for music. Traditional sound-producers did not satisfy him, and he created his own instruments: the prepared piano, in which various materials were placed on the strings of a piano to change the qualities of the sounds; the water gong, which was lowered into water while vibrating to produce a change in tone; etc. Not only did he equate sound and silence so that long passages of silence were integral parts of his compositions, but he pointed out that absolute silence does not exist. (He is fond of describing his experience in a theoretically sound-proof research room in which he heard two sounds: the circulation of his blood and the functioning of his nervous system.) If sound is ever-present, so are the other senses, and Cage has gone so far as to deny the existence of music itself, if music is considered as hearing isolated from sight, touch, smell, etc.

These considerations led to a shift of emphasis in Cage's concerts toward non-auditory elements. Of course the performance of music for an audience is never entirely auditory. Rituals of tuning up, the appearance of the conductor, and the attitudes, behavior, and dress of the musicians are important parts of the experience. Although we enjoy watching performances on traditional instruments (at a piano recital, for example, seats on the keyboard side are preferred), the visual aspects are relatively easy to take for granted (and those who cannot see the keyboard do not feel cheated). A new instrument, such as a water gong, or a new way of playing, such as reaching inside the piano to pluck the strings, calls attention to itself: *how* the sound is produced becomes as significant a part of the experience as the *quality* of the sound itself. This theatricalization of a musical performance exists on an entirely different level from the emotional dramatizations of a Bernstein.

If any kind of sound-producer may be used to make music, and if silence is also music (because the true silence does not exist), it follows that any activity or event may be presented as part of a music concert. La Monte Young may use a butterfly as his sound source; the ONCE group can refer to the performance of a piece which includes the broadcast narration of a horse race (the only primarily auditory element), the projected image of rolling marbles, and a series of people moving in various ways (on roller skates, etc.) as "music."

This emphasis upon performance, which is one result of a refusal to place limits upon music, draws attention to the performer himself. But the musician is not acting. Acting might be defined as the creation of character and/or place: details of "who" and "where" the performer is are necessary to the performance. The actor functions within subjective or objective person-place matrices. The musician, on the other hand, is *nonmatrixed*. He attempts to be no one other than himself, nor does he function in a place other than that which physically contains him and the audience.

Nonmatrixed performances are not uncommon. Although the audience-performer relationship which is the basis of theatre exists in sporting events, for example, the athlete does not create character or place. Nor is such imaginary information a part of the half-time spectacle of a football game, religious or secular rituals, political conventions, or many other activities in "real life." The tendency, however, is to deny the performers in these situations serious consideration either because, like the musician, they are not a "legitimate" and accepted part of the formal experience, or because the works in which they appear are not art. My point is not to change our view of these "common" events but to suggest the profound possibilities and potentialities of nonmatrixed performing for the theatre.

Since acting is, by definition, matrixed performing, why not simply use the terms "acting" and "non-acting" rather than suggesting new and fairly awkward terms? The fact is that non-acting would be equally awkward and less meaningful. Matrix is a larger and more inclusive concept than the activity of the performer, and a person may be matrixed without acting.

Acting is something that a performer does; matrix can be externally imposed upon his behavior. The context of place, for example, as determined by the physical setting and the information provided verbally and visually by the production, is frequently so strong that it makes an actor out of any person, such as an extra, who walks upon the stage. In many cases nothing needs to be done in order to act. The priest in church performing part of the service, the football player warming up and playing the game, the sign painter being raised on a scaffold while passers-by watch, are not matrixed by character or place. Even their specific, identifying clothing does not make them characters. Yet the same people might do exactly the same things in a play involving a scene of worship, a football game, or the creation of a large sign, and become actors because of the context.[1]

This does not mean that there is always a clear line between matrixed and nonmatrixed performing. The terms refer to polar conceptions which are quite obvious in their pure forms, but a continuum exists between them, and it is possible that this or that performance might be difficult to categorize. In other words, the strength of character-place matrices may be described as "strong" or "weak" and the exact point at which a weak matrix becomes nonmatrix is not easy to perceive. But even in the extreme case in which both the work of the performer and the information provided by his context are so vague and nonspecific that we could not explain who he was or where he was supposed to be, we often feel that he is someone other than himself or in some place other than the actual place of performance. We know when we are suspending disbelief or being asked to suspend it.

Nonmatrixed performances which are complete in themselves are referred to as Events. A piano is destroyed. The orchestra conductor walks on stage, bows to the audience, raises his baton, and the curtain falls. A formally dressed man appears with a french horn under his arm: when he bows, ball bearings pour from the bell of the horn in a noisy cascade. A person asks if La Monte Young is in the audience: when there is no answer, he leaves. A man sets a balloon on stage, carefully estimates the distance as he walks away from it, then does a backward flip, landing on the balloon and breaking it. Since Events are usually short, they are frequently performed as parts of longer programs. The Fluxus group, a fairly loose organization which includes most of the people working in the form in New York, has presented many "concerts" composed entirely of Events. The form demonstrates a type of performing that is widely used in the New Theatre and which is one of its most important contributions.

In his music Cage abandoned harmony, the traditional means of structuring a composition, and replaced it with duration. This was logically consistent, since duration was the only dimension of music which applied to silence as well as to sounds. Duration could also be used to structure spoken material, and Cage built lectures with these same techniques. Indeed, duration is the one dimension which exists in *all* performance, and in the summer of 1952, stimulated no doubt by his awareness of the performance aspects of music and by his programmatic refusal to place limits upon the sounds used or the manner in which they were produced, Cage presented a work at Black Mountain College which combined dance, motion pictures, poetry and prose readings, and recorded music. These materials were handled exactly as if they had been sounds. The musical and non-musical elements were all precisely scored for points of entry into the piece and duration—a wide variety of performance materials were "orchestrated."

Theatre as we have generally known it is based primarily upon *information structure*. Not only do the individual elements of a presentation generate meaning, but each conveys meaning to and receives it from the other elements. This was not true of the piece which Cage presented at Black Mountain College. Although some of the elements contained information, the performance units did not pass information back and forth or explain each other. The film, for example, which was the cook at the school and later of a sunset, did not help the spectator to understand the dance any more clearly than if the dance had been presented by itself. The ideas expressed in the poetry had no intentional relationship to the ideas contained in the prose. The elements remained intellectually discrete. Each was a separate compartment. The structure was *alogical*.

The information structure of traditional theatre is not alogical but either logical or illogical. Information is built and interrelated in both the logical well-made play and the illogical dream, surreal, or absurd play. Illogic depends upon an awareness of what is logical. Alogical structure stands completely outside of these relationships.

Of course the structure of all music (overlooking the "waterfalls" and "twittering birds" of program music and the written program itself, which adds its own information structure to the composition) and of abstract or nonobjective painting and sculpture is alogical. It depends upon sensory rather than intellectual relationships. Literature, on the other hand, depends primarily upon information structure. It is this fact rather than a reliance upon written script material or the use of words which makes it so easy and so correct to call traditional theatre *"literary* theatre." As Cage's piece demonstrated, *verbal* should not be confused with *literary*. Nor is the nonverbal necessarily alogical. Information is conveyed by movement, setting, and lighting as well as by words, and a mime play, although more limited in its technical means, constructs the same web of information that a dialogue play does. Both are literary. The spectator "reads" the performance.[2]

A performance using a variety of materials (films, dance, readings, music, etc.) in a compartmented structure, and making use of essentially nonmatrixed performance, is a Happening. Thus the distinction between Happenings and Events can be made on the basis of compartments or logically discrete elements. The Event is limited to one compartment, while the Happening contains several, most often sequential, compartments, and a variety of primary materials.

The name "Happening" was taken by the public from *18 Happenings in 6 Parts* by Allan Kaprow (who had studied with Cage), which was presented in 1959. Since then it has been applied indiscriminately to many performances ranging from plays to parlor games. It has been a fad word, although the small attendance at presentations prevents Happenings themselves from being called a fad. Nobody seems to like the word except the public. Since the name was first applied to a piece by Kaprow, it tends to be his word, and some other artists, not caring for the slightest implication that their work is not at least 100 percent original, do not publicly apply the name Happening to their productions. (I am reminded of the person who said he did not want to go to a particular Happening because he had seen a Happening already. It was as if he was saying that he did not want to read a particular novel because he had read a novel once.) Names are beginning to proliferate: Theatre Piece (Robert Whitman), Action Theatre (Ken Dewey), Ray Gun Theatre (Claes Oldenburg), Kinetic Theatre (Carolee Schneemann). The ONCE group and Ann Halprin perform works which I would call Happenings, but they refer to them as music, dance, or by no generic name. Because nothing better has been coined to replace it, I will use the term Happening.

A dominant aspect of Cage's thought has been his concern with the environmental or directional aspects of performance. In addition to the frequent use of extremely loud sounds which have a high density and fill the space, he often distributes the sound sources or loudspeakers around the spectators so that the music comes to them from various angles and distances. In his presentation at Black Mountain College, the audience sat in the center of the space while some performers stood up among them to read, other readings were done from ladders at either end, Merce Cunningham danced around the outer space, and a film was projected on the ceiling and walls.

This manipulation and creative use of the relationship between the presented performance material and the spectator has been developed extensively in Happenings. Spectators are frequently placed in unconventional seating arrangements so that a performance element which is close to some is far from others and stimuli reach the observer from many different directions. In some arrangements the spectators are free to move and, in selecting their own vantage points, control the spatial relationship themselves. At other times they are led through or past spatially separated performance units much as medieval audiences passed from one station to another.

A major aspect of directional and environmental manipulations is not merely that different spectators experience stimuli at different intensities but that they may not experience some of the material at all. This is intentional, and unavoidable in a situation that is much like a three-ring circus.

If a circus were a work of art, it would be an excellent example of a Happening. Except for the clowns (and perhaps the man with the lions who pretends that they are vicious), the performances are nonmatrixed. The acrobats, jugglers, and animal trainers were merely carrying out their activities. The grips or stagehands become performers, too, as they dismantle and rig the equipment—demonstrating that nonmatrixed performing exists at all levels of difficulty. The structure of a three-ring circus makes use of simultaneous as well as sequential compartments. There is no information structure: the acts do not add meaning to one another, and one can be fully understood without any of the others. At the same time the circus is a total performance and not just the sum of its parts. The flow of processions alternates with focused activity in the rings. Animal acts or acrobatic acts are presented at the same time. Sometimes all but one of the simultaneous acts end at the same moment, concentrating the spectators' previously scattered attention on a single image. Perhaps tumblers and riders are presented early in the program, and a spatial progression is achieved by ending the program with the high wire and trapeze artists. And the circus, even without its traditional tent, has strong environmental aspects. The exhibits of the side show, the menagerie, and the uniformed vendors in the aisles are all part of the show. Sometimes small flashlights with cords attached are hawked to the children: whenever the lights are dimmed, the whole space is filled with hundreds of tiny lights being swung in circles.

But although the acrobat may be seen as an archetypal example of nonmatrixed performing, he can be something else. In Vsevolod Meyerhold's biomechanics, actors were trained as acrobats and gymnasts. The actor functioned as a machine, and the constructivist set was merely an arrangement of platforms, ramps, swings, ladders, and other nonrepresentational elements that the performer could use. But the performers were still matrixed by place and character. Although the set did not indicate a particular place, the dialogue and situations made it clear. Biomechanics were used merely as a way of projecting the characters of the story. An actor turned a somersault to express rage or performed a salto-mortale to show exaltation. Calm and unrest could both be signified on the high wire rather than in the usual ways. Determination could be projected from a trapeze. Although biomechanics used movements which, out of context, were nonmatrixed acrobatics, it used them within place and character matrices created by an information structure.

The nonmatrixed performing in Happenings is of several types. Occasionally people are used somewhat as inanimate objects. In *Washes* by

Claes Oldenburg, for example, a motionless girl covered with balloons floated on her back in the swimming pool where the piece was being presented while a man bit the balloons and exploded them. At other times the simple operation of theatrical machinery becomes part of the performance: in *Washes* a record player and a motion picture projector were turned on and off in plain view of the audience; the "lifeguard" merely walked around the pool and helped with certain props. Most nonmatrixed performing is more complicated, however. It might be thought of as combining the image quality of the first type with the purposeful functioning of the second. At one point in *Washes,* for example, four men dove into the pool and pushed sections of silver flue pipe back and forth along a red clothes line. There was no practical purpose in shoving and twisting the pipes, but it was real activity. Manufactured character or situation had nothing to do with it. The men did not pretend to be anyone other than themselves, nor did they pretend—unlike the swimmers in *Dead End* or *Wish You Were Here*—that the water they were in was anything other than what it actually was: in this case a health club pool with spectators standing around the edge.

When acting is called for in a Happening, it almost always exists in a rudimentary form. Because of the absence of an information structure, the job of acting tends to fall into its basic elements. Perhaps an emotion is created and projected as it was by the exaggerated frenzy with which the man in *Washes* bit the balloons attached to the floating girl. Although the rate or tempo of this action had no necessary connection with character, and the activity could have been carried out in a nonmatrixed manner, it could not be denied that the agitated and mock-ferocious quality that was dominant was acting. The acted qualities stood out and remained isolated because they did not fit into a character matrix or into a larger situation. Other facets of acting—playing an attitude, place, details of characterization—are also found in Happenings, but they are usually isolated and function as a very weak matrix.

This is not to say that emotion of any sort during a performance is necessarily acted. Although much nonmatrixed performance is comparatively expressionless, it would be erroneous to think that this type of performing is without emotion. Certainly feelings are expressed in the nonmatrixed performing of everyday life: in the runner's face as he breaks the tape, in the professor's intonation and stress during his lecture, in the owner's attitude as he handles his dog in a dog show. The important point is that emotions apparent during a nonmatrixed performance are those of the performer himself. They are not intentionally created, and they are the natural result of the individual's attitude toward the piece, of the particular task being performed, or of the particular situation of being in front of an audience. Without acted emotions to mask his own feelings, the performer's own attitudes are more apt to become manifest than they are in traditional theatre.

Of course acting and nonmatrixed performing have certain elements in common. When the production of various kinds of information is eliminated from the actor's task, certain requirements still remain. They are the same requirements which exist for performers of any kind. Concentration, for example, is as important to athletes and Happeners as it is to actors, and stage-presence—the degree to which a person can mask or control feelings of nervousness, shyness, uncertainty, etc.—is equally useful to actors, public speakers, and musicians.[3]

One final point about performance in the New Theatre concerns the question of improvisation and indeterminacy. Indeterminacy means that limits within which the performers are free to make choices are provided by the creator of the piece: a range of alternatives is made available from which the performer may select. Thus in a musical composition the number of notes to be played within a given time period may be given but not the notes themselves; the pitch ranges may be indicated for given durations but specific notes not required. Indeterminacy is used in the New Theatre when, for example, the number of steps a performer should take is limited but the direction is optional or when the type of action is designated but no specific action is given. The choices involved in indeterminacy may be made before the actual performance, but they are most frequently left until the moment of presentation in an attempt to insure spontaneity.

Indeterminacy is not the same as improvisation. Although spontaneity may be a goal of both, it is also the goal of much precisely detailed acting. The primary difference between indeterminacy and improvisation is the amount of momentary, on-the-spot creativity which is involved. Not only is the detail— the apt comment, the *bon mot*, the unexpected or unusual reaction—central to improvisation, but the form and structure of a scene may also be changed. Even when, as was common in *Commedia dell'Arte,* the general outline of the scene is set, the performer is responding to unfamiliar material and providing in return his inventions, which require a response. As evidenced by the so-called improvisational theatres such as Second City, an improvisation loses these values once it has been repeated a few times. It no longer is an improvisation, and most of these groups make no pretense among themselves that it is. In indeterminacy the alternatives are quite clear, although the exact choice may not be made until performance. And the alternatives *do not matter:* one is as good as another. Since the performers usually function independently and do not respond to the choices made by the other performers, no give-and-take is involved. The situation is open-ended as it is in improvisation.

Thus the four men who manipulated the sections of pipe in *Washes,* for example, did no creative work although the details of their actions and procedure were different during each performance. They merely embodied the image of man-and-pipe which Oldenburg had created. They were not, in the true sense, improvising. Only the type of behavior mattered and not the details. Whether they swam for a while rather than working, whether they twisted this length of pipe rather than that one, whether they worked together or individually, did not matter provided they kept within the directed limits. The image was the same each night.

A somewhat related attitude is the acceptance of incidental aspects of audience reaction and environmental occurrences as *part* of the production. One of Cage's most notorious musical compositions is *4' 33"*—four minutes and thirty-three seconds of silence by the musician or musicians performing it. The nonplaying (in addition to focusing the performer aspects of the piece) allows any incidental sounds—perhaps traffic noises or crickets outside the auditorium, the creak of seats, coughing and whispering in the audience—to become music. This exploitation and integration of happenstance occurrences unique to each performance into the performance itself is another common, but not universal, trait of the New Theatre.

One method of assuring completely alogical structure in a work is to use chance methods. Beginning in about 1951 Cage used chance operations such as a system of coin tossing derived from *I Ching*, the Chinese *Book of Changes*. In a method close to pure chance, he determined the placement of notes in certain compositions by marking the imperfections in the score paper. In the Happening which he presented during the summer of 1952 at Black Mountain College the point of entry and the duration of the various performance elements were fixed by chance techniques. Cage's *Theatre Piece* of 1960 can be performed by one to eight musicians, singers, actors, dancers, and is unusual in that it provides an elaborate *method* (including the use of plastic overlays) of determining individual "scores," but it does not designate the actions, sounds, phrases, etc.—several groups of which are selected to be the raw material for the chance operations.

The use of chance and indeterminacy in composition are aspects of a wide concern with methods and procedure in the New Theatre. Another approach to the question of method is illustrated by a *Graphis* by Dick Higgins (who also studied with Cage) in which a linear pattern is marked out on the floor of the performance space with words written at various points. Performers may move only along the lines, and they perform pre-selected actions corresponding to each word when they arrive at that word. Thus the repeated actions and limited lines of movement create visual and rhythmic patterns which freely structure the work in an alogical way.

Jackson Mac Low, another of Cage's students, applied chance methods to the materials of the traditional drama. For *The Marrying Maiden*, for example, he selected characters and speeches from the *I Ching*. The order and duration of speeches and the directions for rate, volume, inflection, and manner of speaking were all independently ascribed to the material by chance techniques. Five different tempos ranging from "Very Slow" to "Very Fast" and five different amplitudes ranging from "Very Soft" to "Very Loud" were used. The attitudes to be acted were selected and placed into the script by the application of random number methods to a list of 500 adverbs or adverbial phrases ("smugly," "religiously," "apingly") compiled by Mac Low. Although the delivery of the lines in *The Marrying Maiden* is more closely controlled than in a traditional script, no movements, business, or actions are given. Staging is left to the director or actors. When the play was presented by The Living Theatre in 1960 and 1961, the physical activity worked out by Judith Malina, the director, was fixed. Other actions were inserted at random intervals by the use of an "action pack" of about 1,200 cards containing stage directions ("scratch yourself," "kiss the nearest woman," "use any three objects in an action") which were given to the performers by a visible stage manager who rolled dice to determine his own behavior.

In many of the works by Dick Higgins the operations of chance shift emphatically onto the performance. In *The Tart,* for example, selection by chance or taste is made from among the given characters, speeches, and cues by the performer or director, who then decides on actions to supplement the chosen material. Since at least some of the behavior or effects which cue the speeches and actions are provided by one or more "special" performers, a complicated cueing situation exists, creating a performance *pattern* which is different each time, although the performance *materials* remain constant.

Since the chance performances of Mac Low and Higgins make basic use of acting, the fundamental material of traditional theatre, there is some justification for retaining them in the play or drama category. They can be called *chance plays* or *alogical drama.* They are not Happenings. As with other definitions in the New Theatre, however, these terms can only be applied by measuring central tendency. Plays obviously use materials other than acting; Happenings may use acting as part of the performance. It then becomes a question of whether acting is the *primary* element, as in a play, or whether the emphasis is on nonmatrixed performing, physical effect, or a balance between several components, as in a Happening.

The recent production of *The Tart* is an example of the difficulty that can result when one tries to categorize a particular performance without making up pointless terms. Reading the script, there seems to be no question that the basic performance element is supposed to be acting and that it is a chance play. In the actual production at the Sunnyside Garden boxing arena in Queens, however, acting was used much less than it could have been, and physical effects were added. Because of this, the emphasis was shifted past the borderline between Happenings and chance theatre. This, in itself, is not important, but the way in which it came about makes clearer how to apply the terms I have been using.

In order to understand the apparent shift away from acting in the performance of *The Tart,* two things must be remembered. In the first place, distinctions between matrixed and nonmatrixed performing are not made on the basis of acting style or on the basis of good or bad acting. Both naturalistic acting, in which the performer disappears within the character, and formalized acting, which makes use of artificial gesture and speech, develop equally strong matrices. The acrobatic performers in *Le Cocu magnifique* were acting. And the poor actor—unless he gives up completely and drops out of character to ask for a line—is, like the good actor, providing a supply of character-place data. The work may be more obvious in one case and the matrices demonstrated or indicated rather than implied, but this is basically an aesthetic question rather than a formal one.

In the second place, neither costumes nor dialogue have any necessary relationship to acting. A costume or a line of dialogue is—like a prop, a particular kind of light, or the setting—merely another piece of information. It may be related to character material which is acted or to other information and thus help to form a strong matrix, but a nonmatrixed performer may also wear a costume or speak.

The Tart makes great demands upon actors. The performers do not speak to each other and play scenes in the way possible, for example, with the alogical verbal material of Jackson Mac Low's *Verdurous Sanguinaria.* The dialogue of *The Tart* usually consists of speeches attributed to some other character, and something of that character is supposed to be superimposed upon the base character when the line is given. Obviously, in order to keep in character, highly skilled actors are needed, and when the performers cannot sustain the base character, as happened in this case, acting disintegrates into disparate lines and actions. Although the performers are required to select their own actions, which can strengthen the character matrix and ease the complicated and difficult acting task, many of them in this production chose to use arbitrary or meaningless movement, which only destroyed any character matrix they might have established. One or two of the performers, experienced in Happenings, made no attempt to act. Thus the final effect was one in which acting was subordinate to effect and to nonmatrixed performing. In performance *The Tart* turned from a chance play into a Happening.

Just as the words "play" and "drama" have a historical usage which should not be replaced with "Happening" or Event" unless the fundamental elements are different, the word "dance" has an accepted meaning which takes precedence over any new terminology. And certain contemporary developments in dance are a very important part of the New Theatre. Although these developments are the result of progressive aesthetic changes within the field, the form has been brought to that point where many formal and stylistic similarities exist between contemporary dance works and pieces presented by nondancers which are not referred to as "dance." Significant creative exchange has become possible between disciplines which have been thought of as isolated. One pronounced and important characteristic of the New Theatre is the tendency to reduce or eliminate the traditionally strong divisions of drama, dance, and opera.

The changes in dance which give it a place in the New Theatre parallel those which are exemplified by Events, Happenings, and chance theatre, but not necessarily derive from them. For example, Merce Cunningham created *16 Dances* by chance method in 1951—the year before Cage's presentation at Black Mountain College. The order of passages and even the order of movements within one passage were determined by tossing coins. (Cage, who has worked closely with Cunningham for many years and was working with chance techniques at that time, composed the music for the piece by setting a fixed procedure for moving on a chart containing the noises, tones, and aggregates of sound that would be used in the composition.) Since Cunningham's early work, much investigation into chance, game, and indeterminacy methods and various other alogical structures has been undertaken by dancers, especially by Ann Halprin's Dancers' Workshop and by Robert Dunn, whose classes at Cunningham's studio in 1960–62 eventually developed into the Judson Dance Theatre.

As structure in dance became alogical and made use of simultaneous performances that were not interrelated (except that they were concurrently presented to the spectator), the manner of performance has also changed. Of course certain types of dancing have always been nonmatrixed. No character or place is created and projected in ballroom dancing (which, it might be pointed out, almost always has an audience, although that is not its orientation), and acrobatic dancing, tap dancing, soft shoe dancing, and the like are all nonmatrixed—unless, of course, they appear as part of the action in a play. But, from the stories of ballet to the psychological projections of modern dance, the dance as an art form has generally made use of character and place matrices. In recent years, however, story, plot, character, situation, ecstasy, personal expression, and self-dramatization have all dropped away, and dance has made use of nonmatrixed performing.

The separation of dance from music is perhaps one of the factors responsible for the shift. Musical accompaniment functions in part as an emotional matrix which "explains" dancers. Think, for example, of how much expression and character can be given to the film image of a blank face or even the back of a head by the music on the sound track. In John Cage's scores for many of Merce Cunningham's dances, music and movement merely fill the same time period without relationship. Some of Mary Wigman's dances just after the First World War and almost all of the dances in the New Theatre entirely eliminated music; thus interpretation is no longer a factor, and the possibility of nonmatrixed performing is increased.

As character, emotional continuity, and a sense of created locale have been eliminated from dance, walking, running, falling, doing calisthenics, and other simple activities from everyday life have become dance elements. No attempt is made to embellish these actions, and it does not take years of training to dance them. Merce Cunningham did a piece called *Collage* at Brandeis University in 1953 in which he used fifteen untrained dancers who performed simple, ordinary movements and activities such as running and hair combing. A number of nondancers are performing members of the Judson Dance Theatre[4] in New York City.

The concern for activity with its concomitant movement rather than for movement in itself—for *what* is done rather than *how* it is done—brings much new dance very close to Happenings and Events. And just as any performance may be called music with the justification that sound is involved, almost any performance may be referred to as dance when human movement is involved. Works which are not formally distinguishable from Happenings have been called dance pieces. Actually the most important differences among many of the performances in the New Theatre—whether done by painters, sculptors, musicians, dancers, or professional theatre people—exist on stylistic rather than formal grounds. One wonders what difference it would make if *Check* by Robert Morris, for example, were called a Happening, and Claes Oldenburg's *Washes* were referred to as a dance.

Certain works have come out of the new theatre and out of the creative climate fostered by Cage which have pushed "performance" beyond the limits of theatre and offer new insights into the nature of performing and of theatre. Cage advocated the elimination of boundaries between art and life. The acceptance of chance is an acceptance of the laws of nature; and life, as illustrated in *4'33"*, always participates in the totality of the perceived work of art. (This way of thinking means, for example, that a painting or sculpture is not the same in the gallery as it is in the studio.)

Performance and audience are both necessary to have theatre. But it might be thought that it is this very separation of spectator and work which is responsible for an "artificiality" of the form, and many Happenings and related pieces have attempted to "break down" the "barrier" between presentation and spectator and to make the passive viewer a more active participator. At any rate, works have recently been conceived which, since they are to be performed without an audience—a totally original and unprecedented development in art—might be called Activities.

In some of George Brecht's pieces the question of an audience seems ambiguous. Brecht's work implies that any performance piece has an aesthetic value for its performer or creator which is distinct from its value for an audience: the performance of *any* piece without an audience is a certain kind of art. Some of his things, such as the untitled child-thermometer-clock piece, are so intimate that spectators are obviously not intended or required.

Activities make it possible to work with time and space dimensions that would be very difficult or impossible in theatre. In *Chair* by Robert Ashley, for example, a wooden chair is variously transformed on each of six successive days. The lines in Stanley Brouwn's *Phone-drawings* exist only in the mind of the performer, who is aware that if the locations he has called on the telephone were connected (in the same way the child connects numbered dots to make a picture appear) the image he has chosen would actually exist on a vast scale. These works emphasize the private, proprioceptive, and cerebral aspects of Activities.

Allan Kaprow has performed pieces which also eliminate the audience but function on a much larger scale. Some of them, using many performers, resembled his Happenings except for the absence of spectators. The more recent pieces, although involving sizable numbers of performers, are more widely distributed through space and time so that the participants are frequently entirely separated from each other. Ken Dewey's recent works have mixed both Activity sections and units in which the assembled people functioned in the traditional passive manner of spectators.

Although these works, like Kaprow's *Eat* Environment, are outside the limits of theatre, they are related to the performance mentality, and they help to clarify some of the attitudes and concepts of the New Theatre as well as providing fresh theoretical positions from which to evaluate theatre as a whole.

John Cage is emphasized as the touchstone of the New Theatre for at least two reasons. In the first place, the body of his work—writings and lectures as well as musical compositions and performance pieces—gives clear precedents for many later developments. Secondly, many of the younger artists in the New Theatre actually studied with Cage, although each creates in his own manner.

But there are at least as many reasons why the formulation I have presented is not wholly true or valid. As a simplification, it glosses over the exceptions and degrees of shading that any complete account should have. Actually, the New Theatre has been in existence long enough for widening aesthetic ripples to spread far from the source. Each artist changes it. It has moved in various directions, making use of established techniques as well as the most recent developments in other fields and disciplines. Many of the artists producing Happenings, for example, are not fundamentally in sympathy with Cage's views, and their work is stylistically very different.

The emphasis on Cage may have implied that he is a completely original artist. This of course is not true. Completely original artists—like Dylan Thomas' "eggs laid by tigers"—do not exist. Actually each of the dimensions of Cage's work was prefigured in the work of the Futurists and the Dadaists, in Marinetti, Duchamp, and others. (Of course, much of this material had been available to everyone for a good number of years. It is to Cage's credit that he saw what was in it while others apparently did not.)

A sketch of the earlier history and origins of the New Theatre would have to begin at least with the Italian Futurists, whose *bruitisme,* the use of everyday sounds and noises rather than those produced by traditional musical instruments, can be traced through Dada, the compositions of Erik Satie and Edgar Varèse, and, finally, electronic music, which has as its material a sound spectrum of unprecedented width and variety. Although the Futurists apparently did not add nonmusical elements to their performances, their theoretical position provided the basis for the later expansion of music into performance.

In addition to their own "noise music" performed by instruments such as baby rattles and jangled keys and tin cans, the Dadaists in Zürich during the First World War and later in Paris read and recited simultaneous poems and manifestos which were an early form of compartmentalization. (These and the Dada distortion of the lecture into a work of art prefigure certain aspects of Cage's lectures.) Unrelated "acts" were often performed at the same time, and the Dadaists presented what would now be referred to as Events: Philippe Saupault in his *Le célèbre illusioniste (The Famous Magician)* released balloons of various colors each bearing the name of a famous man; Walter Serner, instead of reading a poem, placed a bouquet of flowers at the feet of a dressmaker's dummy; in their *Noir cacadou* Richard Huelsenbeck and Tristan Tzara waddled around in a sack with their heads in a piece of pipe; Jean Arp recited his poems from inside a huge hat, and Georges Ribemont-Dessaignes danced inside a giant funnel. The Dadaists even staged a mock trial in front of an audience with witnesses called for the prosecution and the defense.

The intentional use of chance so important to Cage and some of the New Theatre was also used by the Dadaists. Tristan Tzara composed and recited poems by mixing cards with words on them in a hat and drawing out the cards one at a time. Arp and Duchamp used chance in making paintings and constructions.

Surrealism also had its impact on the New Theatre. It proposed the irrational as the material of art and stressed the dream, the obsessive act, the psychic accident; it supported automatism and chance as creative techniques and thus—after being driven from Europe to this country by the Second World War—provided the basis for Abstract Expressionism. (Although Cage accepted this concern with method, he differed sharply with later creators of Happenings such as Oldenburg and Whitman who stressed the unconscious affective aspects in their work.)

The Abstract Expressionist mentality which pervaded the New York art world in the late '50s was one of the contributing factors in bringing painters into the performing arts. The *act* of painting rather than the completed composition had become the creative focus. At the same time painting and sculpture had a long tradition, in which Dada and Surrealism played their parts, of assemblage—the fabricating of a work from disparate objects and materials. Thus the artists found nothing strange about assembling a theatrical work from various types of alogically related performance material.

The New Theatre is not important merely because it is new. But if it is agreed that a work of art may be important if only it is new—an aesthetic position which cannot be elaborated or defended here—then these works deserve serious consideration. Not only should they suggest to any practicing theatre artist new directions in which his work may go, but they represent several of the most significant developments in the history of theatre art.

In this theatre "suspension of disbelief" is not operative, and the absence of character and situation precludes identification. Thus the traditional mode of experiencing theatre, which has dominated both players and spectators for thousands of years, is altered.

As I have tried to show, structure and, almost always, the manner of performing are radically different in the New Theatre. These innovations place theatre—in a very limited way—in some equivalency with the other arts. If painting and sculpture, for example, have not yet exhausted the possibilities of their nonobjective breakthrough (which occurred only three years after the start of this century), and if music has not yet begun to assimilate all the implications of its new-found electronic materials, there is every reason to feel that there will also be a fruitful aesthetic future for the New Theatre.

Notes

1. Of course the behavior in "real life" and on stage might not be exactly the same. A particular emotional reaction to facing an audience in the theatre situation could be expected. But while *created* or acted emotions are part of character matrix, *real* emotions are not. The question of emotion will be touched on again below.

2. Thus it is not essentially the degree of correlation between the written script and the performance which makes a theatre piece literary. Whether or not it began from written material, any production, no matter how alogical, may be described in words, and the description could then be used as the literary basis for another production. On the other hand, there is the additional question of the latitude of interpretation allowed by a printed script—e.g., George Brecht's *Exit*, the score of which consists in its entirety of the single

word with no directions or suggestions for interpretation and realization. *Any* written material, and even nonverbal material, may serve as the script for a performance.

3. The *use* of stage presence is an aesthetic question. Some performances place a high degree of emphasis upon it, while in others it is intentionally excluded or performers are employed *because* they are somewhat ill at ease.

4. Although traditional dance movements and techniques are not excluded, this emphasis on relatively simple kinds of movement has led to the style being labeled "anti-dance." In lieu of a more accurate term, the name has some usefulness, but the intent of the dancers is not to oppose or destroy dance but to eliminate what seems to be unnecessary conventions and restrictions, to approach movement in a fresh way, and to open new formal areas.

6

An Interview with John Cage
(1965)

Michael Kirby and Richard Schechner

Kirby: What's your definition of theatre?

Cage: I try to make definitions that won't exclude. I would simply say that theatre is something which engages both the eye and the ear. The two public senses are seeing and hearing; the senses of taste, touch, and odor are more proper to intimate, nonpublic, situations. The reason I want to make my definition of theatre that simple is so one could view everyday life itself as theatre.

Schechner: Is a concert a theatrical activity?

Cage: Yes, even a conventional piece played by a conventional symphony orchestra: the horn player, for example, from time to time empties the spit out of his horn. And this frequently engages my attention more than the melodies, harmonies, etc.

Schechner: What about a mime troupe or dancers where sound is incidental? Their sound is silence. Would that be a theatrical activity also?

Cage: Yes.

Kirby: You say that absolute silence doesn't exist, so you wouldn't be able to separate seeing from hearing, right?

Cage: Hearing would always be there and seeing too, if you have your eyes open.

Kirby: How about listening to recorded music?

Cage: I find that most interesting when one finds something in the environment to look at. If you're in a room and a record is playing and the window is open and there's some breeze and a curtain is blowing, that's sufficient, it seems to me, to produce a theatrical experience.

Schechner: When I listen to recorded music—I'm really hung up on *The Messiah*—

Cage: Hallelujah.

Schechner:—I lie down and I close my eyes and I fantasy along with the music. That's how I get the most enjoyment out of music. I don't like concerts because I have to sit up.

Cage: When you're lying down and listening you're having an intimate, interiorly-realized theatre which I would—if I were going to exclude anything—exclude from my definition of theatre as a public occasion. In other words you're doing something by yourself that's extremely difficult to describe or relate to anyone accurately. I think of theatre as an occasion involving any number of people, but not just one.

Kirby: You said once, "I try to get it so that people realize that they themselves are doing their experience and that it's not being *done* to them." Isn't all art done to you?

Cage: It has been, but I think we're changing that. When you have the proscenium stage and the audience arranged in such a way that they all look in the same direction—even though those on the extreme right and left are said to be in "bad seats," and those in the center are in "good seats"—the assumption is that people will see *it* if they all look in one direction. But our experience nowadays is not so focused at one point. We live in, and are more and more aware of living in, the space around us. Current developments in theatre are changing architecture from the Renaissance notion to something else which relates to our lives. That was the case with the theatre in the round. But that never seemed to me any real change from the proscenium, because it again focused people's attention and the only thing that changed was that some people were seeing one side of the thing and the other people the other side.

It could of course produce more interesting conversation afterward or during intermission, because people didn't see the same side. It was like the story of the blind men with the elephant. More pertinent to our daily experience is a theatre in which we ourselves are in the round . . . in which the activity takes place around us. The seating arrangement I had at Black Mountain in 1952 was a square composed of four triangles with the apexes of the triangles merging towards the center, but not meeting. The center was a larger space that could take movement, and the aisles between these four triangles also admitted of movement. The audience could see itself, which is of course the advantage of any theatre in the round. The larger part of the action took place *outside* of that square. In each one of the seats was a cup, and it wasn't explained to the audience what to do with this cup—some used it as an ashtray—but the performance was concluded by a kind of ritual of pouring coffee into each cup.

Kirby: Could you describe the whole performance?

Cage: At one end of a rectangular hall, the long end, was a movie and at the other end were slides. I was up on a ladder delivering a lecture which included silences and there was another ladder which M. C. Richards and Charles Olsen went up at different times. During periods that I called time brackets, the performers were free within limitations—I think you would call them compartments—compartments which they didn't have to fill, like a green light in traffic. Until this compartment began, they were not free to act, but once it had begun they could act as long as they wanted to during it. Robert Rauschenberg was playing an old-fashioned phonograph that had a horn and a dog on the side listening, and David Tudor was playing a piano, and Merce Cunningham and other dancers were moving through the audience and around the audience. Rauschenberg's pictures were suspended above the audience—

Kirby: Those were the "white paintings?"

Cage: Right. He was also painting black ones at the time, but I think we used only the white ones. They were suspended at various angles, a canopy of painting above the audience. I don't recall anything else except the ritual with the coffee cup. I remember a lady coming in at the beginning who was the widow of the man who had formerly headed the music department. She had made a point of coming very early in order to get the best seat. And she asked me where the best seat was and I said they were all equally good.

Schechner: Did she believe you?

Cage: Well, she saw that she wasn't getting a reply in relation to her question so she simply sat down where she chose. She had no way, nor did I, of telling where the best seat was, since from every seat you would see something different.

Schechner: One of the consequences of eliminating central focus is that you do away with all the usual texts because they depend on central focus. Let's take a very classical play, something like the *Oresteia* . . . in the multi-focus thing do we no longer attempt the *Oresteia*, or do we restructure it?

Cage: Our situation as artists is that we have all this work that was done before we came along. We have the opportunity to do work now. I would not present things from the past, but I would approach them as materials available to something else which we were going to do now. They could enter, in terms of collage, into any play. One extremely interesting theatrical thing that hasn't been done is a collage made from various plays.

Let me explain to you why I think of past literature as material rather than as art. There are oodles of people who are going to think of the past as a museum and be faithful to it, but that's not my attitude. Now as material it can be put together with other things. They could be things that don't connect with art as we conventionally understand it. Ordinary occurrences in a city, or ordinary occurrences in the country, or technological occurrences—things that are now practical simply because techniques have changed. This is altering the nature of music and I'm sure it's altering your theatre, say through the employment of color television, or multiple movie projectors, photo-electric devices that will set off relays when an actor moves through a certain area. I would have to analyze theatre to see what are the things that make it up in order, when we later make a synthesis, to let those things come in. Now in terms of music I thought of something manually produced, and then of something vocally produced, wind, etc. This includes all the literature. And then I thought of sounds we cannot hear because they're too small, but through new techniques we can enlarge them, sounds like ants walking in the grass. Other sounds are city sounds, country sounds, and synthetic sounds. I haven't analyzed all the things that go into theatre, but I think one could.

Schechner: What are some of them?

Cage: It's extremely complex because it involves, as I said earlier, seeing and hearing. We know, or think we know, what the aspects of sound are, what we can hear and how to produce sounds. But when you're involved with sight the situation becomes more complex. It involves color, light, shapes that are not moving, shapes that are moving; it involves what in Buddhism is called "nonsentient" being and then goes again in relation to what is called "sentient being"—animals, etc. I would refer back to Artaud's thinking about theatre. He made lists that could give ideas about what goes into theatre. And one should search constantly to see if something that could take place in theatre has escaped one's notice.

Kirby: Do you believe that we'll ever get to a point where there won't be any unknowns left?

Cage: I've been reading Buckminster Fuller lately and he said that we live in a finite world, and that the part we see as being relevant to our experience is "definite" and he sees two areas outside of that definite one which are still finite but which are either too big or too interior—too small—for us yet to have noticed and related to our daily experience.

Kirby: We end up the same way, always with some unknowns left.

Schechner: One of the consequences of this line of thinking is that the basic structure of theatre necessarily becomes altered. Once you remove action-focus you change the structure all the way up and down the line: modes of rehearsal to modes of production. In all the work of yours that I have read or heard there is a great feeling for structure. I wonder what kind of structure replaces the focus-structure?

Cage: The structure we should think about is that of each person in the audience. In other words, his consciousness is structuring the experience differently from anybody else's in the audience. So the less we structure the theatrical occasion and the more it is like unstructured daily life, the greater will be the stimulus to the structuring faculty of each person in the audience. If we have done nothing he then will have everything to do.

Schechner: Theatre before this time has depended upon a space structure, of which the focus was the most important thing. Kirby would call it an information structure, though I'm not sure that I would agree. Let's say an information-space structure. Are you suggesting that a duration structure replace the space-information structure?

Cage: I did formerly. In 1952 we had a duration structure with compartments which had been arrived at by chance operations. But in my more recent work I'm concerned rather with what I call process—setting a process going which has no necessary beginning, no middle, no end, and no sections. Beginnings and endings can be given things but I try to obscure that fact, rather than to do anything like what I used to do, which was to measure it. The notion of measurement and the notion of structure are not notions with which I am presently concerned. I try to discover what one needs to do in art by observations from my daily life. I think daily life is excellent and that art introduces us to it and to its excellence the more it begins to be like it.

Schechner: Is there a difference between a group of people deciding to go to the beach and watching what happens on the beach, and a group of people deciding to go to an Event or an Activity and watching or participating in it?

Cage: If a person assumes that the beach is theatre and experiences it in those terms I don't see that there's much difference. It is possible for him to take that attitude. This is very useful because you often find yourself, in our daily life, in irritating circumstances. They won't be irritating if you see them in terms of theatre.

Kirby: In other words if you remove yourself from them?

Cage: Can we say remove, or: use your faculties in such a way that you are truly the center? We've been speaking of the central factor being each person in the audience.

Schechner: Let's take a hypothetical but possible event. I'm involved in an auto wreck in which I'm not hurt but in which my best friend is killed. Well, I imagine that's a few steps above irritating—but if I look at it as theatre, as happening to another but not to me, I can learn from the experience, respond to it but not be in it; then perhaps I can remove the irritants.

Cage: I didn't mean by putting the person at the center that he wasn't in it, I meant rather to show him that he was at the very center of it.

Schechner: I don't see how this can remove the irritation then.

Cage: Do you know the Zen story of the mother who has just lost her only son? She is sitting by the road weeping and the monk comes along and asks her why she's weeping, and she says she's lost her only son, and he hits her on the head and says, "There, that'll give you something to cry about." Isn't there something of that same insistence in Artaud, in the business of the plague and of cruelty? Doesn't he want people to see themselves not in a pleasant world but in something that is the clue to all the things that we normally try to protect ourselves from?

Schechner: Sure. My only quarrel is whether one really enjoys it or not. When the mother gets hit over the head she has two things to cry about.

Another thing about the structure. Isn't the difference between the beach and the theatre that the beach is not rehearsed and the theatre is? The thing that bothered me about the Happenings I've seen is that they were obviously rehearsed but badly done. Either they shouldn't have been rehearsed, or they shouldn't have gone half way. In one Happening there was a man choking another and it became very theatrical for me in a bad way, because I knew that they weren't really choking each other...

Cage: And you knew what the word "theatrical" should mean...

Schechner: Convincingly. Either they should have done it well or not at all.

Cage: I couldn't be in greater agreement. If there are intentions, then there should be every effort made to realize those intentions. Otherwise carelessness takes over. However, if one is able to act in a way that doesn't have intention in it, then there is no need for rehearsal. This is what I'm working on now: to do something without benefit of measurement, without benefit of the sense that now that this is finished we can go on to the next thing.

Let me give you one example. In those boxes over there are some ninety loops on tape. They vary from small loops that are just long enough for a tape machine, to ones which are, say, forty feet long. We gave a performance, last week, at Brandeis, with six performers—the number that turned up at the time that the setup was made—and thirteen tape machines. The performance simply consisted of putting the loops on the various machines and taking them off. Doing this, a complex stage situation developed because we had to set up stands around which the tapes would go, and these things were overlapping. The number of loops made it fairly certain that no intention was involved in putting on one rather than another loop. The number of people and the number of machines also created a situation that was somewhat free of intentions. Another way is by making use of electronic circuits to involve the performers in manipulating the amplifiers. Somebody might be working at a microphone or a cartridge point when another person is at the amplifier altering it. Both people are prevented from successfully putting through any intentions.

Schechner: Both these cases depend upon the use of a machine which will short circuit human intention.

Cage: If you have a number of people then a non-knowledge on the part of each of what the other is going to do would be useful. Even if one of them was full of intentions, if none of them knew what the others' intentions were...

Schechner: Even though each individual thing may be very structured: The combination would be...

Cage:...tend in a non-intentional, unstructured direction, and would resemble what I referred to as daily life. If you go down the street in the city you can see that people are moving about with intention but you don't know what those intentions are. Many many things happen which can be viewed in purposeless ways.

Schechner: How do you take into account the fact that people, as soon as they become an audience, demand structure and impose it even if it's not there?

Cage: Those people coming together to see a play come as it were to a salvation. If there is this lack of distinction between art and life, then one could say: Well, why have the arts when we already have it in life? A suitable answer from my point of view is that we thereby celebrate. We have a history in our culture of special occasions, and I don't see anything wrong with that, and I don't see anything wrong with doing something that's unnecessary.

Kirby: Why didn't you go on doing the 1952 Black Mountain piece? It was given only once. It seems that you were somewhat disappointed with this piece and went in other directions...

Cage: No. One does what one does largely due to circumstances. When I was at Black Mountain I was working on a very time-consuming task—part of a project which involved the making of tape music by other composers: Morton Feldman, Christian Wolff, and Earle Brown. My piece alone took nine months of work, for composing and splicing. While I was working on those tape pieces I received a commission from Donaueschingen in Germany to make a piece for two prepared pianos. I wrote those *Timelength Pieces* for two pianos, and that interested me very much. Then I wrote a part for a percussion player and a part for a string player. My time was much taken up by work with Merce Cunningham and his dancers, by the tours and concerts, and lectures. So the interest in doing a specifically theatrical work was satisfied by the work with Cunningham, and then later by the *Theatre Piece*.

Schechner: How have all these things come together in your mind and work? You work in music, theatre, writing, lecturing, dance...

Cage: Mushrooms...

Schechner: That kind of range is very unusual today.

Cage: Don't you think again we would have to trace circumstances? When I was just beginning I wrote a piece for a clarinet solo. Since I knew it was difficult to play I called up the first clarinetist of the Los Angeles Philharmonic Orchestra. And when he looked at it he said, "That's not the way to write music." He thought I should write like most writers, so he was not going to play it, and advised me not to do the sort of thing that I was committed to doing. Then I made another stab at getting this piece done, and it failed again. That time not because the clarinetist wasn't willing to play it but because he didn't have the time to devote to learning to overcome its difficulties, and didn't choose to overcome them. The circumstances again. Then at just about that time I was called up by some modern dancers at UCLA, who actually wanted me to do something... and so I did it, and in that way I soon learned that if you were writing music that orchestras just weren't interested in—or string quartets, I made several attempts, I didn't give up immediately—that you could get things done very easily by modern dance groups. At the time I was interested in structure because I was fresh from working with Schoenberg. I thought that dealing with noises, as I was, I'd need another structure so I found this time structure and immediately was able to give it to the dancers to work with. Time was a common denominator between dance and music, rather than being specific to music as harmony and tonality were. I freed the dancers from the necessity to interpret music on the level of feeling; they could make a dance in the same structure that a musician was using. They could do it independently of one another, bringing their results together as pure hypothetical meaning. And we were always delighted to see that what we brought together worked. We thought it worked because we had a common structure, as if you, I, and Kirby decided to write a sonnet. We could do it two ways: we could write three sonnets and see that they were related to one another, or we could assign six lines to each, and find the results stimulating on an irrational level. Nevertheless these things do go together and we thought that they were together because of the structure. But then in circumstances that I recounted in a lecture called *Changes,* which is in my book, and also in the *Lecture on Nothing,* we discovered that more and more things we thought were necessary were not necessary. Things can be done without those precautions.

Schechner: How did you move into the theatre thing?

Cage: Experience with the dance led me there. The reflection that a human being isn't just ears, but has these eyes, I think it was this: around 1945, '46, '47 I became concerned about music—I think you know this story—and I determined not to continue with this activity unless it was useful, and unless I found answers that struck me as being sufficient reason to devote one's life to it. I found through Oriental philosophy, my work with Suzuki, that what we are doing is living, and that we are not moving toward a goal, but are, so to speak, at the goal constantly and changing with it, and that art, if it is going to do anything useful, should open our eyes to this fact. Before the *Theatre Piece* I did two pieces for television. One was called *Water Walk* and one was called *Sounds of Venice.* I called it *Water Walk* because of the *Music Walk,* and the *Music Walk,* I think you would agree, is a theatrical work. Before the *Music Walk* was the *Water Music.* Those titles wish to show that all those works are connected. The *Water Music* comes from 1952, I believe—the same year as the Black Mountain show—and was my immediate reaction to that event.

Kirby: Could you describe it briefly?

Cage: The *Water Music* wishes to be a piece of music, but to introduce visual elements in such a way that it can be experienced as theatre. That is, it moves towards theatre from music. The first thing that could be theatrical is what the pianist is looking at—the score. Normally nobody sees it but him, and since we're involved with seeing now, we make it large enough so that the audience can see it. I was working at the time on chance operations and a chart which enabled me to determine what sound pops up at what time and how loud, etc. So I simply put into the chart things that not only would produce sounds but that would produce actions that were interesting to see. I had somewhere gotten the notion that the world is made up of water, earth, fire, etc. and I thought that water was a useful thing to concentrate on. So the possibilities that I put into the chart involved, not exclusively, but largely, water.

Kirby: What were some of these?

Cage: Well, pouring water from one cup into another, using a whistle that requires water to produce sound, making that whistle descend into the water and come out of it.

Kirby: Do you remember any of the non-water images?

Cage: There was a glissando on the keyboard, also a dominant 7th chord. I was already interested at that time in avoiding the exclusion of banal elements. In the development of 12–tone music there was an emphasis on dissonance, to the exclusion or very careful treatment of consonances. Octaves as well as 5ths and particularly dominant 7ths and cadences became things that one shouldn't do. I've always been on the side of the things one shouldn't do and searching for ways of bringing the refused elements back into play. So I included sounds that were, just from a musical point of view, forbidden at that time. You could talk to any modern composer at the time and no matter how enlightened he was he would refuse to include banal musical sounds.

Schechner: When you came to the *Theatre Piece* in 1960...

Cage: Before that came a time-length piece, which is thirty-four minutes for a pianist predominantly. I had been commissioned to write a piece for two prepared pianos, but I introduced an "x" concept of auxiliary noises. Thus I had other groups of noises: one was produced inside the piano, one was produced outside the piano but on it, and then there were noises separated from the piano—whistles. The parts are not in a scored relation, they are independent of one another. Then I wrote a lecture to go with them, involving combing the hair and kiss sounds and gestures that made the lecture theatrical. So I think you could find the theatrical continuing in my work.

In Milan, when I was invited to perform on a quiz show, the first performance was of *Amores,* an early piece for prepared piano, and the next two especially for television. I used the *Fontana Mix.* They are overlaying transparencies involving points and curvy lines which don't cross over themselves. A given line doesn't cross over itself but it goes in curving, meandering ways from one side of the page to another. These curving lines are six in number and are differentiated by thickness (three are dotted) and you simply place them over the sheet with points—one sheet with points and one sheet with curved lines—and then a graph which is a hundred units in one direction and twenty in the other. There is a straight line used to connect a point that is outside the graph with one that is inside, and one measures the intersection of the curved lines with this straight line with reference to the graph vertically, to determine the kind of thing that would happen. The horizontal measurement gives the time. I used the *Fontana Mix* to make a tape piece, and I used it to make television pieces. I don't think I used all six of the lines. I used as many as I thought were necessary. And then I made lists of actions that I was willing to involve myself in. Then through the intersection of those curved lines and the straight line I could see within what amount of time I had, for instance, to put a rose in a bathtub, if that came up. If at the same time playing a particular note—or not a particular note—on the piano came up, those two things had to get done within the time allotted. I ended up with six parts which I then rehearsed very carefully, over and over and over again with people watching me and correcting me, because I had to do it within three minutes. It had many actions in it and it demanded what you might call virtuosity. I was unwilling to perform it until I was certain that I could do it well.

Kirby: You say there were many things you had to do within the three-minute time; could you mention a few of them?

Cage: They're all listed in the score. What is more interesting, I think, is that my chart included far more activity than came up through the measurements, so that a lot of my preparatory planning and thinking was, from a normal point of view, wasted.

Schechner: Have the charts been published?

Cage: You can buy them, you can buy the *Fontana Mix,* and you can also buy the *Theatre Piece.* The *Theatre Piece* carries this kind of activity up to an abstract point, because none of the things to be done are verbalized. But what an actor will do in a given time space is up to him. He follows my directions— and I think many people perform that piece without following my directions—and puts verbs and nouns on cards. He conceals the order from himself by shuffling the cards. Then he lays them out so he can tell which is one and which is two, up to twenty. Reading the numbers, which are the only things which are in my score, he will be able to make a program of action just as I made one for the *Water Walk.* And if he did it as I did it he would, I know, arrive at a complex situation. But what people tend to do is to get ideas of what they think will be interesting and these, of course, are a limited number of things, because their imaginations are lazy and they do fewer things rather than more and they are satisfied to do one thing over an inordinately long duration.

Schechner: Did you originally perform the *Theatre Piece* yourself?

Cage: No. I might be said to have conducted it. I acted as a clock simply because we couldn't lay our hands on a large enough clock for everyone to see.

Schechner: How many people does it involve?

Cage: Eight. And I think it says in my directions that if you want more material you can apply to me for it, or you could take those eight, divide them in half and get sixteen, etc.

Schechner: That was 1960, and that's still a highly structured piece of work . . .

Cage: No. It has what Kirby would call "compartments," but these overlap in a way that is quite complex. The notion of an overall structure is not in the work.

Schechner: But there is on each card a thing, there is a word.

Cage: Each sheet takes up many of these compartments and can amount to as much time as a performer chooses.

Schechner: There's a development from *Water Walk* to this, and during the next five years from this to the position we talked about at the beginning...

Cage: *Theatre Piece* was composed in terms of what I would call process rather than structure. When we do anything and bring it to a performance, it reaches to a point that becomes realization. At that realization point it can be viewed, as we said earlier, as structured, though it wasn't.

Schechner: So the structure is the observer's and not the piece's.

Cage: When I was writing the *Theatre Piece* I started out in terms of process, just overlaying these things and taking measurements, and I went far enough with that concept to put it on paper, but not to specify verbally. I left that up to the performer. I stopped the process before it was realized, leaving the realization up to the individual.

This is why: I had a conversation earlier that year with Karlheinz Stockhausen and he asked, "If you were writing a song would you write for the singer or would you write music?" I said I would write for the singer. He said, "That's the difference between us, I would write music." He was at the time thinking about writing a song for Cathy Berberian and he wanted to make use of as many ways of vocal production as he could think of. He was interested in African clicking, and she was able to do that, so he put it in. He was also interested in whistling. It didn't occur to him that she couldn't whistle. She's absolutely incapable of whistling. So he gave her things to do which she was unable to do. That was why I left the *Theatre Piece* unspecified. I didn't want to ask anyone to do something he couldn't do.

Kirby: The words could be taken by chance from a dictionary...

Cage: Right.

Kirby: Yet they're supposed to be the basis of the action.

Cage: Right. I wanted to leave the performer free. I didn't want him to get involved in a situation that he wasn't willing to carry through.

Schechner: What happened after the *Theatre Piece?*

Cage: At about that time my music was published, and it took a long time to make up a catalogue for it. In 1958 I began some pieces called *Variations*. The first one was involved with the parameters of sound, the transparencies overlaid, and each performer making measurements that would locate sounds in space. Then, while I was at Wesleyan, in the first piece I had had five lines on a single transparent sheet, though I had had no intention of putting them the way I did, I just drew them quickly. At Wesleyan while talking to some students it suddenly occurred to me that there would be much more freedom if I put only a single line or a single notation on a single sheet. So I did that, but it still involved measurement. *Variations III* came along. I had been working very early with structure, with this process which could be seen as structure; it always involved space, which struck me as distinguishing what we now call neo-Dada from earlier Dada. I admired most modern architecture with all its open space. I admired those Japanese gardens with just a few stones. I had been committed to the notion of activity and non-activity, just as earlier I had been committed to sound and silence.

Just as I came to see that there was no such thing as silence, and so wrote the *Silent Piece,* I was now coming to the realization that there was no such thing as non-activity. In other words the sand in which the stones in the Japanese garden lie is also something. Why that had not been evident to me before, I don't know. There isn't any non-activity. Or, as Jasper Johns says, looking at the world, "It appears to be very busy." And so I made *Variations III,* which leaves no space between one thing and the next and posits that we are constantly active, that these actions can be of any kind, and all I ask the performer to do is to be aware as much as he can of how many actions he is performing. I ask him, in other words, to count. That's all I ask him to do. I ask him even to count passive actions, such as noticing that there is a noise in the environment. We move through our activity without any space between one action and the next, and with many overlapping actions. The thing I don't like about *Variations III* is that it requires counting, and I'm now trying to get rid of that. But I thought that performance was simply getting up and then doing it.

Schechner: There is a contradiction here.

Cage: You won't find me logical.

Schechner: No, not that kind of contradiction. You say that these things should be somehow like everyday life. And yet in hearing you talk, or listening to the composition, they're anything but like everyday life. The action may be as random as everyday life, but the visual and audial effect is most unusual and strange.

Cage: Yes, but I think that when non-intention underlies it—even though it is strange and special, and for that reason suitable for a celebration—it does relate to daily life. Many people have told me after a concert that they notice changes in perception of everyday life.

Schechner: Sure it is related and sharpens one's perceptions—simply because it makes one pay attention. But...

Cage: The attitude that I take is that everyday life is more interesting than forms of celebration, when we become aware of it. That *when* is when our intentions go down to zero. Then suddenly you notice that the world is magical.

From a musical point of view, and I'm sure from the visual point of view, one thing makes everyday life far more fascinating and special than, say, concert life. That is the variety of sound with respect to all the other things, including space. When we make electronic music, we have to flood the hall with sound from a few loudspeakers. But in our everyday life sounds are popping up, just as visual things and moving things are popping up, everywhere around us. I would like to imitate that—to present fantastic architectural and technological problems. That's how the theatre will be. We have in America two or three loudspeakers in a theatre, in Europe they have them up in teens, and I think in hundreds in Russia, so that sounds can move or appear to come from any point in space, generally around the shell. I would also like it to appear, as I think it will with transistor means, in the center of the space. And then there's mobility, too. When a fly buzzes past me now I have, from an artistic point of view, a frightful problem. But it's quite reasonable to imagine that we will have a loudspeaker that will be able to fly through space.

Schechner: Amplifications of sounds are so very un-everyday-life-ish simply because they're so amplified.

Cage: I agree with you. I only said what I said in order to show that one needn't agree with you. Alan Watts came to a concert once, and left very shortly because, as he said, "I can hear this sort of thing outside, I don't need to be here."

Schechner: It would be a good thing to take people to watch something out there, to create in the out-there a celebratory situation, if not a play.

Cage: That was so touching in *Miracle in Milan:* people seated in rows to look at the sunset. What is so interesting about modern art and Pop Art in this country is that it has more and more trained our eyes not on the most noticeable things, but on the things generally overlooked.

Schechner: Which are very much there; when we are asked to look at them, they are translated into something they were not intended for. These Madison Avenue images were intended to engage us, and the result of Pop Art is to disengage us. So that when we face them again in reality we're looking at them as themselves and not as what they're luring us to do. The painting separates us from the intention of the billboard. When you see the face or the can or the girl the first time you are moved to do something; you see the painting and then see her again on the billboard, you're moved just to look at her but not do what the sign tells you to do. A very interesting basic freedom is involved in Pop Art... you're no longer compelled to go out and buy. Do these theatre experiences have a similar thrust?

Cage: Yes. We can become more aware and furthermore we can become more curious.

Kirby: When you taught at the New School, around 1956, you worked with performance material as well as with music. What kind of assignments did you give?

Cage: The course generally began with my trying to bring the students to the point of knowing who I was, that is, what my concerns and activities were, and I wanted them to find out who they were and what they were doing. I wasn't concerned with a teaching situation that involved a body of material to be transmitted by me to them. I would, when it was necessary, give them a survey of earlier works, by me and by others, in terms of composition, but mostly I emphasized what I was doing at that time and would show them what I was doing and why I was interested in it. Then I warned them that if they didn't want to change their ways of doing things, they ought to leave the class, that it would be my function, if I had any, to stimulate them to change.

Schechner: Did many leave?

Cage: Well there never were many and they mostly stayed. Eight or ten at the most. Some people did quite conventional musical work, they knew that I would try to get them to budge a bit. And some of them did. After this basic introduction, the classes consisted simply in their showing what they had done. And if I had anything to say I would say it. I also got them to say things about their work . . . but this is a common progressive education practice isn't it? We had very little to work with: a closet full of percussion instruments, a broken down piano, and things that people brought with them. The room was very small, so we simply did what we could do in that room.

I reminded them that because we had so little they had to do things that would nevertheless work. I didn't want them making things that couldn't be done. Practicality has always seemed to me to be of the essence. I hate the image of an artist who makes things that can't be done.

Kirby: Wasn't it surprising to have painters in a music class like that?

Cage: It wasn't surprising to me because I had, before that, in the late '40s and '50s, been part and parcel of the Artists Club. I had early seen that musicians were the people who didn't like me. But the painters did. The people who came to the concerts which I organized were very rarely musicians—either performing or composing. The audience was made up of people interested in painting and sculpture.

Schechner: What kind of dialogue came out of your class?

Cage: You mean what could a painter do with this kind of situation?

Schechner: What *did* they do?

Cage: But you know that. It's a matter of history now. Allan Kaprow introduced the element of time more and more into his work. Normally a musician writes in measures, and then assigns to the unit of those measures a metronomic figure. So we have andante and largo and all those things. In a piece called the *Music of Changes,* which I composed for the *Book of Changes,* all the things I could discern in a piece of music were subjected to chance operation. Among the things I noticed and subjected to chance operation was tempo. If you look at the *Music of Changes* you see that every few measures, at every structural point, things were speeding up or slowing down or remaining constant. How much these things varied was chance determined. David Tudor learned a form of mathematics which he didn't know before in order to translate those tempo indications into actual time. It was a very difficult process and very time consuming for him. After that I altered my way of composing; I didn't write in tempos but always in times. By the time I was teaching at the New School this was one of the facts of my work, and they caught on readily because it gives one enormous facility in the field of time to know by means of a clock when something's got to start.

Schechner: Why do you think this kind of thing turns painters on?

Cage: I think that Kirby has indicated that in his introduction to the book on Happenings.

Schechner: A lot of your own work seems to be very different in substance, if not in underlying theory, from Happenings.

Cage: In Kirby's introduction he searches to do something fairly precisely which I've said I don't like myself to do, namely to make a definition. In making that definition he was brought to excluding the *Motor-Vehicle Sundown Event* of George Brecht from the category of Happenings simply because it didn't involve intention. Am I right?

Kirby: I think at the time I made the definition I was thinking of another category of Chance Theatre. I've changed my opinion somewhat since then.

Cage: And you wanted in the case of Happenings to set up a notion of an intentional theatre that was alogical and nonmatrixed?

Kirby: Yes.

Cage: I have felt the presence of intention in an alogical continuity to be something that doesn't interest me, for this reason: does not the term alogical mean that anything can happen?

Kirby: I was thinking that there weren't any intellectual relationships; it wasn't either logical or illogical.

Cage: That will be very hard to prove. In Kaprow's Happening with the mountain, he says that there is this symbol business about the girl...

Kirby: I agree with you about that piece, as I tried to explain in the introduction to *Happenings*. Most of *The Courtyard* I consider an alogical play rather than a Happening.

Cage: And the Earth Mother. That strikes me as drawing relationships between things, in accord with an intention. If we do that, I think then we have to do it better than people in history did it. Happenings don't do it better because they have this thing we've spoken of as carelessness in them.

Carelessness comes about through—to use your words—"nonmatrixed activity." The only way you're going to get a good performance of an intentional piece, that furthermore involves symbols and other relationships which the artist has drawn in his mind, is to have lots of rehearsals, and you're going to have to do it as well as you can; rather than using one symbol you might find another more effective symbol. You're involved in a whole thing that we have been familiar with since the Renaissance and before.

I think that what we're doing is something else and not that. So when I go to a Happening that seems to me to have intention in it I go away saying that I'm not interested. I also did not like to be told, in the *Eighteen Happenings in Six Parts,* to move from one room to another. Though I don't actively engage in politics I do as an artist have some awareness of art's political content, and it doesn't include policemen.

I think we all realize that anarchy is not practical; the lovely movement of philosophical anarchism in the United States that did quite a lot in the nineteenth century finally busted up because in the large population centers its ideas were not practical. We look at our lives, at the anarchist moments, or spaces, or times, or whatever you want to call them, and there these things that I'm so interested in—awareness, curiosity, etc.—have play. It is not during organized or policed moments that these things happen. I admit that in a policed circumstance I can take an aesthetic attitude and enjoy it, just as I can listen to Beethoven in a way other than he intended and enjoy it on my terms. But why do you think that so many Happenings have become intentional?

I think that those people for one reason or another are interested in themselves. I came to be interested in anything but myself. This is the difference. When I say that anything can happen I don't mean anything that *I want* to have happen.

Schechner: But don't you in some way structure your work?

Cage: You're aiming now at a purity which we are never going to achieve. When we say "purposelessness" we add "purposeful purposelessness." You'll find this more and more being recognized not as double talk, but as truth. That's why I don't like definition; when you succeed in defining and cutting things off from something, you thereby take the life out of it. It isn't any longer as true as it was when it was incapable of being defined.

Kirby: But some people can't do things unless you define them for them.

Cage: That kind of sight is not going to enable them to see. The whole desire for definitions has to do with the Renaissance in which we demanded clarity and got it. Now we are not in such a period and such definitions are no longer of use to us.

The difficulty with the theatre, as I see it, is that it has—because of the complexity involved and probably because of the economics—tended to close the circle around it rather than to open it out. This is true also of the symphony orchestra. Whether or not people inside the circle are going to enter into the dialogue is very much an open question. Occasions will arise when dialogues will occur, but in the case of theatre it's extremely difficult. I was up at Wesleyan University for discussions about the performing arts. There was a man who had performed Hamlet at the Tyrone Guthrie...

Schechner: George Grizzard?

Cage: Yes. And a director associated with him.

Schechner: Alan Schneider?

Cage: Alan Schneider. I certainly wouldn't have gone had I known what was going to take place. It was a warm evening and they began by taking their coats off, and trying to give the feeling of informality, and they went so far as not to use the chairs but to sit on the table which had been placed in front of them. They proceeded to say that they had nothing to tell the audience, that what they wanted were ideas from the audience, in other words they wanted to have a discussion. Of course there were no questions. So they had to chat and supplement one another's loss of knowledge of what to do next. The whole thing was absolutely disgusting: the kinds of ideas and the kinds of objectives, the vulgarity of it, was almost incomprehensible. The chairman of the meeting was also disgusted and at one point he interrupted Schneider and Grizzard and knowing that I was in the audience, asked me to speak my piece. I asked them what they thought of Happenings, and learned that they had no knowledge of them whatsoever. They don't go. They weren't interested. They were concerned with the *Hamlet* situation.

Schechner: This is the difficulty. When a painter comes to a Happening he brings a painting tradition, when a musician comes he brings with him a music tradition, but no one in the theatre brings anything—

Cage: Except a quality of mind, namely a tremendous ego. You could see that in Grizzard. He kept being humble in order to show that he wasn't so stuck up. But it was clear that he was as stuck on himself as he could be, and that he wanted the best thing to happen to him that could happen. He thought it was nice and ethical of him to have preferred to do *Hamlet* instead of something on Broadway. That kind of shoddy ethic is just intolerable.

I said this sort of thing. I was quite heated, I normally don't like to talk against things, but I had been asked to. When we couldn't discuss Happenings because they had no knowledge nor interest and didn't think it was as serious as *Hamlet* and thought they were being virtuous, then I said, "Well, what do you think about TV?" They weren't interested in TV. And yet they're living in an electronic world where TV is of far more relevance than the legitimate theatre.

Why don't we think of those theatre people as what they are? They're a form of museum. And we are going to have museums and we should just be grateful to them for doing what they're doing and not bother them.

Let me add something that I think might illuminate this. What is the primary concern of the dramatist and the actor? It is content, in any way that you interpret content. But Marshall McLuhan in his work on mass media, begins by saying that content is of no importance. He says "The medium is the message." And he says you can only come to this conclusion and this awareness if you divorce yourself from thoughts of content. This is very similar to my statement about divorcing oneself from thoughts of intention, they go very well together. What does McLuhan see as activity for an artist? It's perfectly beautiful, and every time we see it now we enjoy it: he says all we have to do is brush information against information, and it doesn't matter what. By that brushing we will be made aware of the world which itself is doing that.

7

Yvonne Rainer
Interviews Ann Halprin
(1965)

Halprin: I was trained as a traditional modern dancer. The big break came for me about fifteen years ago when I left the scene. I didn't know what I wanted to do except to leave that scene—that's when we built our outdoor platform.

Rainer: Had you been doing solo work before that or collaborating?

Halprin: Solo work. I also had a group.

Rainer: And you choreographed for the group?

Halprin: Yes. I had a studio together with Welland Lathrop, and was part of that tradition of modern dance. But then I felt a break. I was in a New York Dance Festival, an ANTA thing. I wasn't very stimulated, as I had gone to New York as the only dancer from the West Coast, but hadn't seen what was going on in dance. When I came back I wasn't excited about anything. That's when the big break came. The workshop idea started when I left San Francisco and came out to Kentfield. Some of the students who had been working with me in San Francisco followed me. Because I didn't know what I wanted to do, or what I wanted to teach, we set up a workshop situation in which I gave myself permission to explore. Even though I was the catalyst of the group and somehow or other the teacher, I still made it very clear that I wasn't teaching in the usual sense. I didn't feel that I had to know an answer and teach it to somebody.

Rainer: What was the role of the people you brought?

Halprin: They simply wanted to have the opportunity to stay in contact with the kinds of activities I was interested in. They also wanted to explore and work together.

I wanted to explore in a particular way breaking down any preconceived notions I had about what dance was, or what movement was, or what composition was. I began setting up situations where we could rely only on our improvisational skills. Everything was done, for quite a few years, with improvisation. The purpose of the improvisation was not self-expression. I was trying to get at subconscious areas, so things would happen in an unpredictable way. I was trying to eliminate stereotyped ways of reacting. Improvisation was used to release things that were blocked off because we were traditional modern dancers.

Rainer: Was the focus physical? Did you start out with the body?

Halprin: Sometimes it would be purely physical; we worked on technique this way. My training is in anatomy so it was easy for me to go into the bone structure and the muscle structure and to work like a kinesiologist. We would isolate in an anatomical and objective way the body as an instrument. We would improvise with rotation or flexion or other anatomical structures. We would say, we're going to begin to work with how you can articulate this part of the body, isolate it from another part of the body—what is the efficient way to do that movement, do we really need to do this or is it just habit? When we improvised we were finding out what *our* bodies could do, not learning somebody else's pattern or technique.

As the teacher or director of the group, I never told anybody why a movement should be or how it should look. In that sense, too, they had to build their own technique. Even now in our company there is no unified look; there's a unified approach but everybody is different in movement. And we used improvisation to explore space and certain kinds of dynamics. We would set up a situation where two people had a focus that concerned the amount of space between them. They would improvise to get a feeling of what could happen, and what one person did would elicit a reaction from the other. We got involved in cause and effect. After a while we noticed that this was restrictive. But that period gave us a certain technique which is still one of our resources. All of us began to feel the need for another step.

Rainer: How long after was this?

Halprin: I think we worked together for four years using improvisation and starting really from the beginning. Out of that period we evolved compositions which were completely improvised with particular focuses. We began to allow the voice to become an integral part of movement, where breathing became sound or some heightened feeling stimulated certain associative responses and a word came, or a sound, or a shout. Free-association became an important part of the work. This would very often manifest itself in dialogue. We began to deal with ourselves as people, not dancers. We incorporated actions that had never been used in dance before. Works that came out of this period included *Trunk Dance* and *Four-Square.*

Rainer: Were the dances improvised for performance?

Halprin: No. They were improvised in order to get at the result; once that result was there it was fixed. You can see how that would wear itself out. The next step was a system whereby we would be forced to adapt ourselves to some outside direction.

Rainer: In performance?

Halprin: No—now we go back to work. Each performance represents several years' investigation. Each new work represents a new concept, a new system of composition. We have never been a repertory company; we may repeat a piece within the year that we're doing it, but once we have felt the need to explore another area, we drop what we're doing.

We began to explore systems that would knock out cause and effect...

Rainer: You mean between people?

Halprin: Between everything. Anything that had to do with cause and effect got you back into your own resources again. I wanted to find out things that I'd never thought of, that would never come out of my personal responses.

Rainer: Did you find that you moved in patterns?

Halprin: Yes. It wasn't so much repeating patterns, it was a repetition of similar attitudes that didn't lead to any further growth. Improvisation is still a basic part of our technique. Everything we do keeps growing; it's not that we don't do something any more, it's just that the skill is there but it's not used in the same way.

The next step was to find a way to separate the elements that we were using. We had gotten enormously involved in a lot of complex and diverse materials. We were using vocal materials and words, musicians were improvising with us: La Monte Young, Terry Riley, Warner Jepson, Bill Spencer. We were using objects and props—we were using space in a determinist way. I wanted to isolate these elements. I began to work with a system where all these things became independent of cause and effect: in order to get the music to do *this* you didn't have to do *that*.

Rainer: The musicians worked out their things in a different place, or what?

Halprin: We separated from the musicians for a while. I began to chart movement; I put everything on charts; everything became arbitrary.

Rainer: Movement patterns, space patterns?

Halprin: Anything I was dealing with. I could do it with a movement. I have a great pamphlet in which I've taken every possible anatomical combination of movement and put them all on sheets of paper and given them numbers. One sheet had to do with flexion, different joints, another sheet had to do with extension. I would pick off these things and I'd make a pattern. These were movements I hadn't evolved myself. And then I tried to do it. I got into the wildest combinations of movement, things I never could have conceived of. All of a sudden my body began to experience new ways of moving. We applied this in bigger compositional ways. We would experiment with all the elements we worked with, even combinations of people. In *Birds of America* I used a pie-shape and I made pies with a different interval for each one; I put different elements into each pie, and then I'd have another transparent wheel on top of that to mix them up so that each one could be rotated for a different combination. I'd say, "We'll try this combination and we'll make a composition based on these particular elements coming together, now let's see what'll happen."
    Even though I got the composition system formalized, we still worked it out with improvisation.

Rainer: So you invented new movement.

Halprin: We invented new movement possibilities, new ways of combining the elements. But when the dance was finished it was fixed.

Rainer: In arriving at the final product you improvised with those things you had found through manipulating the wheels?

Halprin: That's right. I could have manipulated the wheels several times and gotten any number of versions, and this is what I intended to do, but we got too involved in our next problem so we took another jump before we explored any further. *Birds of America* was about fifty minutes, our first long work. We spent two years doing exercises, exploring things that led to this system; then it took us about three months to compose the work. We performed it once. By that time we had gotten into doing something else. With that system we could have composed other works, but I wasn't interested. Something else was happening.

By chance I happened to become very aware of the space in the theatre, the stage. I just didn't like it, it bothered me, I didn't know what to do. I got this flash: just before performance I put a bamboo pole in everybody's hands including mine, and we had to do the dance that we'd always done, holding bamboo poles.

Rainer: Throughout the fifty minutes?

Halprin: Yes. The poles were very long and they created their own spatial environment. This was the beginning of our next jump. I became preoccupied with movement in relation to environment. I began to feel that we had paid such strict attention to self-awareness, kinesthetic responses, and each other, that we developed a stifling introspection. So we began to extend our focus to adaptive responses in the environment. We had worked with musicians, painters, all kinds of artists...

Rainer: Could you go into some detail about that?

Halprin: In *Birds of America* they came into a situation we had already established as dancers. Their influence was not a real cross-fertilization yet. But the music wasn't accompaniment, we'd gotten away from that when we began to work with separate elements.

Rainer: Background?

Halprin: Not even background. The dance was always first. It was a matter of finding sound, finding costumes—whatever it is that would be suitable to the dance. In that sense the dance was still the focus, but I felt that breaking up the categories would be much more exciting. The people we were working with had many resources and they weren't using them. We were by that time interested in finding out about what there was on the outside that could affect our ideas for movement.

The next big thing was *Five-Legged Stool*. This was a full-length evening, in two acts. This work further developed the cross-fertilization idea. Up until then we had been content with using the space that we had. But I got discouraged with having to be up there in that relationship to an audience. I began to look at the lobby, the aisles, the ceilings, the floor. Suddenly I thought, "Who says we have to stay on that stage, this is a whole building." In *Five-Legged Stool* what happened was that all these independent elements were developed: the use of sound, vocal material, the word and its content, the painter and the way in which a painter became, very often, the choreographer. For example, in Act II I wanted to keep bringing objects out and putting them down and going back, taking objects out and putting them down. The painter we were working with, Jo Landor, kept watching this going on and one day she came in with forty wine bottles and said, "Here, I want you to bring these in." She almost set the kind of movement I did. It's pretty hard for me to know who choreographed that work, Jo Landor or me.

Rainer: Supposing you had not wanted to do what you had to do with those wine bottles?

Halprin: It worked out fine, because I had also gotten attached to the idea that I wanted people to have tasks to do. Doing a task created an attitude that would bring the movement quality into another kind of reality. It was devoid of a certain kind of introspection.

Rainer: I remember that summer I was here with you and you assigned tasks. But as I understood it, the tasks were to make you become aware of your body. It wasn't necessary to retain the task but to do the movement or the kinesthetic thing that the task brought about.

Halprin: Afterwards we became much more concerned with doing the task itself. Then we set up tasks that would be so challenging that the choice of a task would be the idea of the movement.

Rainer: Rather than it being transformed?

Halprin: That's right. Jo was in on all this. The wine bottle task that she gave me was so challenging and so difficult that I was quite content to do it. I couldn't get up and down; I had to stay in a stooped-over position or I'd break my back. Then I had the task of taking these wine bottles, putting them overhead, getting them to disappear in the ceiling. I had to balance on a stool. The task was sufficiently compelling in itself that I was able to turn my full attention to it. It took me forty minutes.

Rainer: Did all the movements in *Five-Legged Stool* have to do with tasks?

Halprin: Yes, and all the tasks were chosen for different reasons. For example, John Graham had a plank that was on a diagonal resting on a ceiling beam. He crawled up to the ceiling and his task was to slide down that beam head first. It was a complete fantasy; it had nothing to do with anything functional. It wasn't the kind of task that had to do with something as recognizable as carrying out a bottle and placing it.

Rainer: Did he do it?

Halprin: Yes. By achieving the impossible he arrived at an incredible bit of fantasy.

Rainer: In that particular piece did being yourselves, not having a character, carry through?

Halprin: Yes, quite automatically. Actually I was very pleased by it. In doing these tasks we were not playing roles or creating moods; we simply did something. By the choice of the objects and tasks we could determine the overall quality. For example, in the first act of *Five-Legged Stool* each person had several gambits that could be done in any combination, even though each time they had to be done the same way. Things like pouring water. I had a big box of colorful material and tin cans, and other things that I had chosen, and just throwing them as high as I could would be another task. There would be a task like changing clothes. There would be another task that had to do with falling, a movement task. Even though these things were repeated exactly the same way in every performance, their sequence changed so that the composition would be different for the audience and the performer. This was the first composition where we had a different performance every night.

Rainer: In looking at the photographs, a lot of the visual impact has to do with the decor and costumes, which were not essential to the carrying out of the tasks.

Halprin: True. There was an enormous amount of juxtaposition in *Five-Legged Stool* and it was done deliberately. There was an attempt to really break down cause and effect. I wanted everything to have such a sensory impact that an audience would not question why. I didn't want anything to look as if it had meaning, or continuity. What we wore had nothing to do with the tasks. We went down to McAllister Street and everybody was asked to collect things that interested them for costumes. I had a jag for dresses from the 1920s, those spangly things, beautiful colors and very luminous. I had a thing about those dresses and I'd go down and collect as many as I could. Other times we used everyday clothing. It was a big thing for us—the first time we hadn't used tights and leotards. They were taboo. We danced with shoes on. I felt like a naughty little girl the first day, because a modern dancer used bare feet, and suddenly I was wearing high-heeled shoes. Leath was wearing tennis shoes.

This was for us a very important breakthrough, and helped us have completely new images of who we were. It was the last time that we ever really thought of ourselves as dancers. The other thing about *Five-Legged Stool* was that we began to use the space; we explored the entire theatre—it was a small theatre—the outside, the corridors, the ceilings, the basement, the aisles, everything. What happened was that the audience was in the center, and the performance went all around them. Above them and below them and in front of them, and outside, sometimes they would hear things out on the street.

Rainer: In that theatre the sidewalk is right outside.

Halprin: Something happened in that performance that we'd never experienced before, and began to establish a next step. We got a violent audience reaction. That's when people started throwing things at us. That was the first time. People would throw shoes on stage. The dance ended with five minutes of just feathers falling from the ceiling, all you saw was five minutes of feathers falling. The windows in the theatre were open so that the street sounds came in, and the wind came in, and just these feathers dropping.

Rainer: Were the performers on the stage?

Halprin: No. Everything was cleared away. This got people quite involved for some reason. I remember one woman said, "Isn't this the silliest thing? I'm just sitting here in this theatre spending my time just looking at those feathers drop." The people would talk, they wouldn't just whisper to each other, they would talk loudly so that everybody could hear.

Rainer: What happened during the performance?

Halprin: They talked all during the performance, they talked to the person next to them as if that person were ten miles away, as if everything they said to each other was a public announcement. There was a definite kind of involvement that we had never experienced before, nor did we know what to do with it, or why it was there.

Rainer: They didn't actually interfere?

Halprin: Often they did. People would come up onto the stage and start to grab the feathers. One time during the bottle dance, when Leath and I balanced on a stool and shouted at each other, people in the audience started shouting and throwing shoes at us. We were completely naïve about what we were doing. We didn't know this would affect anyone else. Everything made complete sense to us because, after all, we spent two years investigating these techniques. We'd worked with juxtaposition, this kind of unrelatedness. We couldn't figure out what was wrong, why everybody was getting so excited. People would walk out in a rage. We gave sixteen performances of this and always got this reaction. When we did it in Rome it was ten times worse. Absolutely violent. When we came back we were concerned about what we were doing to an audience.

Rainer: This was after Rome. What else did you bring to Europe?

Halprin: *Esposizione,* a commission. Luciano Berio saw *Five-Legged Stool* and felt that he wanted to work with us. He had been asked to write a small opera for the Venice Biennale. He asked us to work with him. We started out with the architecture of the Venice Opera House. The first thing that occurred to me was that the stage looked like a fireplace in somebody's living room—if we tried to dance on the floor we'd look like little ants. There were only six of us in the company, we'd be drowned by that space. It's built like a horseshoe, there are five tiers of seats and only two hundred people on the bottom floor. The first problem was how to integrate ourselves into that space. I felt that we needed something vertical, and we evolved the idea of suspending a cargo net across the proscenium, forty feet in the air. The bottoms were stretched out like wings over the orchestra pit and way back into the stage. This is the way in which we were able to alter that proscenium and allow the dancers to be able to move vertically.

Rainer: Was one cargo net enough?

Halprin: Yes, it was a very big one. We built a big ramp, too, on the floor, so that we really had no floor. The floor itself was a slant.

Rainer: You built the ramp out of boards?

Halprin: Out of fiberglass. We cut down eucalyptus trees from Marin County and we shipped them all the way over to Italy because we had worked with this cargo net on those trees and it was real scary forty feet in the air. We weren't about to take any chances, so we shipped our own trees there. That dance evolved out of a spatial idea, an environmental idea. We said the theatre was our environment and we were going to move through the theatre. And we took a single task: burdening ourselves with enormous amounts of luggage. The whole group had this one task, to be burdened with things.

We chose objects for their texture and form; they were all everyday objects: automobile tires, gunnysacks filled with things—at one point we had a big hassock filled with tennis balls—bundles of rags, parachutes that were stuck into containers, newspapers rolled up that were stuck into things, things that could come out and explode. Each person had to carry these things and to allow his movements to be conditioned to speeds that had been set up for him. Some started in the plaza, some started in the prompter's pit; they started all over the place, so that it was like an invasion. The music started at a different time, dancers started at different times. You just didn't have any idea when anything started. The cargo net started going up during intermission, and people couldn't tell if things were starting or if this was preparation. The whole dance—it took forty minutes—was a series of false beginnings. Nothing ever got anywhere. As soon as something got started, something else would be introduced. The dancers' task was to carry things and to penetrate the entire audience. This meant they had to go through that stage area which included the cargo net. One of the most compelling parts of the dance was the effort of carrying those things up that cargo net, because the stuff would fall.

Rainer: It actually did fall?

Halprin: Yes. We had a hassock filled with two hundred tennis balls and one dancer's task was to take that hassock up there and when she got it up there to overturn it, so that the tennis balls came flying down. When we reached the high point—there was an enormous amount of objects there by that time— automobile tires were rolling down, tennis balls were falling, it was just a great crash of things. The tennis balls bounced all over so that the whole space exploded. People's bodies dropped down through the net and were caught by ropes, they would hang on; we turned into acrobats. We worked on that cargo net for a year. We got so that we could fall from one point to another, catch ourselves on a rope, hang upside down. We developed a whole technique to operate on that cargo net. The nine-year-old child who was in it started off at the top of the cargo net, jumped into a perpendicular rope, and swung; she got a big momentum going and she swung clear across the heads of the audience in the first few rows and all the way back into the stage. *Esposizione* was a very bold use of the architectonic concept of space. It also was just a continual repetition and variation of one task.

Rainer: Did people have set speeds that were constant throughout?

Halprin: Yes. We had time scores. Everything was done according to seconds. We never heard the music until the night of the performance and the time score helped us correlate with the music. We had so much time to get from here to here. This is what determined the effort of our movements. Sometimes it was almost impossible to cover a certain terrain in a certain length of time, because of the burdens we carried. We would stumble, it was like a life and death situation.

Rainer: You had cues in the music.

Halprin: No. We never heard the music.

Rainer: How did you keep time?

Halprin: We had five people stationed all over the place who were giving us cues.

Rainer: Vocally?

Halprin: We would keep track of them, we would look and they would give us hand signals. Each person in the dance had his own conductor who managed to get to various spots, and just like musicians we looked at our conductor from time to time and found out where we were. We just jolly well had to be where we had to be when the time came.

Rainer: The conductor would be where you were supposed to be?

Halprin: No. He would be in a place where we could see him. We had worked it out.

Rainer: So they moved around?

Halprin: Yes. It was so important for us to do that task that if necessary we had to drop one of our bundles in order to get somewhere. We left a trail of litter everywhere. Litter in the balconies, in the aisles.

Rainer: Did you take all this stuff over with you?

Halprin: Yes, we did, which was really stupid. We got very possessive about the things we collected. And our costumes were designed in such a way that we could only wear them for the night of the one performance. The cargo net ripped the costumes to shreds. The task, the effort of doing it, the amount of stumbling, and having to get through certain environments would just rip us to shreds. We would start out absolutely beautifully attired.

Rainer: What kind of costumes?

Halprin: The costumes were designed as extensions of our props. Each person was very different. John Graham had a tuxedo and a gold helmet, and it was all black and white. Daria was just full of different transparent, thin things, she was very bulky but very soft and transparent. Each person was really designed as an object. We never wore our costumes until the night of performance. By the end everybody was in shreds. John Graham only had his trousers left. His coat had been ripped off, he was completely bare from his waist up. We had a vocal score in three different languages. We had to sing and speak in Italian, English, and Greek.

Rainer: How was this established?

Halprin: Berio simply gave us the score. At certain times, according to its elements, we said the score, or sang it.

Rainer: You learned it?

Halprin: Yes. The parts were sent to us. John Graham did an amazing thing on the cargo net. I was giving him one task and Berio was giving him another. They were both very difficult. He had to be going as fast as he could up that cargo net carrying this tire and other baggage, and at the same time Berio gave him a score which took seven minutes to read in which he was constantly talking and shouting. He had to alternate speaking Italian and English. He didn't understand a word of the Italian, so he memorized it. It was just this continual bla-bla-bla-bla of words coming out and every word had to be memorized; it had a particular sound value to Berio. It was considered a small opera because we had that much vocal activity. Then he had vocal people— two young boys and a woman—who sang. The only trouble with the vocal material was that we never heard it in performance because the audience shouted so much and responded so excitedly to all the vocal material that you couldn't hear ours as being any different than theirs.

Rainer: Do you know what the vocal material was, I mean in Italian?

Halprin: Yes, we knew. Rona had a passage in which she was sitting out in one of the tiers, blowing soap bubbles and wearing a yellow raincoat, telling a biblical story in Latin. We were trying to get up to the top of that cargo net with all of our baggage falling. We were scrambling and being torn apart. And she was, at that time, sitting out there and telling this biblical story in Latin. These are things that Berio had planned and that became very interesting juxtapositions.

Rainer: You never did *Esposizione* here?

Halprin: We've never done it anywhere else. It was a difficult work because of the musical score and an eighteen-piece orchestra. It was a very complicated thing.

Rainer: What are you doing now?

Halprin: When we came back we took a long rest. Then we began to explore the audience. We wanted to find out what an audience was, to understand a little bit more what we were doing to an audience.

Rainer: I'd like to know. Was it mostly outrage that you experienced in Europe?

Halprin: Not with the cargo dance. They were very excited; they'd never seen anything like that. They had never been so overwhelmed with performers all around them, and so forth. I felt hostility only one time: when the music became very repetitious and monotonous, they started yelling "Basta! Basta!" The press was interested in it as a new form and there was no hostility. They responded to it for what it was, not because it was or wasn't dance. They were appreciating the fact that it was a new form, what Stuchenschmitt called a "sur-naturalism," a new use for dance and movement, that had gone into new areas. There was hostility to *Five-Legged Stool*. It was very controversial in Zagreb. It was almost cancelled after the first performance.

Rainer: Why?

Halprin: "Decadent Western art." That audience didn't say a word. They just sat absolutely still. Apparently there was enormous hostility. In Italy they threw things at us, but asked us to come back. They said they'd never had such a gorgeous scandal. That's apparently what they enjoyed. They didn't care whether they liked the dance, they had permission to misbehave.

Rainer: The response affected you?

Halprin: I was concerned not that it offended me, but that we had this kind of power to stir people up. If we have this kind of power, how should we use it? I was concerned with our own naïveté. In Rome the audience was very hostile; they really knew how to be effective with their hostility. When they threw a shoe it hit. There was no pussyfooting.

Did you hear the famous story about the guy who came twice and waited for the special time when everything was quiet? He marched down and stood in the spotlights and turned and announced to the audience: "It's all Christopher Columbus's fault." And he marched out and everybody applauded. That was clever. These are people who know how to use their power. For the first time I realized there was an encounter going on between audience and performers. This is what we were interested in exploring next. We invited fifty people to join a series. It was announced as *A Series of Compositions for an Audience*. We explored this power: where is it, who has it, and how can we use it? We set up situations where the audience could investigate its role as an audience and learn how to use its power and then we could measure what it did to us.

Rainer: Do you feel that it's a moral issue? Can this power be misused, do people have to be educated?

Halprin: No, it's not a moral issue. It's throwing something away. I never realized that we were stirring people so deeply. I know now why. It gets at their pre-conscious and kinesthetic responses. It's very sensory and primitive. The more we know about this power the stronger we can be in using it. The audience has a power too, and if they can be given an opportunity to use it, we could have an encounter that would really send sparks. At Cal when a girl got up and smashed a lantern, she was using her power as an audience, but because we didn't appreciate the fact that she was using her power we threw it away. Had we responded and allowed the audience to realize that her act was a spontaneous, unplanned, vicious attack—WOW! would they have had an experience! Instead, we just threw it away, by pretending that we didn't really react to it.

Rainer: Describe what happened to you.

Halprin: Let's go back a little. In three works this year, incidents happened. Chuck Ross, a sculptor, brought some big-scale things down the aisles—it was just overwhelming: they're over your head and they're all around you. He blew up great big weather balloons that started flying all over the place. The whole place was full of sound, action, and props. When we did it outdoors in Fresno, it was like a gigantic three-ring circus. People laughed; they had a wonderful time. But when we did it in a closed area, it was always terrifying. These big things were moving around, crashing, flying, and exploding, and the dancers were moving in risky ways.

Rainer: Was this at Cal?

Halprin: Yes.

Rainer: Did it happen over the heads of the audience?

Halprin: Well, the big weather balloon was over their heads, the stuff that was carried in the aisles was going right past them. They could put their hands out and feel the metal. They could see the dancers, they could feel the tension of their movement right at their feet, or balancing on something over their heads—they were that close. It really did get them enormously involved. We knew that it was going to do this; we knew it would stimulate this kind of response in our audience. So it happened. About three-quarters of the way through some girl couldn't stand it and she got up from her seat, rushed onto the stage, took this lit lantern—it was the only light, everything else was black at that moment—and smashed it against a metal frame. Glass and kerosene went flying all over the place. The plastic—there was a lot of it around—could easily have caught fire. The dancers were shocked; they just gathered together and took a bow as if nothing had really happened. The audience thought that this thing was planned. They didn't appreciate their power and we didn't use ours.

Rainer: Stalemate.

Halprin: We learned from that summer that we and the audience had power. What we didn't have was the experience to deal with it when the encounter happened.

Rainer: Could you really prepare for this kind of thing?

Halprin: We did. We had a week of thorough therapy on this. We became completely brainwashed; we analyzed that thing from beginning to end. Now we're just waiting for the opportunity to see how we'll use their power, not throw it away, and not throw ours away.

Rainer: Are you going to deliberately provoke an audience?

Halprin: No. Never. Now we know that because of the things we do and the way we do them, we will stir people up. We've accepted that, we're not naïve about it any more. Now also we have to take the consequences when we stir up an audience, and we have to have an attitude for dealing with it.

Rainer: What was the name of that piece?

Halprin: *Parades and Changes*. It is compositionally one of the most satisfying fulfillments of an idea that was started in *Birds of America*. A very complicated score was worked out by the musician Mort Subotnik and me. It permitted us complete and total flexibility. When we take this to Stockholm in August [1965], we will take absolutely nothing but the score. We will use only the materials that we have in the theatre and collect when we get there. *Parades and Changes* has a set like cell blocks. Each person is in his own medium: the lighting person, the musician, the dancers—everybody has his own series of blocks.

Rainer: Which are not coordinated?

Halprin: They're not coordinated at all. They can last five to twenty minutes. The selection of the blocks was made on the basis of their contrast—there are eight completely different uses of sound. One might be magnetic tape, one might be a lute, one might be live sounds, one might be vocal sounds, another might be a Bach cantata, for example. Each block has been chosen on the basis of the differences.

Rainer: Different lengths?

Halprin: Yes, they're completely flexible.

Rainer: The Bach cantata can go on and on?

Halprin: No, that is the one thing that can't. That's "a set piece." It's exactly four minutes. That's the only one, and it can be coordinated with any number of things. Sometimes the dancers work as musicians, and sometimes the musicians use their material. We are conducted by a conductor. The dancers become musicians and sometimes they are also environmentalists: we work as a crew.

Rainer: What determines when things take place?

Halprin: All these little cell blocks—it's like you arrive with a trunk full of different clothes, and then, depending upon the weather, you decide what you're going to wear that day. This is exactly what we do. We come into that theatre and look at it and study it. What is it? What will work here? So we say, "I'm going to pick out five of my blocks, I'm not going to do two of them because they just won't work here." The musician picks out what he wants, and so forth.

Rainer: No one depends on anybody else?

Halprin: That's right. Then we get together and decide which ones will work in sequence, which things will work together, based on practical matters. Very often a whole new section is invented during the performance in order to make a link between one block and another. Sometimes blocks overlap in a way that they never have before, in order to fill the space or contract the space.

This has been a delightful composition to work with because so far we have given three performances of it and they are so completely different that people that have seen them all don't even know that they are the same dance. It's been a culminating point for us in developing a system of collaboration that we started five years ago.

This is completely different from another work, *Apartment 6,* that we're not taking to Europe because of the language barrier. It's done with a lot of dialogue. It's more of a play than *Parades and Changes.*

Rainer: How long is *Parades and Changes?*

Halprin: It can be anywhere from five minutes to five hours—completely fluid in its duration.

Rainer: And *Apartment 6?*

Halprin: We've done it as a full-length work, a two-hour piece in three acts. This is new for us and it's very hard for me to talk about it because I don't quite know what it came from except that Leath and John and I—there are only three people in it—have been working together for fourteen years. We know each other so well that our relationships are terribly complicated. What happened was that we set up a problem for ourselves: let's use each other as material, let's see what will happen if we don't use any props, music, or anything. Let's just use each other. Let's explore who you really are in terms of me.

Rainer: Are you talking about feelings?

Halprin: Yes—what we really feel about each other. We were in therapy together, the three of us, to explore what our feelings were about each other. We worked on the piece for about two years. We had outside supervision, a psychologist to help us expose our feelings.

Rainer: Why did you think this was important? Artists can work without knowing their feelings, or analyzing them.

Halprin: Partly by chance, and partly by intuition. We felt that unless we began to work this way we wouldn't be able to work together any more. We wouldn't be able to get any feedback from each other any more. We had to go further, otherwise we were finished with each other. Everything that we evolved, we evolved together with Patrick Hickey, Jo Landor, Morton Subotnik, Terry Riley, and La Monte Young. But the three of us, John, Leath, and I, were the nucleus.

Also it was something that we were beginning to feel about everybody. The person who is the performer is working with his body as an instrument, he's making sounds, and he's doing everything as if he were an object, when he's more than an object; he's full of the most fantastic psychological phenomena, but he's completely cutting these off and blocking them. But these are the most unique parts of the performer. The musician can't do this because he's got an instrument between him and the thing he's doing; and the painter has his material. But the dancer and the actor are their own instruments. They can find out why they are different from chairs or flutes or tape recorders.

There was also a desire to find out more about the human interior. To tell you the truth I was scared to death about this whole thing. I don't know if I'm the only one, I don't know how you feel about it, but when you start exposing your unconscious behavior—perhaps that's the wrong word—but when you start exposing your feelings about other people or yourself, you're opening up a lot of areas which are very uncomfortable, and it would be much easier if you just left them alone. It was uncomfortable and torturous. I approached it as a technical problem. I said, "OK, this is just new material that's been buried for a long time. I'm going to expose it, and try to find the skill to use it." There were times when I was upset and depressed because I was beginning to find out things about myself that I'd just as soon not know. I kept working on it from the point of view, "How can I use it as an artist?" That's how *Apartment 6* grew. We set it up as a domestic scene, so that the audience would have definite things to deal with. We cooked. I fixed breakfast for John on stage, we read newspapers, we played the radio, we talked.

Rainer: Your roles in relation to each other, were they what they really are, so you were not acting?

Halprin: I was myself. John was himself. I pretty much knew by then what some of our relationships were all about. We spent three years developing the skill to deal with this. We would set up focuses. I would set a task for myself to do. John would set a task for himself. Each person had something to do, so that we had a very formalized structure. The process of trying to do this task would always be encountered and interfered with by the other person, this is what we couldn't help. We were so aware of how we were using each other.

Rainer: Was it always interference?

Halprin: It was either interference or reinforcement. Both altered the work. Also we developed a technique that we called "three realities." When those three realities went on at different times there would be a fourth reality. One was the simple act of doing something, which could be cooking—I made my pancake mix and I just made it. I followed the directions on the box. People would come to the theatre and they would see John reading the newspaper, really reading what was in the newspaper that day. It was absolute, complete realism. Then there would be another kind of realism—say that Leath is reading the newspaper, John is playing the radio. The radio is beginning to annoy Leath, so he wants to turn it off. He's dealing with another reality at this point. He's beginning to get feelings about that radio which put him in contact with John. All Leath's hostility against John is stirred up by the blasted radio. So he puts the newspaper down and does the most violent movement you've ever seen. He might explode in mid-air. That's how he's feeling about John at that particular moment.

Rainer: It's not what he would do in reality necessarily.

Halprin: No. That's it. We had great limitations. John was allowed to express these kinds of feelings in words, Leath was not, Leath had to express them in movement.

Rainer: Why did you restrict them?

Halprin: It's very complicated. We wanted to guarantee that Leath would be able to make very sudden shifts. If he talked out his feelings, the audience would lose direct touch with what he was feeling because his verbal material came out so sarcastically. But when he used movement he was direct. John uses words, and they come out in a way that transfers.

Rainer: You're making aesthetic judgments on the basis of....

Halprin: On the basis of our particular skills and development at that moment. We were able to bring certain formalized controls to these things.

Rainer: It had to do with effectiveness?

Halprin: It had to do with our skills at that particular moment. At that time Leath couldn't handle words in that situation so he used movement. In certain areas of fantasy he would start using words which would come through fine.
    We got strange juxtapositions of realities going on at the same time. I

might be in an absolute tizzy about my pancakes and go into a terrific fantasy about those pancakes and Leath would be just sitting at the table eating his grapefruit and reading his paper, while John was listening to the radio. Do you see what I mean?

Rainer: Yes. Sometimes people were using different realities at different times. What was the third one?

Halprin: The fantasy. Leath would simply turn into a dog, or a dart board, and John would throw darts at him. But he really fantasized these things, like day-dreaming. So he could do it in action.

The fourth reality is when the other three [realities] come together in their peculiar ways. We had it divided up: Leath and John first, then John and me, then Leath and me. There were three completely different relationships, which became the three acts. The performances were completely different each night. It was the here and now, you couldn't do any pretending. Everything was completely real at that moment. What came out of the radio, what you read in the papers, your feelings about the other person might change a little bit from one day to another. It was very, very exhausting to use your skill at a consistent level all that time. It wasn't until the last, the sixteenth, performance that I felt we had captured what we wanted to do, which was to simply have two hours on that stage of a real-life situation, in which you as performer and you as a person were completely the same thing. That finally happened. It worked for us and it worked for the audience.

Rainer: The Stanislavski Method, as it's taught in New York acting schools, seems close to what you were doing.

Halprin: I don't know anything about it. I tried to read Stanislavski but I don't understand it. It doesn't appeal to me.

Rainer: You don't see any connection?

Halprin: None at all. In our situation there's absolutely nothing pretended. We don't play any roles. We just are who we are. I don't know where it's going to lead to. We use our skills as artists to respond to the material. We use certain structures to guarantee a possibility for the audience to be in on it. We avoid personalizing.

Rainer: Do you feel a necessity to relate what you're doing to dance any more?

Halprin: No. I don't even identify with dance.

Rainer: Do you have another name for what you are doing?

Halprin: No. It's as much dance as anything—if you can think of dance as the rhythmic phenomena of the human being reacting to his environment. Essentially this is what dance is. If the audience accepted this definition, then I'd say yes, it's dance.

Rainer: What was the response of the audience? How did the power thing relate to this situation?

Halprin: There was not any of that. If affected them very differently than *Parades and Changes.* They laughed a lot and they cried a lot. Some people were crying and some people were laughing at the same time. I don't know why. Nobody really cried and felt sorry for anybody. And we cried and our thing on stage was the material we used for our crying. It was a very curious thing. I don't ever remember feeling sorry that so-and-so was crying: "He's crying, that's my material, I really feel it, I'm crying." You may not know why you cry; something hits you and you cry. The audience does the same thing. I never experienced anybody crying before in an audience. I don't really know very much about this yet. There was none of that power bit.

What I heard from people is that they identified with us closely. There were people who walked out, too—who thought they came to see a dance concert. One person had an interesting reaction, she said: "I enjoyed myself thoroughly while I was there but I'll never come again." Patrick asked why. And she said, "It just isn't art."

8

TDR's First Ten Years
(1966)

Robert Corrigan

Probably the most legitimate reason for celebrating anniversaries is that they provide the occasion for that kind of double vision which permits one to look backward and forward at the same time. Such contortions, if practiced on a daily basis, would very quickly lead to schizophrenia, total blindness, and inevitable crack-up. This is as true for a magazine as it is for a marriage. But on these special occasions we can—and we should—step back from our immediate problems; from the vantage point of that still moment outside of time, it is possible for us to see more clearly where we have been and where we might be going.

Looking back over *TDR's* first ten years it becomes apparent almost at once that since its first issue was published in May of 1955,[1] this magazine has been both the herald and the chronicle in America of all that has been important in the theatre. Long before they had become fashionable—and in some cases even heard of—work by and on Artaud, Ghelderode, Ionesco, Vilar, Pinter, Frisch, and the "Theatre of the Absurd" had appeared in these pages; the special issues on Brecht and Genet-Ionesco have yet to be matched elsewhere; the monumental reassessment of Stanislavski in America was as much needed as it was long overdue and these numbers [T25 and T26] are certainly one of the magazine's finest achievements. But for me, two issues stand out as the most significant ones of *TDR's* first decade. They are T1 (October, 1958) and T30 (December, 1965). Looking back, T1 was quite an issue, but unquestionably the most important item in it was Duerrenmatt's "Problems of the Theatre." Only now is it possible for me to comprehend the full significance of our publishing that long essay. On an operational level it was the magazine's first big breakthrough. "Problems of the Theatre" is a major effort by one of Europe's foremost dramatists, who was then still unknown to most Americans. When we published it people all over the world began to take notice of the magazine and from that moment on the struggle to obtain or commission works of equal significance became increasingly less difficult.

But the Duerrenmatt piece has an even greater significance from another perspective. I can think of no single essay which does a better job of defining the manifold dilemmas of the dramatists writing in the mid-twentieth century. Duerrenmatt is writing about "problems," the problems of form and structure, language and style, theme and significance which he and his colleagues in the theatre somehow had to overcome if they were to go on writing. His discussion of these problems is marked by an overriding tone of despairing stoicism. "Creon's secretary closes Antigone's case," writes Duerrenmatt, and in that line one senses the bankruptcy of those Renaissance-humanistic values which have been the foundation stones of the theatre since the time of Shakespeare. We might not have realized it, but the end of one kind of theatre—the kind we know best—was at hand, and in the years that followed *TDR* chronicled its demise and entombment.

But in the death there was—as there always is—a rebirth, and *TDR* has been the herald of these glad tidings. Hence, the significance of its remarkable "Happenings" issue (T30). Already it has raised storms of controversy, and there are many who believe that these bizarre gatherings have nothing to do with the theatre, but are only the faddish, undisciplined, irresponsible, campy, pretentious self-indulgences of a bunch of overaged neo-beatniks. Such charges do indeed have some truth to them, but the outcries of disgust are a little too hysterical: perhaps they mask a deep-seated insecurity. A new theatre is aborning, and the Happenings (and all of the other intermedia experiments) are the harbingers of the shape of things to come. Just what that shape will be, no one knows for certain; but that it will be different seems incontestable to me and those who cannot accept this fact are making the most noise. They—and "they" includes the resident repertory-ites as well as the Broadway establishment—are attempting to revive a ghost by turning to the glories (real and sham) of the past rather than being concerned, as the theatre always has been concerned, with the present and its possibilities. From its inception, although more noticeably now, *TDR* has been committed to the possibilities of the present. This has been its greatest strength and I believe that, more than anything else, this commitment accounts for the magazine's great prestige, its increased circulation, and most important, its ever-widening influence on the American theatre. My own contribution to the celebration of this spirit will appear in a forthcoming issue of the magazine, so for the present I need but hail all those who have nurtured it and by these efforts have brought our theatre to a greater (and sometimes painful) awareness of what its possibilities really are and can be. I am reminded of some of Christopher Fry's lines near the end of *A Sleep of Prisoners:*

> Thank God our time is now when wrong
> Comes up to face us everywhere
> Never to leave us till we take
> The largest stride of soul men ever took.

Fry is describing (accurately I think) the contemporary human condition, but he could have been describing the condition of the contemporary theatre. I can only say, thank God *TDR* is here to urge each person working and (hopefully) creating in our theatre of the necessity to take longer strides than he ever imagined himself capable of taking.

Note

1. The first issue of *TDR* was actually published in May of 1957 as the third and final issue of volume I. The first two issues of volume I were published as the *Carleton Drama Review*.

9

El Teatro Campesino:
Interviews with Luis Valdez
(1967)

Beth Bagby

El Teatro Campesino (The Farm Workers Theatre), founded and directed by twenty-six-year-old Luis Miguel Valdez, deals with the same problems of the San Joaquin Valley that John Steinbeck depicted so graphically thirty years ago. The emphasis, however, is communication to the oppressed, not about them.

The Teatro, as it is usually called, is a bilingual theatre established in Delano, California, during the first months of a continuing agricultural strike. On September 8, 1965, the largely Filipino AFL-CIO affiliate AWOC, Agricultural Workers Organizing Committee, called a strike against the area's grape ranches. On September 16, members of the largely Mexican-American NFWA, National Farm Workers Association, founded by Cesar Chavez, voted unanimously to join the strike. Later, when NFWA had also affiliated with AFL-CIO, the two unions merged and became UFWOC, United Farm Workers Organizing Committee.

The Teatro's early actos, *acts of about fifteen minutes developed out of improvisation, dealt primarily with the significance of the* Huelga *(strike), the NFWA, and why farm workers should join. As the problems of the strike have become more complicated, as its targets have changed, and with the union merger and reorganization, the role of the Teatro and the content of its* actos *have become more involved. In the last few months it has instituted a Monday night film series, drama classes for different age groups, recorder classes, workshops in graphic arts and puppet making, and classes in English.*

The Teatro is always understaffed, and never has more than one actress. Consequently, only a few actos *include female characters. Another factor affecting Teatro material is the necessity of communicating in two languages. Some union members speak little or no English, so actors wear signs—usually in Spanish—designating a character's name or role. Felipe Cantu, forty-five years old and a part-time member of the Teatro, is its best comic actor, but does not speak English. However, he reacts so totally with his voice, face, and body that most of the audience never observes that he does not have any lines. Songs are usually Spanish and introduced with English explanations, although Augustin "Augie" Lira, the first Teatro member, recently composed some in English. Dialogue fluctuates between English and Spanish, but with little loss of meaning—Spanish and English slang are commonly known anyway, and wherever either language is not understood, there is little visual doubt as to the significance of an event.*

Valdez's interest in a Delano strike theatre has been as part of a large migrant farm labor family of Mexican-American descent, a college graduate in drama and a playwright. His unpublished three-act play The Shrunken Head of Pancho Villa *deals with a Mexican-American farm labor family's disorientation in lower middle-class urban life. Working with the Teatro has given him a chance to take some of these problems and propose solutions: first, economic equalization, so that unshackled by poverty and materialistic dreams, the Mexican-American can then establish an identity which integrates those historic and ethnic elements in which he should have pride. The Teatro has been limited to an audience of either farm workers or urban strike sympathizers, but its unwritten* actos *have established dramatic images which will last the lives of its audiences.*

This interview was held in what has been the Teatro's headquarters since last summer, La Azteca, *a former* tortilleria, *on August 30, 1966. The date is important as the day of the first recognized elections for farm labor union representation. The results were a test of the effectiveness of the union organizers, and in the case of the Teatro, of its communication with its audience. UFWOC did win representation for field workers, where they had organized hardest. The Teamsters won representation for non-field workers (truck drivers and grape packers), who constitute a small percentage of ranch employees.*

Valdez: I have been interested in drama since the first grade. I started school at Stratford, a small town about 35 miles from here, where we'd been picking cotton and living in one of the bigger camps. We got stuck there when our old pickup was put up on blocks because it was broken down. It started to rain, and the rain kept on for weeks. Then fall came along and school. I started school in October, I think. The only problem was I didn't know a word of English.

The first English word I remember learning was "crawl," and I'll tell you how it came about. The teacher was in charge of the school play that year, and she had this pet—a Mexican kid, who spoke English. She brought him in one day in a monkey suit, with a monkey mask and—well it was a little suit with a tail, and I was really aghast. This was too much. Then I somehow learned that there was going to be a play, that this was tryouts and this kid was going to be one of the monkeys in the play. It was about the jungle. Christmas in the jungle or something. She told him, "crawl," like a monkey I guess, but I remember "crawl." He started bouncing around, and I wanted to be a monkey. I thought, "If she tells me to crawl, I'll crawl."

I don't remember if I did, but I got the part. I was one of the monkeys, and we started working on the set with the teacher. I was really fascinated by the fake trees we put up and the stage and the curtain; and the papier mâché masks—they turned me on. But my family moved just before Christmas, so I missed being in the play, and I never forgot that. Shortly after, I started organizing my own plays, at school. And then at home in the garage I set up puppet shows.

Bagby: What were the subjects?

Valdez: Fairy tales. I used to dig fairy tales.

Bagby: Did you relate them to the Mexican-American farm worker?

Valdez: No. They were very far out things—the Grimm brothers. They were adaptations, but hardly anything connected with what was going on at home. That continued all through grammar school, and in high school I got in the Speech and Drama Department and was in several plays. I was a very serious student, and I wanted to make it and eventually got a scholarship.

Bagby: To San Jose State?

Valdez: Yes. I was in math and science at that time, and the whole speech and drama thing was a hobby; the bread and butter stuff was mathematics and science. I changed majors in my sophomore year; I went into English, and from there started taking all kinds of courses in drama—literature first, reading all kinds of plays. Then I started writing. Toward the end of my sophomore year, I wrote a one-act called *The Theft*. It won a school prize and a contest that the San Jose Theatre Guild ran. The award was production of the play, and later it was produced at San Jose State.

Then there was a two-year lull, while I worked on *The Shrunken Head of Pancho Villa*. I had a professor working with me from the beginning; I kept working on it and working on it, and he kept asking me to finish. I finally finished a producible version and we got it together and I directed it. After it was produced for the Northwest Drama Conference at San Jose State, there were still very grave faults with the play that I wanted to iron out. I didn't want to stay at San Jose anymore. It was in that spring, too, that I discovered the San Francisco Mime Troupe.

Bagby: When they were in San Jose?

Valdez: Yes. They were doing *Tartuffe* in *commedia dell'arte* style, and I'd never seen anything like it. I was amazed by the possibilities of that type of theatre and wanted to know how it worked, so I jumped into it.

Bagby: Had you at that time started to think of theatre's potential among farm workers?

Valdez: No. Before my play was produced at San Jose State, I hadn't decided whether or not I would go ahead or cut out and start hitting the labor camps. I felt I needed some roots again and wanted to get to the Valley and to people here, many of them my relatives. Then when I got involved in production of the play, I didn't take off as an itinerant farm worker writer.

After the play was produced that idea rolled up again and became very plausible, because it was spring and there would be a lot of work. But it didn't seem right to leave things as they were. I'd made some headway and was writing plays. It was about that time that the idea of theatre and farm labor came together in my mind, and I thought, yeah, it's a possibility—a theatre group for the Valley.

But I didn't have the resources; so when I discovered the Mime Troupe, I figured if any theatre could turn on farm workers, it would be that type of theatre—outside, that lively, that bawdy. That same spring I had heard about the National Farm Workers Association. Copies of *El Malcriado* [bi-weekly, bilingual newspaper of the Farm Worker Press] started to seep through.

Bagby: Through what channels, your relatives?

Valdez: My grandmother lives in Earlimart and came to visit my family in San Jose. She brought a copy of *El Malcriado* with Zapata's picture on it, and that really amazed me. Zapata! That's potent stuff. I maintained an active interest in that; but I was still reworking the play. Then the strike broke—September 8th, 1965. A couple of weeks passed, and we heard there was going to be a march. That seemed like a good enough reason to come down, to participate in the march.

Bagby: Which march was that?

Valdez: The twenty-sixth of September. I came down with some friends—
there were six of us. We were here in Delano that full day and left at night.
We'd marched, with all of those people shouting *Huelga*. There must have
been 1200 people.

Bagby: These were mostly strikers?

Valdez: Filipinos and Mexicans, yes. This was the *fantastic* thing about it. I
couldn't **get** it out of my head for weeks after that. These were Mexicans and
Filipinos, **not** students or citified radicals; these were poor farm workers. I
went back to San Francisco. I thought a lot about a farm workers theatre then.
I knew I had to do something.

Bagby: Were you still with the Mime Troupe?

Valdez: Right. Part of the reason I had to go back and stay in San Francisco
was because their performances of *Candelaio* ran into October, and I was
committed to that. After the march, I talked to Dolores Huerta [one of the
UFWOC's five officers] about whether or not they could visualize, see any
necessity for, a farm workers theatre, and she said, "Oh yes, it's very possible.
Come on down." That immediate reaction was kind of funny, so I didn't
believe her. Then I talked to Cesar Chavez, and apparently Dolores had
already talked to him. He said, "Come on down," so I came on down. We had
a preliminary meeting in the office, and then we set up another.

Bagby: Who was present?

Valdez: Farm workers, some of the student volunteers. There was a crowd of
about thirty-five that night—right there in the little office. They all seemed to
like the idea, but what next? How do we go about forming a theatre group?
One woman wondered if her sons and their rock and roll band could
participate. I couldn't communicate the concept of theatre, because most of
them had never been to a play as such. The only way to really show them what
I meant was to illustrate it. Frank Cieciorka, the San Francisco artist, had
made some signs for me before I came down—*Esquirol* (strikebreaker or
scab), *Patroncito* (grower), *Huelgista* (striker), *Contratista* (contractor).

Bagby: So you had already begun to envision *actos?*

Luis Valdez explains an *acto* to farm workers.
(Photo: John Kouns)

Valdez: Yes. Well, I figured that I'd have to hang signs on them. The second meeting started out very slow. We got about twelve people. About four or five were, again, student volunteers, and I was a little disappointed because I wanted farm workers. And with another five—some were very serious. It seemed dismal.

I talked for about ten minutes, and then realized that talking wasn't going to accomplish anything. The thing to do was do it, so I called three of them over, and on two hung *Huelgista* signs. Then I gave one an *Esquirol* sign, and told him to stand up there and act like an *Esquirol*—a scab. He didn't want to at first, because it was a dirty word at that time, but he did it in good spirits. Then the two *huelgistas* started shouting at him, and everybody started cracking up. All of a sudden, people started coming into the pink house from I don't know where; they filled up the whole kitchen. We started changing signs around and people started volunteering. "Let me play so and so." "Look this is what I did," imitating all kinds of things. We ran for about two hours just doing that. By the time we had finished, there were people packing the place. They were in the doorways, the living room, and they were outside at the windows peeking in. Dolores showed up later. She stood there watching, and I think it got the message across—that you can do a lot by acting out things.

That was the beginning. The effects we achieved that night were fantastic, because people were acting out *real things*. Then I got together an original group of about five, and we started working on skits—this was all done after picketing hours, by the way. Sometimes we wouldn't get started until eight or nine, but we went on every night for about three weeks. We gave our first presentation in Filipino Hall.

Bagby: Did you do any skits at that first formal production that you do now?

Valdez: None that I can remember. The first formal one that we worked out was *The Conscience of a Scab,* and then *Three-Grapes* and *Papelaccion.* The *Conscience of a Scab* involves two actors: the grape worker who "scabs" and the *huelgista.* When the scab hears the striker quote Jack London's *Definition of a Strikebreaker* ("After God had finished the rattlesnake, the toad and the vampire, he had some awful substance left with which he made a Strikebreaker..."), he joins the strike and goes off shouting *"Huelga!"*

The "three grapes" are the green, ripe, and rotten grapes, who come onto the stage walking in a squat. Each grape wants to be picked by the worker, who has not left the field for the strike. Every time the worker begins to inspect a grape bunch before cutting, a *huelgista* comes on with a *Huelga* sign and chases the scab away. When the grower orders him to cut the grapes, even the green one has begun to smell, so is as worthless as the rotten and the ripe, which is now too ripe to pick. When the worker discovers that even the green grape smells, he leaves the field to join the strike. If a grower cannot harvest enough crop, he must concede to strike demands.

Papelaccion translates as paper play or role play. A grower comes out wearing the sign "Smiling Jack" and proceeds to tell his laborer how much he loves his Mexican workers. The grower's sign changes to "Liar," "Gringo," "Jackass," and finally *Huelga* as the worker sees through his boss's platitudes.

After about the first month, the boycott against Schenley Industries started and my two best actors were sent away as boycott organizers. There was a lot of work to be done, and sometimes we were too tired after picketing to rehearse so there was a lull for a month. That was due, in part, to the fact that most of my actors were taken away, and we were involved in picketing and boycotting and chasing trucks. Then we got an offer from Stanford University to perform.

Bagby: Who made the offer?

Valdez: One of the ministers. Canterbury House. We accepted without knowing how we were going to make it—no actors, no nothing. We performed in a student lounge, and there were about fifty people present. It was interesting from the viewpoint that what we had been doing for farm workers in Delano could work outside too, in a university setting. By that time, we had started using a mask, the pig-like mask.

Bagby: Did you have any songs?

Valdez: We had about three *Huelga* songs, and others. The show at Stanford was crude, but they seemed to like it and that established a pattern we started following: going out to the cities to raise money and spread news about the strike, and then performing in Delano at weekly meetings.

Then in March, we started planning a march to Sacramento. It was decided that the Teatro would be one of the big attractions at each night's rally, so we pushed it as such and organized the rallies to include songs and speeches, reading *The Plan of Delano,* and the use of the Virgin of Guadalupe as symbol and Pilgrimage, Penance, and Revolution as themes, with the Teatro at the end as a drawing card. We performed across the Valley in about twenty-five farm worker towns.

We gained a resilience as a result of those twenty-five performances on the march that made us real veterans; so we had our material down pretty well pat for the performance at *The Committee.*

Shortly after, we had a reorganization, and we felt a growing need to get closer to the farm worker. We had been very effective in the march, but then ran into some snags—a couple of performances, for instance, in Yuba City that really made us wonder. We began to think, "How can we influence, get to the farm worker a little bit closer, how can we reach him?" Part of the problem was that we had been too busy touring, going from L.A. to San Francisco, across the Valley and to different farm worker towns. We had gotten away from the situation in Delano.

Bagby: Did you ask for this touring to let up, or by that time did the elections at DiGiorgio Corporation's two ranches—

Valdez: It kind of fell into place again. The elections came and everybody was called into service to help out organizing. The Teatro was drafted to go out in the camps, organize, satirize the competing Teamsters.

Bagby: Had you ever been to a camp as a theatre group before the arbitrators set up the organizers' schedule?

Valdez: Before the first election, June twenty-fourth, Cesar [Chavez] called us to Borrego Springs, and we performed in a park. The purpose was for Cesar to explain why the workers should not vote, why they should boycott the election. The Teatro had only pointed references to the elections; we were intended more for entertainment and color. After that, we performed at DiGiorgio's ranch in Arvin. The performance wasn't actually inside the property; it was right on the property line. There is a small fence about knee-high, and so we pulled the truck right up to it. We had the union banners and flags, the Teatro red and black screen and our own *El Teatro Campesino* banner and a mike. We started about 7:30 p.m. It was still light enough so that people could see, and there's this open space between the fence and the camp. There were some trees, and the workers were all underneath the trees, or around the cabins. We were on the truckbed calling them over, but they wouldn't come, so we started singing and then began our first *acto*—Felipe came out. We started to get some stragglers, and as it got darker more and more people came out. By the time we were into the show, all of the people in the camp were out there—a couple of hundred people. They cheered, they laughed, they applauded. It was probably the most successful performance we've had with farm workers since the march, the great difference being that this time there wasn't the whole impact of the march. There was just the Teatro out there by itself.

We've discovered a number of things about farm workers and what they respond to; it verges on slapstick, but it's slapstick with a purpose; it depends who is slapping who. If a DiGiorgio character is beating a farm worker over the head, it may be funny, but it's serious laughter. If the farm worker starts slapping the DiGiorgio character, then it becomes riotous.

I think humor is our major asset and weapon, not only from a satirical point of view, but from the fact that humor can stand up on its own and is a much more healthy child of the theatre than let's say tragedy or realism. You can't do that on the flatbed of a truck. If you want to get realistic about the problems, you have to do it in indirect fashion, through dramatic images. But if you think that DiGiorgio is living and standing on the backs of his farm workers, you can show it with humor. You get "DiGiorgio" to stand on the backs of two farm workers, and there it is and nobody will refute you.

We use comedy because it stems from a necessary situation—the necessity of lifting the morale of our strikers, who have been on strike for seventeen months. When they go to a meeting it's long and drawn out; so we do a comedy, with the intention of making them laugh—but with a purpose. We try to make social points, not in spite of the comedy, but through it. This leads us into satire and slapstick, and sometimes very close to the underlying tragedy of it all—the fact that human beings have been wasted in farm labor for generations. . . .

I've noticed one thing about audiences. When they see something they recognize as a reality, they laugh. Here in the Teatro we sometimes work up imitations—of personalities, animals, of incidents. Impersonations are funny; why? Just because the impersonation itself comes so close to the reality. People say, "Yes, that's the way it is," and they laugh. If it's a reality they recognize as their own, they'll laugh and perhaps tears will come to their eyes.

When I speak about comic and dramatic images, I'm speaking about visions of reality. Our comic images are directed at the farm worker; they're supposed to represent the reality that he sees. It's not a naturalistic representation; most of the time it's a symbolic, emblematic presentation of what the farm worker feels. But we can't be stuffy about it, so we use slapstick. Very often the slapstick is the image.

There's a dramatic theory—we used to talk about it in the Mime Troupe. I think we've put a different use to it in the Teatro just out of necessity, but it is that your dramatic situation, the thing you're trying to portray on the stage, must be very close to the reality that is *on* the stage. You take the figure of DiGiorgio standing on the backs of two farm workers. The response of the audience is to the very real situation of one human being standing on two others. That type of fakery is not imitation. It's a theatrical reality that will hold up on the flatbed of a truck. You don't need fancy lights or a curtain. This is what we're working toward—this type of reality.

Farm workers laugh at Summer in *The Fifth Season*. We've used various actors as Summer, and they're not physically funny when they come on; but they're wearing this old shirt with money all over it, and I think with that image we've hit something. This is the way farm workers look at summer. As a kid, I can remember my family going north toward the prune and apricot orchards. My image was of leaves and fruit clustered on the trees, and all of this turning into flows of dollar bills. When you see a ripe orchard or vineyard, the limbs boughing down they're so heavy with fruit, this is money. All you have to do is get up and stretch out your hand. That's money; it's a quarter for every bucket, a penny for every apple or pear. It's a vision of paradise; you're going there—the promised land—you're getting there finally.

Then reality creeps in again, and you end up with less money than you started with. But the dream is always there, the dream that you're going to get rich quick. It isn't just reaching up and holding your hand under the fruit which falls into your palm. More often, it's working like a dog with the snot running down your nose; and you're black with dirt and sweat, and with the blood straining your veins. You're lost in your work; you forget what the hell you're doing. And the contractor's truck is a dirty ugly truck; once in a while it strikes you. But what takes you away from that hard ugly reality is the dream that you're going to get rich.

Anyway, that is the background behind the image of Summer coming in with his shirt covered with money. I think that is why farm workers laugh. Not because it's funny, but because they recognize that reality. They've been caught.

We don't think in terms of art, but of our political purpose in putting across certain points. We think of our spiritual purpose in terms of turning on crowds. We know when we're not turning on the crowd. From a show business point of view that's bad enough, but when you're trying to excite crowds to go out on strike or to support you, it gains an added significance.

The *patroncito* (boss) points out his holdings to the *esquirol* (scab) in *The Two Faces of the Boss.*

(Photo: Beth Bagby)

The following excerpts represent an attempt to clarify and update certain points of the first interview. They were taped on February 13 and 14, 1967; the Teatro was preparing for a short tour to raise funds for a newly purchased camper, which will take them back to some of the strike areas in Texas that they visited last fall—"it took us thirty-eight hours to drive. Seven of us and the trunk and the screen in one little car." After they return from Texas, a tour of colleges is planned.

Valdez: The most characteristic thing about the Teatro as a theatre group is that we are dedicated to a very specific goal—the organization of farm workers. That's an advantage and a limitation. Once you accept that reality, the limitation ceases to exist, and that's what I do. . . .

Most of us working here in Delano have realized that what will result is not a series of Delanos, but a national union that at best will be like the United Auto Workers; and even the UAW is pulling some pretty surprising things. There's no doubt that what the people want are new cars, education so they can send their kids to college, a middle-class home, security—the whole shebang, the middle-class line. It's romantic and sentimental to try to accomplish anything else.

Bagby: But you do satirize that reversal of positions. It must be conscious. For example, when the farm worker is given the position of the grower in *The Two Faces of the Boss,* he adopts the values of the boss. Do you think that comes across in Delano, or in the cities?

Valdez: It's hard to say how farm workers look at that. When we did this *acto* on the march, those who had seen it before kept saying, "All right, now take off the mask." We exchanged clothes, and then only the mask was left to change, and they said, "Now the mask, now the mask." They were following the changes in the specific terms of the *acto,* but I don't know if they actually realized what was being said. And I am not sure exactly what was being said, but it was fun putting the farm worker in the grower's place.

We're developing an *acto* on the credit union. This is pretty dull stuff, dramatically. It's beautiful stuff in real life. But you look at the facts, and you can see the problem of communicating them all to farm workers. This is where the Teatro can help, because we can strip the dullness and put up the very heart of the credit union. To do this we are thinking of a contrast between the bank and the credit union. . . .

What we strive for is this image that will outlast the strike and go into other strikes that we're going to have. . . .

The idea that really excites me about the future of the Teatro, and American theatre, is a theatre of political change. Hell, take *MacBird,* which states something that many people feel. It reflects, and people react to that. But of course she's suggesting some very horrible things, and that makes it a political play. That means we need change. I'm talking politics, not art. I'm not talking about the individualized, introspective, personal philosophic view. I'm talking about influencing people, and I sense a hunger in art for this. We're in a political age, and we're going to go further into it, because social problems are increasing. Certainly in labor they are increasing.

One of the things we're forced to do in our form of drama is present the solution. The farm workers say, "We know the problems, what about it?" So in the *acto,* a farm workers grabs the *Huelga* sign and shouts, "*Huelga!*"... We've never done a wholly serious or tragic *acto* because I think the people would laugh anyway. The serious stuff has already been pounded into them for—hell, our meetings start at seven and go as long as three, sometimes four hours.

Bagby: Most of the time you do just one *acto* and some songs at these Friday union meetings?

Valdez: Yes, and this determines the shape and form of our *actos.* On tour we put them together into a program of an hour or an hour and a half; sometimes in chronological order, or in the best order that will tell a story about the farm worker. The problem is that all of these *actos* have been written, not in conjunction with other *actos,* but to stand alone at a weekly meeting and make five or six different points.

Bagby: As a program, I think it works—outside of Delano, too.

Valdez: Yes, but it forces us to think up endings that are basically the same. It's the snap ending; you end with a bang, and certainly with hope. You show some kind of victory even though victory is not immediately forthcoming.

10

With the Bread & Puppet Theatre: An Interview with Peter Schumann (1968)

Helen Brown and Jane Seitz

This interview was conducted over a period of several weeks. The transcripts were assembled, re-ordered, and edited. We hope we have done justice to what is, in our opinion, one of the most significant theatres in the USA. It is very difficult—without seeing for yourself—to capture the excitement and artistry which a performance of the Bread & Puppet Theatre generates.

—*Richard Schechner*

TDR: What are you trying to do?

Schumann: We want to work directly into and out of the interior of people. A demonic thing.

TDR: Why use masks and puppets whose expressions can't change?

Schumann: Oh, they change greatly. Puppets have tremendous possibilities in their faces and bodies and hands. I build them not as sculpture but as actors. I experiment with movement—with their stiffness or floppiness. I moved from small puppets to the huge ones after I visited a Sicilian theatre in which large puppets were used. I saw there a pure and strong line. I only saw a short excerpt from a play that lasted one year—it was performed two hours every night with big, heavy wooden puppets. They played it only for male audiences. When they performed they wore mikes around their necks—so close that I could hear every intake of breath. The puppets were made from solid wood and metal—they made the whole stage shake. There were fighting scenes in which ten puppets would jump in the air and clash together. Every puppet must have weighed eighty or ninety pounds. They were held by heavy iron rods and they would move roughly to the center of the stage. It was the greatest theatre I have ever seen.

By the way, those guys live in Coney Island now—working as mechanics. They don't make theatre anymore. They used to perform on Mulberry Street in Little Italy. But no more.

TDR: What was so good about the Sicilian theatre?

Schumann: It was great because the artists invented a way of telling, a way of translating and creating a reality, that first of all defines reality. Even though I didn't understand a word of the Sicilian dialect I could sense the purity of this theatre. It was necessary. I feel that art in the modern world is generally superfluous. Either we should find a true need for it, or give it up. We named our theatre the Bread & Puppet because we felt that the theatre should be as basic as bread.

TDR: Do you still believe that?

Schumann: I used to hope, and I don't hope anymore. But sure, I still believe it. I've seen a lot of protests, but few movements. Castro in Cuba: that was a movement. But most of the Vietnam War protests? The hippies? The New Left? And I am disturbed at having the Bread & Puppet called a protest theatre. We are all sick of the Vietnam War. But the theatre must do more than protest.

TDR: But your theatre is associated with the politics of protest.

Schumann: Once we were invited to play by the Communist Party. We did. We thought the play was good and had a basic thing to say—but it didn't come across. Later we did the same play for a very square audience and it went beautifully. Our only specific protest material is about the war. We do one play over and over again: *A Man Says Goodbye to His Mother.* But most of our stuff is more general. We are not very interested in ideology.

TDR: Do you use much satire?

Schumann: I dislike satire—it's too easy. When I use a Johnson speech, I use it for documentation, not satire. I like documented dialogue and narration; it has a substance that invented stuff can't have. I like to write with the help of a tape recorder, to hear what people really say.

TDR: I think political satire has been outmoded because the politicians are so much in the public eye they become parodies of themselves.

Schumann: No, that's not so. Our "leaders" have not been shown as fools yet. In this society they are still the movie star figures that they pretend to be. Their power is pathetic, but real.

TDR: I've noticed that the radical theatre—at least in New York—substitutes commitment for craft. So much of the new theatre is worse than the old bourgeois stuff.

Schumann: I think you have it wrong. I believe that if their commitment were sensitive enough, the craft would come up to it. I've seen a number of groups who seemed more interested in insulting people than in getting to them. You can't simply try to shock an audience. That will only disgust them, and it is cheap. If you reach out to an audience with what you want to get from them you're hung up.

We don't necessarily have to revolutionize theatre. It may be that the best theatre—if it comes—will develop from the most traditional forms. A theatre is good when it makes sense to people. A small theatre that tries simply to do that does not exist in this country. We do not yet have our own version of the *commedia dell'arte.*

TDR: I heard recently that you were thinking of leaving New York and going into a rural area. Why?

Schumann: The stink. The thick column that you see when you come into NY, and the dirt under your fingernails.

TDR: Who would be your audience out there?

Schumann: Trees. Farmers. We're not leaving the city so that we can do social action theatre in new environments. We simply want to get out of New York because it's too stinky and dirty. We'll live out in the country and return to the cities when we have to. Also, this business of being a "professional protest theatre" doesn't seem good enough. I don't think our business is to protest but to say what needs to be said or what feels good to say.

TDR: But don't the protests work?

Schumann: Usually not. A person protests because he feels badly about something and he gets up and shouts. It has to be as genuinely spontaneous as

A Man Says Goodbye to His Mother

Set: Three monochromatic backdrops painted on white sheets—an Asian village below the mountains. One drop is center, the others on either side: a drop and wing effect.

Characters: Narrator, standing stage right, down front, wears a skull mask and carries a large sack over his shoulder. He looks like a beggar or a character from the *commedia*. His bag is full of props. A trumpeter stands upstage right, also in a skull mask. A woman in black robes with a silver-gray face mask stands center stage with her son, who wears no mask and is in army fatigues.

Story: The narrator announces that the young man is saying goodbye to his mother and going to a distant land. The son embraces his mother and sets out, facing the audience, walking in time to a drum. As he travels—the narrator tells us—he is shot in the arm by an enemy. The woman who was the mother replaces her mask with another, given to her by the narrator, who tells us that she is now the women of the village in this distant land. She now wears a white mask, of an oriental woman. The narrator describes the land as a dangerous one. "Here, a man needs a gun." He tosses one to the son and a gasmask. Finally, the narrator says that this is a *very* dangerous land—and he gives the son an airplane. The son swings the plane around his head and all the characters make the buzzing sound of an airplane.

The woman stops her work and looks at the sky. The narrator gives the woman a plant. But he says the son poisons the crops: the son drops a cloth over the plant. The narrator tells us that the people of the land hide in their houses. He hands the woman a cut-out of a house which she holds to her face as she cringes. The son lights a match to burn the house. But the narrator stops this action while telling the audience that New York fire regulations do not permit the burning of houses in that building. So the son rips the house up into little shreds of paper. Then the woman is handed a child and the son kills it. The woman puts the dead child on the ground, pulls a pair of scissors from her robe and stabs the son through the heart. The narrator stands over the dead son, covers his face with a sheet; there is a long, silent pause. He and the woman carry the body off. Both the narrator and the woman are now wearing skull masks.

that. When it becomes a profession it feels wrong. A good protest show makes people laugh. And that's a lousy result. For example, when the Teatro Campesino (T36) played Newport they put on a big show about farm workers' troubles—and people stood there and clapped and went crazy with fun. That's the best professional protest can hope for.

TDR: What you're saying seems to negate the role of the Bread & Puppet Theatre.

Schumann: That's right. It's no good as a profession.

TDR: The heart of your theatre is performances in the streets?

Schumann: Yes. But we don't always get a chance—we need permits.

TDR: Does the audience react differently in the street than they do indoors?

Schumann: We've had our best—and sometimes our most stupid— performances in the streets. Sometimes you make your point because your point is simply to be there in the street. It stops people in their tracks—to see those large puppets, to see something theatrical outside of a theatre. They can't take the attitude that they've paid money to go into a theatre to "see something." Suddenly there is this thing in front of them, confronting them.

TDR: Does this confrontation translate itself into action?

Schumann: No one who does a play, or plays music, or gives a speech, has any specific idea of what he wants to achieve with his audience. You say what you want to say and hope you're being understood. The consequences of your activities are pretty much out of your control.

TDR: How do street performances influence your aesthetics?

Schumann: You don't make your point unless a five-year-old girl can understand it. If she gets it, the grownups will too. The show almost has to be stupid. It has to be tremendously concentrated. You need that intensity on the street much more than in a theatre. Indoors you can get by with technique, by sticking to your dialogue, but on the street you come across only if you have your mind on What Has To Be Done. Everything should be focused, and everything will become awkward and lame if your guts aren't in what you're saying. Just look at the peace marches. Hippies happily singing while carrying photos of burnt children. People running around with coffee and sandwiches.

But carrying pictures of burnt children is something very hard to do, something very heavy. And unless you know that you don't get your message across. Most of our street performances taught us how to concentrate, how to get across. We learned how to make large crowds stop drinking cokes and start to listen.

TDR: And the public reacts differently outside than in a theatre?

Schumann: Look at Uncle Fatso. He is a big puppet with a ring on his finger, he looks like Johnson. He looks like everyone's uncle that no one likes. During the peace march most of the right wing groups were peaceful. But when they saw Uncle Fatso they jumped at him. They went crazy.

TDR: Why do you think the public reacts so sharply?

Schumann: When you walk a white elephant through the streets of New York it has a different effect than when you drive a taxi.

TDR: Why are you in theatre, and not some other art form?

Schumann: The other forms seem very hung up in specific materials. In music there's sound and in painting it's the role of the museum and the paint. In theatre you're involved in a political context. You can say what Humphrey said, but say it more efficiently—you can expose and probe. You can say what you want to say so that it gets to the brains and feelings of people.

But we don't take a problem-solving attitude. We just try, with each show, to be a little real.

We want to evoke a direct emotional response to what is happening—like protesting the war or urban society, or telling kids about violence in our children's plays. We have a show, *The Dead Man Rises,* which doesn't prescribe a thing. It's much stronger than protest. It's a clear expression of outrage and disgust with city life. It's an answer to living in the city. It's a celebration of something else, maybe love.

TDR: How do you develop a show?

Schumann: We have many ways of beginning. Sometimes we play around with the puppets, trying out different movements. Sometimes we begin with music and end up with politics. A lot depends on the space, and on whether we decide to use the little hand puppets or the bigger-than-life things.

TDR: Do you use dialogue?

Schumann: Yes. But we don't use scripts as such. We play with the puppets and improvise with the characters. Each of us tries to feel what the genuine speech of our character would be like. We leave the exact words open. Sometimes we use narration accompanied by mute action. Dialogue depends a lot on the size of the puppets. Hand puppets are very good for dialogue. Huge puppets aren't so good—they never look like they are talking. With the large puppets we almost always use a single narrator who is obviously talking for the characters.

TDR: What is the relation between the size of the puppets and the aesthetics of the theatre?

Schumann: The very small puppets are best in comedy. The really large ones—the eighteen foot ones—are also at their best when they are buffoons. The medium sized puppets are very good for drama.

TDR: How did you arrive at the size of your puppets?

Schumann: The eighteen foot ones are the largest we ever built. I wanted big ones. Once we had the set we played around to see what they could do. Puppets have terrific intrinsic power. They can be funny, or scary. They can say things that actors and dramatists can't say—just by their size. I mentioned the Sicilian puppets. Well, they were five feet high, and they looked larger than life.

TDR: Why?

Schumann: Because the movements of the human body are so intricate; the harmonious details of a live body make a smooth totality. But in a puppet there is movement that is simple and uncomplicated. There isn't so much detail, and so there seems to be increased size and power.

TDR: It sounds Brechtian.

Schumann: Yes. Alienation is automatic with puppets. It is not that our characters are less complex. They are just more explicit.

TDR: Is your use of space different from that of the traditional theatre?

Schumann: The biggest difference is that we don't pay attention to space. Professional theatres care a great deal for space and design. They do something new for every play they put on. There are hundreds of designs for *Hamlet* and in *Marat/Sade* they talked about something fancy called "space explosion." We do a show for a particular space—the space we happen to be in. The one space we reject is that of the traditional theatre.

TDR: Why?

Schumann: It's too comfortable, too well known. Its traditions upset us. People are numbed by sitting in the same chairs in the same way. It conditions their reactions. But when you use the space you happen to be in you use it all: the stairs, the windows, the streets, the doors. We'll do any play anywhere, provided we can fit the puppets in. And in each space it will be different.

TDR: Why do your shows work in so many different kinds of spaces?

Schumann: Because the plays themselves are so rough, raw. We don't go in for stylish events that depend on scenic subtlety. Whether an actor walks a short distance or a long distance in this space or that one, that is what makes a play. It is one kind of play on a small platform and another kind on a huge lawn. We've performed in the streets, indoors, on the back of a truck, in the woods, on lawns, in a convent. When we played for the nuns at Manhattanville College we were on a huge lawn. The nuns walked around and looked at the puppets before we began. Then we came right out into the middle of them and they made a space for us. When the action permitted they closed in and came up close to listen. And after the play they followed us and picked up our props and we turned it into a procession.

TDR: Do you think puppetry is more valid than the theatre of live actors?

Schumann: I really don't like the regular theatre much. But there have been theatres that made sense—news reports, religious services: these things communicate. And the Greek theatre, the Egyptian theatre, the Chinese theatre.

TDR: In modern times? The thirties?

Schumann: Our theatre is still in the thirties. We still hang onto that little cultural revolution.

TDR: The Teatro Campesino?

Schumann: Their big hangup is doing their thing Monday through Sunday. They have become too smooth, too professionally arranged. I suspect they are very good in their own environment playing for farm workers. But in a theatre—no.

TDR: Who are your best audiences?

Schumann: Kids. And the people that are just in a place. At Montreal the best audiences were the people who worked at Expo—the people who swept up, the cops. The audience which doesn't go to the theatre is always the best audience.

TDR: How large is your company?

Schumann: I wouldn't consider us a company. There's a large turnover—and the size of each production is different. Last year we did *Bach Cantata* with more than 100 people. And each of the parades was very large. But sometimes we use only 15 people. There's no trouble finding people. On *Bach Cantata* we had 20 people making puppets for three weeks. Very often we are like a carpentry, furniture making, and moving company. There's so much involved!

TDR: How do you make money?

Schuman: No one gets paid. We charge $1.00 for performances indoors. Nothing on the street. We accept contributions. And if we take a commission we get paid. I tried foundations earlier. They didn't give us money, for political reasons.

TDR: Why did you name your theatre Bread & Puppet?

Schumann: Bread means bread. Something basic. We give it out during or after the show.

TDR: Why?

Schumann: We would like to be able to feed people.

11

Six Axioms for Environmental Theatre
(1968)

Richard Schechner

One. The Theatrical Event Is a Set of Related Transactions

The theatrical event includes audience, performers, text (in most cases), sensory stimuli, architectural enclosure (or lack of it), production equipment, technicians, and house personnel (when used). It ranges from nonmatrixed performance[1] to highly formalized traditional theatre: from chance events and intermedia to "the production of plays." A continuum of theatrical events blends one form into the next:

"Impure; life"   "Pure; art"

public events ⟷ intermedia ⟷ environmental ⟷ traditional
demonstrations   (Happenings)   theatre   theatre

It is because I wish to include this entire range in my definition of theatre that traditional distinctions between art and life no longer function at the root of aesthetics. All along the continuum there are overlaps; and within it—say between a traditional production of *Hamlet* and the march on the Pentagon or Allan Kaprow's *Self-Service*[2]—there are contradictions. The new aesthetics is built on a system of interaction and transformation, on the ability of coherent wholes to include contradictory parts. In the words of New York city planner Richard Weinstein, "competing independent systems within the same aesthetic frame." Kaprow might even take a more radical position, doing away altogether with the frame; or accepting a variety of frames depending upon the perspective of the spectator and performer. Surely the frames may change during a single performance, transforming an event into something quite unlike what it started out to be. The end of *Iphigenia Transformed* at the Firehouse Theatre (1966) had Euripides' *dea ex machina* lowered onto the stage, bringing with her four cases of beer. The marriage ceremony that concludes *Iphigenia at Aulis* was performed followed by a celebration that included the entire audience; the party lasted for several hours.

The theatrical event is a complex social interweave, a network of expectations and obligations.[3] The exchange of stimuli—either sensory or ideational or both—is the root of theatre. What it is that separates theatre from more ordinary exchanges, say a simple conversation or a party, is difficult to pinpoint formally. One might say that theatre is more regulated, following a script or a scenario; that it has been rehearsed. Kirby would probably argue only that theatre presents the self in a more defined way than usual social encounters. Grotowski has said that the theatre is a meeting place between a traditional text and a troupe of performers:

> I didn't do Wyspianski's *Akropolis,* I met it. . . . One structures the montage so that this confrontation can take place. We eliminate those parts of the text which have no importance for us, those parts with which we can neither agree nor disagree. . . . We did not want to write a new play, we wished to confront ourselves.[4]

Indeed, confrontation is what makes current American political activity theatrical. To meet Bull Connor's dogs in Birmingham or LBJ's troops at the Pentagon is more than a showdown in the Wild West tradition. In the movies, everything would be settled by the showdown. In our politics, contrasts are heightened, nothing resolved. A long series of confrontations are necessary to promote change. The streets of Birmingham and the steps of the Pentagon are visible boundaries, special places of special turbulence, where sharply opposed styles are acted out by both sides; Grotowski's personal confrontation is converted into a social confrontation. Out of such situations, slowly and unevenly, guerrilla and street theatre emerge, just as out of the confrontation between medieval ceremony and renaissance tumult emerged the Elizabethan theatre.

John Cage has offered a most inclusive definition of theatre:

> I would simply say that theatre is something which engages both the eye and the ear. The two public senses are seeing and hearing; the senses of taste, touch, and odor are more proper to intimate, non-public, situations. The reason I want to make my definition of theatre that simple is so one could view everyday life itself as theatre. . . . I think of theatre as an occasion involving any number of people, but not just one.[5]

Some would argue that Cage's exclusion of taste, touch, and odor is unnecessarily restrictive. In the New Orleans Group's production of *Victims of Duty* (1967) all three "private" senses were important parts of the performance. During a seduction scene perfume was released in the room; frequently the performers touched the audience, communicating to them with hand and body contact; at the very end of the show, chunks of bread were forcefully administered to the audience by the performers, expanding the final gesture of Ionesco's script.

In situations where descriptive definitions are so open as to be inoperative as excluding criteria, one must seek *relational* definitions. Goffman's assertions regarding social organization go right to the heart of the theatrical event:

> ...any...element of social life...exhibits sanctioned orderliness arising from obligations fulfilled and expectations realized.[6]

> Briefly, a social order may be defined as the consequence of any set of moral norms [rules] that regulates the way in which persons pursue objectives.[7]

The nature of the expectation-obligation network and the specific set of applicable rules vary widely depending upon the particular performance. The difference between a relational and a descriptive definition is that the second is preordained while the first is self-generating. Taking a relational viewpoint makes it possible to understand theatre as something more inclusive than literature, acting, and directing. We can integrate into a single, working aesthetic such seemingly far-removed events as Kaprow's *Self-Service* and Tyrone Guthrie's *Oresteia*.

Returning to the continuum, at the left end are loosely organized street events—the October 21 march on the Pentagon, activities of the Amsterdam and New York Provos;[8] toward that end of the continuum are Kaprow's kind of Happenings (such as *Calling*[9] and those included in *Some Recent Happenings*);[10] in the center of the continuum are highly organized intermedia events—some of Kirby's and Robert Whitman's work, for example—and "conventional" environmental theatre productions, such as the New Orleans Group's *Victims of Duty* or Richard Brown's production of *The Investigation* (1967) at Wayne State University. At the far right of the continuum is the traditional theatre. Textual analysis is possible only from the middle of the continuum to the right end; performance analysis is possible along the entire range.

What are the related transactions which comprise the theatrical event?

Among performers
Among members of the audience
Between performers and audience

These are the three primary transactions. The first begins during rehearsal and continues through all performances. In Stanislavski-oriented training the heaviest emphasis is given to these transactions; they are, in fact, identified with "the play" and the theory is that if the interaction among the performers is perfected (even to the exclusion of the audience from the performers' attention) the production of the play will be artistically successful. There are many examples showing that this theory is inoperative. It is simply not enough for the performers to be an ensemble. And where it does work, the art is a special one in which the audience merely watches, "visitors to the Prozorov household," as Stanislavski put it. The performer-to-performer transaction is essential, but it is not exclusive; functioning alone, it is not enough.

The second transaction—among members of the audience—is usually overlooked. The decorum of theatre-going is such that the audience has and keeps strict rules of behavior. They do not leave their seats, they arrive more or less on time, they leave during intermission or when the show is over, they display approval or disapproval within well-regulated patterns of applause, silence, laughter, tears, and so on. In some intermedia and environmental theatre, the audience is invited to participate. In events on the far left of the performance continuum, it is difficult to distinguish audience from performers. A street demonstration or sit-in is made up of shifting groups of performers and spectators; and in confrontations between demonstrators and police both major groups fill both roles alternately and, frequently, simultaneously. A particularly rich example of this occurred during the march on Washington. The demonstrators had broken through the military lines and were sitting in on the Pentagon parking lot. Those in the front lines sat against the row of troops and frequent small actions—nudging, exchange of conversation—turned these front lines into focal points. Every half-hour or so, both the front-line troops and the demonstrators were relieved. Demonstrators who were watching the action became part of it; the same for the troops. Elements of the Pentagon leadership stood on the steps in front of the main entrance, watching the procedure. For someone at home, the entire confrontation was a performance and everyone—from McNamara at his window to the ad-hoc demonstration leaders with their bullhorns—was acting according to role.

Very little hard work has been done researching the behavior of audiences and the possible exchange of roles between audience and performers. Unlike the performers, the spectators attend theatre unrehearsed; they bring to the theatre a decorum that has been learned elsewhere but which is nevertheless scrupulously applied here. Usually the audience is an impromptu group, meeting at the place of the performance and never meeting as a defined group again. Thus unprepared, they are difficult to mobilize and, once mobilized, even more difficult to control.

The third primary transaction—between performers and audience—is a traditional one. An action onstage evokes an empathetic reaction in the audience which is not an imitation but a harmonic variation. Thus sadness on stage may evoke tears in the audience or put into play personal associations which, on the surface, seem unrelated to sadness. Conversely, as any performer will eagerly testify, a "good" audience will make for a different quality performance than a "bad" audience. Good and bad are sliding terms, depending upon the nature of the performance. An active, noisy audience is good for farce but bad for serious plays. The "best" audience is one in which harmonic evocations are present up to, but not beyond the point where the performers become distracted. The traditional theatre barely explores a part of the full range of audience-performer interaction.

As well as the three primary interactions there are four secondary ones.

Among production elements
Between production elements and performers
Between production elements and audience
Between the total production and the space in which it takes place

These are secondary now. They may become primary in a few years. Production elements have been traditionally understood as scenery, costume, lighting, sound, makeup, and so on. With the fullscale use of electronics— film, TV, taped sound, projected still images, etc.—the production elements need no longer "support" a performance. At certain times these elements are more important than the performers. The Polyvision and the Diapolyecran rooms at the Czech Pavilion at Expo '67 introduced new kinds of film and still-image environments that can serve both as background for performers and as independent performing elements.[11]

Briefly, the Polyvision was the total conversion of a medium-size, rather high room into a film and slide environment. Mirrors, moving cubes and prisms, projections both from outside the space and from within the cubes, images which seemed to move through space as well as cover the walls, ceilings, and floors all built the feeling of a full space of great flexibility. The 9½-minute presentation used 11 film projectors, 28 slide projectors, and a 10-track computer tape for programming. The material itself was banal—an account of Czech industry; but, of course, more "artistic" or "meaningful" material could be used in the system. No live performers participated.

The Diapolyecran was not an environment, strictly speaking. It was restricted to one wall and the audience sat on the floor or stood watching the 14½-minute show. Only slide projectors were used. According to the "Brief Description":

The Diapolyecran is technical equipment which enables a simultaneous projection of slides on a mosaic projection screen consisting of 112 projection surfaces. The surfaces are projected on from behind and they may be shifted singly, in groups, or all at once. This enables one to obtain with still images pictures of motion, and the picture groups thus obtained are best characterized as "mosaic projection."

Each of 112 slide projectors was mounted on a steel frame that had three positions: back, middle, forward. The images could be thrust out toward the audience or moved back from it. The mosaic was achieved by complex programming—there were 5,300,000 bits of information memorized on tape; 19,600 impulses were emitted per second.

The theatre, which has restricted its electronic research to sophisticating lighting control (still using old-fashioned fresnel and ellipsoidal instruments) has not begun to tap the resources suggested by the Czechs. But the key to making technical elements part of the creative performance is not simply applying electronics research. The technicians themselves must become an active part of the performance. This does not necessarily mean the use of more sophisticated equipment, but rather the more sophisticated use of the human beings who run whatever equipment is available. The technicians' role is not limited to perfecting during rehearsal the use of their machines. During performance itself the technicians should participate, improvising and modulating the uses of their equipment night-to-night, just as the performers themselves modulate their roles. Here the experience of discotheques is very instructive. The rhythm and content of light-shows is modulated to accompany and sometimes dominate the activity of the musicians and the spectator dancers. During many intermedia performances, the technicians are free to choose where they will project images, how they will organize sound contexts. There is nothing sacred about "setting" technical elements. If human performance is variable (as it most certainly is) then a unified effect—if one is looking for that—will be better assured by nightly variation of technical means.

Thus possibilities exist for "performing technicians" whose "language" is the film strip or electronic sound and whose range of action includes significant variations in where and what is to be done. The same goes for other technical elements. Traditional separation between performers and technicians is eroding as new equipment encourages either the complete programming of all material (as at the Czech Pavilion) or the nearly total flexibility of bits that can be organized on the spot, during the performance. The "performing group" is expanding so that it includes technicians as well as actors.

Once this is granted, the creative technician will demand fuller participation in performances; and at many times during a performance the actor will support the technician, whose activated equipment will be "center stage." A wide-ranging mix is made possible in which the complexity of images and sounds (with or without the participation of "unarmed" performers) is endless.[12]

To achieve this mix of technical and live performers nothing less than the whole space is needed. There can be no further bifurcation of space, in which one territory is meted out to the audience and the other to the performers. The final exchange between performers and the audience is the exchange of space, the use of audience as scene-makers as well as scene-watchers. This will not result in chaos: rules are not done away with, they are simply changed.

Two. All the Space Is Used for Performance; All the Space Is Used for Audience

Perhaps the one convention that has endured from Greek times to the present is that a special place is marked off within the theatre for the performance. Even the medieval theatre, which moved from place to place on wagons, saw to it that the performers stayed on the wagons and the spectators in the streets. Most of the classical Eastern theatre agrees with the West in this convention. And even simple village folk-plays are acted out in marked-off areas, established for the performance and removed when it is over.

To find instances of the constant exchange of space between performers and spectators we must search among ethnographic reports of nonliterate ritual. There, two circumstances hold our attention. First, the performing group is often the entire population of a village; or, if it is just the adult males, females and children are frequently not permitted to watch. Secondly, these performances are rarely isolated "shows." We understand now that nonliterate ritual theatre is entertainment, and accepted as such by those doing it; but, at the same time, it is something more: an integral part of community life, part of years-long cycle plays which, like the Hevehe Cycle of the Orokolo, recapitulate the life experience of each individual.[13]

During these performances the village, or a place near it, is co-opted for the performance. But the performance does not stand still; it ranges over a loosely defined territory. If there are spectators, they follow the performance, yielding to it when it approaches, pressing in on it when it recedes. The Balinese dance filmed by Margaret Mead and Gregory Bateson (1938) shows the spatial give-and-take, as well as the full use of an ill-defined space. The dancers are highly organized. But they do not feel called on to stay in one spot. They chase the "witch" (Dr. Mead's unfortunate term for the villain of the dance) and are chased by him; they move in and out of the temple and all across the village square. The space of the performance is organically defined by the action; unlike our theatre, where the action is trimmed to a space, the Balinese dance creates its own space, moving where it must.[14]

Once one gives up fixed seating and the bifurcation of space, entirely new relationships are possible. Body contact can naturally occur between performers and audience; voice levels and acting intensities can be widely varied; a sense of shared experience can be engendered. Most important, each scene can create its own space, either contracting to a central or a remote area or expanding to fill all available space. The action "breathes" and the audience itself becomes a major scenic element. During *Victims of Duty* we found that the audience would crowd in during intense scenes and move away when the action became broad or violent; they usually gave way willingly to the performers[15] and reoccupied areas after the action had passed by. During the final scene Nicolas chased the Detective all around the periphery of the large room, stumbling over the audience, searching in the audience for his victim. Nicholas' obstacles were real—the living bodies of the spectators—and the scene ended when he caught and killed the Detective. Had someone in the audience chosen to shelter and protect the Detective an unpredictable complication would have been added; but not one that could not have been dealt with. At several points in the performance, a member of the audience did not want to give up a place in which an action was staged. The performers, in character, had to deal with these people, sometimes forcibly moving them out of the area.

These extra tensions may not seem to be a legitimate part of the

Some spectators get out of the way as Nicolas pursues the Detective in *Victims of Duty* by Eugene Ionesco.
(Photo: Matt Herron, Black Star)

performance. Surely they are not part of "the play." But the exchange of place implies the possibilities of conflict over space; such conflicts have to be coped with in terms of the performance. They can be turned to a capital advantage if one believes that the interaction between performers and audience is a real and valuable one. In many intermedia performances, the spectators actively participate. Often the entire space is a performing space; no one is just watching.

The exchange of space between performers and spectators, and the exploration of the total space by both groups, have not been introduced into our theatre by ethnographers. Our model is closer to home: the streets. Everyday street life is marked by movement and the exchange of space; street demonstrations are a special form of street life which depend on the heightened applications of everyday regulations. One marches with or without a permit, an official sanction; in either case, the event is defined by the rules kept or broken. The ever-increasing use of public space outdoors for rehearsed activities (ranging from demonstrations to street theatre) is having its impact on the indoor theatre.

Three. The Theatrical Event Can Take Place Either in a Totally Transformed Space or in "Found Space"

Environment can be understood in two different ways. First, there is what one can do with and in a space; secondly, there is the acceptance of a given space. In the first case, one *creates* an environment by transforming a space; in the second case, one *negotiates* with an environment, engaging in a scenic dialogue with a space. In the created environment the performance in some sense engineers the arrangement and behavior of the spectators; in a negotiated environment a more fluid situation leads sometimes to the performance being controlled by the spectators.

In the traditional theatre, scenery is segregated; it exists only in that part of the space in which the performance is played. The construction of scenery is guided by sight-lines; even when "the theatre" is exposed—as in Brechtian scenography—the equipment is there as an indication that "this is not reality." In short, conventional attitudes toward scenery are naive and compromised.

In environmental theatre, if scenery is used at all, it is used all the way, to the limits of its possibilities. There is no bifurcation of space, no segregation of scenery, and if equipment is exposed it is there because it must be there, even if it is in the way.

The sources of this extreme position are not easy to locate. The theatre of the Bauhaus group[16] was not really interested in scenery. They wished to build new organic spaces in which the action surrounded the spectators or in which the action could move freely through space. Most of the Bauhaus projects were never built. But the environmental theatre learned from the Bauhaus of new audience-performer relationships. Although not a member of the Bauhaus, Frederick Kiesler (1896-1966) shared many of their ideas. Between 1916 and 1924 he designed (but never built) the Endless Theatre, seating 100,000 people. Kiesler foresaw new functions for theatre:

> The elements of the new dramatic style are still to be worked out. They are not yet classified. Drama, poetry, and scenic formation have no natural milieu. Public, space, and players are artificially assembled. The new aesthetic has not yet attained a unity of expression. Communication lasts two hours; the pauses are the social event. We have no contemporary theatre. No agitators' theatre, no tribunal, no force which does not merely comment on life, but shapes it. [17]

These words were written in 1932. In 1930, Kiesler described his Endless Theatre:

> The whole structure is encased in double shells of steel and opaque welded glass. The stage is an endless spiral. The various levels are connected with elevators and platforms. Seating platforms, stage and elevator platforms are suspended and spanned above each other in space. The structure is an elastic building system of cables and platforms developed from bridge building. The drama can expand and develop freely in space. [18]

From the Bauhaus and men like Kiesler, the environmental theatre learned to reject conventional space and to seek in the event itself an organic and dynamic definition of space. Naturally, such ideas are incompatible with traditional scenic practice. Kaprow suggests an altogether different source.

> With the breakdown of the classical harmonies following the introduction of the "irrational" or nonharmonic juxtapositions, the Cubists tacitly opened the path to infinity. Once foreign matter was introduced into the picture in the form of paper, it was only a matter of time before everything else foreign to paint and canvas would be allowed to get into the creative act, including real space. Simplifying the history of the ensuing evolution into a flashback, this is what happened: the pieces of paper curled up off the canvas, were removed from the surface to exist on their own, became more solid as they grew into other materials and, reaching out further into the room, finally filled it entirely. Suddenly there were jungles, crowded streets, littered alleys, dream spaces of science fiction, rooms of madness, and junk-filled attics of the mind.
> Inasmuch as people visiting such Environments are moving, colored shapes too, and were counted "in," mechanically moving parts could be added, and parts of the created surroundings could then be rearranged like furniture at the artist's and visitors' discretion. And, logically, since the visitor could and did speak, sound and speech, mechanical and recorded, were also soon to be in order. Odors followed. [19]

Many intermedia pieces are environmental. Only recently have happeners "discovered" the proscenium stage; a paradoxical cross-over is starting in which the theatre is becoming more environmental while intermedia is becoming more traditionally theatrical scenically.

Kaprow says that his own route to Happenings (a usage he coined) was through "action collage"—not the making of pictures but the creation of a pictorial event. In his 1952 essay, "The American Action Painters," Harold Rosenberg described what it means to "get inside the canvas":

> ...the canvas began to appear to one American painter after another as an arena in which to act—rather than as a space in which to reproduce, redesign, analyze or "express" an object, actual or imagined. What was to go on the canvas was not a picture but an event.[20]

It is but one brief step from action painting (or collage) to intermedia. My own interest in environmental theatre developed from my interest in intermedia. My partners in the New Orleans Group—Franklin Adams (painter) and Paul Epstein (composer)—followed the same path. Our first definition of environmental theatre was "the application of intermedia techniques to the staging of scripted drama." A painter's and composer's aesthetics were added to that of a theatre person's; traditional theatrical biases fell by the wayside. We were not interested in sightlines or in the focused ordering of space. The audience entered a room in which *all* the space was "designed," in which the environment was an organic transformation of one space into another. The spectators found whatever place they could to view the event. In *Victims of Duty* there were "ridges" and "valleys" of carpeted platforms. For those who sat in the valleys vision was difficult; either they did not see all the action or they stood or they moved. Some of the action took place in the valleys, and during these moments only spectators very close to the action could see it.

For *Victims* a large room (about 75' square) was transformed into a living room. But it was not a living room in which all the elements had a clear or usual function. It was, rather, the "idea of a living room." In one corner chairs spiralled to the ceiling; at another place there was an analyst's couch; on a high platform a wooden chair sat under a bright overhead light; a small proscenium stage was built against one wall for the play-within-the-play; trapdoors allowed the performers to play underneath the audience; a trapeze permitted them to play over the audience; certain scenes took place in the street outside the theatre or in other rooms adjoining or over the theatre; stairways led to nowhere; technical equipment was plainly visible, mounted on platforms against two walls; the walls themselves were covered with flats and lightly overpainted so that scenes from previous proscenium productions faintly showed through; on the walls graffiti were painted: quotations from *Victims of Duty*. The scenic idea was to offer Ionesco's formulation that the play was "naturalistic drama," a parody of the theatre, and a surrealistic-psychedelic-psychoanalytic search.

We did not plan the set. The directors, performers, technicians, and production crews had been working for about a month in the space in which the play was to be performed (we had, by then, been rehearsing for four months). One Saturday afternoon we decided to build the environment. We lugged whatever flats, platforms, stairways, and carpets we could find and worked for 10 hours straight. Out of that scenic improvisation came the environment. Very few changes were made during the ensuing weeks of rehearsal. I do not want to make out of this experience a general principle. But I would observe that the close work on the production by more than 20 people led to a felt knowledge of what the environment should be. By not planning at all, by working, we understood well what was needed.

The very opposite of total transformation of space is found space. The principles here are very simple: (1) the given elements of any space—its architecture, textural qualities, acoustics, and so on—are to be explored, not disguised; (2) the random ordering of space is valid; (3) the function of scenery, if used at all, is to understand, not disguise or transform, the space; (4) the spectators may suddenly and unexpectedly create new spatial possibilities.

Most found space is found outdoors or in public buildings that cannot be transformed.[21] Here the challenge is to acknowledge the environment and cope with it as best one can. The American prototype for this kind of performance is the civil rights march and confrontation.[22] The politics of these marches and confrontations have been discussed. Their aesthetics deserves more than passing attention. The streets were dangerous for black people, the highways were not free, and state governments inhospitable. The sit-ins had explored small indoor spaces; the freedom rides had claimed the interior of buses as they passed through the countryside. But the ultimate gesture was the march of thousands in the streets and across miles of highway. The aesthetic fallout of that large gesture was that the streets were no longer places which one used to get from here to there. They were public arenas, testing grounds, stages for morality plays.

Later demonstrations modelled themselves on early examples. The American-Roman facade of the Pentagon was the proper backdrop for a confrontation between anti-war youth and troops. Draft centers and campuses are other natural focal points. What is happening at these places is not properly described as political action. Ceremonies are being performed. Adapting a phrase from Goffman, these are the places where parts of the public act out their reality. It is, therefore, no accident that most street theatre has had a political content.[23]

I helped plan and direct a series of events called *Guerrilla Warfare* which was then staged at 23 locations throughout New York City on October 28, 1967. The scenario for *Guerrilla Warfare* and three accounts of it have been printed elsewhere.[24] Two of the 23 performances are worth considering here. One was the 2 p.m. performance at the Main Recruiting Center at Times Square and the other the 6 p.m. performance at the Port Authority terminal.

The Recruiting Center is a place where demonstrations occur frequently. The police are familiar with the routine. However, our anti-war play attracted a large hostile crowd who closed in on the performers; not threateningly, but aggressively. Some people shouted, many mumbled their disapproval. Because the play was intentionally ambivalent (a super-super patriot would think we were for the war), several teenage kids thought we were American Nazis and from that point of view began to question their own support of the war. The performance went swiftly, some of the dialogue was lost in the open air, the performers were not comfortable. We found that the narrow triangular sidewalk, surrounded on all sides by automotive traffic, and further abbreviated by the pressing crowd, made the performance brief and staccato.

Quite the opposite happened at the Port Authority. Here the large, vaulting interior space was suited for sound. The police were not expecting a performance and acted confused until orders from higher up ended the show seconds away from completion. We began all performances by humming and then singing the Star Spangled Banner. Performers assembled at a central area upon seeing a sight cue and as they gathered they sang louder. In the terminal the swelling anthem seemed to come from everywhere. Because the commuter crowds were not expecting a performance, at first they didn't seem to believe one was happening. One West Point cadet walked through the performance, paused, and walked away only to return several moments later, scratch his head, and stay. Finally, when he realized what was being said, he walked off in disgust. A large crowd gathered; they were curious rather than hostile and they kept their remarks low, questioning each other about what was going on. Standing as we were in front of the Greyhound ticket booths, just next to the escalators, and alongside a display Ford automobile, the performance had a strange surreality to it. But, at the same time, it was far from esoteric. More than in any other location, the terminal performance—if a bit long—was direct and meaningful. Here, where people want to get home, in the bland but massive institutional architecture of our culture, was the place where a symbolic confrontation could take place.

It is possible to combine the principles of transformed and found space. Once a space has been transformed, the audience will "take their places." Frequently, because there is no fixed seating and little indication of how they should sit, the audience will arrange themselves in unexpected patterns; and during the performance these patterns will change, "breathing" with the action just as the performers do. The audience can thus make even the most cunningly transformed space into found space; it is not possible to block actions in this kind of situation. The performers should take advantage of audience mobility, considering it a flexible part of the performance environment.

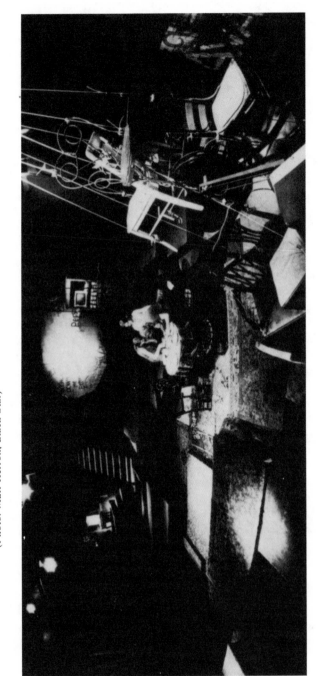

A view of the environment for the New Orleans Group's performance of *Victims*. The performers began eating a meal before any spectators were admitted. Slowly they changed from "themselves" into the "characters." The audience was not certain just when the performance of Ionesco's play began. (Photo: Matt Herron, Black Star)

Four. Focus Is Flexible and Variable

Single-focus is the trademark of traditional theatre. Even when actions are simultaneous and spread across a large stage (for example, the more than 200' proscenium at the Palais de Chaillot in Paris) the audience is looking in one direction. A single glance or a simple scan can take in all the action, even the most panoramic. And within these panoramic scenes, there are centers of attention, usually a single focal point around which everything else is organized. The response of one perceptive spectator should be the response of all.

The environmental theatre does not eliminate this practice. It is useful. But added to it are two other kinds of focus, or lack of focus.

In *multifocus* more than one event—several of the same kind, or mixed media—happens at the same time, distributed throughout the space. Each independent event competes with the others for the audience's attention. The space is organized so that no spectator can see everything. The spectator must move or completely refocus his attention to catch everything that is going on. It is not really the principle of the three-ring circus. In multifocus events happen behind and above and below the spectator. He is surrounded by a variety of sights and sounds. However, it is not necessary that the density of events be "thick." Multifocus and sensory overload are not equivalent terms, though at times they are coincident. Sparse, scattered, low-key, and diverse events may be offered simultaneously. Sensory overload leads to a feeling of a small space which is exploding because it is so full. Sparse events make one feel that the space is unspeakably large, barely populated. The range of multi-focus moves from one extreme to the other and includes all intermediate points.

A performance using multifocus will not reach every spectator in the same way. Reactions may be affectively incompatible with one another because one spectator will put events together in a different way than the woman sitting next to him. In multifocus, the director's role of presenting coherence is largely turned over to the audience. The performers and technicians control the sensory input (and one works painstakingly on this), but the mix of elements is left to the audience.

In *local-focus* events are staged so that only a fraction of the audience can see and hear them. During *Victims*, Choubert went into the audience and spoke quietly to three or four persons. He was saying lines from the play, intimate speeches that asked for a small circle of witnesses and an extremely low vocal level. At the same time as he was speaking to these few people another action—on a larger scale—was happening elsewhere. Later, during the bread-stuffing sequence, Nicholas left the central action (which was staged single-focus) and went into the audience where he picked a young woman at random and began kissing and fondling her. He went as far as he could (and on several evenings a girl was very permissive). He spoke into her ear the private words of lovemaking. He was also listening for his cue—a line by the Detective, who continued the central action of stuffing bread down Choubert's throat. When Nicholas heard his cue, he said to the girl he was kissing, "I'm glad you agree with me." If she had not been cooperative, he said, "I'm sorry you don't agree with me." In either case he left her and rejoined the central action.

Local-focus has the advantage of bringing certain scenes very directly to some members of the audience. A commitment on the part of the performer is possible that cannot be realized in any other way. But what of the other spectators, those who cannot hear or see what's happening? One may offer them their own local actions or a central action. Or—and we used this several times successfully in *Victims*—nothing else is going on. Spectators out of the range of sight and hearing will be aware of some action happening "over there." Some will move to that place; some will look around them at the environment, the other spectators. For those who are neither participating nor trying to participate the moments of local-focus are breaks in the action when they can recapitulate what has gone on before or simply think their own thoughts. We found that these pauses—these pools of inattention—frequently drew spectators further into the world of the performance. Local-focus may be used as part of multifocus. In this case, certain activities are potentially viewable by all the spectators, while other activities are not. In fact, all focus possibilities can be used alone or in combination.

It is very hard to get performers to accept local-focus. They are habituated to projecting even the most intimate situations and language. They cannot understand why the entire audience should not share these intimacies. But once the performer accepts the startling premise that privacy (of a kind) is possible and proper within a performance and that the close relation between a performer and a very few spectators or even one, is valid artistically, wide possibilities open. A low range of subtle actions and volume can be used. Real body contact and whispered communication is possible between performer and spectator. Local whirlpools of action make the theatrical line more complex and varied than in traditional performances. The theatre space is like a city in which lights are going on and off, traffic is moving, parts of conversation are faintly heard.

Five. All Production Elements Speak in Their Own Language

This axiom is implicit in the others. Why should the performer be any more important than other production elements? Because he is human? But the other elements were made by men and are operated by them. While discussing the first axiom, I pointed out that technicians should be a creative part of the performance. In the environmental theatre one element is not submerged for the sake of others. It is even possible that elements will be made and rehearsed separately and that the performance itself is the arena where competing elements meet for the first time.

Portions of the performance can be structured traditionally. In that case, production elements function "operatically," all joining together to make one statement. At these times, a pyramid of supportive elements has the performer at its apex. But there are other times when the performer may find himself in the base of the pyramid; and times when there is no pyramid at all, but distinct and sometimes contradictory elements. Many multifocus situations are structured this way.

The long dialogue between the Detective as father and Choubert as son in *Victims* was played in near darkness with the Detective reading from an almost hidden lectern at the side of a projection booth and Choubert seated among the spectators, his head in his hands. Their dialogue supported two films which were projected alternately and sometimes simultaneously on opposite walls. The dialogue which held the audience's attention was the one between the films.

At other points in the production, the performers were treated as mass and volume, color, texture, and movement. Although they were the only performers there, they were not "actors" but parts of the environment.

Grotowski has carried to the extreme the idea of competing elements, contradictory statements. "There must be theatrical contrast," he says. "This can be between any two elements: music and the actor, the actor and the text, actor and costume, two or more parts of the body (the hands say yes, the legs say no), etc."[25]

Six. The Text Need Be Neither the Starting Point Nor the Goal of a Production. There May Be No Text at All

One of the theatre's most enduring clichés is that the play comes first and from it flows the consequent production: the playwright is the first creator and his intentions serve as production guidelines. One may stretch these intentions to the limits of "interpretation," but no further.

But things aren't that way. Plays are produced for all kinds of reasons, rarely because a play exists that "must be done": a producer has or finds money; a group of actors wants a vehicle; a slot in a season needs to be filled; a theatre is available whose size and equipment are suited to certain productions: cultural, national, or social occasions demand performances. One thing is sure: the play is not the thing.[26] Not that we have much to be proud of in most of our productions. Sanctimonious attitudes toward the text, and production practice that preserves the playwright's words, will yield little, particularly when there is a brief rehearsal period. The repertory—from Aeschylus to Brecht—clogs rather than releases creativity. That repertory will not go away; but need it be preserved, expressed, or interpreted? Cage has put it well:

> Our situation as artists is that we have all this work that was done before we came along. We have the opportunity to do work now. I would not present things from the past, but I would approach them as materials available to something else which we are going to do now. One extremely interesting thing that hasn't been done is a collage made from various plays.
>
> Let me explain to you why I think of past literature as material rather than as art. There are oodles of people who are going to think of the past as a museum and be faithful to it, but that's not my attitude. Now as material it can be put together with other things. They could be things that don't connect with art as we conventionally understand it. Ordinary occurrences in a city, or ordinary occurrences in the country, or technological occurrences—things that are now practical simply because techniques have changed. This is altering the nature of music and I'm sure it's altering your theatre, say through the employment of colored television, or multiple movie projectors, photoelectric devices that will set off relays when an actor moves through a certain area. I would have to analyze theatre to see what are the things that make it up in order, when we later make a synthesis, to let those things come in.[27]

Cage's attitude—treat the repertory as materials not models—is tied to his high regard for technology. That is an understandable bias. Grotowski shares many of Cage's views about the text, while taking an altogether different position on technology. A radical new treatment (some will call it mistreatment) of the text does not depend upon one's attitude toward technology.

> By gradually eliminating whatever proved superfluous, we found that theatre can exist without makeup, without autonomic costume and scenography, without a separate performance area (stage), without lighting and sound effects, etc. It cannot exist without the actor-spectator relationship of perceptual, direct, "live" communion. This is an ancient theoretical truth, of course, but when rigorously tested in practice it undermines most of our usual ideas about theatre.... No matter how theatre expands and exploits its mechanical resources, it will remain technologically inferior to film and television.[28]

A choice is not necessary between Cage and Grotowski. Each production contains its own possibilities. What is striking is that men who have such diverse attitudes toward technology should stand so close in their understanding of the text's function. Cage says the repertory is material; Grotowski practices "montage": rearranging, extrapolating, and eliminating portions of the text.

These practices flow from the premises of the first axiom. If the theatrical event is a set of related transactions, then the text—once rehearsal begins—will participate in these transactions. It is no more reasonable to expect that the text will remain unchanged than that a performer will not develop his role. These changes are what rehearsals are for. But "change" does not precisely describe what happens. Grotowski's *confrontation* is more accurate. I cited Grotowski at the start of this essay, and hope that by now the richness of his suggestion is understood.

> [The actor] must not illustrate Hamlet, he must meet Hamlet. The actor must give his cue within the context of his own experience. And the same for the director. . . . One structures the montage so that this confrontation can take place. We eliminate those parts of the text which have no importance for us, those parts with which we can neither agree nor disagree. Within the montage one finds certain words that function vis-à-vis our own experiences.[29]

The text is a map with many possible routes. You push, pull, explore, exploit. You decide where you want to go. Rehearsals may take you elsewhere. Almost surely you will not go where the playwright intended. Michael Smith wrote of *Victims:*

> I don't, in short, think this was a good production of *Victims of Duty*. It might be described as a very good happening on the same themes as Ionesco's play, using Ionesco's words and structure of action; or as an environment in which *Victims of Duty* was the dominant element. The play was there somewhere . . . but it was subservient to, and generally obscured by, the formal enterprise of the production. Several episodes were brilliantly staged, but what came across finally was not the play but the production.[30]

Smith's reaction is correct, his attitude understandable. (Later, in the same review, he said, "I do think the text of the play . . . is 'the first thing, the original impulse, and the final arbiter.'" We did not "do" Ionesco's play; we "did with it." We confronted it, searched among its words and themes, built around and through it. And we came out with our own thing.

That is the heart of the environmental theatre.

Notes

1. Michael Kirby discusses the distinctions between nonmatrixed and matrixed performances in "The New Theatre," T30.

2. See T39, 160–64.

3. Erving Goffman—a sociologist who looks at behavior from a theatrical point of view—has begun the discussion of expectation-obligation networks in two books: *Encounters* (Indianapolis: Bobbs-Merrill, 1961) and *Behavior in Public Places* (Glencoe: The Free Press, 1963).

4. Interview, published in full in the Fall, 1968, *TDR.*

5. "An Interview with John Cage," *TDR,* Volume 10, No. 2, pp. 50–51.

6. *Encounters,* p. 19.

7. *Behavior in Public Places,* p. 8.

8. A Provo event is described by John Kifner in the *New York Times* of 25 August 1967. "Dollar bills thrown by a band of hippies fluttered down on the floor of the New York Stock Exchange yesterday, disrupting the normal hectic trading pace. Stockbrokers, clerks, and runners turned and stared at the visitors' gallery....Some clerks ran to pick up the bills.... James Fourrat, who led the demonstration along with Abbie Hoffman, explained in a hushed voice: 'It's the death of money.' To forestall any repetition, the officers of the Exchange enclosed the visitors' gallery in bullet-proof glass."

9. See T30, pp. 202–11.

10. *Great Bear Pamphlet* 7 (New York: Something Else Press, 1966). Something Else Press has published many books and pamphlets about intermedia; a great proportion of these includes scenarios and theoretical writings by artists working in intermedia.

11. A complete outline of these techniques can be found in the pamphlet, "Brief Description of the Technical Equipment of the Czechoslovak Pavilion at the Expo 67 World Exhibition" by Jaroslav Frič. One can obtain the pamphlet by writing Výstavnictví, N.C., Ovocný trh 19, Prague 1, Czechoslovakia. Frič is chief of research and engineering for the Prague Scenic Institute. Both the Polyvision and the Diapolyecran were developed from ideas of Josef Svoboda. Some of Svoboda's work can be seen in T33, pp. 141–49.

12. An interesting extension of this idea happened during *Victims of Duty*. There, at several points, the performers operated slide machines and sound sources. At these moments the actors were both technicians and role-playing performers; they modulated the technical environment in which they were performing.

13. The Hevehe Cycle takes from six to twenty years. F. E. Williams, who has written an excellent account of it, believes that the Cycle has been abbreviated since the advent of Western culture in the Papuan Gulf. It seems to me that the Cycle is meant to incorporate the life-span of the Orokolo male. During his life he plays, literally, many roles, each of them relevant spiritually, biologically, and socially. See F. E. Williams, *The Drama of the Orokolo* (London: Oxford University Press, 1940). An extensive, if somewhat haphazard, literature of nonliterate theatre exists. Accounts are rarely organized for use by the theatre theorist or aesthetician; however, I have found ethnographic reading to be of utmost value.

14. The film, *Dance and Trance in Bali,* is available from the New York University film library.

15. On two occasions spectators came to *Victims* with the intention of disrupting the performance. That is an act of bad faith, planning to use a mask of spontaneity to conceal anything but spontaneous participation. One of these occasions led to a fist fight between a disrupter and another member of the audience who was a friend of mine. The disrupter was thrown out, and the show continued without most of the audience being aware that anything unusual had happened. The form of the performance permitted such events to be accepted as part of the show. The man who came to disrupt and who was thrown out was a newspaper critic. Such are the small but real pleasures of environmental theatre.

16. For a full account of the Bauhaus see O. Schlemmer, L. Moholy-Nagy, F. Molnar, *The Theatre of the Bauhaus* (Middletown, Conn.: Wesleyan University Press, 1961).

17. *Shelter-Magazine,* May 1932.

18. *Architectural Record,* May 1930. Ideal theatres are a hobby of architects. See, for example, *The Ideal Theatre: Eight Concepts* (New York: The American Federation of Arts, 1962).

When it comes time to build, the visions are stored and "community" or "cultural" interests take over. The results are lamentable. See A.H. Reiss's "Who Builds Theatres and Why" in T39.

19. *Assemblages, Environments, and Happenings* (New York: Harry N. Abrams, 1960), 165–66. A similar history is presented by Harriet Janis and Rudi Blesh in *Collage* (Philadelphia and New York: Chilton, 1962). Kirby disagrees with these accounts and argues that the movement from painting to collage, assemblage, and environment is but one aspect of the "theatrical" nature of intermedia, and not the most important. "It is in Dada that we find the origins of the nonmatrixed performing and compartmented structure that are so basic to Happenings." For Kirby's discussion see the introduction to his *Happenings* (New York: Dutton, 1965). For descriptions and scenarios of many environmental intermedia pieces see Kirby's book and T30.

20. Collected in Rosenberg's *The Tradition of the New* (New York: McGraw-Hill, 1965), p. 25. The quest for sources can become, in composer Morton Feldman's term, "mayflowering" and as such it is an intriguing but not very productive game. However, since I have begun playing that game, let me add that the work of the Russian Constructivists and the Italian Futurists also bears on the history of environmental staging.

21. It's rather sad to think about the New York Shakespeare Festival or the Avignon Festival. For the first a stage has been built in Central Park which does its best to make an outdoor setting indoors. When the Festival moves around New York it lugs its incongruent stages and equipment with it. At Avignon, the stage built in front of the castle neither successfully hides the facade nor makes productive use of it. In neither case has a negotiation been tried between the large environment and the staged event. Only the Greeks—see Epidaurus—knew how.

22. It remains to be seen whether the riots will offer a new prototype.

23. For an account of one of the best street theatres see the interview with Peter Schumann in T38.

24. The scenario appeared in my essay "Public Events for the Radical Theatre," *Village Voice*, 7 September 1967. Accounts were printed in the *Voice*, 2 November 1967, the *New York Times*, 29 October 1967, and the March, 1968 *Evergreen*. The play we used as the root of the events was Robert Head's *Kill Viet Cong*, printed in T32.

25. Eugenio Barba, "Theatre Laboratory 13 Rzedow," T27.

26. Shakespeare's half-quoted phrase deserves to be quoted in full: "the play's the thing/Wherein I'll catch the conscience of the king." Certainly Hamlet didn't serve the playwright's intentions, but his own independent motives.

27. Cage, *op. cit.*, pp. 53–54.

28. Grotowski, "Towards the Poor Theatre," T35.

29. Interview with Grotowski, published in the Fall, 1968 *TDR*.

30. *Village Voice*, 11 May 1967.

12

A Short Statement on Street Theatre
(1968)

Ed Bullins

Street Theatre is the name given to the play or dramatic piece (i.e., skit, morality or political farce or black "commercial" that subliminally broadcasts blackness) written expressly to be presented upon the urban streets or adapted to that purpose.

When one envisions contemporary America one is compelled to think of faces moving, faces facing upwards, faces in crowds, faces in dynamic mobs—expanses of faces in the streets.

Faces in the streets and in the cities: Broadway, Main Street, Market Street, Broad Street, Grand Avenue, the thoroughfares of New York, Detroit, Providence, Chicago, San Francisco, Philadelphia, Atlanta, L.A.—BLACK FACES.

STREET PLAYS (Black Revolutionary Agit-Prop)

1. Purpose: communicating to masses of Black people. Contact with Black crowds. Communication with diverse classes of people, the Black working class, or with special groups (e.g., winos, pool hall brothers, prostitutes, pimps, hypes) who would not ordinarily come to or be drawn into the theatre.

2. Method: first, draw a crowd. This can be done by use of drums, musicians, recording equipment, girls dancing, or by use of a barker or rallying cry which is familiar and revolutionary and nationalistic in connection (Burn, Baby, Burn). Or this crowd can be gotten spontaneously where masses of people are already assembled—the play done within the mob (mob action—mob act): immediacy—or

done with a minimum of fanfare, in the street, upon a platform or a flatbed truck. The truck can carry the equipment and be used as an object of interest if decorated attractively. Also women can ride atop the truck and aid in crowd-gathering (fishin'). Monitors can circulate throughout the crowd, distributing printed information, doing person-to-person verbal communicating and acting as guards for the performers and crew (The Black Guard).

3. Types of plays: short, sharp, incisive plays are best. Contemporary themes, satirical pieces on current counter-revolutionary figures or enemies of the people, humorous themes, also children's plays with revolutionary lessons are good street play material. Also, startling, unique material, something that gives the masses identifying images, symbols and challenging situations. Each individual in the crowd should have his sense of reality confronted, his consciousness assaulted.

13

Schechner's Farewell
(1969)

Don't You Worry 'Bout Me When I'm Gone. It's a little past two a.m. and way past *TDR* deadline. And this is the last Comment I'll write as editor. Given my personality the combination spells sentimentality. I became editor right out of graduate school (finishing my dissertation just as I was cleaning out Robert W. Corrigan's files). I resigned seven years later to spend more time writing and directing—and also because editing has lost its push for me. This is really not the place to evaluate what I've done. Basically I'm proud of my work on *TDR*. It's a theatre magazine now. Erika Munk was chosen by me and both staff and contributing editors to be the new editor. She's waiting in the livingroom for me to give her this Comment. The readers have helped educate me. I liked opening the circulation mail. I could never understand why foundations didn't give *TDR* more money. I still want to see the theatre get with it. A lot of people worked with me on *TDR* to help make that happen. Thank you all, and goodnight.

—*Richard Schechner*

From the Livingroom. End, continuation, beginning. Richard Schechner made *TDR*—and through it, theatre people—aware of work and ideas which are now part of our general context: multimedia, Grotowski, The Living Theatre, guerrilla performing. There were some false hopes (remember regional theatre?) and new things are being done in directing, writing, film making, acting, composing, dance. Plenty of room for exploration, into the past and future as well as present. In T44, there's no editorial line about either politics or performance, though some basic sympathies are manifest on the next two pages. Major geographic, historical, and aesthetic areas had to be left out for lack of space: Latin American and Asian political theatre will be covered in 1970's two special issues on those regions; material on East Europe, film, and TV will appear in the next few general issues. . . . "In various forms of mask and silence, the artistic universe is organized by the images of a life without fear—in mask and silence because art is without power to bring about this life, and even without power to represent it adequately. Still, the powerless, illusory truth of art (which has never been more powerless and more illusory than today, when it has become an omnipresent ingredient of the administered society) testifies to the validity of its images. The more blatantly irrational the society becomes, the greater the rationality of the artistic universe." Is Marcuse right? And what does that mean to the performances and performers described in this *TDR?*

—*Erika Munk*

14

Media Freaking
(1969)

Abbie Hoffman

Lincoln Park, Chicago, August 27, 1968
Talking to the Yippies

This sure is fun. You know, the city news bureau here in Chicago, where you can always call and get their version of what's happening, is ST2-8100. You might want to take care of a cat named Jack Lawrence from CBS who threw me out while I was fuckin' with their teletype machine last night. That was very unfair. I had some good news items. Now, let's see who else is here. The police, there's some good numbers. OK. Now this is a top secret number that like only a few of the top police have. It's the central number for the police station up here in the zoo. They're very fucked up in there. I've been up there, and you think they're organized, well you're full of shit 'cause their walkie-talkies don't work. I mean they're all stoned up there, tripping over each other, you know, they're rapping, all they want to do is fight and they don't care about all the walkie-talkie shit, they just want to fight, you know. That's their thing. All right, that number is 528-5967. Now—here's the way you use it. There's a Commander Brash of the 18th Precinct who's in charge of the general area of Lincoln Park and there's Deputy Chief Lynsky who's the cop above him. Now, the police have a system of anarchy. See, the Chief might say somethin' is OK, see, then you get some low-level honky cop saying don't do it, you know. The idea is to convince that honky cop on the other end that Chief Lynsky said it was OK, even if you gotta bullshit him a little. You just drop names, like Commander Brash said this was OK, you know, and if Chief Lynsky said this was OK, you know, those cops don't want to lose their jobs. They won't check it out. Cops are like Yippies—you can never find the leaders. So if you're good at guerrilla theatre, you can look a pig right in the eye and

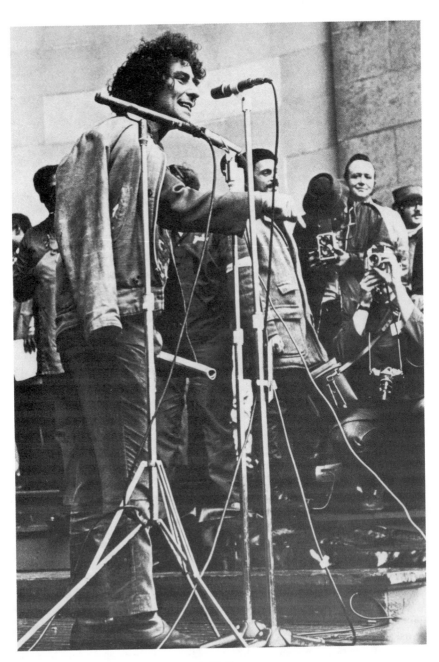

Abbie Hoffman

say that to him, you know, and he'll do it. You know, that's the thing, to get him to do it. You just let 'em know that you're stronger psychically than they are. And you *are*, because you came here for nothin' and they're holdin' on to their fuckin' pig jobs 'cause of that little fuckin' paycheck and workin' themselves up, you know. Up to what? To a fuckin' ulcer. Sergeant. We got them by the balls. The whole thing about guerrilla theatre is gettin' them to believe it. Right.

A guy just said that if you make a call, and just leave your phone off the hook, then that line is tied up. That's groovy. I didn't know about that in Chicago. In New York, that doesn't work. I think we ought to be into jamming up all their lines and everythin' and really fuckin' up their communication thing. 'Cause they broke all our walkie-talkies. They made a definite effort to make sure that we can't communicate with each other so like we ought to start communicatin' with them.

Theatre, guerrilla theatre, can be used as defense and as an offensive weapon. I mean, I think like people could survive naked, see. I think you could take all your fuckin' clothes off, a cop won't hit ya. You jump in Lake Michigan, he won't go after you, but people are too chickenshit to do that. It can be used as an offensive and defensive weapon, like blood. We had a demonstration in New York. We had seven gallons of blood in little plastic bags. You know, if you convince 'em you're crazy enough, they won't hurt ya. With the blood thing, cop goes to hit you, right, you have a bag of blood in your hand. He lifts his stick up, you take your bag of blood and go whack over your head. All this blood pours out, see. Fuckin' cop standin'. Now that says a whole lot more than a picket sign that says end the war in wherever the fuck it is you know. I mean in that demonstration, there was a fuckin' war there. People came down and looked and said holy shit I don't know what it is, blood all over the fuckin' place, smokebombs goin' off, flares, you know, tape recorders with the sounds of machine guns, cops on horses tramplin' Christmas shoppers. It was a fuckin' *war*. And they say, right, I know what the fuck you're talkin' about. You're talkin' about *war*. What the fuck has a picket line got to do with war? But people that are into a very literal bag, like that heavy word scene, you know, don't understand the use of communication in this country and the use of media. I mean, if they give a ten-page speech against imperialism, everybody listens and understands and says yeah. But you throw fuckin' money out on the Stock Exchange, and people get that right away. And they say, right, I understand what that's about. And if they don't know what you're doin', fuck 'em. Who cares? Take this, see, you use blank space as information. You carry a sign that says END THE. You don't need the next word, you just carry a sign that says END, you know. That's enough. I mean the Yippie symbol is Y. So you say, why, man, why, why? Join the Y, bring your sneakers, bring your helmet, right, bring your thing, whatever you got. Y, you say to the Democrats, baby, Y that's not a V it's a Y. You can do a whole lotta shit. Steal it, steal the V, it's a Y. It's up the revolution like that. Keeping your cool and having good wits is your strongest defense.

If you don't want it on TV, write the work "FUCK" on your head, see, and that won't get on TV, right? But that's where theatre is at, it's TV. I mean our thing's for TV. We don't want to get on Meet the Press. What's that shit? We want Ed Sullivan, Johnny Carson show, we want the shit where people are lookin' at it and diggin' it. They're talking about reachin' the troops in Viet Nam so they write in *The Guardian*! [An independent radical newsweekly published in New York.] That's groovy. I've met a *lot* of soldiers who read *The Guardian*, you know. But *we've* had articles in *Jaguar* magazine, *Cavalier*, you know, *National Enquirer* interviews the Queen of the Yippies, someone nobody ever heard of and she runs a whole riff about the Yippies and Viet Nam or whatever her thing is and the soldiers get it and dig it and smoke a little grass and say yeah I can see where she's at. That's why the long hair. I mean shit, you know, long hair is just another prop. You go on TV and you can say anything you want but the people are lookin' at you and they're lookin' at the cat next to you like David Susskind or some guy like that and they're sayin' hey man there's a choice, I can see it loud and clear. But when they look at a guy from the Mobilization [against the war in Vietnam] and they look at David Susskind, they say well I don't know, they seem to be doing the same thing, can't understand what they're doin'. See, Madison Avenue people think like that. That's why a lot SDS's don't like what we're doin'. 'Cause they say we're like exploiting; we're using the tools of Madison Ave. But that's because Madison Ave. is effective in what it does. They know what the fuck they're doin'. *Meet the Press, Face the Nation, Issues and Answers*—all those bullshit shows, you know, where you get a Democrat and a Republican arguin' right back and forth, this and that, this and that, yeah yeah. But at the end of the show nobody changes their fuckin' mind, you see. But they're tryin' to push Brillo, you see, that's good, you ought to use Brillo, see, and 'bout every ten minutes on will come a three-minute thing of Brillo. Brillo is a revolution, man, Brillo is sex, Brillo is fun, Brillo is bl bl bl bl bl bl bl bl. At the end of the show people ain't fuckin' switchin' from Democrat to Republicans or Commies, you know, the right-wingers or any of that shit. They're buying Brillo! And the reason they have those boring shows is because they don't want to get out any information that'll interfere with Brillo. I mean, can you imagine if they had the Beatles goin' zing zing zing zing zing zing zing, all that jump and shout, you know, and all of a sudden they put on an ad where the guy comes on very straight: "You ought to buy Brillo because it's rationally the correct decision and it's part of the American political process and it's the right way to do things." You know, fuck, they'll buy the Beatles, they won't buy the Brillo.

We taped a thing for the David Susskind Show. As he said the word hippie, a live duck came out with "HIPPIE" painted on it. The duck flew up in the air and shat on the floor and ran all around the room. The only hippie in the room, there he is. And David went crazy. 'Cause David, see, he's *New York Times* head, he's not *Daily News* freak. And he said the duck is out and blew it. We said, we'll see you David, goodnight. He say, oh no no. We'll leave the duck in. And we watched the show later when it came on, and the fuckin' duck was all gone. He done never existed. And I called up Susskind and went quack quack quack, you motherfucker, *that* was the best piece of information: that was a hippie. And everything we did, see, non-verbally, he cut out. Like he said, "How do you eat?" and we fed all the people, you know. But he cut that out. He wants to deal with the words. You know, let's play word games, let's analyze it. Soon as you analyze it, it's dead, it's over. You read a book and say well now I understand it, and go back to sleep.

The media distorts. But it always works to our advantage. They say there's low numbers, right? 4000, 5000 people here. That's groovy. Think of it, 4000 people causin' all this trouble. If you asked me, I'd say there are four Yippies. I'd say we're bringin' another four on Wednesday. That's good, that freaks 'em out. They're lookin' around. Only four. I mean I saw that trip with the right wing and the Communist conspiracy. You know, you'd have 5000 people out there at the HUAC demonstrations eight years ago in San Francisco and they'd say there are five Communists in the crowd, you know. And they did it all. You say, man that's pretty cool. So you just play on their paranoia like that. Yeah, there're four guys out around there doin' a thing. So distortion's gonna backfire on them, 'cause all of a sudden Wednesday by magic there are gonna be 200,000 fuckin' people marchin' on that amphitheatre. That's how many we're gonna have. And they'll say, "Wow. From 4000 up to 200,000. Those extra four Yippies did a hell of a good job." I dig that, see. I'm not interested in explainin' my way of life to straight people or people that aren't interested. They never gonna understand it anyway and I couldn't explain it anyway. All I know is, in terms of images and how words are used as images to shape your environment, the *New York Times* is death to us. That's the worst fuckin' paper as far as the Yippies are concerned. They say, "Members of the so-called Youth International Party held a demonstration today." That ain't nothin'. What fuckin' people read that? They fall asleep. 'Cause the *New York Times* has all the news that's fit to print, you know, so once they have all the news, what do the people have to do? They just read the *New York Times* and drink their coffee and go back to work, you know. But the *Daily News*, that's a TV set. Look at it, I mean look at the picture right up front and the way they blast those headlines. You know, "Yippies, sex-loving, dope-loving, commie, beatnik, hippie, freako, weirdos." That's groovy, man, that's a whole life style, that's a whole thing to be, man. I mean you want to get in on that.

When we stormed the Pentagon, my wife and I we leaped over this fence, see. We were really stoned, I mean I was on acid flying away, which of course is an anti-revolutionary drug you know, you can't do a thing on it. I've been on acid ever since I came to Chicago. It's in the form of honey. We got a lab guy doin' his thing. I think he might have got assassinated, I ain't seen him today. Well, so we jumped this here fence, see, we were sneaking through the woods and people were out to get the Pentagon. We had this flag, it said NOW with a big wing on it, I don't know. The right-wingers said there was definitely evidence of Communist conspiracy 'cause of that flag, I don't know what the fuck it was. So we had Uncle Sam hats on, you know, and we jumped over the fence and we're surrounded by marshals, you know, just closin' us in, about 30 marshals around us. And I plant the fuckin' flag and I said, "I claim this land in the name of free America. We are Mr. and Mrs. America. Mrs. America's pregnant." And we sit down and they're goin' fuckin crazy. I mean we got arrested and unarrested like six or seven times. And when we finally got arrested, it was under other names. I'm really a digger, I never was a Yippie. Was always a digger. So I said, you know, A. Digger, Abbie Digger, Mr. and Mrs. A. Digger. They say are you a boy or a girl, I say girl. Right. This is where I wanna go. I don't have to prove manliness by beatin' up 14-year-old girls with nightsticks, you know. Fuck 'em. But ideas, you just get stoned, get the ideas in your head and then do 'em. And don't bullshit. I mean that's the thing about doin' that guerrilla theatre. You be prepared to die to prove your point. You gotta die.

You know, what's life? Life's all that fun shit. Life's doin' what you want to do. *Life*'s an American magazine, and if we hook them right, they're gonna give us 10,000 flowers that are gonna be thrown out of a helicopter tomorrow afternoon. But we'll only allow them to do it if they bring a newsreel person up in the helicopter with 'em. You know, to take the pictures. So we're workin' out that negotiation with *Life* magazine. 'Cause we said, you know, it's called Festival of Life, man, we named it after your magazine. I know that's immoral and I know that's cheatin' and that's stealin'. I wish I was a revolutionist. I wouldn't have these problems. A lot of revolutionists come here, they worry about parking the car. Where we gonna park the car, should we park it in a meter? The meter'll run out, we'll get a ticket. It's a weird revolution. Fuck it. We don't need cars; we travel in wheelbarrows. You see, just worry about your ass. Forget about your clothes, your money, you know, just worry about your ass and all the rest of us's asses. Cars don't mean shit. They grab our walkie-talkies you say yeah, there you go, take it, thank you, it was too heavy to carry.

I think it's a good idea to cut your hair or get a wig or let your hair grow pretty fast or paint your face or change your clothes or get a new hat and a new name. I mean, everybody ought to to have a new name by Wednesday. And like you know we're all one huge happy family with all new names or no names and no faces. 'Cause when we bust out of this park and go down to Grant Park and then go out to the amphitheatre, there are gonna be some mighty strange theatrical events. And you better have your theatre thing down pretty pat.

Well, I've shot my load. I'm for ending the Yippie thing Thursday, killin' it all, 'cause I don't think people are Yippies anymore than they're Mobe or Motherfuckers or whatever they are. They're just people. And I think we oughta burn all our Yippie buttons and laugh at the fuckin' press and say nyah nyah, we took you for a fuckin' ride. That's what we figured when we started this thing back in December—just a couple of speedfreaks hangin' around the cellar sayin' now how are we gonna do this Chicago trip? We ain't got no fuckin' money, you know, we ain't got no organization, we ain't got no constituency. We went to a New Left meeting, they said where's your constituency, you can't talk here, you know, you ain't against imperialism. I said, man, I don't want any pay toilets in this fuckin' country, I don't want to pay a dime to take a shit. SDS doesn't consider that relevant. That's the trouble with the Left you know. Did a trip on a Socialist Scholars Conference, a couple of Hell's Angels guys and I, we went up and had a capgun fight in the Hotel Hilton where the Left has their conferences, it's very interesting. So the heads of the Hilton and the heads of the socialists were gettin' together to decide how to throw us speedfreaks out of the fuckin' place, see. But they didn't, I mean, we stayed to do our thing. The problem with the Left is that there are 10,000 socialist scholars in this country and not one fuckin' socialist. I mean I talk to guys on *The Guardian* and they say yeah, we're working on a serious analysis of the Yippies. I say, that's pretty fuckin' cool, man, that's great. By that time there won't be any Yippies. I mean, what the fuck are you analyzin' for, man, get in and do it.

15

Nauseated by Language
(From an Interview with Peter Handke)
(1970)

Artur Joseph

Joseph: What is the basic idea behind your plays?

Handke: Making people aware of the world of the theatre—not of the outside world. There is a theatrical reality going on at each moment. A chair on the stage is a theatre chair. A broom on the stage may even carry the name of the theatre in which the play is shown. The set is designed so as to place all the objects onstage—what we call everyday objects, a chair, a cupboard—in such a relationship to one another that they'll look like props, objects used for a theatrical performance. They are not set in reality, in the realistic arrangement of a living room, for example. Onstage, a table has its own theatrical function: it is not a table to eat at, to show how a hungry person eats—it is to demonstrate what a table onstage can be good for. A table can serve as an ornament, as a door, as scenery; it can occupy the center of the stage as a symbol of order. The act of sitting down on a chair is broken up into phases, produced in slow motion, so to speak, so that the function seems alienated. The objects are deprived of their normal function in reality. They have an artificial function in the game I force them to play. They are like the objects a circus clown makes factually unreal.

From Artur Joseph, *Theater, unter vier Augen, Gespräche mit Prominente* (Cologne, 1969), pp. 27–39, by permission of Verlag Kiepenheuer & Witsch.

Joseph: What made you write *Offending the Audience,*[1] a play that attacks the theatre and yet is itself theatre? Four speakers "abuse" the audience and analyze the nature of theatre, with abuse moving from a description of what the audience will not see (the usual theatre fictions of time, place, action) to what the audience will see (themselves as fictionless theatre).

Handke: The stage is an artifact; I wanted this play to point out that every word, every utterance onstage is dramaturgy. Every human utterance the theatre presents as natural is not evolved, but produced. I wanted to show the "producedness" of theatre. In *Offending the Audience* I wanted to show that the dramaturgy of the old plays did not satisfy me anymore (that, indeed, it bores me, in the sense that the conventional events onstage are far removed from me). I couldn't stand the pretense of reality anymore. I felt as if the actors were under a glass bell. My point was to use words to encircle the audience so they'd want to free themselves by heckling; they might feel naked and get involved. What is said doesn't really matter. I reduced the play to words because my words are not descriptions, only quotations, and because the only possibility they point to is the one that happens while the words are spoken on the stage. This play, like *Self-Accusation,*[2] came out of an ever greater reduction of means. I had been planning a play with a genuine plot, with a story, a kind of confession—there was constant confessing onstage, in dialogue form. Then this plan was gradually reduced to words, which don't refer to any objects or problems onstage; they merely quote, and what they do least is give the appearance of another reality—rather, they create their own reality of words. It was a reductive process which wasn't arbitrary: it simply came about. The idea was to have the spectators in the orchestra thrown back upon themselves. What mattered to me was making them feel like going to the theatre more, making them see all plays more consciously and with a different consciousness. My theatrical plan is to have the audience always look upon my play as a means of testing other plays. I first intended to write an essay, a pamphlet, against the theatre, but then I realized that a paperback isn't an effective way to publish an anti-theatre statement. And so the outcome was, paradoxically, doing something onstage against the stage, using the theatre to protest against the theatre of the moment—I don't mean theatre as such, the absolute. I mean theatre as a historical phenomenon, as it is to this day.

Joseph: Were you pursuing a political purpose as well?

Handke: Not directly. To say that I was trying to interpret a new social order with this play would be reaching too high, or too low. I was thinking only of the formal, dramaturgical side, of the forms of thought and expression.

Joseph: The rhythms of your plays provide a strong emotional impact. Is that intentional?

Handke: I can't separate the rational and emotional effects. Does a stunning new thought, a new insight, a new view that is based on reason, often make you feel wholly emotional effects? I think what happens is that the novelty, the new perspective, removes the rational view, and emotions come into being—a kind of joy that you could call emotional. However, in *Offending the Audience* many spectators didn't even listen to what was being said. They heard the rhythms, and apparently, rhythms somehow reduce the distance between speakers and listeners. These rhythms turn directly into emotion, bringing objects closer.

Joseph: Does this mean you wish to dissolve the stage as a "moral institution"?

Handke: Morality is the least of my concerns. And the use of the stage as a moral institution gets on my nerves. I'm bothered by this moral presumptuousness of the theatre, by its claim to judge morals. I think the theatre can further morality, but to my mind it cannot function as a moral institution. Especially as I can't use the word morality without reference to social situations. To me, morality in a society that—however moral its pose—is hierarchically organized is simply a lie, an alibi for the inequalities that exist in society. And a theatre that thinks of itself as a moral institution will function as a safety valve for society. Cabaret is often a safety valve. Morality is a sort of appendix of society: you can put up with it, or you can cut it out.

If the theatre makes us aware that there are functions of man's power over man that we didn't know about, functions that we accept by force of habit; if these functions suddenly strike us as man-made, as not at all nature given; and if through theatre, through revelation in language, we are suddenly shown, by grammatical derivations, that the functions of mastery are neither God-given nor given by the state, then the theatre can be a moral institution—but only if the idea is to replace the existing social order with another. I can't accept the theatre as a moral institution when it criticizes individuals on the theory that an additive improvement of individuals might achieve a qualitative improvement of the whole.

Joseph: How do you explain the world-wide success of *Offending the Audience?*

Handke: All you have to do is turn to the spectators and start off; with a perfectly simple shift of ninety degrees you have a new play, a new dramaturgy. Everybody wanted to see it—out of curiosity, perhaps out of a certain masochism. The secret was that people still expected something of the theatre. The kind of immediacy film can't achieve. Now they suddenly felt that theatre spoke directly to them and that this was what they had been missing. Most normal plays disappoint the spectator because they really have nothing to do with his situation in the outside world: they only refer to specific individuals. The dramaturgy doesn't speak to the spectators. The course of events, the mechanics of the dialogue aren't attuned to their acute problems. This dramaturgy is a hundred years old; it runs behind the reality of the day like a rusty bicycle, a tandem. Theatregoers feel that. To put it in geometrical terms: this rectangular relationship, in which people onstage talk to each other while others watch them, is outdated.

You have to credit the staging, too. This play depends on the director's success in stylization and rhythm, in getting an almost musical effect from musical phases of speech, from the suggestive influence of rhythmic speech. It was a verbal rock concert. That made it work. I've adapted structures in rock music that especially struck me, without producing rock-and-roll in my play. A frequent flourish in rock music is a very specific sound sequence that could be described pictorially like this: a train pulls out of the station, gradually moves off, becoming less and less audible—and at the same time another train pulls in and keeps getting noisier. And finally it all stops. This structure, these simple sequences, are often heard in rock. There's a very rapid variation of rhythmic models, and suddenly a break occurs and the models go on in a wholly different time phase. It isn't only in rock that you find this, but there it is very striking. I thought: why can't one use similar phases of speech in a play?

Joseph: What did you want to achieve?

Handke: I wanted to get under people's skins. The rhythmic artificiality was meant as a kind of vehicle to transport the words. It was to bring the words closer to the audience. Speaking in a natural flow of words would have meant only another kind of permanent convention.

Joseph: Did the play's first performance bear this out?

Handke: The staging of the play ought to rely less on movement for its expression than it did in that performance, and less on clowning, and less on surprises in gesture and speech—the play had been loosened up, for fear that the constant speaking might weary the audience. There are infinitely many possible speech phases; you can always keep the audience spellbound. You can always make them listen because they're curious to hear what comes next.

Joseph: Isn't it true that *Offending the Audience* can be shown only once to the same audience—who don't know yet that their traditional expectations of seeing a play with a plot, with characters, with props, will not be fulfilled?

Handke: Some people went two or three times. I don't think the surprise effect is that important. The crux will always be the gradual encirclement, the spectator's encirclement in language, for that is a dramatic action.

Joseph: But how about the average subscription audience, whom a subsidized repertory theatre must take into consideration?

Handke: For me, it would be ideal if the subscription system were abolished, because it doesn't suit my plays. There is simply no way to integrate them. No theatre would dare include *Kaspar* in a subscription repertory.

Joseph: Why not?

Handke: This type of dramaturgy isn't natural enough for people who want art to be natural before they will accept it. Once they find themselves no longer tied to their old expectations of realism they do accept it, because then the play seems realistic to them. When the Berlin Volksbühne put on Ionesco's *The Chairs*, I heard a woman in the lobby say to her husband, "See? That's the way I act with you." She had recognized Ionesco's absurd play as a correct, realistic picture of her situation.

Joseph: Is there a connection between your earlier *Sprechstücke* ("speaking plays") and *Kaspar?* Or were you trying something new?

Handke: It was nothing new, it only evolved because I was again forced to produce plays automatically from pure language, in which the words only illuminate themselves. The words, the pure words which first occur onstage in *Offending the Audience,* are condensed into a character. In Kaspar Hauser I discovered the model of a sort of linguistic myth. The character made me curious. A human being lives in a closet for sixteen or seventeen years, suddenly encounters the outside world, and must get to know that world, although he is unable to speak. After leaving the closet, Kaspar is in a room somewhere and looks out the window. He sees the green trees and thinks they're shutters, because he can't distinguish between planes and space. He can't tell two-dimensionality from three-dimensionality. Can't separate space from time. He can't speak; he's virtually incapable of any correct perception. He sees the world around him as flat, as in a chart; he takes the chairs for wallpaper patterns. To me, this Kaspar Hauser seemed a mythical figure, interesting not only as such, but as a model of men at odds with themselves and their environment, men who feel isolated. He fascinated me from the start. He doesn't know what snow is, and the first time snow falls on him it melts in his hand and burns. And because it's the first white thing he has seen, he calls everything white "snow."

For me, this was a model of conduct, building a person into a society's course of conduct by language, by giving him words to repeat. To enable him somehow to get along in life, to function, he is reconstructed by voices, by language models, and by instructions regarding the objects onstage. There's nothing metaphysical about the voices: they are prompters who appear at the start of the play and climb into the prompter's box in full view of the audience. This makes them theatrical. They gradually build Kaspar. They tell him what to do about the table, the cupboard, the chair; how he is supposed to sit on the stage chair. He doesn't know, after all. He can hardly walk; he's been lying on his back for seventeen years. You can't tell that from the historical account. I took the situation and added quotes from Kaspar Hauser's autobiography. He describes, for instance, how he felt the first evening he came out into the world. He knew only one line: "I want to be a horseman like my father was once." He suddenly wakes up in a strange room in the middle of the night and he aches because he never walked before. He sees a green stove in the room, shining in the night, and wants to communicate with it; so he walks over to it and tells the stove his one line: "I want to be a horseman like my father was once." He doesn't know that objects can't hear him, that they can't answer him. He says that line when he's hungry or when he feels happy. He can't express himself any other way. This is the model.

So a figure comes onstage by crawling through a slit in the backdrop. It has trouble getting through but finally succeeds. And the figure stands there unsteadily, with its one and only line which I made a bit more abstract: "I want to be a person like somebody else was once." He says that over and over. He says it to the chair; he shapes the line into an expression of all kinds of things— help, joy—and since, as far as he could tell, the first chair didn't hear him, he says it to another chair, and then to the cupboard. He says it over and over, to reassure himself when he is frightened because he's so alone. And then, one by one, the prompters begin to speak. And as they speak, they get him over his line. Little by little, his line is dismantled. He gets tangled up in the line. The sentence structure gets more and more disorganized, then the word structure. The words start to sound oddly disjointed and finally he is just uttering letters. Then he only makes sounds, and then he shuts up. That's the first phase. The prompters have silenced him. But at the same time they've managed to make him start speaking all over again, using the right sentences and words this time, the correct models that help an orderly individual to make his way in life.

And so they build Kaspar. They say things for him to repeat; they tease him into speaking. Little by little, he begins to speak. And suddenly he sees everything correctly. He suddenly understands space. He can put things in order—that's the model now. He used to mix up all the objects on the stage, to overturn tables and chairs and throw them on the floor, and now, because he can speak, he sees that everything is in disarray and sets out to create order. He arranges things. He becomes perfect, more and more perfect, a real human being; finally he speaks in verse and, when the greatest possible order has been attained onstage, in beautiful verse. The world has become a poem to him. It has rhyme and reason. Everything has rhyme and reason. Then comes intermission.

After intermission, he gives a kind of self-portrait in rhyme, to show how well he has adjusted and how happy he feels:

> I noticed nothing of what
> was happening
> around me
> before I began
> to come out onto the world.

And that evolves into a hymn; there are new Kaspars coming onstage, joining in the hymn, and the prompters fall in too—then he suddenly stops and says:

> What is it that
> I said
> just now?
> If I only knew
> what it is
> that I said
> just now!

He seems a broken man. Then he gets more and more mixed up—his language is suddenly deranged—until complete schizophrenia sets in; the stage world turns topsy-turvy, and the end is chaos.

Joseph: In *Kaspar* your criticism was aimed less at the theatre—as in *Offending the Audience*—than at society, at the beauties of order, at social organization in general...

Handke: It's hard to say whether, or that, this play criticizes universal society or any society at all, because it consists primarily of sentence games and sentence models dealing with the impossibility of *expressing* anything in language—in other words, of saying something that goes beyond the particular sentence into the realm of significance, meaning. I think a sentence doesn't mean something else: it means itself. What is shown in *Kaspar* is the idiocy of language. In constantly pretending to express something, it expresses nothing but its own stupidity.

In *Kaspar*, I criticize no concrete social model, capitalist or socialist. Instead, in abstracting from modes of speech their basic grammatical elements, I point out the present forms of linguistic alienation. I do not quote clichés as a cabaretist would; I abstract from clichés their original linguistic forms. What this shows is that every sentence not only is a cliché, but has a cliché, like printed matter—or (as I tried to show in my novel *Der Hausierer*): every sentence not only is a story; every sentence has a story. To put it succinctly: in *Kaspar*, history is conceived as a story of sentences.

What bothers me is people's alienation from their own speech. In a way, this is the basic trouble with the young revolutionaries in Germany: they're alienated from their language. It isn't *their* language anymore, so they can't even communicate. The way they speak shows how wretchedly ensnarled they are in themselves.

To me, at least, this is true: when people are alienated from their language and their speech, as workers are from their products, they are alienated from the world as well.

Kaspar is a purely anarchic play: it conveys no social utopia; it merely negates everything it comes across. I don't care whether this yields a positive utopia. The only thing that preoccupies me as a writer—or, to put it less pompously, as a man who writes now and then—is nausea at stupid speechification and the resulting brutalization of people. Of course, it would disgust me to tell anyone how to live. One should learn to be nauseated by language, as the hero of Sartre's *Nausea* is by things. At least that would be a beginning of consciousness.

Translated by E.B. Ashton

Notes

1. *Publikumsbeschimpfung, Selbstbezichtigung* (Frankfurt am Main: Suhrkamp Verlag, 1966).

2. *Kaspar and Other Plays*, trans. Michael Roloff (New York: Farrar, Straus & Giroux, 1969).

16

TDR Statement
(1971)

Michael Kirby

TDR does not pretend to cover theatre from every possible viewpoint and attitude. That would probably be impossible for any quarterly to do in depth, and we feel there is strength in specific and clearly defined goals. Since we would like our editorial policy to be as clear as possible to readers and potential contributors, a few words about the contents of this issue of *TDR*—an introduction, if you will—may help to clarify our preferences and aversions.

In its inaccuracy, the name of our journal suggests some of these. *The Drama Review* has not been limited merely to drama for some time, and it will no longer be involved in "reviewing" productions. With the so-called "Happenings issue," at least, *TDR* showed an interest in the wider scope of performance in general, rather than dealing exclusively with that type of performance involving characterization and narrative. This interest in other forms of presentation as well as drama will be continued.

"Reviewing" a performance means evaluating it. We are not interested in opinions and value judgments about what is "good" and what is "bad." We feel that the detailed and accurate documentation of performances is preferable and gives sufficient grounds for a reader to make his own value judgments. Of course we realize that implicit value judgments on our part are involved in the selection process itself, but these can be intellectual rather than emotional, and they should not be involved in the presentation of the material.

Reviewing usually, although not necessarily, involves interpretation. We are not interested in interpretation, in the explication of "meaning," in the explanation of one thing in terms of another. These processes are subjective and personal; although they may make interesting reading, they are not very useful. There is no need for documentation or theory to be impressionistic.

We would like to present material that is useful to people who actually work in theatre—material that provokes, stimulates and enriches that work. In part for this reason, we prefer articles by people who actually work in the theatre. There is no rule, of course, that critics and independent writers cannot make an important contribution, but there are certain advantages to the writing of practitioners. They tend to know, and therefore deal with, the problems of performance better than observers, and what they write may—whether they intend it to or not—provide insights into their theatrical work. Thus Richard Schechner's piece "Audience Participation" is more than a description of certain objective changes in the performance of *Commune*. It documents a creative process and provides a practitioner's motivation and evaluation.

(It may be parenthetically pointed out that there are several pieces in this issue on various approaches to audience participation. I am well aware that some people—mostly those who never accepted it in the first place—dismiss audience participation as a fad and passing fancy. This is a superficial view. Many serious, intelligent and important directors are concerned with exploring this area. There are many aspects of it yet to be discovered and much work yet to be done. Perhaps someone involved in the work can understand most easily that an available and labeled category does not preclude subtle and innovative investigation.)

Little Trips and the *James Joyce Memorial Liquid Theatre* are both particular, distinctive and rather extreme investigations of audience participation. *Little Trips* is an unusual performance that, in its "trick," changes from one style to another; its overall structure does not depend on narrative, although narrative is involved in the segments. With its tendency to eliminate spectators, *Liquid Theatre* moves away from theatre but not from performance, although the "audience" does most of the performing.

Among other things, the material on the Company Theatre of Los Angeles should demonstrate that *TDR* does not intend to limit itself to those American productions presented in New York. The significance of a performance does not depend on where it is given, on whether it is professional or non-professional, on how many times it was presented, on how many people attended, and so forth. Marjorie Strider's *Cherry Smash* was given twice, and *OEDIPUS, a New Work by John Perreault* was presented once; both were done for small audiences.

These two works—one created by a painter/sculptor and the other by a poet—can be seen as examples of *TDR*'s interest in performances done by artists primarily involved in other fields. The investigations of these interconnections and influences among the arts is another way to expand our view from drama to performance in general.

TDR is interested in the documentation of trends and movements in theatre as well as in the documentation of significant performances. As Dan Issac's piece "Theatre of Fact" demonstrates, this kind of analysis may involve the social, and even political, context of the work, as well as an examination of its purely aesthetic dimensions.

TDR's interest in the history of theatre can be seen in "From the Bauhaus to Black Mountain," which provides new information on the performance activities at the Bauhaus. Schawinsky's early work does not fit the geometrically pure image, created by Schlemmer, that is usually associated with Bauhaus theatre. The piece also documents how a great range of concepts conceived at the Bauhaus were brought to this country before World War II and were developed and demonstrated at one of our leading experimental colleges.

As Schawinsky's "spectodrama" *Play, Life, Illusion* indicates, *TDR* will be publishing scripts. We are interested in scripts of historical importance and in scripts, historical or contemporary, that document significant performances. Schawinsky's scenario fits both of these criteria. Although it was written in an idealized and perfected version sometime after the presentation at Black Mountain College and cannot be taken as a true outline of the actual performance, it does retain many of the scenes that were presented and the general structure.

As a rule, however, we will not be publishing unproduced scripts—even my own. This would involve a literary judgment, and we are concerned with performance, not literature. In part, this position may derive from a belief that the dominance of the script has made our theatre overly literary, word-oriented and unimaginative. In part, we would like to emphasize the nonliterary aspects of performance. After all, it is possible that any script could contribute to an effective performance when used creatively by a strong director.

And, of course, as my own piece "On Style" demonstrates, *TDR* will be concerned with performance theory. Unfortunately, much writing that would like to be taken as theory either re-works old, and frequently outdated, ideas, or it is merely disguised criticism that offers opinions, appreciations and interpretations instead of attempting objectivity. At the same time, it is probably not a coincidence that a certain recent upsurge in the vitality of theatre as an art has coincided with an increase in the amount of performance theory published and with certain changes in the nature of that theory.

These are only some of our interests, as exemplified by articles in this issue of *TDR*. They, of course, should not be taken as final and binding statements of policy. They indicate where our thinking is at the moment, and we reserve the right to change. If you disagree with our orientation and/or have suggestions, we would appreciate hearing from you.

We also welcome contributions—which should be accompanied by a self-addressed stamped return envelope—and queries describing possible articles. For the future, we are preparing two special issues: one on actor training and one, edited by Richard Schechner, on "Communal Performance and Ritual." Although the latter will not appear for more than a year, we would particularly welcome specific suggestions and material for these issues.

17

Women's Theatre Groups
(1972)

Charlotte Rea

Women's theatre groups in the United States have developed during the last five years as a means of exploring and expressing women's identity, potentialities, and the nature of oppression. By dramatizing their conflicts and joys, the women in these groups seek to make other women feel good about being female and to experience outrage at what they consider to be the gross injustices in the relationship between the sexes.

Feminists began forming their own theatre groups because they felt stifled by male domination in both the traditional and experimental theatre worlds. The groups, most in the New York area, vary in performing style, intent and internal structure from the traditional mode of *The New Feminist Theatre,* a group with a well-defined leader, to the collective arrangement of the *It's All Right to Be Woman Theatre,* where feminism is expressed through the structure of the group and theatre pieces. *The Westbeth Feminist Collective* of playwrights, a women's acting class at Bard College, and ad hoc women's political theatre groups also use the collective structure, but with variations.

While the collective structure has been adopted by many feminists, their groups differ in one important aspect from their male-dominated counterparts. This difference is the absence of a leader or director. Almost without exception, heterosexual groups evolve into a leader/followers political structure. The leader is the person acknowledged, even if only implicitly, by the other members to be the most insightful, most creative, most objective, most powerful person in the group. Since women for centuries have felt themselves to be less creative in the arts, less important, and less powerful than men, feminists feel that to allow their groups to evolve into the accepted power structure would be to perpetuate the thinking that has kept women from realizing their own potentialities for creative expression. It is better to develop each member's ideas to a limited degree, they reason, than to pursue fully one person's vision, while the other performers exist only as tools for the transmittal of the director's ideas. If every member must depend on her own creative output instead of relying passively on the leader/director for inspiration and guidance, then the theatrical forms that the group produces must convey to the women in the audience that they, too, possess untapped potential for artistic creativity.

Each feminist group has its own philosophy as to what kind of political and artistic statement it should make. And, as mentioned earlier, the commitment to collective creation has by no means been adopted throughout the women's theatre movement. The first of the feminist theatre groups, *The New Feminist Theatre*, was developed primarily through the efforts of its director, Anselma dell'Olio, to give a dramatic voice to the new feminist movement.

Dell'Olio believes in the necessity of the director/leader because, "I care more than anyone else.... The energy comes from me"; the director is needed to help the performer shape her responses to the material and to determine what is working for the audience and what is not. She feels that the idea of non-authoritarianism, one of the basic tenets of women's consciousness-raising groups, is dogma and that dogma cannot be transposed to the theatre.

"Dogma makes for poor theatre and poor art," dell'Olio contends. "Outrage, on the other hand, which affects the artistic sensibility, can produce art in its highest form."[1] She also feels that the responsibility of feminist theatre is to reach as many people as possible with feminist material, not necessarily to seek new forms of expression.

Dell'Olio's entry into feminist theatre began while she was working in a political cabaret, the DMZ. She started taking feminist material to the (male) director, who found it unsuitable at that time for the DMZ. Dell'Olio, however, was convinced that feminist theatre was a "dynamite idea." She then called a meeting and announced that she was starting a feminist theatre group to do experimental repertory with women. Initially, finding women actors proved to be a problem, since it was mostly writers who expressed interest in joining the new group. But acting classes eventually yielded the necessary talent, and the group was formed with both men and women participating.

The group began by reading material, some original, some from outside the group, such as Jules Feiffer's *Marriage Manual*. Their method of working with a script was to read it together, then put it down and do improvisations around it. Dell'Olio directed and acted. The improvisations led to the realization that the men were not as good at unstructured work as the women, partially, dell'Olio feels, because they were being directed by a woman. The group engaged in theatre games about the men's tightening up in the improvisatory work, but the outcome was that the men still had trouble asserting themselves under the leadership of a woman.

The major playwright for the group was Myrna Lamb. The group did her early plays—*What Have You Done for Me Lately, In the Shadow of the Crematorium,* and *Scyklon Z*—in their first public performance, which was a benefit for the Redstockings, a feminist political group. It was held at the Washington Square Methodist Church in March of 1969. After the Redstockings benefit, Jacqueline Ceballos and dell'Olio joined forces to promote a successful benefit for the National Organization for Women at the Martinique Theatre in May of 1969. The *New York Times* critic, Roz Regelson, commented on May 16th that *"The New Feminist Theatre* . . . is really working at what other radical theatres pretend to be doing—searching for a path in uncharted territory."

What Have You Done for Me Lately encourages empathy with women's fight for abortion-on-demand. It puts a man in a woman's place: he awakens to find he has been implanted with a pregnant uterus. Panicked, he tells of his important plans that will be disrupted, how sick he feels, how trapped, and how desperately he wants to be rid of the fetus inside him. As the man comes to some realization of the tragedy an unwanted pregnancy can be, the initial harsh lighting softens and a woman comes on stage for a confrontation. There is little stage movement because the emphasis is on the message carried by the words.

After the N.O.W. benefit, *The New Feminist Theatre* played evenings (Mondays) of plays and songs for several months at the Village Gate, until internal conflict broke the group apart. The actors demanded contracts for an assured share of profits and for job security. Dell'Olio felt they were trying to sabotage the presentation by being late, undisciplined and by giving ragged performances. She responded to their demands by saying she had not made any money from the show and that if they felt they no longer needed a director, they could continue without her. The group soon disbanded, but the experience proved to dell'Olio that feminist theatre was a great idea.

The Cabaret of Sexual Politics is the current presentation of *The New Feminist Theatre,* which has continued only in the person of dell'Olio, who, with two men (a composer and lyricist) and another woman perform songs and sketches about feminism. The large audience of housewives and businessmen who support the establishment theatre are the people the *Cabaret* hopes to reach. They feel that feminist theatre can work within the traditional framework and can be commercially successful.

The best known of the alternative or non-establishment theatre groups is the *It's All Right to Be Woman Theatre,* which is based in New York and which was founded in 1970. The primary objective of this group is to make women feel that the condition of being woman (not an individual woman but collective woman) is *all* right—hence, their title.

The group reserves many of its performances for women only: it has found that all-female audiences enable the evening to develop more successfully. The effect of performances on an all-woman audience is one of arousal for each spectator to new feelings of identity, solidarity and lack of competition with other women.

The powerful effect the group has on its audience is due in part to the willingness of individual members to use their own lives as the basis for the material they perform. Each theatre piece is derived directly from the life of one of the members of the group. This self-exposure means that performances are often difficult for the women involved. Their performances are often preceded by tears and near-breakdown of some of the members because of the difficulty of acting out their personal conflicts and anxieties. Performances often start late or may even be canceled because of the emotional reactions of one or more members of the group. However, the intensity of their performances as a result of the emotional involvement with the material creates a theatre experience that transcends aesthetic considerations and becomes an event that can change lives.

The quality of the actual performances varies from evening to evening. One night the performances and improvisations are "clean" and communicate well; at other times, they are sloppy and unclear. Certain pieces are not shaped well enough to hold audience attention, or to make a statement consistent with the group's commitment. To an outsider, it seems that their focus in rehearsal is not always to make the most theatrical statement but to express their feelings. Consequently, when a piece has not been sufficiently developed, its effect is diminished.

Before setting material for performance, the *It's All Right to Be Woman* group worked together for many months at consciousness-raising, movement and acting exercises. From their talks, they took particular life experiences they felt should be presented and did improvisations about them. Every member of the group functioned as director, writer, and actor; no one person stood back from the piece and judged what was working and what was not. By resisting the temptation to allow one person to assume authority and by spending long hours working through highly emotional conflicts, their work achieves a cohesiveness and power that reflects their own commitment to feminism and to doing feminist theatre.

All decisions and actions of the group are made with collective approval. In order to report on the group's activity, this writer had to meet with almost half the members—everyone who was available. When it became necessary to have the material checked for accuracy, the whole group was consulted.

The eleven women who comprise the group begin each performance by sitting in a circle, improvising music and chanting. The melodies are simple and sung in unison. They are accompanied by percussion instruments and a guitar. Their theme song is taken from a poem by Marilyn Lowen Fletcher: "It's all right to be woman, to be woman, to be woman/ A chant for my sisters, big belly, dishwasher, strong back, swollen ankles" (In *Sisterhood Is Powerful,* Vintage Books, 1970).

The audience joins the singing as they file in, either by clapping, singing or humming. The participation happens automatically; nobody prompts it, nobody insists on it.

The singing ends when one of the performers stands up and begins touching her body; when she touches her breasts, a kazoo sounds. She can touch her head or hands or arm but not her genitals. She frowns, and the kazoo goes. Her movements finally become completely doll-like, mechanical. Audience and performers sing: "Our faces belong to our bodies, our bodies belong to our lives."

Another performer stands, indicating controlled anger, then rearranges her face into an acceptable, feminine smile; then another performer rises directly in front of her and mimes putting on the smiling mask of makeup; then another performer does the same in front of her. "How are you feeling?" someone from the group asks. The performer nearest the audience sits down; then the one behind her, revealing the last, with agony on her face, "behind the smiles." They sing again: "Our faces are stunted; our bodies are blunted/ We cover our anger with smiles."

A performer then stands in the middle of the circle, and the group starts telling her: "It's not ladylike to be angry; you have nothing to be angry about; oh, isn't she cute when she's angry." She is teased until she ends with an anguished scream. Another performer says: "She's everything but angry when she's angry." The group and the audience then sing again; another performer rises and begins moving mechanically, gradually loosening up her movements to the accompaniment of women singing. With the help of the other women, she is no longer bound by social restrictions.

This first sequence of theatre pieces is done almost every performance. Following the first section, one of the members introduces the group, explains their way of working, and informs the audience that dream plays are next.

In the dream plays, a performer tells of a dream, while the other members of the group, who have not heard it previously, act it out in pantomime. A scarf is placed in the middle of the group on the floor and whoever picks it up pantomimes the part of the dreamer. The other members of the group become the characters, props, and scenery of the dream. There are no words or arranged signals between them. They then invite a woman from the audience to tell her dream; invariably there are volunteers, and the pantomimes that result range from serious re-enactment to clowning, depending on the tone of the dream. The physicalization of the dreams by the performers is almost always very clear, and the improvisatory responses are direct and immediate.

The sequence of pieces varies from performance to performance, with the group maintaining a total repertory, adding works as they are developed. A "cranky" might be the next piece. A "cranky" is a long sheet of white paper with pictures on it, something like a paper television set or a long horizontal scroll. A performer tells the story illustrated on the cranky. Gretchen's cranky is a story from her life called *Sags and Supports*. Gretchen tells the story and turns the cranky; others assist from time to time with appropriate ad libs and drum rolls. *Sags and Supports* is the story of Gretchen and her bra. Humiliated when she was told by the other kids in the sixth grade that she needed a bra, Gretchen took her sister's bra and wore it until she was able to get her own. For fifteen years she strapped herself in, the straps cutting into her shoulders. Then Women's Lib arrived and she liberated herself. Now she has been told that not wearing a bra may produce cancer in big-breasted women. Whom should she believe—the fashion magazines, the women's movement, the often-contradictory medical profession? Gretchen laments at the end of the piece: "I don't know. And now I know that I've never known."

Another piece deals with the story of one woman's love for another. Married, committed to the peace movement but with all the restrictions of middle-class life, this woman began to turn to her feminine friends for companionship and comfort when her husband went to jail for burning draft cards. She soon realized that she had always felt closer to women. Special feelings developed toward one particular friend. Their relationship blossomed into a sexual one. They felt their life was good, even beautiful, but those around them were horrified. Their friends tried to counsel them to "get straightened out," tried to make them feel their life was perverted and ruinous. The couple, however, were committed to each other and their life together. Other pieces deal with the themes of drug addiction, rape, the dependency of women on men, and the responsibility of child rearing.

The chanting that begins the performance also ends it, with songs and tableaux that are direct expressions of women's attitudes. "I, I am, I am a woman/ I am a woman giving birth to myself/ I am growing stronger." "I've been down for a long time." As the chant ends, the audience joins the performers dancing and clapping, finally forming a circle of solidarity.

Other workshops, such as the women's faction of *The Burning City Street Theatre*, are involved in developing performance material, but as yet none are giving public performances. The *Burning City* group rehearses as the Women's Interart Center in New York City; the Interart Center is also developing its own theatre group to do feminist plays.

Feminist theatre is also being developed through women's acting classes of various universities and colleges. Roberta Sklar of the Open Theatre, for example, teaches an acting class at Bard College, where students demanded a women's theatre course for the spring term, 1972, despite tremendous opposition from the male faculty and students. According to Sklar, the class sought to acknowledge they were women and "to try to find theatrical forms to express what that means." While trying to avoid the pressure of creating a performance and with the idea of exploration, the class met several hours a week but without knowing exactly where the experience would lead. The class began by asking itself: "What are the images of women that are set before us to model ourselves after?" The students then examined television commercials trying to determine the nature of the images of themselves.

The responses of the Bard College class to the material presented by individual students acted as the guiding force in trying to develop the work. Sklar believes that "women's acting classes are a form of their own, an exploratory form, a research form."

Another type of performing collective has been created by larger political women's organizations. These groups do plays only as an adjunct to political action; their intention is to make women dissatisfied with existing laws or political situations. The skits done are demonstrations of women's demands concerning a particular issue, such as abortion.

The *Vancouver Women's Caucus,* for example, was formed in 1970 by women who wanted to reach the university and high school women in the area in an effort to draw them into the fight for legalized abortion. The theatre group's main concern at the time was women's lack of control over their bodies. Their four demands were: nationalization of the drug industry in Canada, community control of clinics, free birth control devices and information, and free abortions on demand. They developed skits as needed for whatever political action was coming up. As part of the rehearsal process, they did yoga exercises, movement exercises, and body isolation work. They worked improvisationally and collectively but never from their own lives.

The first skits created were for demonstrations at the University Student Union and at the provincial Parliament in Victoria, B.C., Canada. A series of three skits formed the nucleus of these demonstrations. All three were pantomimed with placards noting place, time or characterization when necessary. The performers (all women) wore whiteface makeup and appropriate costumes.

A long, large piece of cardboard with holes for faces and hands and with doctors' uniforms painted on in black was the setting for one abortion skit. A placard read "Medical Review Board" (the reference was to the Medical Review Board of each hospital that had to pass on a woman's application for abortion; at that time, very few applications were accepted). Women in different stages of pregnancy would come in asking for a legal abortion, such as a child who had been raped; she would be refused. Then a poor woman dressed in tatters would enter. A woman with measles might be the next; she, too, would be refused. Then a woman would offer the cardboard wall of doctors a bribe. She would be accepted.

Shift after Shift was aimed at the working woman. A woman would come on stage wearing several layers of clothes. As she went to each of her "jobs," a layer of clothing would be removed. She would go to work, come home, prepare dinner, feed the children, dress for her husband's return, put the children to bed, feed her husband, wash the dishes, do some cleaning, go to bed, and, finally, entertain her husband in bed.

The third in the series was another abortion skit. It emphasized the various ways women try to rid themselves of an unwanted fetus, i.e., internal medicine, a coat hanger, a vacuum cleaner, an illegal abortionist, a "medicine man."

Musical instruments, drums, bells and rattles were used to tie the scenes together and to emphasize rising tension. Songs were an integral part of the show with sometimes as many as ten songs for each series of two or three skits. The lyrics usually reflected the theme of the skits: "Women in chains for a long, long time/use the body, ignore the mind." Banners, used for the demonstration, were also held up during the performances: "One out of every four women over twenty-five has had an abortion"; "2,000 women die each year of illegal abortions" [Canadian statistics].

The group's *Red Tape* skit was particularly meaningful for the Canadian audience because of the bureaucratic procedure necessary for obtaining an abortion. In the skit, a woman goes to a doctor, who ties one of her hands with red tape. She then goes to the Abortion Committee, with each member of the committee putting a little more red tape on her. Then, she goes back to the doctor for more red tape. By the end of the skit, she is completely covered with red tape but is still pregnant.

These skits and several similar ones were used by the *Vancouver Women's Caucus* during a large cavalcade in 1970 from Vancouver to Ottawa to demonstrate at the Canadian Parliament. The theatre group headed a caravan that took ten days to travel across the country. They stopped in a different town each night and performed their skits.

When the caravan reached Ottawa, on the Saturday before Mother's Day, 1970, their tactics changed from performance *per se* to theatre of disruption. Entering the Parliament building as visitors to the gallery, they waited until the ministers began to speak; then they hurled down banners reading "We are furious women" and began talking loudly about the injustices of the abortion laws.

That evening, they crashed a police barricade and paraded in the streets with a black coffin, symbolizing the deaths of thousands of women from illegal abortions.

On Monday, many women in the movement obtained passes to Parliament and seated themselves on the four sides of the gallery. At 2:30 p.m. a demonstration began outside and inside the Parliament building. The women inside chained themselves to their seats and stood up one by one around the gallery, delivering speeches about the horrors of the abortion laws. Pandemonium broke out in the House when guards began dragging the women away, pulling their legs out of the chains. The women were forcefully escorted out the back door, where they were greeted by journalists and television cameramen.

The theatre group finally disbanded in 1971, mainly because their demands about abortion were met—abortion is now obtainable in Canada through the hospital abortion committees, and very few women are refused.

The Women's Guerrilla Theatre of Los Angeles is another group that has used theatre to make their political demands felt. Sandra Lowell, in *Women: A Journal of Liberation,* Volume 2, No. 1, says: "As for people who say that theatre and politics don't mix, that theatre is ineffectual, that is bullshit.... theatre can open people up to new experiences. It can bring out feelings that straight propaganda might only negate. Remember, we are not competing with the other media, we are creating our own."

The women's guerrilla group has created two scenarios called *Elevator Plays.* They require for production an office building, an elevator, bosses, and dissatisfied secretaries. *Elevator Play No. 1* suggests actions such as women storming each elevator, carrying steno pads and other personal belongings, and announcing that they are quitting and telling why: "The boss yelled at me again," "I can't take all the drudgery," etc. At the ground floor, the women rush out of the elevators shouting: "I can't take this crap any longer," burning their steno pads. A lower-keyed version, which was actually performed, had performers discuss grievances and miseries about typing and being underpaid and under-appreciated all the way down in an elevator in order to get other women and bosses thinking and talking.

Elevator Play No. 2 offers the option of getting the group into as many elevators as possible, stopping at each floor and singing whatever song fits the occasion, usually to a well-known tune such as "Three Blind Mice." Suggested lyrics: "Let your husband/ Do half the housework/ He can take care/ Of the kids, too."

Although performing collectives represent the major kind of women's theatre group, women playwrights at Westbeth have formed a collective and are producing their own plays. The group, *The Westbeth Feminist Collective,* was originally formed as a tenants' association to bargain with the landlords at the Westbeth Artists Residence on the west side of Manhattan. But the group eventually turned from political action to doing readings of their own plays. Actors—male and female—were called upon to do readings so that the playwrights would have the opportunity of hearing their work performed. Although feminism was never discussed as an issue in early meetings, the group's own consciousness became apparent. Members began writing plays about specific themes, such as rape. The writings about rape showed a common attitude—that of the desire to seek revenge for the ultimately unavengeable crime of rape.

These works developed into an evening of women's plays entitled *Rape-In*, produced in the Assembly Theatre in May of 1971. The playwrights themselves assumed responsibility for the production. They hired the actors, directors, and production people. The progress of the work was slowed repeatedly by problems with the directors. Since they were working within the traditional theatre structure, with actors and directors interested in their craft, not in the cause of feminism, they were unable to achieve a common viewpoint for the production. Only the thematic content of the plays made the evening one of feminist theatre.

Gwen Gunn's play, *Across the Street*, illustrates the rage women feel about the humiliating comments made by construction workers as women pass work sites. This time, the rage was turned into effective action: "She" walks by, is yelled at, stops to chat and invites "him" up to her place to fulfill his previous suggestions. As he tells it afterwards, ". . . they had an orgy on me. They used me in disgusting ways, like I was nothing."

Sally Ordway's *Crabs* has the woman remain true to her role of giver— "She" gives him the crabs that she got from his best friend. She also gives him grief about the arrangement between them that calls for her to type all day so he can be a brilliant filmmaker.

There's a Wall between Us, Darling is about a woman's revenge again— this time she cannot forgive him for ruining her career, so she ties him up, gags him and walls him in the basement with his dog, pipe, books and slippers.

Women's ultimate defenselessness against the rapist is one of the themes of Dolores Walker's play, *Abide in Darkness*. Esther's neighbor comes for a get-acquainted visit but is put off by Esther's over-anxious behavior: "I am sorry. I did not mean to be rude, asking who you were; but since IT happened, I am very careful. I do not have a phone; I do not use this as my mailing address." Esther, during their talk, adds more and more clothes, until Ellen pleads errands to do and leaves. Esther calls after her; then opens the curtains, strips down to her slip, and waits. "It is my imagination. It is always my imagination . . . Nothing is happening. Nothing at all," she says. The sound of breaking glass is heard.

After the experience of *Rape-In*, the Westbeth playwrights group began to work more and more on purely feminist material, developing into a true collective. This collective works in a non-authoritarian manner, refusing even to appoint a coordinator or spokeswoman for the group. Their common goal is not to make anyone famous but to develop individual crafts through a commitment to feminism and to the group.

Besides endeavoring to work within the non-authoritarian group structure as an expression of their feminist convictions, the playwrights are also exploring the female consciousness in their scripts, trying to develop serious, three-dimensional roles for women. An indication of the slight treatment that women have gotten in the past is a remark made to one of the Westbeth feminists, Gwen Gunn, by a playwriting teacher. Gwen said she automatically wrote plays about men when she first began writing and was specifically advised to do so because "men can do so much more." Women's liberty to do more is at the heart of the feminist struggle, and the playwrights are reflecting this change by finding themselves and their sisters to be fascinating, complex subjects for dramatic exploration.

The Westbeth playwrights next presented *Up! An Uppity Revue* at the Westbeth Cabaret in February and March, 1972. They found a woman to direct the plays; she used male and female actors.

The revue explored the various roles that women are forced to play in life. Within the sketches, several of the actors switch back and forth from the created character to their own reality. In *Family, Family* by Sally Ordway, the

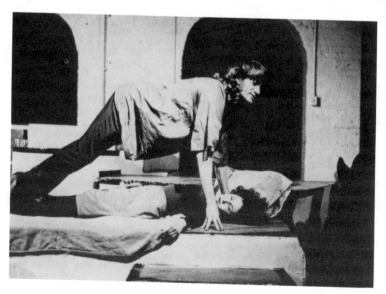

A scene from the *Westbeth Feminist Collective*'s evening of plays, entitled *Up! An Uppity Revue*
(Photo: John Kelly)

nuclear family is brought on stage, but the men and women take opposite roles. Their interaction documents the daughter's growing up: "Don't whine; it's not ladylike; your brother gets the wishbone because he's a growing boy"; "Boys love a good listener; don't let them know you're smarter than they are." The actor playing the daughter finally gets fed up with the asinine things he has to say and steps out of character to denounce the part.

In *Interview* by Dolores Walker, a woman comes in to be interviewed by a machine (performers). She is qualified and could do the job, but she wants to be a chief someday. Sorry, the machine says, it can't use her. Another qualified woman comes in; she began as a Rockette and worked her way "up" to being a secretary and would, besides being sexy, be right for the job. She gets the job offer until she says she wants to advance. Then, no job. The third woman—middle-aged, a Ph.D.—could do the job and has had much previous work experience; in fact, she designed the machine. No job for her—unless she wants to be the office mother. She agrees and is hired.

The individual sketches are joined together by singing, led by two women with guitars in the back of the house. By the end of the show, the whole audience is joining in the women's folk songs.

Although exploration by the revue of the changing roles between the sexes gave the audience an insight about what it is to be a woman, the sketches did not live up to the collective's intention of developing three-dimensional roles for women. The emphasis in the pieces and the production was on entertainment through short sketches that make their point with humor and theatricality, consistent with the revue form.

The polarity that exists between the theatrical emphasis of the *Cabaret for Sexual Politics* and the Westbeth group and the psychological/socio-logical emphasis of the *It's All Right to Be Woman Theatre* is linked to the degree of acceptance by each group of the traditional theatrical framework. The groups that are seeking new forms to reach women and are committing themselves to an internal structure expressive of their consciousness tend to affect the audiences more intensely than the groups whose framework and commitment is to feminist theatre within traditional forms. The groups that express their feminism through humor and lightheartedness make an important intellectual and verbal statement but they do not have the power of engagement that the often erratic *It's All Right* group has, which is a result of its more complete commitment to express a new awareness through new theatrical styles.

Note

1. This quote was taken from "The Founding of the New Feminist Theatre" by Anselma dell'Olio in *Notation from the Second Year: Women's Liberation,* 1970, p. 101.

18

Foreman's *PAIN(T)* and *Vertical Mobility*
(1974)

Kate Davy

> *All of my art is concerned with the problem of consciousness, the structure of consciousness, and specifically, with the problem of making art.*
>
> Richard Foreman

In order to deal with an artist's rehearsal techniques, it is necessary to discuss a particular system or process; in Richard Foreman's work process is important. Foreman has been producing his plays for five years and, although there have been changes, his esthetic and style have remained distinctively constant; partially because he is concerned with the problem and process of making art. He wants the spectator to notice not only the art that is made but also that art is being made. "The realm of art is trying to be clear about its materials which in turn, as you watch it, helps you to be clear about your own watching."

Hence, Foreman's art is basically self-referential in that it treats as subject the process of art. This involvement with process can be seen in the making of his two recent works *PAIN(T)* and *Vertical Mobility: Sophia = (Wisdom) Part 4*. The plays were performed in repertory during April and May, 1974. Because there is no collaboration in this work—every aspect of Foreman's art is done for himself and by himself—his creative process includes writing the text, designing and building the setting and props, recording the tape score, directing the rehearsals, and conducting the performances.[1]

Richard Foreman during a rehearsal
(Photo: Kate Davy)

The three-month rehearsal period commenced in a large loft on January 2, 1974. Rehearsals began promptly at 7:00 every weekday night and continued, without interruption, until 10:00. One play, whichever required the most attention, was rehearsed on three successive nights, and the other rehearsed on the remaining two nights. Occasionally Foreman rehearsed scenes from *PAIN(T)*, involving only two performers, on the weekends.

Because Foreman is not concerned with a virtuosity of acting, he prefers to work with nonactors and uses anyone who wants to participate in his productions. There were nine performers in *PAIN(T)* and eight in *Vertical Mobility*. Four people performed in both plays, and three of these had worked in Foreman's past productions. There were four performers in each play that were not written into the script, and Foreman referred to them as "crew people."

At first there seemed to be nothing extraordinary about Foreman's rehearsal procedures; he passed out scripts to the performers, assigned the speaking roles, and began what appeared to be traditional blocking rehearsals. The rehearsal time for *PAIN(T)* and *Vertical Mobility* was entirely devoted to placing the performers on stage, because for Foreman "placement is nine-tenths of the staging." However, his staging approach and the process involved in his placement is quite different than that of traditional theatre, as well as that of other experimental theatre groups.

The approach is different partially because, in addition to staging the script, Foreman stages the process of writing. "I'm basically interested in staging what's going on in my head while I'm writing the play." Although he is most often described as primarily a visual artist, he personally feels that his scripts are complete and self-sufficient. The words of the text do not function as mere background for the visual placement of the performers but are an integral part of his staging of how the mind operates when writing a play.

When he writes, Foreman thinks about the "kind of room" and the "feel of the space" that the play exists in. He sees the props and other things in the room and "the activities of the body." He does not think of the characters' personalities or faces, because "I really think they are all me." The characters are shades, "like De Chirico figures with the faces wiped out," that come and go in his consciousness. In one line, a character may be a "real flesh-and-blood Rhoda, who is someone I know, saying a real thing to me" and in the next line "Rhoda may become an echo, sort of a memory in my mind, of a certain aspect of the woman." Often, a line spoken by a character is actually Foreman's reaction to the line he has written.

Voice: Oh, it says what happened to Max's red feet.
Rhoda: —Why am I thinking about it now.

Vertical Mobility

Foreman's texts are very personal and self-referential, because they are a documentary of his consciousness in the act of writing.

The Space, Setting, and Props

> *Theatre is about the text and the performer relating to the given architectural space. That's where the key to my performances is.*
>
> Richard Foreman

Vertical Mobility and *PAIN(T)* were rehearsed and presented in the same large, rectangular loft. The space was divided across its width. An audience seating section (bleachers) was placed behind and between two poles at one end of the space, with the stage area directly in front of it. The spectators viewed the stage in a traditional picture-frame arrangement, with the two poles providing a proscenium. These two poles were architectural features of the actual place: the loft. When building the setting, Foreman takes the play's space and superimposes it on the architecture of the given, actual place. He builds the play's decor so that the actual place shows through. Hence, both places are evident simultaneously and overlap each other. His intention is to clarify the space so that when a performer is placed in a specific position, the spectator can see exactly where that body is in spatial relation to both the setting and the theatre/loft. "Rehearsal is all a matter of placement in context. The crucial thing is making each moment completely clear."

Foreman thought originally that *PAIN(T)* would be staged in a very unorganized "gym-like" atmosphere, where the spectator could see the sets for *Vertical Mobility* shoved up against the walls. When rehearsals began, the *Vertical Mobility* setting had already been designed and built, while the *PAIN(T)* setting, except for a few movable set pieces, had not been designed. Foreman soon decided that *PAIN(T)* needed a setting of its own; it was based on the *Vertical Mobility* setting and took shape during the rehearsal period.

Although *PAIN(T)* and *Vertical Mobility* had different designs, basic characteristics were common to both; one or two dominant colors were employed; walls, set pieces, and furniture were generally placed at right angles or parallel to the audience; the space was changed from shallow to deep by using curtains or flats placed parallel to the audience; and finally, the space was redefined several times throughout the performance by the placement of set pieces and the positions of the performers.

During the rehearsal period, many set pieces and props were invented and added to the basic design. Foreman is not a skilled carpenter, and yet he

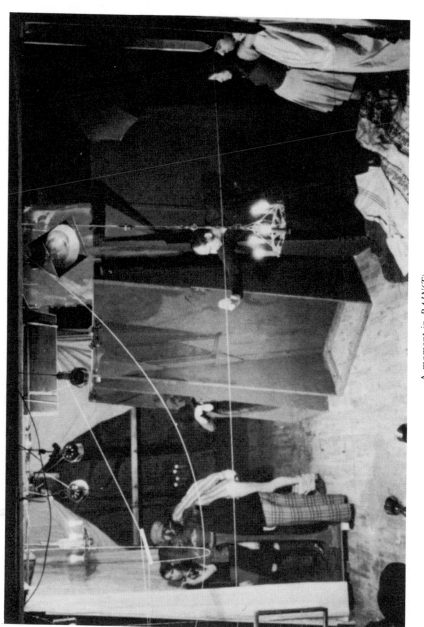

A moment in *PAIN(T)*
(Photo: Kate Davy)

built most of the setting and props himself. "I want everything to look as if I myself made it." Whether or not an object appears slick and professionally built does not concern him, because he is involved with the process of building. When he makes a bed or a wall, he wants the spectator to notice how they were put together and just what decisions were made in the building process.

In all of his technical work, Foreman aims for *bricolage*. The term *bricoleur* is used by Lévi-Strauss to define a kind of handyman who invents in the face of specific circumstances, using whatever means and materials are available. Before and during the rehearsal period, Foreman devised several uses for a large quantity of white sheet material. It was used to make the curtains that comprised the basic setting, and it covered the long narrow table, pyramids, and other objects throughout both plays. Rhoda wore it as a headdress that trailed on the floor. It was used to make long, draping flags, and to cover performers lying on the floor. In *Vertical Mobility,* a ghost costume, a toga, a nightgown and nightcap were made from it. A stage direction at the end of *PAIN(T)* read, "Enter people under white sheets." These costumes resembled Ku Klux Klan outfits with tall, pointed hats and masks, all made by Foreman and from the same white material.

The Placement Process

> *While the texts are carefully written, the*
> *rehearsal process is a trying of every*
> *conceivable alternative to make the text*
> *say what I think it secretly wants to say.*
> Richard Foreman

Perhaps the most distinguishing feature of rehearsals was the meticulous attention to, and accumulation of, detail. Foreman controlled every aspect of the work. The performers neither improvised nor initiated activity. The director did not explain to them why it was necessary to carry out an activity in one way rather than another; they seldom asked questions and rarely suggested solutions. He expected of the performers only that they write down all their actions, positions, and pauses; memorize them; and carry them out as precisely as possible. Often what seemed to be an instruction to a performer— "Register how the word relates to the wait (pause)"—was actually Foreman in the process of thinking out loud or talking to himself. His staging process is closer to that of an artist working in private—painting, writing, or sculpting— than that of a theatre director.

The rehearsals are rather austere and can be very tedious for the performer, because Foreman's placement process involves rigorous attention to the most minute details of staging. He works until every moment is completely clear in the context of the piece. Basically, placement involves the careful blending of three fundamental elements: (1) content—the implication of actions and positions in relation to dialog and the functioning of the consciousness in the process of making art; (2) space—the actual place the piece is performed in and the designed space of the play; (3) performers—the physical relation of the performers to all the visual elements combined. "My task in making art is to make my art reflect everything that I have experienced—it all should be there."

For the most part, Foreman's instructions to the performers were simple and direct. Often he would demonstrate how a certain position should look or how an action should be done. He instructed them to deliver the lines flatly and in a normal speaking voice. No attempt was made to project or interpret the lines. Occasionally, in order to inject a moment of color, he gave a performer a specific way to deliver a line, telling them to do it like "a school teacher scolding a child" or "in a sing-song manner."

Foreman's placement procedure resembles that of a painter: "I tend to think in a very frontal, picture-plane way." Many of his visual arrangements are composed of pictures and tableaux that emphasize the two-dimensional picture plane. When he staged the first dance sequence in *Vertical Mobility*, he arranged four performers standing next to each other, a few feet apart, in the same plane across the stage, facing the audience. A second row of four performers was positioned in the same manner a few feet behind the first row. Foreman paced out the dance for the performers and described it as "a sort of Groucho Marx flapping of the arms, etc...."

The performers were to place their hands on their hips, bend their knees a little, and bend slightly forward from the waist. In this position, they all walked in unison four steps directly to their left. Then, with hands still on hips, they moved (flapped) their elbows back and forth four times. Next, they turned completely around in place using four steps, made another movement with their arms on the count of four and walked four steps directly to their right. They repeated this activity several times, moving from left to right across the stage. Thus, the dance was performed in two planes of the playing space. The dance was accompanied by music. Before he staged the dance, Foreman recorded a banjo instrumental on one channel (track) of the tape. He distorted the sound by recording the music at a slower than normal speed and by adding a sound "overlay": he recorded an additional sound on a second channel of the tape. Foreman placed the microphone close to his mouth and repeated a brief whistle on the dominant beat of the banjo music. Thus, the four dominant beats that the performers danced to were accentuated by added sound.

After a few rehearsals, Foreman made one change in this dance pattern. A couple of the performers, after performing the pattern described above two

A scene from *PAIN(T):*
"Try stuffing the word painter up your ass."
(Photo: Kate Davy)

A scene from *PAIN(T):*
"This was one version of the painting."
(Photo: Kate Davy)

A scene from *PAIN(T):*
"We each have a part of the picture we like best."
(Photo: Kate Davy)

A scene from *Vertical Mobility:*
"Oh, oh, I don't want to look at anything."
(Photo: Kate Davy)

A scene from *Vertical Mobility*:
"We are all terribly shy."
(Photo: **Kate Davy**)

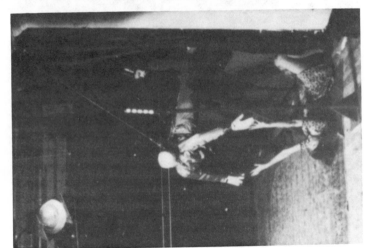

A scene from *Vertical Mobility*:
"Is this really good for people?"
(Photo: **Kate Davy**)

or three times, were instructed to take their four steps forward, toward the audience and their next four steps directly backward, still facing the audience. This was carried out in unison and simultaneously with the other dancers, who continued their movement from left to right. Thus, although the pattern was momentarily extended out of the two single planes, this movement tended to emphasize the horizontal pattern and stress the logical, deliberate division of the playing space.

Foreman described the dancers as "large hostile birds" and told them to "glare at the audience in a hostile manner" throughout the dance, "essentially asking the spectators what they are doing about this piece of art they are watching." The performer forces the spectator to notice where he is by implying with his stare "I am here, where are you?" "Having to notice where one is, is very exhilarating." This technique is related to the Brechtian alienation effect and is employed to distance the viewer from the performance. Foreman wants the spectator to savor the work from afar rather than become involved with it as he is involved with events in life.

In addition to static pictures and movement across and through the space, placement may involve the slight, subtle movements of a performer. In another scene from *Vertical Mobility,* Kate Manheim (Rhoda) performed a sequence of words and positions sitting in a chair that directly faced the audience. Foreman worked with her for several hours so that her feet, legs, torso, arms, hands and head were placed in the essential and most precise positions in relation to the words she delivered. Equally important was the direction in which her eyes were focused with each position. Each shift in position was slight but very exact. For example, Manheim said, "Weight," "Ramp," "Airplane," "Caught," "Ice," "Tilt," "Cave," "Avenue," with pauses between each word. Foreman altered the position of her body in relation to each word—feet to one side, one foot on the chair, head tilted, eyes looking down, legs spread, one hand on opposite thigh, mouth open. At one point he told her to move her lips silently and then said to himself, "This is much better, much more neurotic." Foreman explained to her that the timing had to be exact and the positions precise, because "there is a big difference in the slightest shift in position."

Originally for this scene, the chair was positioned downstage, on the right side. A performer covered completely in white material, like a ghost figure, was placed upstage, on the left side, directly in front of the rear white curtain. "It is hard to know, moment by moment, when to do something because it simply pleases you and when to do something because, whether it pleases you or not, it follows a process or pattern you think important." In the eighth week of rehearsal, Foreman moved Manheim and the chair directly upstage so that they remained on the right side but placed on the same plane as the ghost figure.

While Foreman worked with Manheim on positioning, he added other elements to the scene. The constant, monotonous "tick" of a metronome was heard, and a tape recording of Foreman's voice said, "Notice that each new position of the body implies a different structural extension of the preceding thought...." The performer wearing the ghost costume was given a bell and specific times to ring it. He rang the bell by shaking his entire body under the white material. Foreman added an artificial flower to the top of the ghost costume; later, during a run-through, he left his seat without stopping the rehearsal, walked to the ghost figure, ripped the flower off the costume, and threw it away.

Another distinctive feature of the rehearsal process was the continuous addition of "framing devices." A framing device is anything that punctuates, frames, emphasizes, or brings into the foreground a particular word, object, action or position. For example, in *Vertical Mobility* a crew person attached a string to one wall, about three feet from the floor, drew it horizontally across the stage, parallel to the floor, and attached it to the opposite wall. Max, one of the principal characters, was lying on the floor, and he raised his leg so that his toe touched the string. At a rehearsal, Foreman added a "frame" to the foot by instructing a crew person to attach a rectangular piece of white material to the string directly behind the foot—framing the foot.

Sometimes framing devices were added to framing devices and used

A scene from *Vertical Mobility:*
Max lying on the floor
(Photo: Kate Davy)

simultaneously. A picture and frame were built into the rear wall of the *Vertical Mobility* setting. At one point in the play the picture popped out of the frame leaving the frame and a square-shaped opening. Later, Sophia stood behind the wall, looking through the opening so that her face was framed. During a rehearsal, Foreman added the beam of a flashlight so that her face also was framed by a small circle of light.

Two flashlights mounted on a board, controlled from above and behind the spectators, were used to spotlight individual faces and objects throughout both performances. In rehearsal, Foreman experimented with aiming the flashlight beams while deciding which elements he wanted to emphasize. For example, in *PAIN(T)*, a performer was lying on the floor in the rear of the space with a lighted chandelier on the floor next to him. The lights were dim; there was activity occurring downstage. After several rehearsals, Foreman added a small beam of light around the face of the performer lying in the rear. This device helped to emphasize the depth of the space and at the same time bring the face closer.

A built-in framing device shared by both plays was a small mirror hanging close to the ceiling, facing the audience, and angled toward the floor. Spectators could watch the activity occurring on the floor in the reflection of the mirror. However, because of its size, the mirror reflected and framed only fragments of the total action.

Foremen experimented with many framing devices, but his primary vehicle for framing lines and activity was the tape recorded words, music, and noises that accompanied every rehearsal and performance. Although a few noises were specified in the text, most were added during rehearsals; they included foghorns, thuds, pings, boings, glass shattering, drum rolls, bells, whistles and screams. For example, Foreman added these sounds to the dialog in *Vertical Mobility:*

Rhoda: *(Pause.)* He cannot speak openly, huh. *(Pause.)* Oh, Max, I do not recognize—
Max: What.
Rhoda: the room. *A "ping" added against the word "room."*
Max: Look. *(Pause.)* It became very beautiful. Oh, Rhoda. *A "thud" added against the word "beautiful."*
All: Shhhhhh.
Max: *(Pause.)* We are now in Paradise. *A "thud" added against the word "Paradise."*
Rhoda: I know it.
Max: *(Pause.)* Is it beautiful enough.
Rhoda: No. *A loud "No!" added immediately after Rhoda's "No."*

Often noises were added to provide cues for the performers. At one rehearsal, Foreman told them, "For the change (in position) I'll put in a boing." Until he got around to recording the sound, he shouted "cue!"

Eventually, his shouting became part of the piece, and the "boing" was never added. Several times during the performance, Foreman shouted "cue" from his booth behind the bleachers.

For the most part, the tape-recorded words and speeches in both plays were not written in the text but were improvised and added during the rehearsal period to clarify sections that Foreman felt needed explanation. Most of the voices were his. For example, after a few weeks of rehearsal, Foreman added a tape of his voice to the beginning of each play: "This play is about making art (pause) from a certain energy (pause) which most people use (pause) most of the time *(PAIN(T))*," and, "The play focuses on Max who has given up writing...*(Vertical Mobility)*." At several points in *Vertical Mobility*, Foreman added, "The important word is...showing." The "important word" would change with each repetition depending on which word Foreman wanted to bring to the foreground.

The tape allowed Foreman to interrupt the performance and address the spectator directly. "It's like sitting there next to somebody and saying, 'Look, don't you see this?' and 'Are you overlooking that?'" He continued to add to the tape recording throughout the rehearsal period, and, because he wanted the spectator to understand what the plays were about, many of the tapes took on an "explaining" function.

Some did not. Foreman rarely did any technical work during rehearsals that did not directly involve the performers, but at one *PAIN(T)* rehearsal he gave the performers a five-minute break while he recorded and made a "tape loop." He placed the microphone against the outside of a large glass bowl and threw two pennies into the bowl, against the side. When the sound was recorded, he spliced the end of the tape together, making a loop. This loop ran continuously between the two reels of a tape recorder and was used to repeat the sound in a rhythmically precise way.

While *Vertical Mobility* evolved gradually and without major changes in the setting and text, *PAIN(T)* sustained radical changes during the rehearsal period. Foreman tried a different approach to staging each scene almost every night. By the end of the fourth week of rehearsals, he was at a peak of vacillation with the piece. When he came to rehearsal he told the performers that he was going to try some experiments with the fifth scene. The scene involved Rhoda and Eleanor positioned on the bed. The stage direction read: "Now both on a high, rolling table, each head at a different side, legs together and overlapping." The bed was placed center and parallel to the audience, a few feet from the front row, making the space very shallow and crowded. First, Rhoda and Eleanor were to say the lines through long, narrow, cardboard tubes. Foreman watched this for a few minutes, said, "This is no good," and eliminated the tubes. He added music and instructed the performers to look at each other when saying the lines. Next, he discarded the

A scene from *PAIN(T)*:
Rhoda and Eleanor on the bed
(Photo: Kate Davy)

music and told them to look upstage and deliver the lines. Finally, when nothing appeared to be working out, he said, "There is something about these positions that doesn't make sense with these lines." He changed it all again, deleting many of the lines from the text. At the next rehearsal he said, "I've been doing my homework and have finally figured out how to deal with the second part of this play." He added the lines that were deleted at the previous rehearsal, changed the position of the bed, and worked on the scene again. It wasn't until the seventh week of rehearsal that *PAIN(T)* began to take shape and appear as it would in its final form.

Because the setting was not complete when rehearsals began, the placement process was affected by the adding and subtracting of both large set pieces and props. After a few rehearsals, Foreman added a tent structure, shaped like a tower and made from the same white material mentioned earlier. It was hung from the ceiling and extended to the floor with an opening so that a performer could stand inside of it. He tried different ways of using the tent, but eventually it was eliminated and did not appear in the final production. Since it was always true that performers were placed in strict relation to set pieces and props, the placement of performers was restaged if an object was added or discarded.

Individual performers also had an effect on the placement process. For example, the performer playing Ida in *PAIN(T)* was replaced by a different performer mid-way through the rehearsals. Positions were changed somewhat because of the visual difference between the two people. This was true partially because, with the exception of a few deliberately constructed costumes, the performers wore the same clothes in performance that they wore every night to rehearsals. Hence, the colors a performer usually wore affected the way Foreman placed him in the space.

In rehearsal, Foreman works solely to please himself rather than a prospective audience. "Most theatre is built on people trying very consciously to manipulate the audience's response. I'm certainly not trying to do that. Really, I'm just trying to make an object that I'll end up loving." Along with the work of many other artists, his pieces have been labeled "experimental theatre." An experiment is defined as a test, trial, or tentative procedure carried out in order to discover or prove something. The experimenting in Foreman's work occurs only in rehearsal. Consequently, when the rehearsal period is over, the testing is over, and his plays are exactly as he wants them to be.

Note

1. For a description of Foreman's *Sophia = (Wisdom) Part 3: The Cliffs,* see T58.

19

Post-Modern Dance:
An Introduction
(1975)

Michael Kirby

The New Dance has been one of the most radical innovations in the performing arts in our time. Yet what we have been calling The New Dance is no longer new. It began around 1962, and *TDR* published material on it ten years ago in 1965 (T30). Perhaps it therefore would be better to use a term that already has had some usage and refer to this recent work as "post-modern dance." This at least has the advantage of making a historical point: post-modern dance is that which has followed modern dance.

In *The Rise and Fall and Rise of Modern Dance*, Don McDonagh tries to avoid this kind of thinking by juxtaposing discussions of the work of people such as Merce Cunningham, Alwin Nikolais, Meredith Monk, and Yvonne Rainer under the single rubric "modern dance." (He does refer to work from the nineteen-thirties as "historic modern dance.") What, however, are the characteristics that make certain contemporary work so different from modern dance, as it is generally known? Hoping to clarify these significant differences, we have asked several of the early practitioners of The New Dance to write about their work and the ideas behind it. The attempt has been to join observable form (what the spectator perceives) to the intent of the creator (what the dancer wants to do).

Although Merce Cunningham had some influence on this new work, he never broke completely with modern dance. He has continued to use "dancy" movements, selected for certain esthetic qualities such as lightness, smooth flow, grace, etc. In this kind of thinking, one movement looks better than another for some reason. In the theory of post-modern dance, the choreographer does not apply visual standards to the work. The view is an interior one: movement is not preselected for its characteristics but results from certain decisions, goals, plans, schemes, rules, concepts, or problems. Whatever actual movement occurs during the performance is acceptable as long as the limiting and controlling principles are adhered to.

This rejects the musicalization of movement that typifies modern dance. Although Cunningham separated movement from the actual musical accompaniment, a "melodic" flow and a musical phrasing of his movements kept the music internalized in the behavior of the dancers. Post-modern dance ceases to think of movement in terms of music.

In the discussion of their work, the post-modern dancers do not mention such things as meaning, characterization, mood, or atmosphere. As Noel Carroll illustrates in his article about anti-gravity dancers, their work, unlike almost all modern dance, is not about anything. Dance is not used to convey messages or make statements. The dancers are merely themselves, they do not personify individuals, types, forces, and so forth. This means, among other things, that they use costume only in formal and functional ways. Their clothing does not send messages or represent. Unlike Merce Cunningham in a piece such as *Winterbranch,* they never use lighting to suggest an imaginary place or to invoke a particular scenic atmosphere. Lighting functions only as illumination, not in terms of mood or effect and many of the post-modern dance pieces are done outdoors in natural light.

Leaving a performance given by Alwin Nikolais at the Brooklyn Academy of Music, a man, who may have attended because he had purchased a season ticket, was overheard to say loudly and authoritatively to the three women he was with, "Well, it may be alright, but the question is 'Is it dance?' " This question would never have occurred to a theatre person. To most, Nikolais' work is a clear example of modern dance. But some might question whether what we are calling post-modern dance is dance at all, since it eschews so many of the elements, including the musicalization of movement, that traditionally have been found in dance. The practitioners themselves probably would not care very much if their work were not referred to as "dance." After all, the distinctions between various art forms are primarily intellectual aids rather than value judgments; dance is not better or worse than other modes of performance. But the presentations of post-modern dance are concerned primarily and fundamentally with movement. One might say that movement is important, too, in the works of Meredith Monk and Robert Wilson, for example, but there the movements exists for other purposes. An actor moves to create character, situation, and so forth. This result is primary. The movement in post-modern dance is an end in itself. If a definition can be made only in terms of a continuum rather than in absolute prescriptive terms, movement is certainly the polarity around which dance focuses.

In her time, Loie Fuller also questioned the accepted definition of "dance" and increased its scope. Although movement was central to her work, some apparently felt that "dance" applied only to the human body, and it was Fuller's silks that did most of the "dancing." (Not long afterward, the Futurists were to suggest that a machine, too, could dance.) Fuller's work was at least one of the earliest examples of modern dance. Unlike post-modern dance, it did not reject the externally validated, expressive image. But it did shift the attention away from the expressive potentials of the human body and, from a creative point of view, emphasized the intellectual constructs necessary to shape the dance.

In this issue, we also include documentation on three unusual performances, none of which make use of acting. Perhaps it should be pointed out that we do not consider Kaprow's piece, which is one of the three, to be theatre. It had no audience and was not intended to be observed. It was a performance, however; three different sets of participants performed Kaprow's "plan." (In T30 and in *The Art of Time,* I explained how this type of performance—one in which the esthetic material or medium is the doing itself—could be called an Activity.) The way in which Kaprow uses rules to structure his pieces is similar to the way instructional limits shape certain performances in post-modern dance.

20

The Life in a Sound
(1976)

Andrei Serban

We attempt to create a sound—a sound which grows and turns into a cry. We try to find the energy which produces this action and to become aware of it.

I see the sound as an image. I see what is enclosed in it—a column of air trying to break open. In the effort to produce the cry I attempt to replace heaviness with spontaneous vitality. The cry becomes either an expression of freedom and awakening or a sign of imprisonment; it all depends on how the sound is controlled and directed from inside.

At the beginning of this research real calm is required. One must accept the risk of passing beyond one's accustomed realm of habitual expression. One must try to discover an image, to nourish this image with something concrete, a taste, a smell. Without ever forcing it one must allow oneself the immense pleasure of bringing to life very little known vibrations and energies, of discovering each sound as if for the first time.

This exercise, centered on the desire to free the voice, unveils an enormous field of possibilities.

Not only with words but with fragments of words, with each consonant and each vowel—every sound is charged with particular activity and a specific color. Deepening this search is like delving into the unknown. One is always afraid, and courage is needed. But if you make the commitment, you soon discover that each combination of letters gives a new meaning and each letter shapes the letter that follows. Nothing, in fact, is accidental because everything is interconnected.

We all find ourselves faced with the same difficulty in this attempt, which is to understand something that is very simple. The core of our search is to try to work as if the whole world existed in a single word and each word represented a fragment of life.

We perceive that in the theatre which uses comprehensible language, the word is used mostly to transmit something on the level of information or the level of psychology. People are not terribly interested in other dimensions of the word. When we approach an ancient language it is impossible to discern a literal meaning, but in this apparent lack of sense one rediscovers, perhaps, a greater potential for expression. In an immediate, concrete relationship with the word, the sound, one can perceive rhythms, energies, and impulses of a different order.

We know nothing about the lives of the people who pronounced these words two thousand years ago. We know nothing of the training they underwent. We do not know what their voices were like or what sorts of movements they made. Nonetheless, we are sure that this was possible: that human beings with arms, feet, and chests like our own found a way to master the invisible energy of communication over a great distance. By reading learned volumes on the history of ancient theatre or certain archeological studies, we might learn something. But the actor has the possibility, through his work, of finding that reality far more directly. Approaching this material, he tries to capture the quality of a vibration, of a sound which someone else once made. The entire research consists of rediscovering this sound, this word, of serving it by looking at what it formerly could have been.

The ancient Greek language is perhaps the most generous material for actors that has ever been written. At that time, poets felt the need to invent a poetic language to try to accomplish an enormous task: to send messages through words over great distances in a space open not only to the assembly of Athenian citizens but also to the sea, air, and the stars.

We can imagine, therefore, that these words must have carried within them a certain force and energy to make possible and sustain this contact.

When we speak ancient verse, it is not only the rhythm which comes alive but the entire imagination which begins to stir in many directions. We try *to see* the images in the sound. We believe that we become those who first pronounced the words. Hidden vibrations start to appear, and we begin to understand the text in a way truer than any "analysis" would have afforded. It is not only the imagination but our entire being which lives through the words. It is a matter of discovering the paradox that the head, the heart, and the voice are not separate but connected with each other. The entire body is a complex, sensitive instrument which must be tuned if we wish to use it. For the sound to emerge properly, it is necessary to search for and become aware of a source, to find within oneself a support which allows the sound to grow. To develop the potential for a complete affirmation. Movement and voice rediscover one another in a common effort. Gesture and breathing exist mutually indispensable as the expression of a whole.

This potential cannot be realized by means of any technique, but rather through the opening of a particular sensibility.

What is it then that touches us in *Electra?* What is its message transcending time? What does Electra say during her long lament? It is difficult to determine. Let us take a word that she often repeats: "eee." It is simply what one hears: a prolonged "e." What does this continual repetition of a vowel mean? Nothing that can be translated; "e" means nothing other than "e." The meaning is in the sound itself. The fundamental character of the tragedy can be rediscovered in this unique sound—impossible to translate.

The word is written to be experienced at the moment it is spoken, in an immediate relationship with the sound, with an infinite possibility to create moods and situations as music does. It exists on its own. It comes from somewhere—and it goes away. We sense its vibration. We hold onto it. We can try to make it vibrate inside us.

Translated by Eileen Blumenthal, in consultation with Andrei Serban

21

The Welfare State Theatre
(1977)

Theodore Shank

The itinerant "fringe" or "experimental" theatre groups supported by the Arts Council of Great Britain can be divided into those concerned solely with esthetic expression and those that aim at social efficacy. The latter can be further divided into those with "political" intentions and those with "social" objectives. There are revolutionary socialist theatre groups, often comprised of Marxists, who play almost exclusively for trade union members at meetings and workingmen's clubs, attempting to raise political awareness with respect to the worker in a capitalist society and to stimulate discussion about political problems. And there are theatre groups that do not consider their work overtly political who make plays dealing with the problems of certain constituencies such as teachers, children, old people, prisoners, women, or gays, sometimes involving them in theatrical activities as a kind of therapy.

In 1976–77 the largest Arts Council subsidy received by a "fringe" or "experimental" group went to the Welfare State Theatre, which refuses to be placed in any of these categories. (They receive 40,000 pounds for the year; each member is paid twenty-five pounds per week.) Their social objectives do not grow out of a liberal concern with social service nor a Marxist aim at changing society. Nonetheless, the director of the group, John Fox, is keenly aware of a need they would fill in the lives of their audiences. They refuse to condescend or patronize by adapting their work to specific audiences. They present the same work for children and adults, for well educated artistic sophisticates at art festivals, often on the continent, and for those in small towns and the ghettos of large cities with little education who may never have attended live theatre or an art gallery. The reactions of their spectators range from adulation to stoning.

John Fox considers much of what is done by groups with social aims as "baby minding, to keep children off the streets, but it has nothing to do with art or theatre or poetry." And much of the political theatre, he says, "is patronizing to the working class because it comes from a university intellectual position. It does not come from understanding the situation from within, but is lecturing from without." Furthermore, the audience "doesn't have to be told the landlord is a bastard, they already know it." Regarding his own work he says:

> I feel I'm totally selfish. I follow my own visions and make them concrete in a form which is accessible to as many people as possible. Nevertheless I care enormously about the audience. It's not good enough to give them platitudes. I don't want to give them easy entertainment, because most of the time all they get are substitutes for the "Top Ten," bad beer, bad food, bad radio and television. What I can do for them is to give them the very best I can make from my own head, the best possible structure that comes out of an exploration of my own psyche, often in very troubled and difficult areas. And I come back from those very personal explorations to make that vision objective, to make it accessible to a lot of people. But that doesn't involve making it thin or easy; often it is quite difficult. But I've never found an audience incapable of taking something that is difficult.

Welfare State has a conscious policy of performing for people who otherwise would not have access to theatre, but John Fox is determined that their work not be reduced by the audience. He thinks that some theatre groups dedicated to performing for culturally deprived audiences begin to focus on a social duty rather than making art. It has become fashionable, he says, for some theatre workers with social or political objectives to dismiss the artist as a "raving individualist." He believes the result of denigrating the artist and focusing only on social commitment is the loss of artistic excellence.

> John Fox: We are attacked by both the Right and the Left. The Right says we are anarchists and the Left says we should be preaching to the workers. But if we are about any kind of political statement, it is about being very strong and free individuals.

Since its formation in 1968 Welfare State has attempted to create myths and legends that can provide for its audiences the sense of mystery and wonder that they feel must have been an important part of the lives of early Britons and has been lost. They aim to create myths that unite the individual and the natural world. The performers do not create a fictional world that is separate from the real world as traditional realistic theatre attempts to do. They do not make the spectator lose his sense of self by becoming completely submerged in an illusion. Instead, they present images that are seen as part of the real world somewhat as a sculpture in a gallery is seen as an object in the real world. Welfare State has made two kinds of performances. They have made large outdoor environmental spectacles incorporating regional mythology and invented myth-like images for audiences of 3,000 or more, and they have presented small performances intended for no more than forty spectators.

In the fall of 1972, the twenty-five members of the company presented a month long performance in the form of a pilgrimage following in reverse the 150 mile legendary route of King Arthur. A procession of ten brightly decorated vehicles, ranging from a converted army rocket trailer to a hearse, made the trip, stopping along the way for the performers to present a variety of events incorporating images from the life of its fictional hermaphrodite hero Sir Lancelot Icarus Handyman Quail. Such performances were presented on the roadside, in fields, in town squares, in pubs, and in the circus tent they carried with them. Finally, having reached the Cornish coast, the company boarded a boat that took them to a waiting submarine, and they disappeared.

In May 1973, the Welfare State hero reappeared in the form of Icarus in an environment built on a disused rubbish tip on the outskirts of Burnley, a small industrial town in the north, where the company lives part of the year in their caravans. Using the entire area, which included a hill, they constructed a labyrinthine village representing evil, which was contrasted with an empty circus tent with a patterned sand floor representing beauty. The spectators were led through the outdoor and indoor spaces by Icarus who told how his airplane had crashed, how he had been taken prisoner by the inhabitants of the labyrinth, and how he had escaped. Leading the audience to the top of the hill, he pointed out several other villages which could be seen in the distance, thus relating the entire landscape to the created environment.

In October 1975, for the Festival of Open Theatre in Wroclaw, Poland, the group presented another large environmental performance for about 3,000 people, who withstood the freezing cold of the evening in an open area approximately 100 yards square near the Odra River. The spectacle included, among other images, a twenty-foot tower of fire, an eight-foot figure made of ice, dancing paper figures twelve feet tall, music, and a mummer's play. At the end of the performance Sir Lancelot Icarus Handyman Quail led the 3,000 spectators to the river, where he put a torch to the straw man that he carried on his back and put it in the river. The audience watched the burning figure float downstream until it eventually faded from view.

These events are not structured around a plot. Instead, the physical environment provides the structure for what John Fox sometimes calls "animated sculpture with music." The images and environments are usually made of natural elements, especially water, ice, fire, and earth. And the spirit is that of a mysterious fair or carnival with strange archetypal figures and images giving one a sense of a past time when mythology and legends had a real presence that impinged upon the lives of prehistorical Britons.

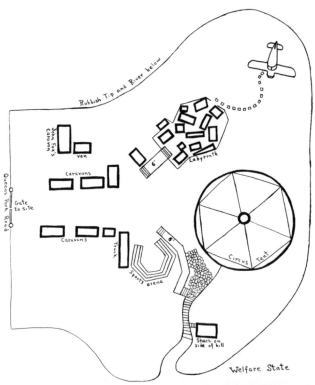

Labyrinth

John Fox's Caravan

Van

Caravans

Queens Park Road

Gate to site

Caravans

Truck

Sports arena

6'

6'

Rubbish Tip and River below

Circus Tent

Shack on side of hill

Welfare State

The Welfare State Theatre at Burnley in May 1973
Top: Labyrinthine village representing evil
Bottom: Icarus relates his experiences.
(Photo: Ted Shank)

In the summer of 1976 several members of Welfare State left to form a new group, and this brought about a change in the original organization. Previously Welfare State had a large semipermanent company ranging upward to twenty-five visual artists and musicians. Although John Fox was the director, they worked as individuals within general conceptions developed by him for each work. His control over the resulting work varied, and sometimes there was little rapport between him and some of the other artists. Since the split in the summer of 1976, John Fox and the associate director Boris Howarth have resolved to limit the permanent members to a nucleus of about seven people including a musical director, an administrator, and a technical engineer, and to add other people as specific projects or tours require. It is clearly understood, however, that they work under the director. Fox is especially interested in foreign artists because he believes that a company made up of several nationalities results in images of greater universality. For a few months in the summer and fall of 1976, six people from a Dutch group called the Idaho Company worked with the Welfare State nucleus.

Since the change in the organization of Welfare State, they have concentrated on smaller, more focused, performances. John Fox says that he became less certain the big events were achieving anything profound because the spectacle tended to take over.

John Fox: I also think that temperamentally I needed to make something that I was more able to control. With a large company of people working in different directions, I became frustrated because the work was sometimes contrary to my own personal vision. After working ten years in theatre, I wanted to make something as perfect as possible.

From the beginning Welfare State intended some of its work for smaller audiences, but the recent work has become more focused. The early work was nearly always outdoors and often the audience moved from place to place, which tended to dissipate the focus. For example, in a child-naming ceremony the audience, who were the participating children and parents, climbed a hill during the course of the ceremony. In the big spectacles, there had sometimes been a short play in one part of the environment, but again it was nearly always competing for attention with other constructed images as well as the natural environment. Their most recent work is performed in a white canvas enclosure, without a roof, about thirty feet square, which seats a single row of spectators in the shape of an "L" on two sides of the acting area. The enclosure is intended to be set up outdoors where, through a large window-like opening in one canvas wall the spectators can see an actual landscape that, like the sky, becomes part of the work.

The white enclosure is only one of several discrete units intended to comprise a large environment somewhat like a fair with several sideshows. One or more of these can be set up in an open place such as a park, playground, field or vacant lot, creating in the community an interest and suspense somewhat like that of an old-time circus coming to town. In addition to the white space, an environment called *The Secrets of the Iron Egg* has been built inside an enclosed nine-ton truck trailer approximately 10 feet by 25 feet. One side of the trailer is covered entirely by a large painting depicting in detail three strata of fantasized archeology. The lowest level is filled by the skeleton of a dinosaur-like beast. The middle level is a wasteland of industrial buildings and smokestacks, and the upper level shows a lush jungle surmounted by a spaceship. Inside the trailer there are display cases with tableaux relating to a story about the appearance in the countryside of a huge iron egg. The environment inside, described by John Fox as "a confused chaotic hell," provides a sharp contrast to the pure simplicity of the white space. Other elements being built are a ghost train that will travel through the fair-like area where the enclosures are set up and a food tent where exotic food will be served. Between these structures will be a courtyard that might be used for dancing.

The Secrets of the Iron Egg is a kind of prolog for a cycle of short plays called *The Island of the Lost World.* Each of the stories comprising the cycle is self-contained but related to the others by theme, atmosphere, and iconography. The group considers it an "epic cycle" that "reaches towards a full and modern iconography." The six stories developed so far are intended for presentation in the white space. The number of plays presented at a performance varies, and the order depends upon the circumstances. For example, if they expect an especially rowdy group of young people, they do the most frightening play first, which, according to John Fox, terrifies them and makes them attentive. When the entire cycle is complete, it will include twelve plays of about fifteen to twenty minutes each.

The great majority of Welfare State performances are for people who live in small towns or in the ghettos of large cities—people who have had little, if any, experience with the arts. Often the performances are sponsored by local community centers, and under these circumstances most of those who attend the performances are of school age. The attitude of these children at the outset is often aggressive and sometimes violent.

John Fox: The young people have so much energy that is completely unfulfilled. And the parents have had very little choice over their own lives and are working at jobs that are very dull, which leads to apathy. So you have energy from the children and lack of control from the parents. It's clear that if energy is not channeled or allowed to be creative it'll become violent, because violence is the only form of personal creativity they know. The first act of any creation is to destroy the existing situation. When you see the environments that people

Painting on trailer used in *The Secrets of the Iron Egg*
(Photo: Roger Perry)

are put into . . . In Glasgow, for instance, there is a high rise of flats and immediately next to it a chemical factory which for eight years has been pumping out toxic fumes. We tried to rehearse in a space a hundred yards from the flats and we couldn't because we were puffing and spewing from the fumes.

Welfare State had worked for a week in the Denistone area of Glasgow during August, 1976. John Fox says that their fourteen performances of five plays from the *The Island of the Lost World* cycle seemed to be the only distractions. There were no cinemas, play spaces, or community centers. During the week, they were stoned several times, a car window was broken, and three of their bikes were stolen. Even the children who became "trusties" and helped patrol the Welfare State camp lied, stole, and cheated as a matter of course. Children of seven were seen drinking whiskey, and one of the "trusties" casually burned his sister's arm with a cigarette.

John Fox believes that their performances often release the energy of the children, who lack any other activities on which it can be expended. It is similar to the violence that happens at football matches where so much energy is released that it cannot be controlled.

Our society is about curbing energy, brainwashing people, manipulating them so they will be good factory workers—so they will go to the factory and work eight hours a day without any pride at a mindless bloody job when they could be enjoying themselves—and so that they will buy the crap that the factories produce. But you cannot forever suppress human energy. I don't think we set out with the intention of releasing energy, but we live in such an energyless society, a death culture, that if you do anything with vitality, if you project energy as we do, it's bound to release energy because people suddenly discover something they have been without for years. I think it's inevitable, because we do our work with spontaneity and belief and conviction. Any group of people who are able to be free, who aren't inhibited or jumped on or oppressed, are able to have those qualities.

However, John Fox believes that, for the many people in their audiences who are not free, the performance or procession or football game comes to an end and they have no way of fulfilling the energies that have been released except in a violent upheaval.

In September, 1976, performances of plays from *The Island of the Lost World* cycle were sponsored by a community center in Halewood, a town of about 25,000 in the north of England where a Ford factory is the principal employer. On Tuesday (September 7) Welfare State set up the white canvas enclosure in an open area of the town and were immediately troubled by children. The first performance was scheduled for Wednesday evening, but on Wednesday morning rocks were already being thrown and there was danger the canvas could be ripped and children hurt. They took down the enclosure and decided to do only processions in the streets, beginning at 5:00 that afternoon. By the time they had done three processions with breaks between them, the children were becoming dangerous. Rock throwing became more frequent, they were clinging to the back of moving vehicles, there was an attempt to steal a Welfare State bicycle, one of the children was hit by a frustrated member of Welfare State and an argument ensued with the child's mother. It was decided that processions were not a good idea as they were raising energy and giving the kids expectations that would not be fulfilled by performances. So they decided to perform away from Halewood and bring the children to the performances by bus, sixty at a time.

On Thursday it was beginning to rain. The group dispersed to find a new site. Near Burtonwood, ten miles away, the discovered a nearly deserted U.S. Army base, where they set up the white canvas enclosure inside a warehouse. Their first performance took place on Friday evening, and three more were given on Saturday afternoon and evening.

Welfare State audiences are always greeted in some fashion at the entrance to the area. For some productions, the Welfare State band, including most of the company, meets the arriving spectators at the entrance gate. At the U.S. Army base, the bus loads of spectators from Halewood were met outside the warehouse by a member of the group dressed in a seedy old-fashioned black tuxedo. The audiences consisted predominately of children between the ages of six and fourteen, but there were also some babies and adults. They were led into the warehouse where a labyrinth had been set up leading into the white space.

A Guide, with a craggy green-and-white face that looks as if the makeup had been applied with a palette knife, gestures silently with his bamboo hand for the spectators to follow him through the labyrinth. In the semidarkness, they are confronted by a series of grotesque figures and sculptures. Later a four-year-old girl was asked what she thought of the experience. She replied, "It was lovely. There was a man with a funny hand." When asked if she had been frightened, she said, "Oh no. It was lovely, he was all gooey in the face. He told me where to come." A three-year-old, holding tightly to her mother's neck, sobbed quietly during most of the first play, looking only briefly at the performance. A woman, sitting some distance from one of her charges, called instructions to him throughout the performance. In one performance, a man of about thirty-five who was there for the second time felt compelled to share his preknowledge with his friends, telling them what was about to happen, warning them and making jokes.

From the time the spectators enter the labyrinth they hear live music being played on saxophone and strung piano frames that have been removed from their cases. When the audience is seated, a woman dressed as a mythological bird appears in the window-like opening in the canvas wall and sings the song that is used at the beginning and end of the performances:

As the wind ties skeins
In the heart of a tree
So the wind
Blows seeds in the air.

As the wind folds petals
In the Lattice of bone
So the wind
Blows men to the stars.

As the wind drives smoke
To the edge of a field
So the wind
Finds fire in the sky.

The purpose of the song, says the director, is to charge the space, to define it with music at the beginning of the performance and, at the end, to defuse the space and return it to what it was.

In each of the forty-minute Halewood performances, the song was followed by the same three plays from the cycle, separated only by the entrance of a "Blue Priest" wearing a cowl, who set up or removed props. The first two plays, *King of the Ditches I* and *II*, are based on Ghelderode, but the story probably goes back to the Middle Ages. In the first, the King of the Ditches with white face, skull cap, costume of coarse brown material, and feet wrapped in rags, enters carrying a two-foot wooden boat in which there are three pilgrim dolls made of brown burlap. The entire play is a monolog by the King of the Ditches, who also speaks for the Pilgrims who are on their way to Rome. The King taunts them and tortures them with a knife, making them sing and dance. He pulls them around on their boat and finally makes "a miracle" by burning one of them at a stake. A five-year-old in the audience, sitting on the lap of a man, kept asking, rather calmly, "Is he going to cut us with the knife?" A thirteen-year-old relieved his fear by making a joke about buying a pair of "shoes" like the King's.

In *King of the Ditches II,* all of the characters are played by human performers. Two blind pilgrims enter, clinging to each other. Their costumes seem to have been collected from medieval castoffs and their makeup is grotesque. The brightly costumed King of the Ditches (John Fox), with bones and feathers for a headdress and a dried beet root for a nose, gives them advice. None of the roads leads to Rome; they are in the ditch country not having left their native land. He offers them shelter, but the pilgrims mistrust him, first thinking he is an echo; then, thinking he intends to harm them, they swing at him blindly with their sticks, hitting each other. Finally, the pilgrims step in a hoop representing a ditch. The king says,

Sue Fox as the Woman in *The House That Flew Away*, one of the plays from *The Island of the Lost World* cycle
(Photo: Roger Perry)

I can do nothing
The ditches are deep
The blind will not sin
They have come to the

The ditches are nothing
The blind are asleep
The road will not sing
They have come to the end

The final play of each performance was
described in a handout as "a lyrical but strange
work of Welfare State, this was developed by ti
subjective poetic conception by John Fox, which
catalyst. This is the scenario that the director wrote
Sue Fox, his wife, Daniel Fox, his seven-year-old sc
who were to perform it:

A man is building a house with wood. This can be interpreted
model or a full scale sculpture.
  A woman dressed in black with sequined madonna mask is crying
mechanical contrivance to make it cry. She is lighting a grass fire.
child is pushed in by the blue priest on a painted cart (very small). A v

I dreamt I was in a boat
On a sea-green sea of fruit
With a cow
And a horse
And a spotty dog's collar
And a rope that was just afloat.
I dreamt I was in a cart
On a loam black ridge of earth
With a hen
And a duck
And a tabby cat's coat
And a chain that was in a moat.

The child is pulled out.

Pierre Schwartz, who played the Man, is a sculptor who works in metal,
so he made the two-foot square house out of rusted sheet iron rather than
wood. Another member of the group, Maggie Howarth, who plays one of the
pilgrims, made plain expressionless masks—a white one for the Woman and a
tan one for the Man. (John Fox said he wanted the Woman masked so as to
distance the emotion.) The Child does not wear a mask, but his face is made-

up white. The performers made their own costumes, which, according to the director, "always come first, because until you have the costume, you don't have the image and you don't know how to move around." The costumes of the Man and Woman are dark earth colors—brown, blue, and black—and they have a rustic peasant style. The Woman's skirt has small sacks suspended from the waist in which she carries some of the props she uses in the play. The Child wears a white tunic, red tights, and a beret. Once the costumes were completed, the performers improvised in the white space. They performed it for Peter Hall, one of the composers in the group, who wrote melancholic music for the piece which was played on a soprano saxophone. Although the director had little to do with the developing of the piece beyond the brief scenario he had written, he did talk with the performers and the composer about the mood it should have.

The play is performed slowly, as in a dream, in a pensive melancholic mood, without expression of emotion by the characters, and the dialog is sparse. The Man and Woman enter carrying the rusted house, which has no floor. When they place it on the ground, it is supported by two-foot-high thin iron legs. The Man lies stretched out on the ground. Apparently he goes to sleep. The Woman takes dry grass from one of the sacks suspended from her waits, places it under the house and lights it. She lights two candles that are inside the house. From another sack she takes small white stones, each with an eye painted on it. Slowly, one by one, she places these on the floor about six inches apart in an outline around the Man's body. She lifts the house from its legs and places it over the Man's head so that the doorway to the house is like a guillotine over his neck. She places a bunch of leaves in each of his outstretched hands. The Man becomes animated. With his head still held in place under the house, he waves his arms and legs about. After a short time he lies motionless again, the Woman kneeling at his head. The Child, sitting on a small cart with his legs under him, is wheeled in by the Blue Priest. The Child, motionless, half sings and half speaks the song that was in the original scenario. He is wheeled off. Loud strident music is heard from the piano frames. The Woman lifts the house from the Man's head. The Man rises, takes the house from her, and smashes it on the ground, breaking it into pieces. From the pieces the Man makes a ship, which the Woman places on his head as a kind of headdress. The Woman picks up a pitcher. The Man sings a folk song in Dutch that has a heavy rhythm, and the Woman dances around him, spinning so that the sacks at her waist swing out. During slower portions of the song, the Man and Woman walk formally as she sprinkles water from the pitcher on the ground. The Man and Woman slowly exit, taking one step forward, a half step back, until they are out of view. The strings of the piano frames are plucked several times; then the song that opened the entire performance is sung off stage.

When the song is finished, music from the Welfare State band is heard coming from the entrance to the warehouse, and the spectators get up from their seats and go toward it. The band, playing, leads them out of the warehouse to the bus that brought them. The band continues to play as the bus departs for Halewood. As the bus drove away following one of the performances, a twelve-year-old boy shouted, "Rubbish!"

John Fox says that when *The House That Flew Away* was performed in Milton-Keynes, a new housing city populated by people who have been moved from nearby urban areas, the audience thought the play was about their relocation. "But it is about change, about a man and woman trying to make a domestic situation work, which is a universal archetype." Like all of his plays, *The House That Flew Away* derives from an autobiographical source.

> That's our job: to put into a form our own personal emotion and hide it, to make the form sufficiently objective and universal and interesting to others. The danger is you can produce sentimental cliché or emotional crap that is simply autobiographical. It must be made totally separate from yourself. That's what art is.

The play is also "about building structures for yourself which inhibit you or limit you." At the time John Fox wrote the scenario, several people with whom he had worked for a long time were leaving Welfare State. The play derives from the sadness felt concerning this change and the recognition of change in his own family as his children grow older.

> It's about a family that builds something together and then traps themselves in what they have built. The child is the force that liberates the family because the presence of the child gives them courage, perhaps because of his innocence. (We can't ignore the fact that the children are growing, that the caravan where we live is too small.) The child, having changed their lives, makes it necessary to do something.

This play, like their other work, is in part an attempt to restore ceremony to the lives of their spectators. John Fox believes that, since religion has become "moribund and decadent," the quality of ceremony in our lives has deteriorated. Religious ceremonies such as funerals have been reduced "to piped music and sleazy nightclub curtains in a desperate attempt to annihilate death, as if it doesn't exist and isn't a positive force. But if you can't treat death as a positive force, you can't treat life as a positive force." He points out that in the early church the plays presented the iconography of the believer in a form that was accessible. Now, we have no spiritual basis.

> No one knows what the new spiritual consciousness is about. We are making an iconography, symbolic parables of a philosophy which we don't know, which doesn't exist. So we make stories about transition like *The House That Flew Away*. Change is the only conscious understanding we have.

The esthetic objectives of Welfare State precede their social objectives. They are not making plays in order to accomplish a social end. However, having made the best work they can, they are determined to perform it not only for those who are already predisposed to their kind of work but for people who have little or no experience with the arts. They are not taking culture to the provinces, they live in the provinces; and they do not condescend to their audiences by thinking that Halewood will accept work that is inferior to that acceptable in London. They do not have an intentional political objective, but a political attitude is implicit in their work.

John Fox: If you choose to read it as such, there is a very clear political statement in the energy of our performances, the fact that we show ourselves open in making them, and that we are committed to our art and our lives being together. We are showing that although we are intellectuals, we work with our hands and discover that every moment of the day is different from every moment of the previous day, so we are learning and growing all the time. That is an enormously important political message in a death culture. But we do not use the techniques of a death culture, which are to make a lecture or a didactic statement about something, canonizing and fossilizing it. Instead, we are actually doing it.

22

The Theatre of Memè Perlini
(1978)

Rino Mele

After having worked with Giancarlo Nanni as a scenographer, Memè Perlini began his career as a director in 1973 with a signal work in the history of Italian experimental theatre, *Pirandello, Chi? (Who's Pirandello?)*. The production is based entirely on the relationship between light and objects. It does not interpret a script. On the dark stage, the actors move as though in a performance for themselves, hidden from the spectators, revealed only by flashes of light. It is a darkness full of phantoms—like the unconscious of the representation, like the deep structure from which emerges traces of violent struggle.

In the dark theatrical space, Perlini, from the front of the stage, works with small projectors on the magma of unknown actions. He cuts out square and rectangular pieces of light—very precise areas in which he captures details, parts of bodies, parts of objects. Moving the projectors, he follows moving figures. Light expands and contracts, goes on and off. The rectangles of light make images emerge from the darkness and tie them together. Light selects images from (and between) objects, cuts out portions of figures, articulates small details. Light creates unexpected relationships whose only bond is simultaneity or temporal succession. The light, suddenly finding an object, isolates it from its obscure context; things, characters, and theatrical objects undergo a compression—they become images. In *Pirandello, Chi?* everything is entrusted to light.

There are also fixed light sources. There are brief moments of diffused light in which one can reestablish a rapport with the whole stage. Or the stage may capsize, lit alternately in rapid succession at either side. This only proves the presence of a unitary world beyond the fragment, a world that is suddenly absorbed in darkness again.

To the fragmentary visions is added fragmentary dialog from *Sei personaggi in cerca d'autore (Six Characters in Search of an Author)*. Work was begun on that play, but it no longer exists. (However, the title, *Pirandello, Chi?*, is explained.)

There is also aggressive simultaneous musical support: a main piece by Philip Glass on which is superimposed, at times, Pink Floyd. It is a deafening musical continuum that gives the spectator a connected structure to refer to, easing the tension caused by the visual lacerations.

The operation obeys two codes: the theatrical and the filmic. A primitive kind of film is created in the theatrical space and accomplished with theatrical means for observers who are expecting theatre. In Perlini's theatrical film, the fixed lighting and the moving projectors he operates substitute for the movie camera. The actors and objects—the total space in which *Pirandello, Chi?* is performed is itself an object—are "shot" from the top, the bottom, counterlighted, and so forth. The spectator is forced to assume the suggested point of view: the changing beam of light becomes the camera's angle-shot. A character sits on a swing and swings toward the audience and away—as if zoomed by a movie camera. The rapid alternation of lights above and below the swing creates a strange vertical reverse-shot that gives a sudden depth to the entire theatrical space.

Space itself is an object to decompose. Outlines replace the concreteness of things, fragments replace the unity of objects, a multiplicity of angle-shots replaces the central perspective. This is Perlini's idea of space, and he develops it coherently in his successive works, revealing the same premises through apparently contradictory means.

In 1974, the year after *Pirandello, Chi?*, Perlini produced three works: *Tarzan, Candore giallo con suono dimare (Yellow Whiteness with the Sound of the Sea)*, and *Otello*. These three pieces appear to contradict the language of his first work, but in reality they interpret and intensify it.

Tarzan is produced in two adjacent spaces: a semicircle and a rectangle tangent to it. The first is covered with a black cloth, the second by a white sheet blown by a strong wind that lifts it and fills it. Although their passage is broken by the alternation of white and black, the actors are seen completely. Yet even when the stage is well lit, Perlini uses projectors—i.e., a useless probing on walls already too well illuminated.

The two spaces alternate in containing the actions that appear to cross them, depositing the traces of distressing violence. Among the characters are a paralytic who screams in a wheelchair, two topless girls, a small black car occupied by two quarreling people that crosses the stage back and forth, an almost totally naked man whose face is covered by a lion mask, a girl with a small umbrella burning in her hands, an asexual with a dead seagull between his teeth. Bodies either struggle with each other or find serenity in absurd gymnastic exercises.

It seems that in *Tarzan* the most important change, in relation to *Pirandello, Chi?*, is a passage from the fragmentation of objects and bodies to the fragmentation of actions. There is, however, something more important: application of the fragmentation to space. The schizophrenia of vision is transferred from perception to that which is being perceived. This will be even more evident in Perlini's succeeding works.

Yellow Whiteness was staged at Pescara for two performances; it was never repeated. It starts in an enclosed theatre made of cement—bare and low, resembling a bunker. It continues on a beach and, simultaneously, on a nearby pier, on a cement strip parallel to the pier, on a wooden platform built in the sea a few yards from shore, and, finally, on another pier, farther away, that seems the spatial counterbalance of the first one.

The action is always violent, not so much for what takes place but for the violence it suggests. A rooster is beheaded. A girl circles about tied around her waist; she unwinds herself as if escaping some danger; characters wrapped in gauze move awkwardly like astronauts. Girls writhe on the beach. Actions are disconnected, and, even though they are not extracted from darkness by light, they seem to come, by chance and without design, from a dark shapeless magma.

As it was in *Tarzan*, the theme of childhood is strongly evident. Here it is entrusted to words rather than only to images. Long stories and long verbal sequences of associations and memories create a continuous sound. It is not easy to understand the text—although one hears the screams and captures a sense of anguish, of fear. Perlini lets his actors speak the dialect of Romagna; only rarely do they speak Italian. (More and more often in future productions, he will, in addition to the dialect of his childhood, use French, English, German. In *Locus Solus* Perlini even uses Latin.)

With *Otello*, staged for the first time at the 1974 Venice Biennale, the first stage of Perlini's work is concluded. Its violence now seems to be diluted into a story or a group of stories that have Romagna as their locale, although they could as easily take place in any agricultural society. Perhaps one should not speak of violence but of the anguish violence engenders.

There are in *Otello*, as well, various spaces in which the staging occurs. There is an area covered with clods of earth in which there is an uprooted tree, a bed on top of which lie the long legs of a mannequin, and, farther away, an anvil and a table. On the left, there is a wooden cage with a chair inside. A door-window in the back leads to the outside. A large piece of black cloth covers one of the playing areas. At the center hang two enormous grills that swing back and forth, causing huge shadows.

A naked black man lights a candle at the end of a long pole and tries to stick it through the bars of the cage to strike the inside; a woman screams at each stroke of the pole. In the back, a door opens to a void of light. In front of the door, the two grills keep oscillating out of phase, creating gigantic shadows in square patterns that take over the entire space—but only for a moment. In the lighted emptiness, an old lady appears to yell out incomprehensible words. A fat man rails against the old lady. A naked woman lies next to a girl dressed in red.

With this production, Perlini begins a collaboration with Antonello Aglioti, a visual artist. Perlini now incorporates color in his inward-directed theatre, opening it toward the outside. Aglioti stands at the edge of the space using an overhead projector. The projector enlarges the colors drawn on its translucent surface and projects them on the walls and on the actors. Color appears to enhance the actions, but it is easily erased and disappears again.

The cage hit with the pole, the swinging of the grills, the voice of the old woman, the projected colors: each of the images seems to solicit the others. The screams of the fat man blend with the cries of the woman, which become louder while the shadows expand and become threatening. Suddenly there is darkness and silence, followed by the soft and distant sound of horses' hooves. The concept of nullification is very important in *Otello*. Throughout, there is a continuous falling back to darkness, the use of curtains that hide, the cancellation of characters and objects by the overhead projector.

In 1975 Perlini produced one work, staged, but never completely presented, at Chieti. For *Paesaggio N. 5 (Landscape Number 5)* he used the entire slope of a valley that extends into a meadow. The spectators sit at a long table that crosses the meadow.

There is a build-up of unrelated actions. Nuns ride bicycles downhill. A bride approaches, wrapped in veils. A group of men dressed as brides sit at a table farther away. A bride climbing a tree, a woman with an armful of flowers, a barechested youth clinging to a pole up in the air are posed, unmoving characters. Pieces of sentences are repeated; the furious iteration of words focus the attention on one figure and then another, moving it like a piece on a chess board.

The space of the valley seems to be coherent. In reality, it is continuously broken. The greenery and softness of the slope are not enough to unify the fragmentary actions. *Landscape Number 5* is another example of how the fragmentation of objects in Perlini's work has become fragmentation of theatrical space.

The performance is never finished; spectators, some of them students, invade the playing area, yelling, "Perlini, Perlini, la terra ai contadini!" ("Perlini, Perlini, to the farmers the land!")

Locus Solus of 1976 was adapted from the novel by Raymond Roussel. Set in a barren rectangular stage space its floor covered at times with sand, it is again a journey through a past (childhood) and a plunge into an ancient agricultural society that is always allaying its fears by attacking a single person, the most defenseless one. Again it is filled with violent images: three girls who aggressively stride after each other miming a sexual quarrel, a girl possessed by a sort of ferociously obscene dance, the whipping of the floor as if a body was being whipped. But here there is always a single character who finds himself facing all the others—assassins, executioners, the representatives of a crazy tribe. The choral or the tribal moment contrasts with the individual one in an obsessive, repetitive way. In one long section, for example, a long line of actors walks back and forth across the width of the stage; during each passage, a single actor remains behind, alone, and indulges in idiosyncratic and compulsive acts—scratching his hand, wrapping his head in a veil, etc. At the end of the play, the stage is empty. There is only a small wooden model of the setting itself. Perlini, sitting at his control board in front of the audience, throws stones at the model.

In *La Partenza dell'Argonauta (The Departure of the Argonaut)*, also in 1976, Perlini is tempted by the big show, the spectacle, rather than the representation. To totally autonomous music by Panni, he juxtaposes vivid colors, costumes, a particular use of lighting, and complicated and strange props; hollow rotating columns in which cellists are hidden, a rolling sphere, chairs used as crutches, a huge mask that descends from the ceiling, horses, small beds floating in the air, enormous *papier mâché* statues that close the proscenium opening only to be "erased" by square patterns thrown by the overhead projector. Perlini has found his childhood love: "My first rapport was with the circus, not theatre," he says.

In *Tradimenti N. 1 (Treacheries No. 1)*, at an elementary school in Montepulciano, Perlini uses the entire building as a scenic machine, creating a container of strange passageways and disorienting spaces—more like a game of hide-and-seek than a game of chess. The spectator moves through the building with the hesitation of the searcher who is "it," afraid to make the wrong move.

On the ground floor, the dining room is ready for supper, but the dishes are empty. A cellist sits in a chair on a table; in front of him, another chair hangs in the air. In one of the classrooms, the desks, the small chairs, and the teacher's desk all hang suspended, tied with many cords. In another long and narrow classroom, wooden planks six feet above the floor support a series of short plants such as cypresses, creating a false perspective toward the window; there, as if drawn on the sky, is (suggested by a Magritte painting) the outline of a cellist. Musical pieces become superimposed and follow each other like memories without sense from classroom to classroom.

One of the frequently used elements is string, cord, ropes. It suspends objects, holds them together, relates them to one another, indicates itineraries, sets limits. Another ever-present element is a tightly woven metallic net. It is used to mask and obscure things, like a filter. One finds it in front of a classroom door or along the floor of a hallway with a body squirming under it. It is used to cover classroom windows that face the schoolyard where some actors are rehearsing a traditional play. The whole building seems to be inside out.

Translated by Nella Carravetta

23

Notes toward a Semiotic Analysis
(1979)

Patrice Pavis

There is no question, in these few pages, of presenting methods of semiotic analysis applied to the theatre or even of completely describing a performance and its structural principles. Rather, beginning with some theoretical concepts and a montage of photographs we simply would like to develop some thoughts on a performance and its semiotic analysis and to try to find a middle ground between concrete description and abstract semiotic theory: an approach, therefore, determinedly practical *and* theoretical that could contribute to a new phase of theatrical semiotics. Following some indispensable epistemological reflections on the justification of an approach derived from linguistics and structuralism, and following the examination of general models of theatrical functioning, it is imperative that the facts and the hypotheses be verified by comparison with precise analyses and practical observations of theatrical production.

The example chosen for this comparison is *Disparitions (Disappearances)*, a work written by Richard DeMarcy, directed by the author and Teresa Motta, performed in Paris at the Centre Pompidou, then at the Théâtre de la Tempête in March and April 1979 (with A. Aithnard, Cyril Bosc, V. Esteves, D. Lesour, L. Merino, B. Spiegel; lighting by P. Rovai). The piece is a free adaptation of texts by Lewis Carroll, in particular, *The Hunting of the Snark*. Besides being very original, this production lends itself easily to semiotic experimentation, not only because DeMarcy is one of the first theatrical theoreticians to be interested in semiotics (cf. his *Eléments d'une sociologie du spectacle*, Paris, U.G.E., 1973) and it is always extremely interesting to look for traces of his thought in his productions, but especially because a purely narrative or dramaturgical analysis would take into account neither the specific nature of this performance nor its plastic and musical composition.

The Scenic Space

Seated frontally in tiers, the audience looks down onto the performance space, which contains a large expanse (230 m^2) of shallow water. This aquatic surface is not a mimetic representation of a river or a lake but an artificial pond with clearly defined limits that is used as a performance surface. The objects (tents, car, table, chairs, desks) are not at all nautical: they seem to signify chiefly by their deceptively random geometrical arrangement. This surface creates an impression of frightening emptiness, the emptiness of the white sheet of paper before the creative act, an emptiness that the performers do not try to fill with situationally motivated movements and activities. The reflections from this sheet of water are projected onto the three walls, which have been broken up into innumerable screens, positioned in different directions in order to catch the images of the reflections and the shadows (photographs 3 and 4). This space, flattened out in three dimensions, immediately suggests the metaphor of a space to be filled with visual impressions, of a polymorphous space that will have to be occupied, and of a musical score/partition into which the performance is going to flow. This musical metaphor is very quickly confirmed by the spatial arrangement of the six performers. Under the direction of the Captain, "metteur en scene" (director) and "metteur en abyme" (condenser of images) of the story, they position themselves in front of their respective implements. In a semicircle, from left to right, there are: the Baker, in front of an old sewing machine; the Butcher, sharpening his knife at a bench; the Beaver, conscientiously watering the pool of water; the Captain moving from one "musician" to another and organizing the snark hunt. The text, especially when it touches on the leitmotif of the snark, passes from one character to another, and in each case it is delivered according to a specific mode of diction, gesture or action. As in the poem by Lewis Carroll, the text is divided into eight fits ("crises") that recount the misadventures of the crew. The same mathematical division of the whole space produces the effect of a puzzle made up of words, gestures and images. Whenever the mise-en-scène centers on it, each element, visible from the beginning, merely "pushes aside" the others. Two points function as poles of attraction—the tent and the car: everything takes place as though these two objects draw all the other objects and all the action into their magnetic fields.

No performance description is ever without subjective elements that influence the fundamental understanding of the work. In attributing to the scenic space, as we have just done, the function of a *basic system* onto which the other signifying systems (text, gestures, lighting, music, etc.) are grafted *a posteriori*, we are guiding the reading of the mise-en-scène toward what seems to us to correspond to the general *composition* of the mise-en-scène in the sense that S.M. Eisenstein gave to this term: "the construction which, in the

Photograph 1

first place, serves to embody the author's relation to the content while at the same time compelling the spectator to relate himself to the content in the same way" ("La non-indifférente nature," U.G.E., p. 81). This compositional principle (the grafting of all the systems onto a *space-score/partition)* is justified by the fact that the Carroll/DeMarcy text does not "make up" an exterior referent and visualize it in the space; rather, it is the production of images that channels the energy of the performance and integrates the text as one of the scenic "accessories." The space or, more precisely, the water, functions as a mode-effector *(modalisateur)* and as a reading code; it becomes a means for the interpretation of the other scenic systems. Although, like a musical key, this spatial system remains in effect throughout the whole performance, it is not always the basic system. It is replaced at times by music, by an ensemble of gestures or by a monolog. In general, a theatrical performance presents as a perpetual dialectic of the various systems, a more or less stable *hierarchization* of these different elements. In addition to this organizing and structural principle of the space as *score/partition* (segmentation and support of the writing), there is the thematic value of the water and its capacity to produce a hypersign of which the signifier will be "water" and the signified "hunt." In all its possible forms, the signifier "water" generates an infinity of signifieds: the water becomes the place of reflections, of monsters, of the elusive, of fantasy, of writing, etc.

The Theatrical Sign

We are almost at the end of the voyage. In spite of the energetic leadership of the Captain, the snarkers disappear (the Baker), take flight (the Barrister), die (the Banker) or, like the Butcher in photograph 2, collapse. In this moment of prostration, it is possible to discern the mechanisms for the construction/ destruction of a theatrical character as well as the character's potential as a *carrier of signs.*

But, in the theatre, what is it exactly that *constitutes* a sign? At first, the semiotics of performance explained the formation of meaning by the accumulation of minimal signs (or units) that were defined as the shortest segments endowed with meaning and isolable in the scenic continuum. Currently, attention is moving away from this theoretical search for the minimal unit (too fragmenting), toward the grouping of signs according to a shared semiotic objective (or signifying function). In this way, in order to isolate the signified "explorer," it is enough here to add up the signifier "rifle," "helmet," "shorts," "whiteness," etc. Every performance reading proceeds by a back-and-forth motion between translation of the signifiers and the signifieds and attempts to find signifiers with which to corroborate the signifieds already identified. This rapid reading is done all the more easily when the spectator is put in a position where he need only pay attention to relevant signs and can

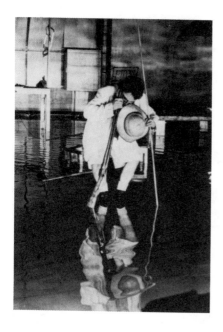

Photograph 2

group them according to a semiotic objective which is closely related to dramaturgical ends. (Here the explorer comes immediately to mind as he is identified with the narrative and thematic development of the hunt.)

To reintroduce the dimensions of its referent into the sign, it has sometimes been tempting to go beyond Saussurianism (where the emphasis is on the relationship between the signifier and the signified) into a three-term system such as Peirce's model (sign, object, interpretant) and by a trichotomy based on the relationship between the sign and the object (icon, index, symbol). The theoretical debate is far from being over, and it is futile to try to reduce the Saussurian model to that of Peirce. It is possible, however, to integrate the two semiotics in the following opposition:

1) Indexical function: this function depends upon the place of the sign in the message, on the enunciation, on the stage and the performer as sources of ostension and physical presence—in all, on the use of the sign in the general discourse of the stage. In the example of the explorer, this indexical function clarifies the necessity and the situation of this episode in the total story.

2) Iconic and symbolic function: this function is related to the object that the sign refers to in the story. The relationship to the object is more or less mimetic, it produces an effect of variable reality and fluctuates between a communication by conventional means and by referential illusion. This function is that of the structure and the nature of the sign: in the example above, it indicates the identity of the character and the reason for this metaphor of the disheartened explorer. (On these questions see F. Deak, "Structuralism in the Theatre," T 72).

Photograph 3

Metamorphoses and Networks of Signs

Here we are in the midst of the action during the second fit: Under the anxious gaze of the Captain, the Beaver, the Butcher and the Judge have just changed into pigs. This metamorphosis is one of the gestural highlights of the performance; it is the first time that the characters come into direct contact with the water. Apart from the pleasure of watching them flounder about in the water, this episode has an additional impact that stems from its placement at the intersection of several isotopies (that is, thematic and signifying conductor threads). The signification of the scene rests on a series of semantic oppositions: water-surface of the Captain/water-element of the pigs; humanity/animality; sleep/hyperactivity; uncontrollable movements/tense orchestral direction; furniture for grown-ups/children's objects; closed and protected spaces/open spaces (water). These oppositions belong to several sign systems that come together and result in a kind of synthesis or tying-up of meaning. Another example: when a fish tank full of water and heteroclite objects comes down from the ceiling toward the Beaver, several sign systems are reiterated and summarized (rectangular shape; oppositions between full/empty, dry/wet) and this ordinary object functions "en abyme" (a condensed image within an image) as the concentration and the emblematic image of the performance.

Here we have an essential characteristic of *Disparitions* and, more generally, of every performance where there is a concern with signs. Every visual sign is part of one or several networks of oppositions; it is transformed and produces new signs; its presence and its "sting" vary at different moments of the mise-en-scène, depending on the rhythm and the dynamics of the stage action. (In contemporary productions, the function of objects becomes all the more important when they are no longer related mimetically to their referent but have a syntagmatic value within the signifying systems.) With this type of image-production, the spectators have a great deal of freedom to reorganize these isotopies and to reconnect the disparate elements. Some spectators will respond to the system—water and movement—while others, for example, will follow the thematic chain of the *bird* (sea-gull, Beaver-swan, Judge-raptor, Captain-parrot, blood-red feathers, which denote the death of the Banker...). Throughout the performance, the accumulation of these scenic images and signs constitutes a sort of *visual discourse* that circulates beneath the surface of the play. Separated from the plot (moreover, quite loosely structured) and from the logical continuity of the action, this visual discourse finally becomes a visual current that captivates the attention because it is detached from linguistic-discursiveness and connected with the structure of fantasy and imagination.

Citations

After the mad chase, comes a lull. Fallen asleep in uncomfortable positions, the snarkers are quite deaf to the encouragements of their Captain, as he urges them not to give up and as he holds forth on the "five unmistakable marks" by which to recognize a genuine snark ("Fit the Second: The Bellman's Speech"). This seems like a rather unexceptional sequence but only if one fails to perceive the signifying work of the image: its capacity to comment, to repeat, to parody—in short, to *cite*.

The citation is a technique that brings together two discourses, one of which lets the other speak in order to confirm its own text. However subtle a citation may be, it must always somehow suggest the fine line that separates the original text and the text quoted. In *Disparitions* the visual citations are more like *collages* than montages: they bring together incongruous elements, heterogeneous materials, antagonistic styles. On the other hand, the plot of the piece is closer to a *montage*—repeated or parallel sequences, the development of tensions in spite of the fragmentary structure, epic progression toward the "last word" of the story. The most effective examples of citations are the *portmanteau-word* and the *portmanteau-image*.

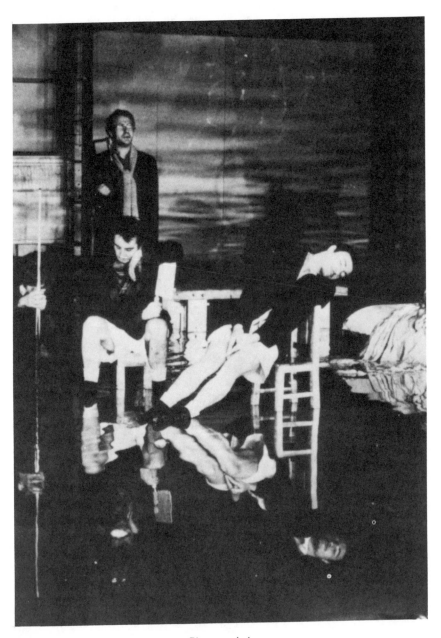

Photograph 4

Portmanteau-image

The Judge is dining in the trunk of a very official and ominous, black Peugeot 404 with the registration plate *Snark 161.* The Banker is fiddling around with the engine. This image of the car-snark constitutes the prototype of what could be called a *portmanteau-image* if we apply to it Carroll's conception of *portmanteau-words.* This theory of Carroll brilliantly foreshadows the work of Freud, Jakobson and Lacan on *condensation (Verdichtung)* and *displacement (Verschiebung),* metaphor and metonymy. The portmanteau-word is a verbal creation from two words which, when put together, produce a new sign and a new concept (snark equals snake plus shark). We know, since Freud, that the process of dreaming proceeds either by the condensation of two dream elements (by metaphorisation) or by displacement of one sign toward the other (by metonymy). In their theatre work, DeMarcy and Motta have developed this practice (without, of course, always doing so consciously or systematically), and if note were taken of all the rhetorical figures of the performance, they would show very many condensed images, extremely fertile for the interpretation of symbols (for example, the world of birds-men, of the Beaver-swan are obtained by the condensation of a horserider, a cyclist, a child and a lively small animal). This principle of condensation is especially valuable for the production of images and for experimental work with words, gestures and new rhythms.

As for the stage image created by *displacement,* it is much more rare and seems to be utilized especially in the arrangement of the plot elements. In effect, the play is conceived on a metonymic basis, a metonymy of verbal and theatrical creation. The sounds of typewriting machines that are heard at the beginning of the play, and with which the performance ends, relate to the original work now translated into text and image. These sound effects *displace* the attention from the creative act to the creation itself. In the same way, as object and as auditory leitmotif, the *snark* continually resists identification, and resists finally, therefore, our apprehension of a definitive meaning.

Considering the stage as a producer of more or less conscious images, and still trying to find a formal method with which to apprehend its signifying functions, semiotics has recourse to ancient rhetoric, to the study of dreams and the unconscious, to the analysis of the networks of images in the *performance text.*

Action, Text, Gesture: Correspondence

No matter how structured and dynamic they may be, the networks of signs, visual citations and portmanteau-images will not hold together without a cementing element to bind them. This cementing element is the *action*—not action in the sense of plot progression or the development of situations, but as

Photograph 5

a current that "unifies word, actor, costume, scenery and music, in the sense that we could then recognize them as different conductors of a single current that either passes from one to another or flows through several at one time" (Honzl). In *Disparitions,* the action is more *scenic event* than plot; it is not wholly dependent on the text but uses the text as one of its components. Apart from functioning as a support for the plot, the Carroll/DeMarcy text works in two diametrically opposed ways: on the one hand, as a metatextual commentary on the language (for example, the Baker's monolog of *portmanteau-words,* photograph 6); and, on the other hand, as a play on sounds, a verbal and poetic creation that has no obvious referent. These are two extreme limits of all theatrical discourse: a commentary external to the director and the spectator that is intimately connected with the words of the characters; a complete absence of meaning that leaves the stage open to every critical interpretation of the audience. These two extremes of theatrical discourse are both present in *Disparitions.* Sometimes a character will philosophize on his own speech act. More often yet, the text, as rewritten by DeMarcy, seems to be concerned only with its own signifying materiality; it becomes a poetic play on linguistics and sound patterns, an extended onomatopoeia. This kind of discourse seems to be propelled by the all-engulfing oral energy of the characters, who take delight in swallowing the text, in gargling with rich, repetitive sounds, in giving in with pleasure to this verbal gluttony, to these calisthenics of the mouth. The boundaries between gesture, body, diction and text are done away with, as though the whole performance—or at least those sequences where *portmanteau-words* flourish—tended, under the sign of *Gestus,* toward the discovery of correspondences.

When the Baker is reciting his poem of *portmanteau-words,* his accompanying gestures are not an imitation of the object of the discourse (which, moreover, has no definite referent), neither are they an accompanying phatic movement. The performer creates gestures, that by their fullness, their intensity, their halts, suggest the action of his discourse in a plastic manner. He brings back to the text a phrasing and a *Gestus* (a Brechtian expression) that tries to find a correspondence for the linguistic rhythm, the physical action and the plastic image. Discourse becomes physical action, and the body can be read like a text. Here we touch on the concept of correspondences. (Is there a unification of the scenic arts in the work, as in a *Gesamtkunstwerk,* or rather autonomy and reciprocal distancing of the stage systems?) It is unquestionable that a fixed code of equivalence between a sound, a color, a word and a gesture does not exist. But in spite of that, we sense that in a good mise-en-scène there is a relationship between the rhythm—or the *Gestus*—of all the theatrical elements (cf., the research of Eisenstein or of Adorno and Eisler: "Composing for the film").

This experimentation with systems of gestures is part of the more

Photograph 6

extensive framework of research into "plastic music" (Eisenstein), the relationships between pictorial composition, music and text. Many sequences of the performance are essentially nothing more than attempts to constitute signifying correspondences between several scenic systems. Even if there is never a true organic fusion of sound and meaning, image and text, we are deeply moved by some scenes precisely because they do come near to this organic fusion (the Beaver, dressed as a ballerina, riding a bicycle, accompanied by a very lyrical and exhilarating song by Neil Diamond; or the delirious Barrister taking off, physically and lyrically, to a piece of music by Purcell, etc.). The placement of the performers in the scenic space gives a clear view of the focusing, the exchanges of eye contact, the composition of the characters through the interplay of looks, glances and attitudes (photograph 6). Each performer makes all his movements according to his own given system of gestures; each actor complements the other, creating an impression of rhythmical balance.

The Discourse of the Mise-en-Scène

The most difficult aspect of the semiotic approach to performance is that of not only pointing out signs but of demonstrating their evolution and their syntagmatic arrangement, of describing the rhythm of the mise-en-scène and the "flow" of the movement from one sequence to the next. Often, semioticians fail to take into account the question of tempo (of rhythm, and even, as we have seen, of *Gestus*)—at least those semioticians who are too intent on static descriptions of a few different scenic systems or fixed moments. And yet, every theatre lover is well aware that the rhythm and the phrasing of the scenic discourse are very closely associated with the elaboration of meaning, especially in a piece like *Disparitions,* when the whole composition is so "musical." The *discourse* of the mise-en-scène is punctuated by silences, narrative breaks, changes in the mode of gesture, and, especially in this piece, by musical interludes.

The music does more than add emotional illustration to a scene, it also segments and articulates the narrative, and indicates the movement from one word to another. The eclecticism of the music (Purcell, Mahler, Neil Diamond, musical comedy, Genesis, Barry Lyndon, sound effects, etc.) suits the very variable rhythmical style, while the precision of its associational codes, including the *Leitmotif,* functions as a sort of automatic pilot for the spectator and brings about a perception of the performance at a nonverbal, subconscious level.

To describe the discourse of the mise-en-scène is also to define the mediating structure of the *performance text* and to become aware of the networks and the forms of signs. At the level of the story, the spectator follows the articulations of the narrative as well as the extratextual elements that are part of the plot structure. In *Disparitions* the discourse is structured around each fit, with one of the six performers as the organizer of his own narration and his own story. Each mini-plot includes and goes beyond the others, and in the story of the Captain-Metteur en scène-Author, all the narrative material is brought together and recomposed.

The scenic discourse also influences the parallel arrangement of the scenic systems: how they are brought together during the performance, the structuring design of each of the individual systems and, in particular, their reciprocal relationships of divergence and reconciliation.

Very often, it is the *out of sync,* the absence of harmony between parallel scenic systems, that brings about the greatest esthetic pleasure and produces meaning. The delay or the advance of one stage element in relation to the others always indicates an esthetic intention. The "tying up of meaning" happens at a focal point when a signifying system unites several isotopies (narrative, thematic, visual), or when the network of sign transformation no longer opens up into something new. In practice, fortunately, this end state is never reached because the spectator always has the capacity of combining other elements, of picking out new signs and of developing new signifying relationships. In this way, semiotics has a means of avoiding the frequent accusation that it freezes the actor, the performance space and the event into a system where everything is foreseen, where every element is semiotized — trapped in the grip of an infernal signifying machine. But in the theatre there are always those elements that are unpredictable, that happen by chance, that are non-signifying. The body of the actor, the rhythm of the diction, and — in a mise-en-scène as open as that of *Disparitions* — the interpretive participation of the spectator, vary from one evening to another. Any preconceived system where every sign is marked in advance would be quite useless. If semiotics wants to do justice to the *event-structure* of theatrical performance, it must be open to hermeneutics and to the esthetics of audience participation. Semiotics must integrate the act of reception into an interpretive circuit and allow the interpreters the freedom to make mistakes and to manipulate the signs according to their own conscious and unconscious desires. The task, however, is far from being simplified. From now on, in addition to the precise methods of linguistics, the semiotician of the theatre must develop an understanding of rhetorical stage movements, a flexible circuit model that takes into account the subjectivity of the spectator, and, finally, the capacity to apply the semiotic approach to the mechanisms of cognition and ideology. This is an extensive project but one that attracts and challenges us, especially when a work of the quality of *Disparitions* formulates — in practice — both the questions and the answers. It is an enormous prey, also, which could easily attract all the snarks in the semiotic waters.

Translated by Marguerite Oerlemans Bunn

24

Intercultural Performance:
An Introduction
(1982)

Richard Schechner

This is a brief note. The issue I've edited speaks its own language, and I don't want to introduce it with any lengthy essay or manifesto. Except to say that the world is learning to pass from its national phase to its cultural phase: the markers that are increasingly meaningful are not those that distinguish nations but those that distinguish cultures. If nations jealously defend their boundaries, cultures have always been promiscuous, and happily so.

For example, the Yaqui of Mexico and Arizona celebrate a ritual calendar that is quintessentially Yaqui. But this yearly rotation of festivals, clowning, religious observance, and other kinds of performing is made from Catholic, Hispanic, and Yaqui-pre-contact elements and the Catholic elements themselves—the story of Jesus, the Passion and Resurrection—consist of syncretic events from Near Eastern, Mediterranean, and European cultures. As with the Yaqui so with everyone: somewhere along the line contacts among peoples leads to borrowing; and often the items borrowed—things, customs, songs, dances, whatever—are so nicely knit into the receiving culture that everything seems "whole" and "native." Who remembers that spaghetti was originally Chinese and not Italian, or that the violin used as a "classical" instrument in southern Indian music was introduced some centuries back by the Portuguese?

But even at a more fundamental level interculturalism operates in the postmodern world. I mean: peoples are going to have to learn to be intercultural if our species, and many of our sister species, are to survive. Clearly nationalism, and its rivalries, armaments, boundaries—culminating in the nuclear catastrophe of mass extinction—is something we humans are going to have to learn to get rid of.

Learn to be intercultural? More like: unlearn what is blocking us from returning to the intercultural. For as far back as we can look in human history peoples have been deeply, continuously, unashamedly intercultural. Borrowing is natural to our species. The swift adoption of Western technology by non-Western peoples is only a recent example of very ancient patterns of acculturation. What is borrowed is swiftly transformed into native material— at the very same time as the borrowing re-makes native culture. So human cultures—the most traditional even—when viewed holistically, are something like the earth viewed from near-space: a whirling mass of constantly changing patterns, incorporating what is introduced, sending out feelers into the surround: very active, yet very well organized. Syncretism and the making of new cultural stuff is the norm of human activity.

Only with the advent of a particularly virulent form of Western European-American exploitative nationalism, and its ideological outgrowths (including Soviet Marxism), was interculturalism foreclosed. We must work to make this foreclosure temporary. Thus, I am arguing for both an experiment and a return to traditional, even ancient, values. This argument has been implicit in experimental art for a long time: it is the root of that art's "primitivism." Interculturalism is a predictable, even inevitable, outcome of the avant-garde, its natural heir.

As systems of communication and transportation—information systems actually—grow more flexible, people will be able to adopt "cultures of choice" in addition to their cultures of birth. This issue gives some examples of that. Some very contemporary modes of cultural exchange—such as tourism—are going to be included in our "serious" thinking, and not just as a negative. We think nothing of eating Thai food one day, northern Italian cuisine the next, and Japanese the next. This is not "unnatural," but part of the expected benefits of cosmopolitan life. Thanks to efficient transportation and tourism Americans can experience the performances of many cultures—sometimes by going there, sometimes by importing artists from there. The time is coming— Victor Turner's article is a harbinger—when people will practice other cultures the way some people now learn second verbal languages.

I'm not Pollyanna about all this. Wayne Ashley's article shows just one way in which values collide. And some very sinister forces are present in interculturalism. First off, it is people from the economically advantaged places that are able to travel and import. Areas are culturally advantaged because of extensive and long-term exploitation of other areas. Many tourists, as well as some impresarios importing performances, are philistines, or worse. Also multinational corporations who seem to be succeeding the nations as the Princes of the Earth are not any better equipped morally or ethically than their predecessors in government. I trust not Mobil. The multinational network has only one advantage: it is not in these conglomerates' self-interest to promote global war. It wasn't always that way. And "small wars," as well as the "arms industry," are still very good, and very evil, business. Good if you want to make a buck.

I am opposed to these trends toward one world under the aegis of state capitalism, corporatism, or international socialism. But I am opposed, too, to the national and ideological fervor that has brought us to the edge of nuclear annihilation—that has pushed us over the edge of squandering energy, wealth, and resources on the death industries.

So where does that leave me?

The more contact among peoples the better. The more we, and everyone else too, can perform our own and other peoples' cultures the better. To perform someone else's culture—as at the McBurney Y Powwow, for example—takes a knowledge, a "translation," that is different, more viscerally experiential, than translating a book. Most essentially, intercultural exchange takes a teacher: someone who knows the body of performance of the culture being translated. The translator of culture is not a mere agent, as a translator of words might be, but an actual culture-bearer. This is why performing other cultures becomes so important. Not just reading them, not just visiting them, or importing them—but actually doing them. So that "them" and "us" is elided, or laid experientially side-by-side.

The work reported in this issue of *TDR* has breadth and depth. The breadth is geographical, and the depth is historic. I also tried to enlist a few people who would write about intercultural activities occurring close to home: among Native Americans, Swiss Americans, American experimental theatre. Lest this seem to be a bootlegging of nationalism, I look at it the other way round: a means of undercutting our own jingoism by reminding everyone that there is no such thing as "an American." We are "the Americans," in a world that I hope will be ever more intensely pluralistic.

25

Theatre Anthropology
(1982)

Eugenio Barba

Where can an Occidental actor turn in order to find out how to construct the material bases of his art? This is the question which theatre anthropology attempts to answer. It consequently neither responds to the need to scientifically analyze what the "actor's language" consists of, nor does it answer the question, fundamental to those who practice theatre: how does one become a good actor?

Theatre anthropology does not seek principles which are universally *true*, but rather directions which are *useful*. It does not have the humility of a science, but the ambition to uncover that knowledge which can be useful to an actor's work. It does not seek to discover "laws," but rather to study the rules of behavior.

Originally, the term anthropology was understood as the study of man's behavior not only on the sociocultural level, but also on the physiological level. Theatre anthropology consequently studies the sociocultural and physiological behavior of man in a performance situation.

Similar Principles/Different Performances

Different actors, in different places and times, in spite of the stylistic forms specific to their traditions, have used some principles which they have in common with actors from other traditions. To trace these "recurrent principles" is the first task of theatre anthropology. The recurrent principles are not proof of the existence of a "science of the theatre," nor of a few universal laws. They are particularly good bits of advice, information, which are very likely to be useful to theatrical practice. To speak of a "bit of good advice" seems to indicate something of little value when contrasted with an expression like theatre anthropology. But entire fields of study—rhetoric and morals, for example, or behavior or arts and crafts—are likewise collections of "good advice."

The bits of good advice are particular in this way: they can be followed or ignored. They are not inviolate laws. Rather—and this is perhaps the best way to use them—one respects them so as to be able to break and overcome them.

The contemporary Occidental actor does not have an organic repertory of advice which can support him and with which he can orient himself. He generally has as a point of departure a text or a director's instructions. He lacks the rules of action which, while not restraining his artistic liberty, aid him in his different tasks. The traditional Oriental actor, on the other hand, bases himself on an organic and well-tested body of absolute advice, that is, rules of art which resemble the laws of a code: they codify a style of action closed unto itself and to which all the actors of a particular genre must conform. Needless to say, the actor who works within a network of codified rules has a greater liberty than he who—like the Occidental actor—is a prisoner of arbitrariness and an absence of rules. But the Oriental actor pays for his greater liberty with a specialization which limits his possibilities to go beyond what he knows. A set of precise, useful, and practical rules for the actor seems only to be able to exist through being absolute, closed to the influence of other traditions and experience. Almost all masters in the Oriental theatre enjoin their pupils not to concern themselves with performance genres different from their own. Sometimes they ask them not even to watch other forms of theatre or dance. They maintain that it is in this way that the purity of the actor's and dancer's style is preserved and that their complete dedication towards their own art is thereby demonstrated. This defense mechanism has as least the merit of avoiding the pathological tendency which the awareness of the relativity of rules brings with it: a lack of any rules at all and the falling into arbitrariness. Thus, in the same way that a Kabuki actor can ignore the best "secrets" of Noh, it is symptomatic that Etienne Decroux, perhaps the only European master to have elaborated a system of rules comparable to that of an Oriental tradition, seeks to transmit to his students the same rigorous closedness to theatre forms different from his own. In the case of Decroux, as in that of the Oriental masters, it is not a question of narrow-mindedness nor of intolerance. It has to do with the awareness that the bases of an actor's work, his points of departure, must be defended like his most precious possessions, even at the risk of isolation, otherwise they will be irremediably polluted and destroyed by syncretism.

The risk of isolation consists in paying for purity with sterility. Those masters who isolate their pupils in a fortress of rules which, in order to be strong, pretend to ignore their own relativity, and therefore the usefulness of comparison, certainly preserve the quality of their own art, but they jeopardize its future.

A theatre can, however, open itself to the experiences of other theatres not in order to mix together different ways of making performances, but in order to seek out the basic principles which it has in common with other theatres, and to transmit these principles through its own experiences. In this case, opening to diversity does not necessarily mean falling into syncretism and into a confusion of languages. It avoids the risk of sterile isolation on the one hand, and, on the other, an opening-at-any-cost which disintegrates into promiscuity. To consider, even if in an abstract and theoretical way, the possibility of a common pedagogical base, does not mean, in fact, to consider a common way of making theatre. "The arts," Decroux has written, "resemble each other through their principles, not through their works." I could add, "So it is with theatres." They resemble each other through their principles, not through their performances.

Theatre anthropology seeks to study these principles: not the profound and hypothetical reasons which might explain why they resemble each other, but their possible uses. In doing so, it will render a service both to the person of the Occidental theatre and to one of the Oriental theatre, to he who has a tradition as well as to he who suffers from the lack of one.

Lokadharmi and *Natyadharmi*

"We have two words," Sanjukta Panigrahi says to me, "to describe man's behavior: one, *lokadharmi,* stands for the behavior *(dharmi)* of man in daily life *(loka)*; the other, *natyadharmi,* for his behavior in dance *(natya)*." In the course of the last several years I have visited numerous masters from different theatres. With some I have collaborated at length. The purpose of my research has not been to study the characteristics of the different traditions, nor that which rendered their arts unique, but to study that which they had in common. What began as my own almost isolated research has slowly become the research of a group consisting of scientists, scholars of European and Asiatic theatre, and artists belonging to various traditions. To these latter goes my particular gratitude: their collaboration has manifested a form of generosity which has broken through the barriers of reticence in order to reveal the "secrets" and almost the intimacy of their professions. It is a generosity which at times has become a form of calculated temerity as they put themselves in work situations which obliged them to search for something new and which revealed an unexpected curiosity for experimentation. Oriental actors, even when they give a cold, technical demonstration, possess a quality of presence which immediately strikes the spectator and engages his attention. For a long time I thought that this was because of a particular power which the actor possessed, acquired through years and years of experience and work, of a particular technique. But that which we call technique is in fact a particular use of the body.

Sanjukta Panigrahi looking at herself in a mirror
(Photo: Nicola Savarese)

The way we use our bodies in daily life is substantially different from the way we use them in performance. The daily techniques are not conscious ones: we move, we sit, we carry things, we kiss, we agree and disagree with gestures which we believe to be "natural" but which are culturally determined. Different cultures teach different body techniques according to whether people walk with or without shoes, whether they carry things on their heads or with their hands, or if they kiss with the lips or the nose. The first steps in discovering what the principles governing the actor's scenic *bios,* the actor's "life," might be, lies in understanding that the daily techniques of the body are opposed by extra-daily ones, that is, techniques which do not respect the habitual conditionings of the body. Those who put themselves in a performance situation have recourse to these extra-daily techniques.

In the Occident, the distance which separates daily body techniques from the extra-daily ones is often neither evident nor consciously considered. In India, on the contrary, the difference between these two techniques is obvious, even sanctioned by nomenclature: *lokadharmi* and *natyadharmi.* The daily techniques generally follow the principle of least effort; i.e., obtaining a maximum result from a minimum expenditure of energy. When I was in Japan with the Odin Teatret, I wondered about the meaning of the expression with which the spectators thanked the actors at the end of the performance: *otsukaresama.* The exact meaning of this expression—particularly meant for actors—is "you are tired." The actor who has interested and touched the spectator is tired because he has not saved his energy. And for this he is thanked.

But a waste, an excess in the use of energy, is not sufficient to explain the power that is perceived in the actor's "life," in his scenic *bios.* The difference between this "actor's life" and the vitality of an acrobat is evident, and the difference is also evident in certain moments of great virtuosity in the Peking Opera and other forms of theatre or dance. In these latter cases, the acrobats, the dancers, show us "another body," a body which uses techniques very different from daily ones, so different in fact as to apparently lose all contact with them. Here it is no longer a matter of extra-daily techniques but simply of "other techniques." In this case there is no longer the tension of distance, no longer a dialectic relationship, but pure distance: the inaccessibility, finally, of a virtuoso's body. The body's daily techniques have communication as their aim; the techniques of virtuosity aim for amazement and the transformation of the body. The aim of extra-daily techniques, on the contrary, is information; they literally put the body in-form. Herein lies the essential difference which separates extra-daily techniques from those which merely transform the body.

Balance in Action

The observation of a particular quality of presence which Oriental actors often possess has led us to distinguish between daily techniques, virtuosic techniques, and extra-daily techniques. It is these latter which concern the actor. They are characteristic of the actor's life even before he represents anything or expresses anything. This is not easy for an Occidental to accept. How is it possible that a level of the actor's art exists in which he is alive and present without either representing anything or having any meaning? Perhaps only those who know Japanese theatre can accept this statement at face value. This state of being powerfully present even without representing anything is for an actor an "oxymoron": a contradiction in terms. But Moriaki Watanabe defines the "oxymoron" of the actor's pure presence in this way: the situation of an actor representing his own absence. This might seem to be nothing more than a mental game, but this in fact is a fundamental aspect of Japanese theatre.

Watanabe points out that in Noh, Kyogen, and Kabuki, there is a character who lies between the two possibilities—that of representing either his real identity or a fictional identity. This intermediary character can be perceived by the spectator through the *waki,* the secondary actor in Noh, who often represents his own non-being. He engages a complex extra-daily body technique which he does not use to express himself, but which draws attention to his ability not to express. This negation is also found in the final moments in Noh, when the main character—the *shite*—disappears: this actor, now stripped of his character, is nevertheless not reduced to his daily identity; he withdraws from the spectator without wanting to express anything, but with the same energy he had in the expressive moments. The *kokken* as well, the men dressed in black who, in Noh and Kabuki, assist the main actor in a given scene, are asked to "perform absence." Their presence, which neither expresses nor represents anything, draws so directly from the sources of the actor's energy and life that connoisseurs say that it is more difficult to be a *kokken* than an actor.

The examples which Watanabe has analyzed (his study on the "fictional body," *kyoko shintai,* has been published in Japan) show that there exists a level on which the extra-daily body techniques engage the actor's energy in a pure state, that is, on the pre-expressive level. In classical Japanese theatre, this level is sometimes openly displayed, sometimes concealed. It is, however, always present in every actor and in the very basis of his life. To speak of an actor's "energy" means using an image which lends itself to a thousand misunderstandings. We give the word "energy" many concrete meanings. Etymologically it means "to be in work, at work." How does it happen, then, that the actor's body enters work, as an actor, on pre-expressive levels? What other words could replace our word "energy"?

Translating the principles of the Oriental actor into a European language involves words like energy, life, power, spirit, to translate terms like the Japanese *ki-ai, kokoro, io-in, ko-shi,* the Balinese *taksu, virasa, chikara,* the Chinese *shun toeng,* the Sanskrit *prana, shakti.* The practical meanings of the principles of the actor's life are obscured by big words, imprecisely translated.

I tried to move ahead by going backwards. I asked certain Oriental theatre masters if, in the language they used for their work, there existed words which could translate our term "energy." "We say that an actor has, or does not have, *ko-shi* to indicate that he either does or doesn't have the right energy while working," the Kabuki actor Sawamura Sojuro replied. *Ko-shi* in Japanese is not an abstract concept, but a very precise part of the body, the hips. To say "he has *ko-shi,* he does not have *ko-shi,"* means "he has hips, he doesn't have hips." But what does not having hips mean? When we walk according to daily body techniques, the hips follow the legs. In the extra-daily techniques of the Kabuki actor, and of the Noh actor, the hips, on the contrary, remain fixed. To block the hips while walking it is necessary to slightly bend the knees and, engaging the vertebral column, to use the trunk as a single unit, which then presses downwards. In this way two different tensions are created in the upper and lower parts of the body. These tensions oblige the body to find a new point of balance. It is not a matter of a stylistic choice; it is a way to engender the actor's life. It then only secondarily becomes a particular stylistic characteristic.

In fact, the actor's life is based on an alteration of balance. When we are holding ourselves erect, we can never be immobile: even when we appear to be so, we are in fact using many minute movements with which to displace our weight. There is a continuous series of adjustments with which we move our weight, first in the toes, then in the heels, now on the left side, then on the right side of the feet. Even in the most absolute immobility, these micromovements are present, sometimes condensed, sometimes enlarged, sometimes more or less controlled, according to our physiological condition, our age, our profession. There have been experiments done with professional actors. If they are asked to imagine themselves carrying a weight while running, falling or climbing, for example, it is found that this imagining in itself immediately produces a modification in their balance, while however not leaving any trace in the balance of a nonactor, for whom imagination remains an almost exclusively mental exercise.

All this says much about balance and the relationship between mental processes and muscular tensions, but, however, it says nothing new about the actor. In fact, to say that an actor is accustomed to controlling his own physical presence and to translating his mental images into physical impulses simply means that an actor is an actor. But the series of micromovements revealed in the scientific laboratories which measure balance put us on another track: they constitute a kind of kernel which, hidden in the depths of

Jas, a young Balinese dancer, demonstrating extra-daily walking technique
(Photo: Nicola Savarese)

the body's daily techniques, can be modelled and amplified in order to increase the power of the actor's presence, becoming thus the basis of extra-daily techniques.

Anyone who has seen a Marcel Marceau performance will certainly have stopped for a moment to consider the strange fate of the mime who appears alone on the stage for a few seconds, in between one number and the next, holding up a card on which is announced the title of the piece Marceau is about to perform. "I agree," one might say, "mime is a mute form, and even the announcements, in order not to break the silence, must be mute. But why use a mime, an actor, as a notice board? Doesn't it mean that he is trapped in a desperate situation in which he can, literally, do nothing?" One of these mimes, Pierre Verry, who for a long time presented the cards announcing the names of Marceau's vignettes, one day related how he sought to achieve the highest degree of scenic existence during the brief instant in which he appeared on the stage without having—and without being able—to do anything. He said that the only possible way to achieve this was to make as strong as possible, as alive as possible, the position in which he held the card. In order to reach this result in the few seconds of his appearance, he had to concentrate for a long time to achieve "precarious balance." This immobility became not a static immobility but a dynamic one. In the absence of anything else, Verry was forced to reduce himself to the essential and he discovered the essential in the alteration of balance.

The basic body positions in the various forms of Oriental dance-theatre are likewise examples of a conscious and controlled distortion of balance. The actors of the various Oriental traditions deform the positions of the legs and the knees, the way of placing the feet on the ground, or they reduce the distance between one foot and the other, thus reducing the body's base and making balance precarious. "All the technique of the dance," says Sanjukta Panigrahi, speaking about Odissi dance but implying a principle of general application to the actor's life, "is based on the division of the body into two equal halves, according to a line which crosses the body vertically, and with unequal placements of the weight, now more on one part, now more on the other." That is, the dance amplifies, as if by putting under a microscope, those continuous and minute shifts of weight with which we remain in immobility and which laboratories specialized in the measuring of balance reveal by means of complicated diagrams. It is this *dance of balance* which actors and dancers reveal in the fundamental principles of all forms of theatre.

The Dance of Oppositions

The reader should not be surprised if I use the words actor and dancer indiscriminately just as I pass with a certain indifference from the Orient to the Occident and vice versa. The life principles that we are in search of are not

Positions of precarious
equilibrium in actors of
different cultures
Left: A commedia dell'arte
character
Right: An Indian dancer
from Odissi

limited by the distinction between what we define as "theatre," "mime," or "dance." Gordon Craig, scorning the contorted images used by critics to describe the English actor Henry Irving's particular way of walking, simply added, "Irving did not walk on the stage, he danced on it." The same shift from theatre to dance came to be used, but this time in a negative sense, to deprecate Meyerhold's research. After seeing his production of *Don Juan*, some critics wrote that what he had done was not real theatre but ballet. The rigid distinction between dance and theatre, characteristic of our culture, reveals a profound wound, a void of tradition, which continually risks drawing the actor towards a denial of the body and the dancer towards virtuousity. This distinction is absurd to an Oriental artist, as it would have appeared absurd to European artists in other historical periods: to a jester or a comedian of the sixteenth century, for example. We can ask a Noh or Kabuki actor how he would translate the word energy into the language of his work, but he would shake his head in amazement if we asked him to explain the difference between dance and theatre. "Energy," said the Kabuki actor Sawamura Sojuro, "could be translated by *ko-shi*." And according to the Noh actor Hideo Kanze, "My father never said, 'Use more *ko-shi*,' but he taught me what it was all about by making me try to walk while he grasped me by the hips and held me back." To overcome the resistance of his father's grasp, he was forced to incline his torso slightly forwards, bend his knees, press his feet on the floor and glide them forward rather than taking a normal step. The result was the basic Noh walk. Energy, like *ko-shi*, is revealed not as a result of simple and mechanical alteration of balance, but as a consequence of the tension between opposing forces.

The Kyogen actor Mannojo Nomura remembered that the Noh actors of the Kita School said: "The actor must imagine that above him is suspended a ring of iron which is pulling him upwards and against which it is necessary to resist in order to keep one's feet on the ground." The Japanese term which designates this opposing tension is *hippari hai,* which means: to pull towards oneself something or someone, at the same time as this other person or thing is trying to do the same. *Hippari hai* occurs between the upper and lower parts of the actor's body, as well as between the front and the back. There is also *hippari hai* between the actor and the musicians, who do not in fact proceed in unison but seek to move away from each other, alternately surprising each other, one breaking the tempo of the other, all the while not going so far apart as to lose the contact between them, that particular bond which puts them in opposition.

Expanding this concept, we could say that in this sense the extra-daily body techniques have a relationship of *happari-hai,* or antagonistic traction, with the techniques of daily use. We have seen in fact that the extra-daily techniques depart from the daily ones, but maintain a tension with them, without becoming separated and estranged from them. One of the ways the actor's body reveals his life to the spectator resides in a tension between opposing forces: this is the principle of opposition. Around this principle, which obviously belongs also to the experience of the Occidental actor, the codified traditions of the Orient have built various composition systems.

In the Peking Opera, the actor's entire movement system is built on the principle that every movement must begin in the direction opposite to that in which the movement will ultimately be carried out. All the forms of Balinese dance are constructed composing a series of oppositions between *kras* and *manis. Kras* means strong, hard, vigorous. *Manis* means delicate, soft, tender. *Kras* and *manis* can be applied to various movements, to positions of different parts of the body in a dance, to successive movements in the same dance. If one examines a basic Balinese dance position, one will observe this relationship, which to the Occidental eye may appear to be bizarre and extremely stylized, but which is the result of a consequential alternation of parts of the body in the *kras* position with parts in the *manis* position.

The dance of opposition characterizes the actor's life on many different levels. But, generally speaking, in the search for this dance the actor has a compass with which he can orient himself: unease. "Mime is at ease in un-ease," says Decroux, and his maxim is echoed by theatre masters from all the traditions. Katsuko Azuma's master told her that she could verify that a

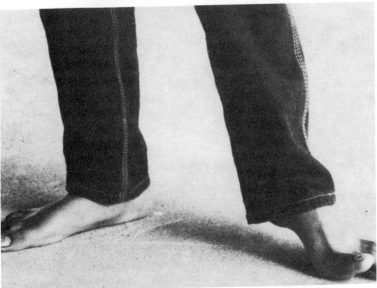

Examples of the play of *kras* and *manis* tensions in a Balinese actor.
In the hand, the index finger is *kras*, while the rest of the fingers are
manis. In the foot, the big toe is *kras*.
(Photo: Nicola Savarese)

position has been correctly assumed if she felt pain when in that position. And she added, smiling, "But if it hurts, it doesn't necessarily mean that it's right." Sanjukta Panigrahi, the masters of the Peking Opera, and those of classical or Balinese dance reiterate the same idea. Un-ease, then, becomes a system of control, a kind of internal radar which permits the actor to observe himself while he is acting. Not to observe himself with his eyes, but by means of a series of physical perceptions which confirm for him that extra-daily, nonhabitual tensions are at work in his body.

When I asked the Balinese I Made Pasek Tempo what, according to him, might be the principal talents of an actor or dancer, he responded that it was the *tahan*, the capacity for resistance, endurance. This same awareness is found in the working terminology of the Chinese theatre. To imply that an actor has mastery, it is said that he has *kun-fu*, which literally means the "capacity to hold fast, to resist." All this brings us to what in an Occidental language we might mean with the word "energy": the capacity to persist in work, to endure. But once again this word is in danger of becoming a trap for us.

When an Occidental actor wishes to be energetic, when he wants to use all his energy, he begins to move in space with tremendous vitality. He develops huge movements, with great speed and muscular strength. All this is associated with the image of "fatigue," of "hard work." An Oriental actor (or a great Occidental actor) can become even more tired almost without moving. His tiredness is not determined by an excess of vitality, by the use of huge movements, but by the play of oppositions. His body becomes charged with energy because within it is established a whole series of differences of potential which render the body alive, strongly present, even with slow movements or in apparent immobility. The dance of oppositions is danced *in* the body before being danced with the body. It is essential to understand this principle of the actor's life: energy does not necessarily correspond to movement in space.

In the *lokadharmi*, the different daily body techniques, the forces which give life to the actions of extending or withdrawing an arm or leg, or the finger of one hand, act one at a time. In the *natyadharmi*, the extra-daily techniques, the two opposing forces (of extending and withdrawing) are in simultaneous action; or better, the arm, the legs, the fingers, the spine, the neck, extend themselves as if in resistance to a force which then obliges them to bend and vice versa. Katsuko Azuma explains, for example, which forces are at work in the movement—typical both of Buyo dance and of Noh—in which the torso inclines slightly and the arms extend forwards with a gentle curve. She speaks about the forces which are acting in the opposite direction to what one observes: the arms, she says, do not extend to make the curve, but rather it is as if they are pulling a large square box towards the chest. In this way, the arms, which appear to move away from the body, in fact push towards the body, just as the torso, pushed inwards, in reality opposes resistance and bends forward.

The Virtue of Omission

The principle which is revealed through the dance of opposition in the body is, in spite of all appearances, a principle which progresses through elimination. Actions are isolated from their context and are thereby revealed. Dances, which seem to weave together movements much more complex than everyday ones, are actually the result of simplification: they compose moments in which the oppositions governing the body's life are manifest at the simplest level. This occurs because a well-defined number of forces, that is oppositions, are isolated, eventually amplified and mounted together or in succession. Once again, it is an uneconomical use of the body, because daily techniques tend to superimpose different processes, with a subsequent saving of time and energy. When Decroux writes that mime is a "portrait of work" composed with the body, what he is saying can be also assumed from other traditions. This bodily "portrait of work" is one of the principles which preside over the life of those who then conceal this very state, as for example classical ballet dancers who hide their weight and labor behind an image of lightness and ease. The principle of oppositions, because opposition is the essence of energy, is connected to the principle of simplification. Simplification in this case means the omission of certain elements in order to put others into relief; these other elements then appear to be essential.

The same principles which sustain the life of the dancer—whose movements are evidently far removed from daily movements—can also sustain the life of the actor, whose movements seem to be closer to those of daily use. Not only, in fact, can an actor omit the complexity of the daily use of the body in order to allow the essence of his work, his *bios,* to manifest itself through fundamental opposition but he can also even omit extending the action in space. Dario Fo explains how the power of an actor's movement is the result of synthesis: that is, either of the concentration of an action which uses a large amount of energy in a small space, or the reproduction of only the elements necessary to the action, eliminating those elements which are considered to be superfluous. Decroux, like the Indian actor, considers the body to be essentially limited to the trunk. He considers the movements of the arms and the legs as being accessory (or anecdotal) movements, only actually belonging to the body if they originate in the trunk.

One can speak of this process—according to which the space of the action is restricted—as a process of the absorption of energy. This process of the absorption of energy is developed from the amplification of oppositions, but also reveals a new and different route by means of which we can specify one of the "returning principles" which can be useful to theatrical practice. The opposition between one force which pushes towards action and another force which holds back is converted, according to the working language of the Noh

Ingemar Lindh gives examples of the play of
tensions in Decroux mime.
(Photos: Nicola Savarese)

and Kabuki actor, into a series of rules which oppose an energy employed in space with an energy employed in time. According to one of these rules, seven-tenths of the actor's energy should be used in time and only three-tenths in space. The actors also say that it is as if the action doesn't actually finish where the gesture has stopped in space, but continues much further.

There exists in both Noh and Kabuki the expression *tameru*, which can be represented by a Chinese ideogram meaning "to accumulate" or by a Japanese ideogram meaning "to bend" something which is at the same time flexible and resistant, like a cane of bamboo. *Tameru* defines the action of holding back, of conserving. From this comes *tame*, the ability to keep energy in, to absorb into an action which is limited in space the energy necessary to carry out a much larger action. This ability becomes a way of describing an actor's talent in general. In order to say that a pupil has or doesn't have sufficient scenic presence, the necessary power, the master tells him that he has, or doesn't have, *tame*.

All this may appear to be the result of a complicated and excessive codification of the actor's art. In reality it derives from experience which is common to actors from different traditions: the compression into restricted movements of the same physical energy, which would be set in motion in order to accomplish a much ampler and heavier action. For example, to light a cigarette mobilizing the entire body, as we would mobilize ourselves when we have to lift, say, not a little match, but a huge box; to nod with the chin and to leave the mouth slightly ajar using the same force that would be used to rush at someone and bite them. This uncovers a quality of energy which makes the actor's entire body theatrically alive even in immobility. It is probably for this reason that so-called "stage business" is often developed into the greatest scenes of famous actors. When these actors were obliged not to act, when they had to stay on the sidelines, while other actors were developing the principal action, they were able to absorb into almost imperceptible movements the force of actions which they were not permitted to carry out. It is precisely in these cases that their *bios* stood out with a particular force and left its mark on the spectator's memory. "Stage business" does not belong only to the Occidental tradition. In the 17th and 18th centuries, the Kabuki actor Kameko Kichiwaemon wrote a treatise on the actor's art entitled "Dust in the Ears." He says that at a given moment in certain performances, when only one actor is dancing, the other actors turn their backs to the audience and relax. "I do not relax," writes Kameko Kichiwaemon, "but perform the entire dance in my mind. If I do not do so, the sight of my back is not interesting to the spectator."

The theatrical virtue of omission does not consist in letting oneself go into undefined nonaction. In the theatre and for the actor, omission means rather to withhold, to not spread around in an excess of expressivity and vitality that which distinguishes real scenic life. The beauty of omission, in fact, is the beauty of indirect action, of the life which is revealed with a maximum of intensity in a minimum of activity. Once again, it is a question of a game of oppositions, but at a level which goes beyond even the pre-expressive level of the actor's art and which thus goes beyond the limits which we proposed at the beginning of this article.

Intermezzo

At this point one might ask if the principles of the actor's art which I have described do not take us too far from the theatre which is known and practiced in Europe. Are those principles actually good advice, useful for theatrical practice? Does drawing attention to the pre-expressive level of the actor's art separate us from the real problems of the European actor? Is the pre-expressive level perhaps only verifiable in theatrical cultures which are highly codified? Is the European tradition not perhaps characterized by the lack of codification and by the search for individual expressivity? These are undoubtedly binding questions and rather than demanding immediate answers, they invite us to stop and rest for a moment.

So let's talk about flowers.

If we put some flowers in a vase, we do so in order to show how beautiful they are, in order to enjoy them. We can also make them take on ulterior meanings: filial or religious piety, love, recognition, respect. But as beautiful as they might be, flowers have a defect: taken out of their own context, they continue to represent only themselves. They are like the actor of whom Decroux speaks: a man condemned to resemble just a man, a body imitating a body. This may well be pleasing, but to be considered art it is not sufficient to merely be pleasing. In order for there to be art, adds Decroux, the idea of the thing needs to be represented by another thing. Flowers in a vase are irremediably flowers in a vase, sometimes subjects of works of art, but never works of art themselves.

But let's imagine using cut flowers to represent something else: the struggle of the plant to grow, to move away from the earth into which its roots sink ever deeper as it strives upwards to the sky. Let's imagine wanting to represent the passage of time, as the plant blossoms, grows, develops, and dies. If we succeed with our intention, the flowers will represent something other than flowers and will constitute a work of art, that is to say, we will have made an *ikebana*. *Ikebana* means, if one follows the sense of the ideogram, "to make flowers live." The life of the flowers, because of having been interrupted, blocked, can be represented. The procedure is evident: something has been wrenched from its normal conditions of life (this is the state flowers are in when we simply arrange them in a vase), and the rules which govern these normal conditions have been replaced and analogically rebuilt using other rules. Flowers, for example, cannot act in time, cannot represent in temporal terms their blossoming and withering, but the passage of time can be suggested with an analogy in space. One can bring together—that is, compare—one flower in bud with another fully blossomed. With two branches, one thrusting upwards and the other downwards, one can underline the direction in which the plant is developing: the force which binds it to the earth, and the force which pushes it away from the earth. A third branch, extending along an oblique line, can evidence the combined force which results from the two opposing tensions. A composition which seems to derive from refined esthetic taste is the result of the analysis and dissection of a phenomenon and of the transposition of energy acting in time into lines extending in space.

This transposition opens the composition to new meanings different from the original ones: here the branch which is reaching upwards becomes associated with Heaven, the one reaching downwards with the earth, and the branch in the centre with the mediator between these two opposing entities, Man. The result of a schematic analysis of reality and its transposition following principles which represent it without reproducing it becomes the object of a philosophical contemplation.

"The mind has difficulty maintaining the thought of the bud because the thing thus designated is prey to an impetuous development, and shows—in spite of our thought—a strong impulse not to be a flower bud but a flower." These are words which Brecht attributes to Hu-jeh, who adds, "Thus, for the thinker, the concept of the flower bud is the concept of something which already aspires to be other than what it is." This difficulty in our thinking is exactly what *ikebana* proposes: an indication of the past and a suggestion of the future, a representation through immobility of the continuous motion through which the positive turns into the negative and vice versa.

The example of *ikebana* shows us how abstract meanings are born from the precise work of analysis and transposition of a physical phenomenon. Starting from these abstract meanings, one would never reach the concreteness and precision of *ikebana,* whereas starting from concreteness and precision, one does attain these abstract meanings. As for the actor, he often tries to proceed from the abstract to the concrete. He believes that the point of departure can be created from the things to be expressed, which then implies the use of a technique which is suitable to what one wishes to express. A symptom of this absurd belief is supplied by the diffidence shown towards the codified forms of theatre and towards the principles for the actor's life which they contain. These principles, in fact, are not esthetic suggestions made to *add* beauty to the actor's body. They are means whereby the daily automatisms can be stripped from the body to prevent it from being no more than a human body condemned to resemble itself, to present and represent only itself. When certain principles return with frequency, in different latitudes and traditions, one can assume that they "work" in our case as well.

The example of *ikebana* shows how certain forces which develop in time can find an analogy in spatial terms. This substitution of the forces which characterize the daily use of the body with analogous forces is the basis of Decroux's mime system. Decroux often gives the idea of a real action by acting in a way exactly opposite to the real action. He shows, for example, the action of pushing something not by projecting the chest forward and pressing with the back foot, as occurs in the real action, but by arching the spine concavely, as if instead of pushing he was being pushed, bringing the arms towards the chest and pressing downwards with the front foot and leg. This radical inversion of the forces with respect to how they occur in the real action restores the work, or the effort, which comes into play in the real action. It is as if the actor's body was taken apart and then recomposed according to rules which no longer follow the rules of daily life. At the end of the work of recomposition, the body no longer resembles itself. Like the flowers in our vase or like Japanese *ikebana*, the actor and dancer are cut from the "natural" context in which they usually act, are severed from the domains where the daily body techniques dominate. Like the flowers and the branches of the *ikebana,* the actor, in order to be theatrically alive, cannot present or represent what he *is*. In other words, he must abandon his own automatic responses.

The different codifications of the actor's art are, above all, methods to break the automatic responses of daily life.

Naturally, this rupture of the automatic is not expression. But without this rupture there is no expression. "Kill the breathing! Kill the rhythm!" repeated Katsuko Azuma's master to her as she worked. To kill breathing and to kill rhythm means to be aware of the tendency to automatically link gesture to the rhythm of respiration and music, and to then break this link. The Japanese are perhaps those in whose theatrical culture the breaking of the automatic of daily life has been the most consciously and radically done.

The precepts which, in the working terminology used by Katsuko Azuma's master, demand the killing of rhythm and the killing of breathing, show how the search for opposition can be finalized in the rupture of the automatic responses of the body's daily techniques. To kill the rhythm in fact implies creating a series of tensions to prevent the movements of the dance from coinciding with the cadences of the music. To kill the breathing means to withhold the breath even in the moment of expiration—which is a moment of relaxation—and to oppose the exhalation with a contrary force. Katsuko Azuma said that it was actually painful for her to see a dancer who, as happens in all cultures other than the Japanese, follows the tempo of the music. It is easy to understand how, for her, according to the particular solutions of her culture, a dance which follows the rhythm of the music might be something which makes her uneasy, because it shows an action which has been decided from the outside, from the music, or from daily behavior. The solution which the Japanese have found for this problem belongs to Japanese culture alone, but the problem which is illuminated concerns actors everywhere.

A Decided Body

There exists in many European languages an expression which might be chosen to epitomize what is essential for the actor's life. It is a grammatically paradoxical expression, in which a passive form comes to assume an active meaning, and in which the indication of an availability for action is couched in a form of passivity. It is not an ambiguous expression, but an hermaphroditic one, combining within it action and passivity, and in spite of its strangeness it is an expression found in common speech. One says, in fact, *"essere deciso,"* *"être décidé,"* "to be decided." And it does not mean that someone or something decides us or that we undergo decision, nor that we are the object of decision. It doesn't even mean that we are deciding, nor that we are carrying out the action of deciding.

Between these two opposite conditions flows a current of life which language does not seem to be able to represent and around which it dances with images. Only direct experience shows what it means "to be decided." In order to explain to someone what it means to be decided, we must refer to innumerable associations of ideas, to innumerable examples, to the construction of artificial situations. Nevertheless, we all believe that we know very well what this expression means. All the complex images, the whole gamut of abstruse rules which twist around the actors, the elaboration of artistic precepts which seem to be—and are—the result of sophisticated esthetics, are the vaultings and acrobatics of the wish to transmit an experience which in its real sense cannot be transmitted, cannot be transported from hand to hand, but which can only be lived. To explain the actor's experience really means to artificially create, with a complicated strategy, the condition in which this experience can be reproduced.

Let us imagine one more time that we can penetrate the intimacy of the work which takes place between Katsuko Azuma and her master. The master is also called Azuma. When she judges that she has succeeded in passing on her experience to her student, she will also pass on her name. Azuma, then, says to the future Azuma, "Find your *ma*." *Ma* means something similar to dimension in the sense of space but also duration in the sense of time. "To find your *ma* you must kill rhythm. Find your *jo-ha-kyu*." The expression *jo-ha-kyu* represents the three phases into which all the actions of an actor are subdivided. The first phase is determined by the opposition between a force

Katsuko Azuma: transforming immobility into action
(Photo: Nicola Savarese)

which tends to increase and another which holds back *(jo* = to withhold); the second phase *(ha* = to break) occurs in the moment in which one is liberated from this force, until one arrives at the third phase *(kyu* = rapidity) in which the action reaches its culmination, using up all of its force to suddenly stop as if face to face with an obstacle, a new resistance.

To teach Azuma to move according to *jo-ha-kyu,* her master would hold her by the waist and then suddenly let her go. Azuma would work very hard to make the first few steps (while being held), bending her knees, pressing the soles of her feet to the ground, slightly inclining her trunk. Then, released by her teacher, she would advance quickly to the specified limit of the movement, at which point she would suddenly stop as if a deep ravine had opened up a few centimeters in front of her. What she did, in other words, was to execute the movement which anyone who has seen Japanese theatre is accustomed to recognize as being typical. When an actor has learned, as his second nature, this artificial way of moving, he appears to have been cut from the everyday space-time relationship and appears to be "alive," he is, yes, decided. Etymologically, "to be decided" means "to cut away." The expression "to be decided" assumes then yet another facet: it is as if it indicated that one's availability to create also includes cutting oneself off from daily practices.

The three phases of *jo-ha-kyu* impregnate the atoms, the cells, the entire organism of Japanese performance. They apply to every one of an actor's actions, to each of his gestures, to respiration, to the music, to each theatrical scene, to each play in the composition of a Noh play. It is a kind of code of life which runs through all the levels of organization of the theatre.

René Sieffert maintains that the rule of *jo-ha-kyu* is a "constant in the esthetic sense of humanity." In a certain sense this is true; even if a rule dissolves into something insignificant when it ends up being applicable to everything. From our point of view another of Sieffert's statements seems more important: that *jo-ha-kyu* permits the actor, as Zeami explains, to apparently break the rule in order to establish contact with the audience. Here is a constant in the actor's life: the building up of artificial rules, hand in hand with their infraction. An actor who has nothing but rules is an actor who no longer has theatre but only liturgy. An actor who is without rules is also without theatre: he has only the *lokadharmi*—the daily behavior—with its boredom and its necessity for direct provocation in order to keep the spectator's attention awake. All the teachings which Azuma the master gave to Azuma the student are directed to the discovery of the center of the latter's own energy. The methods of the search are meticulously codified, the fruits of generations and generations of experience. The result is impossible to define with precision, different from person to person.

Today, Azuma says that the principle of her life, of her energy as an actress and dancer can be defined as a center of gravity which is found at the midpoint of a line which travels from the navel to the coccyx. Every time she dances, she tries to find her balance around this center. Even today, in spite of all her experience, in spite of the fact that she is a student of one of the greatest masters and that she herself is now a master, she isn't always able to find this center. She imagines (or perhaps it is a question of the images with which her teacher tried to transmit the experience to her) that the center of her energy is a ball of steel which is found at a certain point on a line going from the navel to the coccyx, or in the center of the triangle formed by lines between the hips and the coccyx, and that this steel ball is covered with many layers of cotton. I Made Pasek Tempo, the Balinese dancer, agrees, "Everything that Azuma does is really just that, *kras* covered by *manis,* vigor covered by softness."

In the Occidental tradition, the actor's work has been oriented around a network of fictions, of "magic-ifs" which deal with the psychology, the behavior and the history of his person and that of the character he is playing. The pre-expressive principles of the actor's life are not cold concepts only with the physiology and mechanics of the body. They also are based on a network of fictions, but fictions, "magic-ifs," which deal with the physical forces which move the body. What the actor is looking for, in this case, is a fictional body, not a fictional personality. In the Oriental traditions, in ballet, in Decroux's mime system, in order to break the automatic responses of daily behavior, each of the body's gestures is dramatized by imagining that one is pushing, lifting, touching objects of determined weight and consistency. It is a question of a psycho-technique which does not attempt to influence the actor's psychic state, but rather his physical state. It has therefore to do with the language with which the actor speaks to himself, and even more so, with what the master says to the student, but which has no pretense of meaning anything to the spectator.

To find the extra-daily techniques of the body, the actor does not study physiology but creates a network of external stimuli to which he reacts with physical actions.

In Indian tradition, among the ten qualities of the actor there is one which has to do with knowing how to see, how to direct the eyes in space. This is the sign that the actor is reacting to something precise. We can watch an actor who is apparently carrying out the exercises of his training in an extraordinary manner, but whose way of seeing is not precisely directed, and his actions have no power. On the other hand, the body can be relaxed but if the eyes are active—that is, if they see in order to observe—then the actor's body is brought to life. In this sense one can say that the eyes are like the actor's second spinal column. All the Oriental traditions codify the eye movements, the directions they must follow. This doesn't concern only what the spectator sees, but also the actor himself, the way in which he populates the empty space with lines of force, with stimuli to be reacted to.

At the end of his diary the Kabuki actor Sadoshima Dampachi, who died in 1712, writes that there exists an expression according to which "one dances with the eyes," implying that the dance one is performing can be compared to the body and the eyes to the soul. He adds that a dance in which the eyes do not take part is a dead dance, while a living dance is one in which the movements of the body and of the eyes participate together. In the European traditions as well, the eyes are the "mirrors of the soul" and an actor's eyes are considered as the half-way point between the extra-daily techniques of his physical behavior and his extra-daily psycho-techniques. It is the eyes which show that he is decided and which make him be decided.

The great Danish physicist Niels Bohr was an ardent Western film fan, and he wondered why, in all the final shootouts, the hero shot fastest even though his adversary was usually the first to reach for his gun. Bohr asked himself if some physical truth might not lie behind this convention. He came to the conclusion that such a truth did indeed exist: the first to draw is the slowest to shoot because he decides to shoot, and dies. The second lives because he is faster, and he is faster because he doesn't have to decide, he is decided.

A Million Candles

"True expression," said Grotowski in a recent interview, "is like that of the tree." And he explained, "If an actor has the will to express, then he is divided: there is a part of him doing the willing and another part doing the expressing, a part which is commanding and another which carries out the commands."

Having followed the trail of the actor's energy, we have reached the point where we are able to perceive its nucleus:

1) in the amplification and the putting into play of the forces which are at work in balance;
2) in the oppositions which determine the dynamics of movements;
3) in an operation of reduction and substitution where what is essential in the actions emerges and which removes the body from daily techniques, creating a tension, a difference in potential, through which energy passes.

The extra-daily techniques of the body consist of physical procedures which appear to be based on the reality with which everyone is familiar, but which follow a logic not immediately recognizable.

In the working terminology of the Noh, "energy" can be translated with *ki-hai* which means "profound agreement" *(hai)* of the spirit *(ki)*, with the body. Here spirit is used in the sense of spirit as pneuma and breath. In both

India and Bali the word *prana* is equivalent to *ki-hai*. These are all images which inspire, but they are not advice capable of guiding us. In fact they allude to something which is beyond the master's intervention: that which we call expression, or "subtle fascination," or the actor's art.

When Zeami was writing about *yugen*, the subtle fascination, he used as an example the dance which carries the name of Shirabioshi, a woman who danced in Japan in the 13th century dressed as a man, a sword in her hand. The reason why so often, especially in the Orient, but also in the Occident, the culmination of the actor's art seems to be reached by men who are playing female characters, or by women playing male characters, is because in these cases the actor or actress is doing exactly the opposite of what an actor who today dresses as a person of the opposite sex does: he or she does not disguise themselves but divests themselves of the mask of his or her sex to allow a soft or vigorous temperament to shine through, independent of the schema to which a man or woman in a determined culture must conform.

In the theatrical works of different civilizations, masculine and feminine characters are represented by those temperaments which the different cultures identify as being "naturally" appropriate to the masculine or feminine sexes. The representation of the distinctive characters of the sexes is therefore, in theatrical works, the most subject to conventions: it is a question of such a profound conditioning as to render almost impossible the distinction between sex and temperament. When an actor represents a person of the opposite sex, the identification between the determined temperament of one or the other sex cracks. It is perhaps the moment in which the opposition between *lokadharmi* and *natyadharmi*, between daily behavior and extra-daily behavior, slides away from the physical plane and reaches another not immediately recognizable plane. A new physical presence and a new spiritual presence reveal themselves through the rupture, which in the theatre is paradoxically accepted, of masculine and feminine roles.

Once when I was talking with Sanjukta Panigrahi, the most apt and least usable translation of the term "energy" when applied to the actor emerged. It was the least usable because it translates the experience of a point of departure as well as a great result: it does not translate the experience of the process of achieving the result. Sanjukta Panigrahi says that energy is called *Shakti:* it is creative energy, neither masculine nor feminine, but which is represented by the image of a woman. For this reason only women in India are attributed with the title *Shakti amsha,* meaning "part of Shakti." But an actor, independent of his or her sex, says Sanjukta Panigrahi, is always *Shakti,* energy which creates.

The moment of arrival, the end-product, when the actor creates, is not a moment with which we here in these pages can occupy ourselves. But, after speaking of the dance of opposition on which the actor's life is based, and after

Theatrical "barter" by Eugenio Barba's Odin Teatret in Peru
(Photo: Tony d'Urso)

considering the contrasts which the actor voluntarily amplifies, after discussing the balance which he voluntarily makes precarious and puts into play, the image of Shakti can perhaps become a symbol of that of which we have not spoken here; the fundamental question: how does one become a *good* actor?

In one of her dances, Sanjukta Panigrahi shows *Ardhanarishwara,* Shiva half male, half female. Immediately after her, Iben Nagel Rasmussen presents *Moon and Darkness:* we are in Bonn, at the end of the International School of Theatre Anthropology, where for a month teachers and students from different continents have worked together on the cold, technical, pre-expressive bases of the actor's work. The song which accompanies Sanjukta's dance says:

> I bow before you
> You who are both
> Male and female
> Two gods in one
> You whose female half has the vivid color
> Of a Champak flower
> And whose male half has the pallid color
> Of the camphor flower
>
> The female half jingles
> With golden arm bracelets
> The male half is adorned
> With bracelets of serpents
> The female half has love-eyes
> The male half meditation-eyes
>
> The female half has
> A garland of almond flowers
> The masculine half has
> A garland of skulls
> Dressed in dazzling clothes
> Is the female half
> Nude, the male half
>
> The female half is capable
> Of all creation
> The male half is capable
> Of all destruction
>
> I turn to you
> Linked to the God Shiva
> Your wife
> I turn to you
> Linked to the Goddess Shiva
> Your husband

Iben Nagel Rasmussen, on the contrary, sings the lament of a shaman of a destroyed people. She immediately reappears as an adolescent stammering joyously on the threshold of a world at war. The Oriental actress and the Occidental actress seem to be moving far apart, each one in the depths of her own culture. Nevertheless they meet each other. They seem to surpass not only their own personalities and sex, but even their own artistic skill, showing something which is beyond all this.

An actor's master knows how many years of work are at the source of these moments, but still it seems to him that something is flowering spontaneously, neither sought for nor desired. There is nothing to be said. One can only watch, as Virginia Woolf watched Orlando, "A million candles burned in Orlando, without him having thought of lighting even a single one."

Translated by Richard Fowler

26

The WOW Cafe
(1984)

Alisa Solomon

The WOW Cafe is a force more than a place. Unlike many East Village performance spaces, WOW, at 330 E. 11th Street, did not begin as a location seeking work to produce but was born the other way around. Women who had been producing a vast variety of work all over the East Village sought a permanent home. Recently, during one of their weekly open staff meetings, the 15 or so women who make up the Cafe's anarchic organizing collective spoke about the origins of their café. In typical WOW fashion, women periodically wandered in and out. The Cafe's oral history, recounted at this meeting for the first time, is rich—and long enough that the tellers disagree about the details of their story. At the same time, WOW's creatively amorphous organization includes enough newcomers that some women were surprised to hear there was an extensive past.

WOW began with a dream shared by Lois Weaver and Peggy Shaw. Touring in Europe in the late '70s with Spiderwoman Theater and Hot Peaches, they met several companies who wanted to perform in the United States. They also attended many women's theatre festivals in Europe and thought it was about time one took place in America. "It became clear," says Weaver, "that if it was going to be done, we were going to have to be the ones to do it." They began to mention their vision to European companies, making it clear that the American system did not permit conditions equivalent to the ones they enjoyed in Europe; they would be unable to invite groups into a theatre that could pay even a small fee or accommodate them. "You would have to come and produce yourselves; that's how we do it," Weaver told them. Peggy Shaw, tossing in wry interjections throughout Weaver's narrative, adds with a sigh recalling exhaustion, "We didn't think they'd really fall for it. We said we'd do it, and then, all of a sudden, we had to."

And all of a sudden is how it happened. They had the idea in May 1980, and the first Women's One World (WOW) Festival took place the following October. Without any personal capital or funding, and not enough time to apply for grants, Weaver and Shaw, forming "Allied Farces" with Jordi Mark and Pamela Camhe, began to work fanatically to create a festival that would feature international groups but also highlight national and New York women performers. Acknowledging that music and dance already had healthy circuits in place, they concentrated on theatre, with the European festival as their deliberate model. There, one could pay one admission to see two or three shows, a movie, sit in a café and talk, and dance afterwards. "We wanted to create that sort of multimedia environment," says Weaver, "so we did. God only knows how."

One tactic was to amass a crew of volunteers, who became the backbone of the project. Throughout the summer of 1980, they produced benefits, usually in the form of wild costume parties, in donated spaces. In addition to giving the festival exposure, these benefits acquainted the women with the vagaries of producing, accustomed them to the technical demands of their performance space, and collected a following. "We didn't raise much money," Weaver says, "but it did give us a lot in the long run in terms of exposure and experience, and we developed an audience."

Working out of the Allcraft Center on St. Marks Place (the old Electric Circus), Allied Farces had to put up their sets right before they went on and break them down the same night. By the time the festival arrived, they had acquired an adept technical crew. The festival ran for two weeks with two, sometimes three, performances a night and occasional afternoon shows. Groups came from Europe, paying their own way and sleeping on floors of friends of the festival. "We couldn't offer much," Weaver explains, "but just having a spot to perform in New York was a big deal for them. And we got them some press. That actually generated enough interest that they could come back on their own later, as Beryl and the Perils did." "We couldn't pay them," Shaw adds, "but they got a lot of attention and made a lot of contacts."

When the festival ended, the Allcraft management, pleased with its success, offered its organizers the space to keep going. " 'Why don't we do *what?*,' we said," explains Weaver, "but space was at a premium, and we felt that if someone was offering us a women's performance space, we couldn't very well refuse." They stayed until March.

In the ensuing months, they produced dance, theatre, and poetry by women every Wednesday night and sometimes on Thursday nights, splitting the receipts with the performers. As word about the space got out, resumés and brochures from performers barraged them. But just as their reputation was growing and their procedures were taking shape, they got locked out of the Allcraft Center. One night the Flamboyant Ladies, a black lesbian group, performed a show that Weaver describes as "very, very hot, very sensual." "It was beautiful," says Shaw, "but a little too sexy for the Center." It happened that near the end of the show there was a fire in the building next door that had nothing to do with the performance, but it caused some damage to the Allcraft. The next time the WOW staff came to the space, they found padlocks on the door.

There is no animosity between WOW and the Allcraft manager; the women understood that Allcraft had been under investigation by the CETA Board that funded them and were afraid of losing money. "There had been some growing tension, some homophobic kind of tension, because of that," says Weaver, "but they really had been generous. We did pay them a portion of our proceeds but not nearly as much as they could have made if they had rented the space out."

Weaver, Shaw, and the current WOW organizers do not seem disconcerted by the implicit indirect censorship from the CETA foundation. They had, after all, if not by design, acquired a reputation for producing lesbian work and expected certain attacks. Though their policy was to produce any work written or directed by a woman, or that presented a woman's sensibility, many of their benefits depended on creating environments that, depending on the theme, might include such attractions as kissing booths. However, they made no deliberate attempt to appeal exclusively to lesbians. "You didn't have to be a lesbian to get into the shows," explains Shaw, "but most of the people who came were." Then she adds jokingly, "Most either came that way or ended up that way."

Locked out, in any case, but booked for the next three months, the WOW brigade searched for a space and eventually found the ballroom at the Ukrainian Home on 2nd Avenue. It was difficult to create a congenial atmosphere in the cavernous, 86-year-old theatre, but bringing in platforms, folding chairs, and electricity enabled them to produce a month of Wednesday performances and some benefits. In the meantime, they made a connection with the University of the Streets when it was still, in Shaw's words, "just a tacky little storefront," and they staged benefits there as well.

By now it was April 1981, and time, they felt, to plan another festival. This time, they knew they wanted to include an all-day café space where performers and spectators could hang out, and they immediately made arrangements with University of the Streets. Wanting to expand the festival's scope, they also booked other spaces. Again they worked without substantial funding: The October 1981 WOW Festival budget amounted to $2–3,000. Each of its 11 days was packed with performances: "Pasta and Performance" at University of the Streets every day at 6:00 p.m., mainstage shows at 8:00 and 10:00 at the Ukrainian Home, 11:00 performances at Theatre for the New City, midnight Cabaret at the Centre Pub, and occasional films at Millennium.

After a year, WOW had become a full part of the international network of women performers and attracted groups from Finland, Sweden, New Zealand and all over Europe. Some got money from their own countries, but most came over on their own just because they had heard about the previous WOW Festival.

After the second festival, artists felt that something was missing and realized that they did not want to give up the inspiration that working together had generated. "It was like there was energy left over," Weaver explains. "There had been a place where you could drop by and always run into someone you knew. Not only people who had been working, but also people who had been spectators missed the energy after the festival finished." So this arbitrary group of people—including a huge production team of designers and technicians—who had come together for the festival, began having brunches together on Sundays and talked about creating a permanent café. According to Weaver, "This was something we always hoped would happen, and it seemed like the perfect outgrowth of the festival."

This ad hoc brunch committee began to organize benefits at Club 57: costume affairs like the Freudian Slip party to which guests came dressed in lingerie, a Debutante Ball, and "X-rated Xmas"—which brought back one of the most controversial performers from the festival. Diane Torr, a performance artist making her living as a go-go dancer in New Jersey, created a piece with her colleagues in which they danced and talked about their lives. Many women were upset by the show, Shaw thinks, "because they didn't know how to act, how to react, or how to be with these women. A lot of women loved it, but many objected to it politically." Never shying away from controversy, they invited Torr to work on a benefit in which she performed for an all-women audience and invited them to participate. Other benefits included a Medical Drag Ball attended by people in costumes dripping with blood and gore, who danced with their I.V.s. Club 57, an old horror movie house in the basement of a church at 57 St. Mark's Place, was one of the first clubs in the area to feature crazy theme parties. Appreciative of WOW's purpose and zaniness, they rented them the space for $75 a night.

These benefits had financial, albeit modest, success. "All of a sudden we had five or six hundred dollars in our hands that had been raised for a café, so we started looking for spaces," says Weaver, "and one afternoon we found 330 E. 11th. We had to talk the landlord into renting it to us because he didn't really want any little lesbian theatre in his building." "We told him we wanted it for a women's resource center," Shaw explains, "but," adds Weaver, "he took one look at us and said, 'Oh. I have a son who's gay.' We had learned by then that you have to be up front right from the start because we didn't want to put our hearts into something and end up disappointed."

Since opening in March 1982, the WOW Cafe has presented innumerable poets, performers, plays, films, videos and art exhibits. Continually reconsidering the Cafe's purposes, the staff molds its flexible shape to meet its constituents' changing interests and needs. They began literally as a café, serving coffee and toasted brie sandwiches, simply as Mo Angeles says, "because we had called it a café. So we had to serve coffee."

The space was named "WOW at 330" to signify both its address and the hour, as Weaver puts it, "when girls get out of school and go out looking for fun." It was open from 3:30 until 11:00 p.m.—a feasible prospect since everyone on the staff had a key—and truly became a social center. "But what we really wanted," says Weaver, "was a women's performance space. We also wanted a hangout, a girls' social club." Unsure of their institutional identity, the dozen or so amorphously organized staff (anyone who showed up to an open staff meeting automatically joined the staff) argued over whether to have a pool table, what color to paint the ceiling, and whether paintings should be left on the walls during performances. "We eventually learned," Shaw says, "that you could do anything you wanted in the space when nobody else was there." Every time they would come in, they explained laughingly, someone else's paintings would be newly hung.

Without explicitly declaring their intentions for 330, its organizers expressed their plans when one of the first things they did was to construct a platform stage at one end of the room and hang a curtain. The stage, like the entire space, is barely 10 feet wide. With its floor of octagonal ceramic tiles, patterned along one side, the room seems like it might have been someone's vestibule or, even earlier, half a dining room. Now, impossibly narrow and maybe 20 feet long, it hardly contains a dozen or so rows of folding chairs. The homemade lightboard of household dimmers sits in the center of the room, controlling a handful of small, outdoor-type reflector lamps—all the electrical system can accommodate. The backstage area is a ten feet by ten feet jumble of old props, bits of costumes, and chunks of sets. The Cafe's original excuse, an enormous coffee maker, is stashed in a corner.

In its early days, the Cafe kept afloat by selling food and memberships. For $60 a year, members got half-price admissions to performances. Although this was not much of a bargain since performances were not yet very regular, it offered patrons a way to support the Cafe where they hung out. Membership reached 120 within a few months. Performance booking remained erratic until Holly Hughes emerged to take on the management of the Cafe. She instituted a number of regular events that increased the Cafe's visibility, brought more regular customers, and attracted more writers, comics and actors. She orchestrated a number of brunches, for instance, and created the popular "Talking Slide Show," where artists would show their slides and talk about their work. Variety nights also caught on, providing opportunities for many inchoate artists to work on material without having to face the risks and mechanics of mounting entire productions. Countless East Village performers got their start in these casual shows. Hughes herself developed her first piece, "Shrimp in a Basket," at the Cafe, and then "Well of Horniness," which went on to become a popular Lower East Side cult piece, playing at the Pyramid Club, Limbo Lounge and on WBAI Radio. Tammy Whynot, a character in Split Britches' most recent play, *Upwardly Mobile Home,* first appeared at a talent night. And Carmelita Tropicana, a persona created by Alina Troyano, was born almost by accident. Troyano, drawn to the Cafe because of its sense of humor, went on for an emcee who did not show up one night and, she proclaims, never came off. Recently she performed at the Chandalier and the Limelight.

After about a year, Holly Hughes was exhausted by her nonpaying, full-time management of the Cafe and decided to leave. Therefore, in the spring of '83, the roughly 15 women who still comprised WOW's collective management called a retreat to determine their next steps. "What happens, unfortunately, when one person is in charge of all the details," Weaver says, "is that the collective sort of vanishes and leaves all the little decisions up to that one person. So we had to regroup. This meeting was really a turning point for the Cafe."

The women who gathered for the weekend were tired and knew that something had to change. "We were no longer just a café," says Weaver. "Now we wanted to be serious about being a performance space, a cultural center." So they sat around a big table, and each person recommended what she would like to see happen in the coming season. They drew up a month-by-month list of the suggestions, and produced every one of them the following year.

Worried about Hughes' departure, the WOW collective remained uncertain about the Cafe's definition and wondered whether all of its functions could coexist gracefully. "We wanted to be an art space, a theatre space, a hangout, and have as much input from the community as possible," Troyano remarks, "but how do you maintain that?" As usual though, things fell into place. Because they had sketched out a calendar for the season, Weaver believes, "each month just materialized. It wasn't as if anyone was there holding us to it, it just sort of happened because the calendar had to be filled in each month ahead of time, so we just did it; it was pretty magical."

That magic was replaced by a less ethereal if equally powerful force in Fall, 1983 when Susan Young took over as booking manager. "I had just moved here," she relates. "I didn't know any of these women, I hadn't seen any WOW festivals or really knew that they had existed. But I came here and saw Split Britches perform and knew immediately that this was where I wanted to work." Since then, she has been designing WOW productions and carrying out day-to-day managerial tasks. Under her direction, informed by the collective, the Cafe has turned in slightly new directions. While continuing to book anyone who requests space, Young has also set up some regular events whose management she turns over to the groups involved. Each Sunday night from September 1984 until Christmas, for example, is directed by the Asian Lesbians of the East Coast. "Instead of taking individual bookings for a jam session here, a film showing there, we decided that this group would put together its own evenings. The outcome has been incredible: films, videos, poetry readings, music." This arrangement also serves a growing aim of the Cafe: to reach out to a more racially mixed audience.

At the same time, caféniks are beginning to rethink their policy of allowing anyone with an interest to book the Cafe, not only because they want to put their energy into producing their own work, but also because they are sometimes displeased with the results. "We still want to provide a producing service to the community," says Young, "but women come in expecting a great deal and don't give anything back to the space. There are a lot of women who aren't regulars here who come in and perform, put holes in the wall, break our lightboard, and split, and don't even think of ever coming to a staff meeting or even to a performance by another woman."

More abstract issues such as the risks that works will be artistically bad, politically inconsistent with the Cafe's tacit feminism, or just poorly executed increasingly concern the staff. Yet they would rather tolerate occasional disasters than audition women for the space; that, they believe, would amount to censorship. "We're always criticized for not auditioning," Shaw complains. "We're told, 'Now that you've been around you have to have quality work.' But we feel the minute you start auditioning you become just like anybody else."

These issues may become less pressing as the Cafe moves toward its year-long goal of putting on work from within its own community—a priority not as cliqueish as it may sound since anyone who hangs around is absorbed into that community. Facing some of the difficulties posed by outside performers, Young explains, "We wondered, why are we breaking our backs producing so many other women when our own work is not a priority?" This past season they decided to rectify the situation and to make concrete proposals for in-house bookings. Just as booking a calendar the year before provided the structured impetus to keep the Cafe going then, this new commitment generated creative work and pushed WOW women toward inventing and finishing new projects.

The most experienced of the WOW regulars is the Split Britches company, comprised of Lois Weaver, Peggy Shaw and Deborah Margolin. Their recent work-in-progress, *Upwardly Mobile Home,* has been shown twice at the Cafe, once in the Spring of '84 and again, further developed, in the

Fall. Though there is probably no such thing as a typical WOW performance, Split Britches crystalizes some of the distinguishing qualities from which one might be able to infer a WOW sensibility.

Upwardly Mobile Home takes place in 1986 after Reagan's re-election. Three actors in the theatre company, who are preparing a production of a '20s hit, *Shanghai Gesture,* are camping out under the Brooklyn Bridge, homeless. There, one woman peddles her old clothes, another sells instant coffee over the phone, and all three fantasize, argue and rehearse their show. A bizarre sense of humor combines with a barrage of intersecting ideas to create a complex criticism of American myths. Formally inventive, the piece follows a day in the life of these actresses, with overlapping monologs, songs and play-within-a-play sequences.

Other WOW productions so far lack Split Britches' dramatic sophistication. But *Heart of the Scorpion,* "a lesbian Harlequin Romance" by Alice Forrester, also reflects some of WOW's typical energetic zaniness. Forrester's production also came out the Cafe's recent push to produce more in-house work. Another reason for this shift in emphasis is that the Cafe might lose its lease at 330 E. 11th when it comes up for renewal in March. "We wanted to be sure we would still have definition even if we lose the space," explains Weaver, "so we created a number of regular projects to fall under the umbrella of WOW Productions." In addition to Split Britches' and Forrester's work, these projects have included the Lower East Side Girls' Chorus, a loose collection of women who got together to sing; "Holl's Dolls," a group directed by Holly Hughes that is currently working on a new version of *Bye Bye Birdie;* "High Fiber Comedy," featuring the comic Reno; and the Working Girls Repertory, a newly-formed ongoing women's repertory. Working Girls Repertory premiered in December with an adaptation of Hans Christian Andersen's *The Snow Queen,* adapted by Shaw and directed by Weaver. Incorporating story-telling techniques with dramatic representation, the play offers a subtly feminist revision of the fairy tale.

If the Cafe has not declared any manifestos to define the nature of WOW productions, some common themes and esthetics have emerged. Feminism and lesbianism appear in the shows not as issues but as givens. If there is an overriding artistic impulse, says Young, "it's simply to invent from what we have. We can't afford to go out and buy things, so our limits determine our creativity." What is true literally of the sets and costumes applies equally to the material of the plays—it is drawn from the women's lives. The stylistic result is an attention to detail, an approach Weaver calls "a feminine esthetic because its details are often forgotten or stepped over in male-dominated works. But little parts of our lives are as important as the big climactic events that usually make dramas." Often, for instance, they work from simple images or from examining a single day in a character's life. Their method of working also reflects a feminist intention with its implicit rejection of mainstream hierarchy; jobs are defined and individuals take responsibility for specific tasks, but everyone contributes to creative processes in discussion, and anyone can become part of the Cafe staff simply by choice.

Working within limitations may be a fruitful challenge, Shaw is quick to point out, but she thinks they would do just as well with plenty of money and a big space. But chances are they won't ever have to worry about money cramping their creativity because they have slim prospects of ever acquiring much cash flow. Members of the WOW staff disagree about applying for grants. Some, like Troyano, believe that no one wants to bother sitting down to write proposals. Angelos likes the idea of grants, but found when she did some research that "the kinds of things I thought we might be able to get money for were not really the kinds of things we wanted to do." And Shaw worries that "grants change you. You get grants, people come in and *judge* you, and you start thinking that you better not do anything that will make them take your grant away." "Butch and femme night?" someone chimes in referring to a past extravaganza, "Forget it."

To compensate, WOW still throws benefits now and then; some of the best ones, the staff claims, have been rent parties. And some of them have been known to beg on the street, in Shaw's words, "guilt-tripping our friends into writing checks." It does not help that the Cafe has been robbed periodically. "Don't publish that we just bought a new projector," Angelos jokes. The life of Cafe property has averaged three or four months. They had speakers for only a month and have lost many bicycles. Shaw says, "They used to come here and even drink our beer, throw the cans on the floor, and leave the toilet seat up. But that stopped many months ago. Things feel safer."

The Cafe is even safer in a figurative sense. Anyone is encouraged to get up and perform at WOW and, says Weaver, "that encouragement creates a freedom to express oneself. Once a performer feels safe, you can train her." Troyano agrees and considers the support she gets from her WOW colleagues a crucial element of her progress. "People here will be critical of your work," she says, "but they'll criticize in a positive way that's helpful when you go out to perform in the other theatre world."

Though several of the WOW women refer to "the real theatre world," they do not really feel isolated or illegitimate. A number of WOW technicians and designers are hired by Equity productions, and the Cafe is known as a resource for good stage managers and technical people. But what gives WOW its strength is its independence: it needs no external sanctioning in order to survive because it has a loyal, critical audience of women of various backgrounds who consider the Cafe vital. "We do want criticism," Weaver points out. "We don't want to be ghettoized, but we also like the safe, growing atmosphere." "It's a place to learn the craft," says Troyano, "while you're doing it." Above all, Weaver continues, "the WOW Cafe is community theatre in the best sense—it's creating theatre of, for and by the community. If we have a big show to put on, we don't go outside to find a more talented actress, for instance, or a more talented and expensive lighting designer. We pull all the resources from the community as it continues to form itself." That's why WOW will survive even if they have to leave 330 E. 11th. WOW's community is defined by a force bigger than geography.

An Evening in the East Village
(1984)

TDR felt that one way to understand the characteristics, scope, range and diversity of performance in New York City's East Village would be to consider all of the presentations on a given evening. The evening we chose was Friday, November 30, 1984. Here are reports documenting the performances of that evening. We might have published them in an order that followed a possible walking itinerary from one club to another. Since the performances were more-or-less simultaneous, however, and no one could have seen all of them, the reports are presented in alphabetical order according to the names of the clubs. Readers may choose their own itinerary.

—The Editors

Carmelita Tropicana Chats
at the Club Chandalier

Jill Dolan

When an innocent spectator at the Club Chandalier's bar ordered a J&B on the rocks, the bartender yelled, "J&B on the rocks? What do you think this is, the Mayfair Hotel? This is Avenue C!" Located on Avenue C between 8th and 9th Streets, Club Chandalier is anything but high class. Without the street number, the club would be impossible to find. Luckily, the number 120 is pasted on the door, which is partially ajar by 10:50 p.m. on Friday, November 30. The club is a room on the second floor to the right of a long set of steep wooden stairs. The door opens onto a long narrow room, the front half of which serves as the performance space and seating area. The back half houses the wooden bar with several wobbly stools, a fireplace that doesn't seem to work, and piecemeal old furniture where spectators sit waiting for the performance to start.

Before the show, the bar is the center of activity. A small glass chandelier that looks slightly dusty and yellowed hangs low above the bar and seems to provide the club's name. The bartender, who is later billed as New York's meanest, is a woman wearing black lipstick, a black leather short skirt, fishnet stockings strategically ripped, and a deep-plunging, black sleeveless top with thin straps. A snake tattoo crawls up from between her breasts, and her cleavage is marked by a seashell. Her neck is ringed by a studded black leather collar. In an unabashedly loud New York accent, she seems to be the night's warmup act: "You just passing the time of day, or do you want to order?" "Are you just here to ogle me, or do you want to order a drink?" There is some confusion about what to charge for the Blatz or Rolling Rock beer and jug wine, but after collecting from customers, the bartender noisily rattles her large tip jar until customers donate.

The crowd is mostly women, many of whom are recognizable from the 8:30 show at the WOW Cafe. The spectators mingle freely; many seem to know each other and are comfortable in the space. Performers are difficult to distinguish from spectators. One woman wears a black mask, another wears a formal tux and carries a small stringed instrument. Others wear what look like fright wigs or have strangely colored punk-style hair. There is some traffic between the room with the bar and a back room, where the performers seem to be getting ready.

Before the show begins, an eclectic set of color slides is projected on a screen hanging from the ceiling across from the bar. Burnt out buildings, many recognizable from the walk to the club, are superimposed with abstract graphic shapes. Geometric plexiglass pieces sit on the mantelpiece above the fireplace. Pseudo-Greek sculptures are strewn about. Several plaster heads on long white poles are gathered in a kind of umbrella stand, lit with blue light. The entire low ceiling is covered with a dark, plastic material speckled with dayglo paint. The covering dips in places where it isn't securely fastened. A Harlequin-type character is suspended from the ceiling above the spectators; it holds a long tube from which a headless G.I. Joe doll hangs. To its right, also suspended, is a large canvas shape from which a light shines. The ceiling is so low, the three fresnels hanging directly in front of the shallow performance space appear to be part of the club's decor. A mirror covers the wall to the right of the space, and a makeshift curtain marks off a "backstage" corner.

The pre-show music—tapes played from a cassette deck above the refrigerator behind the bar—ranges from reggae to Muzak. The club fills up quickly; people jam into the 50–75 folding chairs, and the overflow stands in the back and along the sides of the space. The audience clearly anticipates *Carmelita Tropicana Chats*. As soon as the lights dim, the spectators begin to laugh. Lou, a woman with a crew cut, wearing a tie, who has mingled freely with spectators and seems to know everyone, introduces Carmelita as "part-time talk show host and feminist." To wild applause, Carmelita appears in a low-cut, flaming red evening gown covered with large black and green printed flowers. A black feather boa is draped around her shoulders. She wears a flower behind each ear and dangling earrings that look like miniature disco balls. Her dress is partially unzipped in the back.

Carmelita greets the crowd with Cuban flair and a wide, toothy smile, and they respond by yelling phrases like, "I love it when you talk dirty." Carmelita, in Mike Douglas fashion, warmly informs the crowd that she will begin with a medley of her greatest hits, and relates that she's recently won an award for her singing. In an unself-consciously off-key voice, she sings old standards like "Que Sera Sera" and "You Light Up My Life," pronouncing the lyrics with the Cuban accent she maintains throughout the performance.

Carmelita's solo segment is a lesbian parody of the standard talk show formula. After her tuneful beginning, which immediately wins the spectators, Carmelita offers a cooking lesson, since after all, "the way to a woman's heart is through her stomach." With a white paper bag on her head to serve as a chef's hat—although it quickly falls off—Carmelita lays out a Japanese mat to demonstrate her brand of Japanese-Cuban cooking. A raw chicken is used for the lesson. Carmelita insists you have to become friends with the chicken before you cook it, and she dances with it a bit before she hacks it up with a large, Samurai-type knife. She asks for a "beautiful audience helper" to accompany her rhythmically by banging on a pot while she garnishes the chicken with paper parasols.

Tammy Whynot, a famous country-western singer, is Carmelita's first guest. Carmelita invites her out for some "chick chat," and to "talk about her life as a womans." The two women sit next to each other on a single row of old theatre seats and discuss Tammy's recently published autobiography. The exchange is impromptu, if not improvised. Carmelita ad libs her interjections while Tammy narrates most of her life history in a twangy country accent. Tammy wears a tight sequined gown, and her hair is piled into layers of blond white curls. On Carmelita's prompting, Tammy reads a poem from her book, dedicated to her children. It chronicles events in their childhoods that Tammy missed while she was touring ("Mama was out of town"). Delivered with saccharine sentiment in forced rhyme, the poem parodies the mainstream opinion of the working mother's dilemma. At the end of Tammy's visit, Carmelita joins her in an off-key duet, and the two reveal that they will soon be starring together in a television special.

The next segment is filmmaker Holly Hughes' "dyke-umentary." Hughes introduces the super-8 film, projected on a cloth suspended from the ceiling. She says the film was funded by the National Geographic Society, since it is a study of flora and fauna in Provincetown, Massachusetts. The spectators, who seem aware of Provincetown's reputation as a lesbian and gay summer retreat, are prepared for the shots of women cavorting on the beach, and laugh appreciatively. The film is shot as a home movie—Hughes and her lover

Becoming friends with the chicken: Carmelita dances with the bird before she hacks it up in her demonstration of Japanese-Cuban cooking. (Photo: Kate Davy)

appear being knocked down by waves, and most of the spectators recognize many of the other women in the film. Halfway through, Carmelita re-appears in a black tuxedo as Julio, the popular Latin singing sensation. She is joined by another woman, who does an impersonation of Willie Nelson. Together, they sing "To All the Girls I've Loved," forgetting most of the lyrics and building to a dramatic, off-key finale as the film ends.

As Julio, Carmelita introduces her next guest, Sherry Baby, who appears in a tux and a slightly loose bow tie to present "Easy Music Lesson 15: Latin Rhythms." Standing in front of a music stand on which oversized sheet music rests, Sherry plays chords and progressions on a zither-like instrument, and talks about "trying to get rid of the mystique" of learning to play music. With a smooth, low, deadpan delivery, Sherry pontificates around musical themes: "Many have gone deaf trying to amplify the obvious." Her remarks are vaguely sarcastic and point out certain semantic absurdities. For instance, she talks about keeping time, "as if one could keep time."

For "Tattle Tale," the show's final segment, Carmelita introduces three "famous" couples, who are asked various personal questions about their relationships in the style of *The Newlywed Game*. Uzi Parnes and Ela Troyano (the owners and operators of Club Chandalier, who also live above the space) sit front to back facing away from the spectators and barely answer questions. Holly Hughes sits on her lover Bonnie Sue Katz' lap and plays dumb in response to most of the questions. Lou and Margaret (the woman wearing the black mask) are openly affectionate with each other and answer the questions a bit too honestly to produce the intended comic effect. Carmelita is joined by the bartender: together, they become the fourth famous couple. The bartender's outlandish responses to the questions bring them the spectators' vote—indicated by wild applause—as the couple with the most interesting relationship.

The surprise Mystery Guest who ends the performance is pushed from backstage hidden in a large cardboard box. When the lid is removed, Carmelita jumps out, holding a birthday cake, which she presents to Sherry. The performance becomes a party for spectators inclined to stay.

Most of the spectators do remain in the club, since the atmosphere throughout the evening has been more like a party than a performance. The context for *Carmelita Tropicana Chats* is clearly a mix of invention and a kind of twisted reality that might not be easily distinguished by the uninitiated. Tammy Whynot, for instance, is a character Lois Weaver plays in Split Britches' *Upwardly Mobile Home* at the WOW Cafe. Weaver arrived at Club Chandalier in full costume and remained in character before and after the performance. The bartender maintained her persona both behind the bar and during her performance stint, leading one to doubt that she was "acting." The performers seemed to be merely exaggerating parts of themselves, as people at parties entertaining friends might do to get laughs.

Darinka

Danny Sandford

Darinka is a small performance club located at 118 E. 1st Street between Avenues A and 1st. Formerly an after-hours club, Darinka, which is a woman's name meaning "gift giver" in Serbo-Croatian, opened to the public in Summer 1984. Club owner Gary Ray Bugarchich envisioned a space that could provide quality performance art and new music in a relaxed, intimate atmosphere. He intended to create an environment that "made people feel like they were at a party. Not necessarily a disco, but a no-pressure situation."

Though the club is part of the new phenomenon sweeping the East Village, it does not share the geographical or urban characteristics of its counterparts. Instead, it lies on the edge of "alphabet town," embracing a part of E. Houston Street that remained relatively unaffected by the demographic changes and urban blight that transformed much of the neighboring area during the 1970s. Thus, Darinka is in a more stable neighborhood, the latest incarnation in a succession of private clubs, rather than the product of creatively "adjusted" space. Because of this, it needed little, if any, interior remodelling. And, loyal to its exterior environment, it sought to integrate itself with the now flourishing neighborhood.

Darinka is easy to miss unless one is looking for it. The only beacons are some unobtrusive spray-painted letters over a brick wall and the number 118 in black. No light, no bric-a-brac, no large sign. The door, a few steps below street level, is hidden behind a set of black metal stairs that lead to apartments on the first and upper floors of the building. As one descends the few steps to a landing beneath the metal staircase, there is the faintly illicit feeling of entering a private domain. The space is small but intimate. As the patron enters, he or she is greeted by either Gary or a door person who relates the cover charge for the evening (usually $3 or $4, depending on the night of the week). On the right wall of the inside landing area is a black cloth with a sheet announcing the evening's fare. By contrast, the opposite wall is a smorgasbord composite of flyers and notices of past and upcoming events. Three more steps lead down to the audience space, which resembles someone's oversized living room. It is cozy. The walls are painted white, covered with paintings of different sizes. The ceiling is low and embellished with a light stucco effect. The floor is a neat, solid chequer of black-and-white linoleum tiles. The room has a satisfying sense of grace and elegance without being pretentious or overly elaborate. On the right is a bar with ample storage space behind it for stocking cases of beer. The stage lies on the opposite end. A corridor, leading straight to the back, divides the stage from the bathroom area. This corridor leads to a small open backstage room used for storing props and instruments between shows, or for performers who prefer not to mingle with their audience before show time. The corridor opens to the backyard that has been covered up with wood planking and serves as an auxiliary lounge area. Two spotlights illuminate the backyard, sparsely furnished with a few chairs and a simple table or two.

The audience space is an informal, open area conducive to milling about, talking and just simply socializing. Chairs are usually not set up. They are brought out from the back and left for the patrons to arrange. It is unclear whether the paintings are for sale or not since Darinka is not really a gallery. But their presence lends a degree of artiness to the space. Along the east wall, a built-in bench extends the length of the room, from stage to bar. On the western wall, a much smaller carpet-covered version serves a similar purpose.

The performing area is a raised stage with the only entrance at the left side. It measures 11 feet by 10 feet at a height of six-and-one-half feet. A square, supporting pillar separates the hallway from stage and frames the proscenium. General lighting fixtures include two orange bubble lights fixed to both sides of the stage. Three bare spotlights complemented by two angled clip-lights provide virtually the stage's only illumination. The light is harsh and white.

The bill for Friday, November 30th included *Darkness,* a set of three short one-act plays; the music of Laraaji, playing a zither-like autoharp; and two Englishmen who call themselves "Fast Forward" playing steel drums. At 9:00, the scheduled time for *Darkness,* there were 35–40 people in the club. Twenty-five minutes later, when the show began, another 10 had arrived. The chairs had been carefully arranged in rows facing the stage for this performance. The audience was quiet, expectant, well-behaved. It seemed to be a theatre crowd, there solely because of the first group.

Darkness: **First Play**

A bearded man comes onstage with a chair that has only three legs. He places the chair on the floor, sits in it and promptly collapses. Half surprised, he exclaims from the floor, "I don't want to." He gets up, moves the chair to another location two feet away and gingerly sits down. This time he does not fall and echoes part of his previous statement in a more subdued tone: "Want to." He rises and places the chair in the first location, falls down again, says "sleep," gets up, moves to the second location and so on, repeating the same pattern of actions throughout the following soliloquy: "I don't want to...sleep...don't touch it...it's in pain...I can't sit on it...it'll break...silent song...friend." He drags the chair off. End of piece.

Darkness: **Second Play**

Folding chairs are brought on and arranged in three rows with a middle aisle, facing the audience. A woman and man, both clad in nondescript brown shirts and pants, come onstage and sit in the front row on different sides. They stare directly ahead into the audience as if watching a film.

The bearded man enters and in a whimpering manner asks the man seated up front to move, claiming the seat is his. The first man logically refutes his claim. They continue talking until the arrival of two more women, dressed in the same drab clothes, interrupts their conversation. The women sit in the back row, on opposite sides of the aisle. One of them complains, in a tired voice, of not being able to see the screen. The other woman chides her in a German accent, and asks her to leave or to ask the men to move. A fourth woman appears. She sits next to the woman up front. She is tense and complains in a highpitched voice to the woman next to her that she can't hear or see the screen. Her interlocutor responds in a thick Brooklyn accent and tells her to be quiet.

In each pair, the complainant is recognizable by the white pallor on their face, while the stronger partner has a reddened face. The dialog is circuitous and totally absurd. Their world is a Beckettian setting presided over by a film they cannot see or hear.

At one point the women in the back row move to the middle row, sticking out their heads to see around the people in front of them. Each character has a characteristic tic or movement pattern that they employ intermittently.

> *Hypertense Woman:* I can't see.
> *Tough Brooklyner:* Close your eyes. What do you see?
> *Hypertense Woman:* Nothing.
> *Tough Brooklyner:* Open them. Now what do you see?
> *Hypertense Woman:* Same thing.

The characters all rise: The bearded man starts whining loudly. The others try to quiet him.

> *Hypertense Woman:* I've run out of ideas.
> *Tough Brooklyner:* That's redundant.
> *Whimpering Man:* The lights have gone out.
> *Logical Man:* No there's no one here to turn them out. . . .

The cast then takes a deep breath and says in unison "breathe." As the lights start to fade, they all quickly and repeatedly blurt out "excuse me," overlapping each other. End of piece.

Darkness: **Third Play**

A woman wearing a black leotard, black pants, boots and a large grey, Mexican-type wool sweater comes out on stage. She stands. She takes a position. Isn't sure of herself. Feels uncomfortable. Tries to execute a series of movements. It's awkward. She loses balance and moves to another position. She repeats the movements but again loses balance. Third attempt. She succeeds. She emits a cry of triumph and raises her hands to the ceiling. End of piece.

Jo Andres' *Liquid TV*
at 8BC

Norma Adler

8BC, as the name suggests, is a club located between Avenues B and C, at 337 E. Eighth Street. After paying the cover charge at the door, one passes on to an area—similar to a foyer—approximately 12 feet long by eight feet wide. Promotional material for upcoming events at the club is located here, as are the entrance to the soundbooth and a small alcove where people play cards. The soundbooth is painted with balloons, squiggles and semi-nude women. Decals in various shapes also adorn the booth. To reach the main floor, where the bar, tables and chairs are, one descends from the foyer about five feet via a wide staircase. Directly opposite, and at the same height as the foyer, is the proscenium stage. It appears as though the main floor—between the foyer and stage—was excavated, thus creating an unusual arrangement of levels within the club.

The stage spans the entire width of one wall. The other three walls are exposed brick; some of the brick is painted, but most of it is bare. Along one wall is a row of tables and chairs; opposite is the long low bar. The mural hanging above the bar depicts women, bare to the waist, chased by vicious dogs along the beach. Three slender columns extend from floor to ceiling, approximately 20 feet high, on the main floor. There is seating for about 30 people; by the time *Liquid TV* commences, there will be almost 100 people in the room.

On the wall near the tables, approximately four-and-one-half feet above the floor, is a mounted rail, on which an art exhibit is mounted. The exhibit consists of five figures. They are constructed from discarded items easily found on the streets and vacant lots in the East Village. The heads are made from cardboard boxes and are designed to look like birds and fantastic creatures. The bodies are made of cloth, black plastic bags, wooden slats, and other items. While the heads are reminiscent of totem-pole figures, the bodies appear more like scarecrows.

At 11:40 p.m. the crank curtain goes up and Jo Andres' *Liquid TV* begins. On the stage, three small portable television sets face away from the audience. Mimi Goese and Lucy Sexton, dressed in black tank tops and pants, manipulate plexiglass tubes shaped like batons to taped electronic music. With stylized movements, they threaten each other with the tubes. Handing the tubes to assistants in the wings, the women perform percussive, angular, dance-like movements, mostly in unison. Occasionally, they stamp the floor. Retrieving the tubes, they put fluorescent blue lights inside. The stage lights grow dim, and we see two eerie blue glowing objects moving about the stage. Suddenly, Goese and Sexton blow the blue lights out of the tubes. The stage lights return.

A second taped song is played, and Jo Andres, dressed like the others, joins the two women. They do similar percussive movements, both in unison and in counterpoint to each other, sometimes striking a position reminiscent of Auguste Rodin's sculpture *The Thinker*.

At the conclusion of the second song, musician Bob Gale begins to play his electric cello. Patterned lights sweep over him, then return to the three women on the stage. Two hold red shields and the other holds a green one. They manipulate the shields through a bolt of tulle or netting that appears to be wisps of smoke in the blue-gray lights. Patterns are projected onto the fabric, and red fish, people, multicolored fish and a skeleton float across the fabric. The tulle is moved through the lights as though it were mist that could be controlled.

One woman goes offstage while the other two manipulate the fabric. The first one returns wearing what appears to be outsized cardboard feet on top of her own. In the light one can barely see the women—rather, the impression one receives is that of giant feet moving through a sea of smoke or mist.

The women retrieve their plexiglass tubes, and the cardboard feet are removed. Green and blue lights are inserted into the tubes. After making patterns in the darkness with the lights, they all blow the colored lights out of the tubes.

In near darkness, the three approach the small television sets. They reach for glowing makeup in front of the screens and apply it to their own faces, hands, arms, clothing and hair. They do some dance moves, throwing off bits of the glowing matter onto the stage, audience and each other.

Vampire Lesbians of Sodom
at the Limbo Lounge

Arnold Aronson

Although it is a Friday night, E. 9th Street between Avenues B and C is virtually deserted. Not all the street lights work, so there are stretches of darkness along the block. Some of the apartment buildings along the street seem to have been recently renovated, attesting to the gentrification of the East Village, but there are still gutted ruins along the way. A "people's park" has been created amidst the rubble of some vacant lots across from the Limbo Lounge.

The Lounge itself is not easily spotted. Looking down the street from Tompkins Square, there are no bright lights, no crowds of people. There is little to identify the theatre from the outside except a small sign on the wall above the door saying "Limbo." Otherwise, it looks pretty much like the other tenements and storefronts of the neighborhood.

Inside it is crowded, though strangely subdued. The show is scheduled to begin at 10 p.m. The doors open at 9:30, and by 9:40 all of the 75 or so metal folding chairs are filled. Immediately inside the door is a small lobby area

The Limbo Lounge, on E. 9th Street between Avenues B and C

where money is taken and programs are handed out. You then proceed down a short hallway past the restrooms to the theatre. Although a basically long and narrow space, the theatre seems cavernous because of the extremely high ceiling.

One of the first impressions upon entering the Lounge is the violet glow. The whole space seems suffused in dim violet or purple light. The space itself is spare: there is no architectural detail or decoration, although some walls are covered with large paper murals painted in crude comic book style, depicting a somewhat profane version of Little Red Riding Hood. To one side of the space is a bar with a crude frame—like a peaked roof—over it, and decorated in small white Christmas lights. The stage is a simple raised platform with a white back wall framed in black drapes.

As more and more people arrive, they stand in the back or in the aisle. Some hang around the bar. A few people in the audience are drinking Rolling Rock beer from bottles purchased at the bar. There is a lot of cigarette smoke. While the atmosphere is extremely informal, it is clearly a theatre. Quiet, recorded music is playing in the background. People sit quietly or talk softly waiting for the performance to begin. The audience is primarily gay and conservatively dressed; this is not the East Village Punk scene one sees on the street a block or two away. It is a cult audience familiar with the work of playwright/actor Charles Busch, and with the high-camp style of this company. It is not a "theatre audience"—by and large, these spectators are not familiar with nor interested in the range of avant-garde theatre available elsewhere in the city. It is a young audience and many are not familiar with the early work of John Vaccaro, Ron Tavel, Charles Ludlam, and Hot Peaches, which is a clear precedent for this performance. This is an audience out for simple entertainment.

By the time the house lights dim, there are perhaps 150 people sitting and standing in the theatre. As the lights go down, corny movie music from the '30s is heard—something appropriate for old vampire films. The audience laughs at the music, which continues for two or three minutes. The house lights finally dim completely, and the same music repeats; more laughter. The plot is simple. Scene one occurs in ancient Sodom where a monster, the Succubus—a vampire (played by one of the two women in the cast)—demands young virgins. Two scantily-clad young men bring her a virgin in the person of Charles Busch in drag. Scene two takes place in '20s Hollywood where the Succubus and her victim have become rival film stars. Scene three is set in current-day Las Vegas, where the two rivals meet again, this time in the form of an aging star and a scrub woman. In this scene, three chorus boys get to do a take-off on a disco number from the film *Flashdance*.

The acting style throughout is purposely "bad," though obviously very controlled. The performers are almost always grouped at the center of the bare

Julie Halston (left) and Charles Busch (right) in *Vampire Lesbians of Sodom*

stage, the white background throwing them into relief. Most lines are delivered to the audience rather than to the other performers. Poses are carefully struck. Gestures and line readings are broad, melodramatic and campy. The script, of course, is written in a parodistic style reminiscent of old movies in which emotion and plot contrivance took precedence over logic and verisimilitude.

The audience seemed to be a participant in the performance, not through any physical involvement, but through enthusiastic, spontaneous responses to performers, characters and lines. Lavish costumes, favorite actors (several performers were clearly known to the audience from other shows), in-jokes and clever parodies brought cheers, raucous laughter, and applause. The line between performer and character was tenuous, at best, and while the "illusion" was never broken, the performers were adept at playing to the audience.

After the curtain call, Busch stepped forward to introduce the cast and crew and to make announcements about upcoming events, mailing lists and the like. His speech emphasized the intimacy and informality of the event. The violet houselights came back on, and loud music began to play.

Beth Lapides'
A Good American Novel
at P.S. 122

Amy C. Ward

Billed as "the Einstein of performance art" and "a cross between Bill Murray and Judy Garland," Beth Lapides opened her newest performance, *A Good American Novel,* at P.S. 122 on Friday, November 30. P.S. 122 is a versatile space, and for this performance, it was converted into a quasi-club atmosphere. The spectators had three seating choices: folding chairs on conventional risers, seats at small, round cloth-covered tables, or foam cushions on the floor in front of the tables. The performance area consisted of a rectangular raised platform stage about four feet high and an open semi-circular floor space in front of that. Behind and to the left of the open area was a synthesizer and sound system, and a projection screen hung centered behind and above the stage.

Before the performance officially began, the audience's participation helped to shape Lapides' show. Along with programs, spectators were given ballots on which they were instructed to nominate three books for the Great

American Novel. The winners would be announced by Lapides during her performance. A P.S. 122 representative stated that beer was available for $2.00, information that did not go unheeded. Many spectators seemed to know one another, and as they drank their beer and mingled, the space took on the ambiance of a club, rather than the more formal aspects associated with a theatre event.

Lunatune, a four-woman *a capella* group, began the evening with four original compositions. Their off-beat, comical numbers ranged from a piece connecting a Dear Abby column and nuclear war to a satirical look at women victims in popular love songs. Using fedoras, baseball caps, sunglasses and other paraphernalia, Lunatune's characters alternated between a variety of ages, genders and occupations.

Following their set, Lunatune collected the audience's ballots, and a 10-minute intermission gave everyone a chance to chat over another beer. Two microphones were set up on the stage for Lunatune, who assisted Lapides with the music in her performance.

Lapides casually strolled out, and the lights dimmed. She wore a white suit, red shirt and socks, and a blue tie. She carried a clipboard and, flipping her long brown curls behind her, began constructing a story, "Mad Lib" style. The audience supplied Lapides with words for locations, foods, smells, emotions and so on, and she filled in the blanks. The bulk of the story, about a woman's search for the meaning of life, had already been written by Lapides. When the audience's improvised information was inserted, parts of the story were hilariously cock-eyed, others amazingly appropriate.

Next, Lapides performed a song accompanied by a synthesizer and Lunatune, who appeared above and behind her on the platform. A mirror ball with a baby doll stuck in its center dropped from the ceiling and began to spin. This connected the song to the Mad Lib story, which ends when the heroine meets two babies, one of whom tells her that life is a river, the other insisting that it is not. Lapides' song concerned the qualities that make a hero, something she said no Great American Novel could be without.

Allowing Lunatune to do most of the singing, Lapides danced free-form around the space, combining spins, twists and boogie steps. Her voice is strong but atonal, so her singing sounded more like chanting, especially when juxtaposed with Lunatune's tight harmonies. She seemed well aware of her off-key singing and appeared disinterested in convincing the spectators that she possessed great vocal ability.

In fact, the entire tone of Lapides' performance contained this off-the-cuff quality. Although much of her text was probably pre-determined, she performed it without polish or glitz. Lapides has been described as a stand-up comic, but *A Good American Novel* had none of that genre's hard-edged tendencies. The feeling was one of intimacy, as though Lapides was an old friend who simply wanted to share some thoughts about heroes, good books and, as she put it, "maintaining your sense of self in the face of it all."

She explored the notion of heroism throughout the piece, telling the story of Hero and Lysander, which is the etymological origin of the word "hero." As she described the tale's action, she demonstrated it physically, first playing Lysander, then running across the space to play Hero. As the story built, so did Lapides' movement, becoming more and more frantic.

Her ability to perform two characters simultaneously, story-theatre style, was also exhibited in an interview with herself. She set up two folding chairs and grabbed a handful of index cards containing questions. Slides of Johnny Carson with a guest were projected onto the screen behind her. As she switched between asking a question and nimbly jumping to the other chair to answer it, additional slides were superimposed over Carson's and his guests' faces so that interviews occurred between, among others, Porky Pig, David Brenner, Ed Koch and Yoda. As soon as she had read a question, Lapides flung the index card over her shoulder, and by the time her self-interrogation was finished, the floor was strewn with questions.

Then came the moment to announce the winners of the Great American Novel election. First, Lapides read a list of honorable mentions. Next, a member of Lunatune marched out, bearing an envelope marked "second runner-up." Lapides peeked inside and exclaimed, "Oh great! I was hoping this would be one of them." She then stuffed the envelope inside her pocket, making the audience wait to hear the title. "Before I read it," she explained, "I want to talk a little more about what makes a novel great." She began a story about life with Gregory, her boyfriend. Halfway through it, she stopped and, based on the "palpable audience expectancy" she said she felt, decided to get on with announcing the winners. The second runner-up was *Catcher in the Rye,* and the first runner-up was *Huckleberry Finn,* "a great novel about life being a river," she commented, "just like the little baby said." The winner, presented with a flourish by Lunatune, sent Lapides into gales of laughter. It was *Moby Dick,* a book she said she had never gotten through but was currently reading because, "I knew it would be a winner in the performance."

A Good American Novel continued with another story from Lapides' everyday life. She recreated the experience of sitting in her living room in the evening and hearing the people around her practice various skills. First she hears a piano student playing scales, then a violinist's exercises, then a vocalist and, finally, a group of Hell's Angels on the street below, revving up their motorcycle engines. As Lapides spoke, the sounds she described were played over the speakers, creating an accumulation of musical and mechanical noises. As the sounds faded, Lapides reflected on whether or not people and their societies are getting better. "I guess, with all this practicing going on," she said, "we must be at least *trying* to get better."

Lapides' performance ended with another song, again accompanied by Lunatune. As she danced, hair flying in all directions, she sang lyrics like:

> We're trying to get better
> We read a lot of books
> Heroes they have defects
> Be your own hero
> Be your own hero
> I just want to tell
> my own story

The song ended, and Lapides thanked the audience for coming. "I hope you enjoyed this," she said. "Thanks for letting me tell my own story."

Ethyl Eichelberger in
Souled Out (or *Dr. Mary Faustus*)
at the Pyramid Club

L. George Odom

Walking down Avenue A, it wouldn't be difficult to pass the entrance to the Pyramid Club. Two heavily barred windows frame a single black metal door. There is no name, no sign, except for a black-outlined, stacked-stone pyramid painted over the door. The doorman, who sits just inside the door next to a small table littered with performance flyers, collects the cover charge (which on some nights can now be $10).

The long and narrow bar area is currently decorated in what could be called "new wave surrealism" with an overlay of Cocteau. Broken framed mirrors with dripping blood cover the long wall across from the bar; a sculpted and splattered black cat in a flimsy cage hangs over the bar's service area; a mannequin's leg projects through a hoop that hangs from the ceiling midway along the mirrored wall. In the center of the ceiling is a large beach umbrella, striped and starred in circus colors with Christmas twinkle lights around its perimeter. A line of yellow and orange painted flames moves across the top of the bar's back wall, in the center of which is a rough cartoon portrait of President and Mrs. Reagan topped by two American flags. Just below, three green-painted fish on sticks circle mechanically, appearing to "jump" over and again through a box of painted water. The ceiling is studded with irregularly sized and spaced mylar diamonds.

In contrast to this imposed decor are the actual fixtures themselves. The heavy old wooden bar runs the length of the front room. The mirrored

The Pyramid Club, at 101 Avenue A between 6th and 7th, with the stone-stacked pyramid over the entrance

backing and bar service area are (besides the superficial trimmings) relatively unchanged. The tile floor is almost worn through. Old-fashioned lamps hang over the bar, the only illumination except for the twinkle lights above and the beams of colored light aimed about the room.

The crowd on November 30, 1984, is as incongruous and mixed as the surrounding decor. New neighborhood people mix with old neighborhood people. Three young men at the end of the bar in New Wave garb (black pants, jackets and boots) are having a serious discussion over beers beside three other guys (in designer jeans, sweatshirts and sport shoes) who are laughing about one of their girlfriends. At 8:30 p.m. (very early for the Pyramid) the crowd also includes a dozen or so other people, most in dark clothes, all with idiosyncratic hairstyles. They seem to group rather than divide into couples. Everyone seems oblivious to the crashing loud music issuing from the two huge speakers hung over the bar at each end of the room. Conversations are conducted either from mouth to ear, or shouted over the music.

The show is to start at 9 p.m., but no one seems to grow restless as the hour comes and goes. Periodically, sounds from the other room (staple guns, banging chairs) indicate the performance is not yet ready. Two large barn-like doors separate that room, usually used for dancing, from the bar; a fiery sign over the doors announces "DANCING."

At around 9:20, the barn doors are opened to carry something in and are left open. A group just arriving (including a tall blonde woman in a big black coat escorting a small white dog in a white sweater and red bow) enter the bar and head directly for the performance area. This begins a slow drifting of bar patrons into the other room. Where there used to be platforms and tables and chairs on each side, there are now narrow standing counters bolted to the exposed brick walls. The stage area is at the far end of the room—an eight feet by ten feet raised platform with exit stairs to the left side. A costumed figure is still staple-gunning drapes to the set: the gold front cloth is attached, then a side drape to cover the folding partition that masks entrances on the left. A projection screen hangs mid-room over the left side of the audience.

The white backcloth covering the wall behind the stage is painted with wild flames up to the ceiling (which is only about 8 feet above the stage). A small table along the back wall has a large, inverted, clear-glass light fixture on it, filled with a few strands of multicolored Christmas tree lights. A piano sits on the floor to the left in front of the exit screen. The stage manager's chair is against the right wall, a large Chinese gong suspended over it. Two accordions are set near the front of the stage, one left and one right.

At around 9:30, the seats begin to fill (only about 40 have been set up). Though some chairs remain empty, half a dozen people stand along the walls during the show. The projectionist takes his place half-way up a ladder at the rear of the room alongside the $1 coat-check booth. Several people stand at the entrance to the area just inside the closed doors. (Throughout the performance, people wander in and out of the room and stand at the sides and back.)

While the audience is talking, a large man in a black leotard, short black skirt, black tights and heels appears at the front. His whitened face has eyes and brows heavily outlined in black. He wears his hair pulled back into a snood and has an oversized "happy face" button for an earring. His name is Happy. Greeted by cheers, he introduces the play we are about to see and names the players. As each of their names is mentioned, they strike a pose on the stage; all but Dr. Mary Faustus (Ethyl Eichelberger) who seats her(him)self at the piano and plays the opening number. Eichelberger is accompanied throughout by a woman seated facing the stage to the right who plays conga drums and a recorder.

The story follows the traditional Goethe plot of Faust's dilemmas, yet with wild and campy sidetracks. Dr. Mary Faustus is tempted by Mephistopheles, then set straight by St. Angeles. They duel over her soul, each offering what he/she can. Dr. Mary Faustus is drawn one way, then the other. Wearing a golden, Greek-style drape and spiked headdress (reminiscent of the Statue of Liberty), Dr. Mary Faustus speaks in a deep, sonorous voice with the elocution of a turn-of-the-century Shakespearean actress. Breaking through this voice, at times of confusion and comedy, is a higher, nasal twang.

St. Angeles, covered in clouds of white tulle and net, also uses two voices—a soft, sweet, almost Confucius-like voice broken by sharp, piercing snaps of Brooklynese. Mephistopheles—in black fake-fur shorts, a tank top, tights, orange zapped wig, and voluminous red cape—uses a slimy, malevolent, sneering voice, touched at times by hints of Groucho Marx.

Dr. Mary Faustus is constantly being misunderstood by her two guardians. Because of her poetic and often verbose speech, St. Angeles and Mephistopheles periodically make indignant exclamations about what they think she said. For example, when speaking of Helen of Troy as "the face that launched a thousand ships," Dr. Mary Faustus is misunderstood to have said "fish and chips."

As the debate over Dr. Mary Faustus' soul rages in the first act, various songs are interjected, most accompanied by Eichelberger on the accordion. There are no segues into the songs. They are abruptly presented at the appropriate moment, in the style of old film musicals. Some mention is made of this technique in the dialog itself, with comments like, "That seems like a good time for a song." Of course, whenever Eichelberger reaches down and straps on an accordion, the audience has a pretty good idea that a song is close at hand.

Lines from other shows, famous names, and well-known places are used proliferously in the script. Any snatch of dialog that can be twisted and punned upon usually is. Mephistopheles tries to put Dr. Mary Faustus to sleep using the voice of the Wicked Witch of the West saying, "Sleep, sleep." At the mention of nirvana, St. Angeles breaks into a chorus of "Nirvana, nirvana, I love ya, nirvana . . ." to the tune of "Tomorrow" from the Broadway musical *Annie*. Keith Haring's name is slipped into the dialog along with other current headliners. Very apropos to the playing space, Dr. Mary Faustus is at one point to protect herself by placing herself inside a "pyramid." She holds a small mirrored one, and the stage manager constructs a crepe paper outline of a tetrahedron around her (at some length, with other players making comments about how long this is taking).

Later, the troupe makes its way down through the seas to Atlantis. The movie projector shows a short film of New York City buildings on the screen over the audience. As Dr. Mary Faustus describes Atlantis' great towers and wonders, she suddenly proclaims, pointing to the screen, "There's Atlantis!" At this point (whether or not it was planned) the film image changes to that of a metal sphere being struck by lightning bolts. Upon seeing this, Dr. Mary Faustus stops in mid-sentence and says in a confused, sarcastic tone, "That's not Atlantis." No attempt is made to reconcile the film with the dialog, or to explain what the image is meant to be.

While for the most part the three characters remain relatively stationary, maybe exchanging places or advancing forward or back, there is little room for stage blocking. Most of the dialog is spoken directly to the audience. Every line is accompanied by grand, sweeping gestures of the hands and arms and, of course, grand sweeps of attached fabric.

Although there is little conventional blocking, there is choreographed movement during some of the musical numbers. While Dr. Mary Faustus sings "I want to know if life is worth living," Mephistopheles and St. Angeles waltz in the background. On the third chorus, both join in harmony and the recorder plays a descant. As Mephistopheles sings "Each soul has a label...and a price," holding a portable stereo that is blasting a congested conga beat, Dr. Mary Faustus and St. Angeles do a sort of conga chorus line in the rear. When Dr. Mary Faustus sings a love song to Helen (played by St. Angeles in padding and an overlaid cape), pumping a great oomp-pa-pa melody from a large pearl accordion, Helen sways in time beside her as Mephistopheles disgruntledly looks on. On the third chorus, they all sing, counterpointing melodies from the rest of the show. Mephistopheles yodels. At the song's end, all three improvise convoluted cadenzas, Dr. Mary Faustus holding out the longest—then the big Act I finish.

It's intermission. The audience stays seated (or standing) and watches the set being altered. Happy tells us what they are doing and asks us to wait. In the meantime, he will entertain. He begins an impromptu song and dance routine to "When You're Smiling," but gets stumped on the words. People from the audience and someone from the stage try to help by shouting out the lyrics, but the song is abandoned. Happy hits upon a new idea—a song from "my new album." With a flourish of stomps and kicks, he performs a song about "a girl named Happy" to the tune of the theme song from *The Beverly Hillbillies*. As the audience applauds, lights come up on the stage, and the second act begins.

Act II opens with Dr. Mary Faustus tied with mesh material to the plumbing pipes in the ceiling. She is to be tortured and tempted with the Seven Deadly Sins. She encourages Mephistopheles to bring them on; she can resist them. One by one Mephistopheles carries in small stick-puppets that represent each of the sins. Dr. Mary Faustus recognizes each of them in turn, gives a short commentary on its evil properties, then sends it away. Near the end, she weakens and is tempted to sell out. St. Angeles pleads with her, singing, "Don't do it." Mephistopheles, getting desperate, pulls a gun on Dr. Mary Faustus and tries to force her to submit and sell her soul. He sings, "I've won, I've won, I've got a gun," a slower ballad. A fight ensues. Mephistopheles and Dr. Mary Faustus yank two long vertical plastic rods filled with now-lit Christmas lights out of the floor and use them as swords (shades of *Star Wars*). The light tubes go out and are discarded.

Dr. Mary Faustus calls to St. Angeles to help her subdue Mephistopheles. They wrestle him down and try to tie him up. Everyone but Mephistopheles is caught in the swaths of fabric hanging from the ceiling.

Realizing the situation, Mephistopheles takes the net and ties himself in it, proclaiming, "No, don't tie me up." Dr. Mary Faustus calls for help from Happy, who bounds onto the stage and ties up Mephistopheles, getting tangled in the web himself.

At this point, Dr. Mary Faustus realizes that they are all caught up together in the net—inseparable. She sees that she does not need to battle with these different forces, but that they are all a part of her, the good and the bad. Now, it's "all for one, and one for all." Tied together, Happy too, they belt out the final song.

There is a good deal of extended applause, and the room lights come on. One of the bar workers announces the performance is over and that the floor will soon be open for dancing. He asks everyone to fold their chairs and place them against the walls. The audience does so. The stage manager starts clearing the props, and the cast mingles with the crowd near the stage. The music and conversations from the bar area, which have been subdued yet constant during the show, now rev up again, and the large doors connecting the two rooms are opened.

The Shuttle

Judy Levine

The Shuttle Club is located in a basement at 523 E. 6th Street between Avenues A and B. At the top of the stairs is a sign: TO BE ADMITTED INTO "THE SHUTTLE THEATRE" EVERYBODY IS REQUIRED TO BE A MEMBER OF THE "INTERNATIONAL CENTER FOR URBAN RESOURCES." THE MEMBERSHIP IS ONLY GIVEN TO PEOPLE INTERESTED IN ART AND POPULAR CULTURE. Anyone who wants to enter the club can become a member.

Directly to the right of the sign, a cylindrical black light is glowing, and that, along with the small bulb at the desk at the bottom of the stairs, provides the only illumination for the trip down the wooden planks. Inside the theatre, there is a profusion of color. Clip-on lights—one lime green, another hot pink—are on all the walls. The performance area in the front of the space is red and blue; behind it, the wall is painted with streaks and drips of white, pink, red and light and dark turquoise. The ceiling is low, and the space is filled with columns, each one with large dots—pink, gray or black. There is the feeling of being closed-in in a highly colored place, the lights and walls compensating for the gray concrete floor. The 11 square tables have black formica tops; on each is a clamshell ash tray. The four red metal folding chairs around each table have rental-agency stickers on the back. Several "no smoking" signs are posted on the walls. There is a large couch in one corner; antique dresses with numbers on them hang above it. They seem like the numbers on objects at an auction, but the dresses are not for sale.

Art work decorates the unpainted walls. Black metal cutout figures dance wildly, two or three to a wall, and a large zig-zag strip made out of wood appears in several places. A bar selling coffee, wine and beer is in the back of the space, and near it is a large table with clothes, books and other odds and ends for sale. The proceeds of this sale go to a fund set up by the residents of the building to buy the building from the city. They, including the Shuttle Theatre, are still squatters at this point.

There's another art exhibition in the back near the bar: masks of jazz players and a musical sculpture. The entire exhibition is part of a new project by Sandro Dernini, the club's co-director, called JAM (Join Art and Music). The art installation changes weekly (this week's is by James McCoy), and this exhibition will culminate in a sound concept (Dernini's term) in which musicians will perform over the entire space of the club. McCoy has also made instruments, such as a drum carved from a tree stump that is played as part of the artist/musician collaboration project.

Dernini hopes that the work on the walls will become a stimulation for the music. In the same vein, next week, an artist is coming to sketch the musicians as they play. Dancers perform regularly with musicians on Sunday nights, and the Nuyorican Poet's Cafe also has readings on Sunday.

The music on Friday, November 30, the Roy Campbell Ethnic Trio, was scheduled to start at 11 p.m. Between 11 and 12:30 not much happened. A tape of recorded music played jazz, improvised synthesizer music, African music, Latin music and reggae. At 11:30, Campbell started warming up on saxophone. People straggled in, first several middle-aged people from the neighborhood, then a few of the musicians' friends, and then a few young people. No one was drinking anything from the bar. There was no heat, and the basement became colder and colder. People put their coats on.

Dernini started the music at 12:30 a.m. with an apology for being so late. "We are trying to be on time more," he said. The Roy Campbell Ethnic Trio was made up of William Parker on bass, percussion and the flute, Zen Matsura on drums and percussion, and Roy Campbell on trumpet and percussion. They play improvised avant-garde jazz, not based on existing song forms but growing out of the interaction between players. Typical of the four pieces played *(Imhotet, Emergence, Vigilance* and *Sketches of the Morning Moons)* was the opening composition *Imhotet.* This was a half-hour improvisation, the sections of which were differentiated by instrumentation, featured player and rhythmic character. All three players participate equally in the characteristic structure. There are usually three types of rhythms happening over one steady pulse. Campbell plays melodically, usually on trumpet, but also on French horn and South American bamboo flutes and reed pipes. Parker and Matsura are more active rhythmically, sometimes working together to create a unified line that builds with Campbell's solos, at other times working independently to create a richly layered shimmering contrapunctual texture. Layering is crucial to the feel of this trio—even when the texture becomes thinnest, in one of Parker's bass solos, Campbell accompanies him on bells.

When Campbell solos on trumpet, he starts with long melodies that build into a series of bursts of notes. These flurries of activity are often reiterated in Matsura's drums. Throughout Campbell's solos, Matsura and Parker phrase with him, creating patterns moment by moment that change almost before they can be recognized as patterns. The three players listen closely to one another.

The audience hushes each other on the solos and is generally attentive to the musicians. People have been steadily arriving, and by 1 a.m. the club is, while not crowded, filled. The crowd is about half black and half white, with many people appearing to know the musicians and each other. The ongoing pulse of the music has permeated the room, and people tap their feet as the space becomes more animated. Several tall black men with dred locks wander in and out of the club, talking to the man at the door. Dernini, dressed in corduroy pants, a shiny vinyl jacket and sunglasses, talks animatedly to a woman who has been snapping pictures. The bartender, not doing much business, talks to two men sitting at the bar. Dernini has kept this a membership club, not wanting to get involved with the problems (legal and otherwise) that commercialization and renown would bring. The club opened in July, and Dernini has been careful not to antagonize his residential neighbors. "We are not another gentrification group," he has stated categorically, comparing his club on the Lower East Side in 1984 to those in Harlem in 1926. The Shuttle Theatre has a strong identification with the black and Puerto Rican cultural movements, and the chairman of Plexus (the parent nonprofit corporation) is Richard Bruce Nuggent, once chairman of the Harlem Council of Art.

At 1:50 the music ends. Some people have left earlier, but now most stay. The atmosphere has become one of cordial, intense talk. The art surrounding the people adds to this intensity, and the talk seems to pick up what is lost when the music ends. The temperature in the club is almost freezing, but people seem to accept that. The evening's progression from cool to hopping has begun to reverse, and settles into a calm social buzz. The musicians pack up and leave, and people begin to drift out. Many will be back tomorrow.

**Heart of the Scorpion
at the WOW Cafe**

Kate Davy

Unlike other East Village performance spaces, the WOW Cafe is not located on one of the virtually deserted blocks in what has become known as "ABCland." It is on E. 11th Street, a well-lit, frequently traveled block between 1st and 2nd Avenues. WOW is a women's performance space, and a woman would not hesitate to walk there alone at night.

To find the theatre it is helpful to know the address, since the storefront that houses it does not call attention to itself—there is no sign on the building indicating that it is a theatre, only some flyers and photographs taped to the inside of the picture window and the window of the door. Although a performance was scheduled for the coming weekend, there was no way to know about it short of walking by the theatre at 330 E. 11th Street to read the unadorned, handwritten poster in the window that announced it.

The poster stated that a play entitled *The Heart of the Scorpion* by Alice M. Forrester would be playing at 8:00 p.m. The performance was neither advertised nor listed in the newspapers, and because the theatre has a pay telephone, there is no way to look up the phone number or get it from directory assistance. Clearly, word of mouth was the primary vehicle for attracting an audience to this particular performance, presumably an audience already familiar with the theatre.

At ten minutes to 8:00 there was no one outside the theatre and the door was locked. A woman answered the door and said that the show would begin at 8:30; a rehearsal was in progress. When asked if it was permissible to shoot photographs during the performance, the woman said that she would check with the director. But a woman standing behind her said, "No, no. The stage manager handles that." "O.K.," the first woman responded. Then she turned to head toward the stage, stopped, turned back, and asked, "Who is the stage manager?"

By 8:30 some spectators are seated while others are entering the dark doorway to pay the $5.00 admission at a small "ticket table" to the left of the door, lit by a single, glaring light. Although WOW calls itself a "café," no beverages are served.

The space is small and narrow, about 20 feet to the stage and only 10 feet wide. A very high ceiling lessens the room's potential to create an acutely claustrophobic feeling. The house seats about 25 people in rows of gray folding chairs, four chairs to a row. There is a name in black block letters on the back of each chair, ostensibly the names of women who donated the money to buy the chairs. Most of the names are unfamiliar, but one of them is "Katharine Hepburn."

At the far end of the room is a platform stage with no front curtain. The focal point of the setting is a twin-sized bed on the left side of the stage. The foot of the bed is downstage, the head is steeply raked upstage, facing the audience. Next to the bed, and comprising the back wall of the set, is an open clothes closet. The clothes hanging in it have been shoved to one side, revealing a curtained doorway that leads to the backstage area. On the right wall are a dressing table and a mirror—it has the look of a "girl's bedroom." On the right side of the stage, on the floor in front of the platform, is a large, black leather easy chair. A video monitor rests on a table directly behind and above the back of this chair.

Many of the spectators know each other. They chat quietly among themselves or read one of the several flyers, available at the door, that announce coming events, such as poetry and fiction readings, an evening of "Films by, for and about women at work," and the Working Girls Repertory Company's production of *The Snow Queen:* "a WOW holiday faerie tale." The flyer for this evening's performance, *The Heart of the Scorpion,* is printed in black ink on hot pink paper and combines a frilly valentine image with images of women and girls—the left arm of a woman wearing a bridal veil, for instance, is superimposed with the flexed arm of a muscle-bound male weight-lifter, and two little girls are pictured in ponytails and wearing skirts with their right arms up in the "right on" or "power to the people" gesture. The text reads:

a harlequin romance for the girls

the romantic notions...every mother's wish for her little girl...to find that perfect woman...run away to the Greek islands...and live happily ever after.

Who lives happily ever after, anyway?
Is there the perfect woman for your dreams?
What does your mother know anyway?

The four-page program for the performance is mostly filled with less-than-serious bio's of the actors, designers, film and video makers, and technicians. Some audience members chuckle as they read biographies such as:

CARMELITA TROPICANA (SUPER 8's)
I forgot to ask A.T. for a Bio, so I'll make one up. She is filthy rich and lives in Rio most of the year. She likes fast cars, fast women and Barry Manilow songs.

DIANE (JEEP) RIES (KIT)
After flunking out of college for brain surgery, she became a butcher. In her spare time, between slicing loins, she acts and sings barbershop quartets.

KATHY THOMAS (STAGE MANAGER)
Major garbage picker, plant assassin (hates green things) and stems from Brooklyn, NY.

As people chat and read—some seated, a few gathered around the small ticket table, some outside the door smoking cigarettes—a woman noisily clumps across the stage through the closet's curtained door to the backstage area and back again a few moments later to a seat in the audience. No one pays much attention. The general feeling is as much that of a social club as it is one of an audience waiting for a performance to begin.

Apparently, few people take the curtain time seriously as spectators continue to arrive until nearly 9:00 when the performance begins. As the lights dim, there are 20 people in the house. The audience is primarily lesbian.

Near the front of the seating section are the sound and lighting controls. The woman running tech for the show turns on a tape recorder and a Super 8 movie projector. Traditional Greek music can be heard along with a film shot from a car traveling down a tree-lined suburban street to a house. It is projected on a screen hanging over the stage. The film is accompanied by a woman's voice reciting a corny monolog about "home." The audience laughs through most of this short film, which ends with a pan from the house to a full-length shot of a white horse in the yard. As the horse walks directly up to the camera, its mouth is moving in such a way that it appears to be delivering the monolog. The film ends as its nose fills the screen.

The performers make little effort to be quiet as they take their places in the blackout that follows the film. When the lights come up, the play begins. It is fitting that the focal point of the stage is a bed, since the story that unfolds is typical of Harlequin romance novels, except that all the players in this love story are women, as well as all of the characters they play. Unlike some gay male theatre where men perform in drag in order to portray heterosexual couples, women do not play men in this production: the couples are lesbian. There is only one man in the story, and he is represented by a life-size, homemade-looking stuffed dummy with a somewhat pig-like face. He has no lines.

While the plot focuses on a college student, Annabelle, and her unrequited love, Ran, it is frequently interrupted by romantic subplots. The play is comprised of many short scenes in several locations, as the action moves from Annabelle's hometown to a cruise around the Greek Isles. All locales are indicated by pieces of furniture and played in front of the bedroom setting. A lawn lounge chair, for instance, indicates that the scene is taking place on the deck of a ship.

Both Annabelle and the woman she loves, Ran, are performed by the playwright, Alice Forrester. Ran appears only on the video monitor, so that when the two characters speak to each other, Forrester is talking to a video image of herself. Because the monitor is centered right above the back of the black easy chair, and because Ran appears only in a head and shoulder shot, the image "reads" as Ran sitting in the chair. Furthermore, because the chair is large and seems to have a video monitor for a "head," even when the monitor is turned off Ran's presence in the action is felt—a kind of physicalization of the obsessive quality of unrequited love. Ran is always "there"—thought about, if not talked about.

The fact that the lovers are played by the same person seems not so much a comment on narcissism as an interesting staging technique and, perhaps, a statement about the sameness of same-sex relationships. Making all of the couples women not only parodies the Harlequin romance formula, but heterosexual relationships as well, in so far as they are grounded in polarities of sexual difference. Some of the play's biggest laughs come at moments when this similarity/difference dichotomy is thrown into relief, as it were, simply by virtue of all of the lovers being the same sex. Although, clearly, the production is devised primarily for entertainment, the intent to undermine the social and sexual values of the romance genre is evident.

The performing style is an exaggerated version of television soap opera acting. It is purposely bad, fairly consistently sloppy, and draws laughter from the audience in and of itself. Performers frequently deliver lines as if they are fishing for them. Toward the end of the play, a performer playing the role of Kit says to Ran, "Agree to that, Kit.... I mean Ran." During a dinner scene, the performer playing the role of the mom serves a salad to each person at the table and then shoves a plate of lettuce under Ran's nose, that is, in front of the video monitor. In proposing a toast, Annabelle holds her glass up and mimes clinking it together with Ran's glass which, of course, is on video—the tape recorded "clink" follows the action by a couple of beats.

Casual is the word for the way everything is handled. Some of the performers sit in the audience and enter for their scenes from these seats. At one point a performer exits down the aisle to a space near the ticket table behind the audience. Hearing rustling noises back there, some spectators turn around and see this performer near-naked in the process of changing her costume. Early in the performance, as the characters prepare for their Greek cruise, another short film is projected of a marina, obviously shot on Long Island or in New England rather than Greece. The camera pans by a boat with the name "Bad Girl" painted on its side. There may have been more film in the production, but the movie projector broke down after the marina sequence.

The audience laughed with, as opposed to laughing at, the performance throughout the evening. The curtain call brought warm, enthusiastic applause. Many spectators seemed to know the cast and stayed to talk with the performers. People involved in the show were busy spreading the word that there was another performance worth seeing about an hour later that night at the Club Chandalier.

The Wooster Group's *L.S.D.*
(...Just the High Points...)
(1985)

Arnold Aronson

The Wooster Group has been one of the most provocative and significant performance collectives of the past several years. As a descendant of The Performance Group, they continue to operate as an ensemble with all members contributing to all aspects of a work's evolution. Yet under the leadership of director Elizabeth LeCompte, they have evolved an esthetic closer in style and spirit to performance art or conceptual art. The acting at times approaches an intensity more often associated with the expressionistic style of many ensemble groups of the late '60s; the raw material and subject matter of the pieces often evolves from instinctual or subconscious sources; and at the same time the structure—the most dominant aspect of the performances—is highly formal and abstract.

Although not overly influenced by the deconstructionist theories of Derrida and others (LeCompte says she is aware of this critical movement but has not read any of the sources), the Group's recent work provides virtually the only example of deconstructionist ideas put into practice in the American theatre. Beginning with *Nayatt School*, the third part of *Three Places in Rhode Island,* and continuing through *Point Judith, Route 1 & 9* and now *L.S.D. (...Just the High Points...),* the Group has taken modern classics *(The Cocktail Party, Long Day's Journey into Night, Our Town* and *The Crucible)* as raw material upon which to construct theatre pieces. Out of these sources come fragments of scenes, characters, dialog and thematic material which are explored, reworked, echoed, quoted, blended and juxtaposed with fragments from popular, cultural and social history as well as events, ideas and situations that emerge from the personal and collective experiences of members of the Group. The staging also quotes the Group's performance

~~DADAIST/MANIFESTO/(1920)~~

L.S.D. MANIFESTO

~~Art~~ (Theatre) in its Execution and Direction is dependent on the Time in which it Lives, and (Theatre) Artists are creatures of their Epoch. The highest ~~Art~~ (Theatre) will be that which in its ~~conscious~~ Content presents the thousandfold Problems of the Day, the Art which has been visibly shattered by the Explosions of last Week, which is forever trying to collect its Limbs after yesterday's Crash. The best and most extraordinary Artists will be those who every hour snatch the tatters of their Bodies out of the frenzied cataract of Life, who,/~~with/bleeding/Hands/and/Hearts,~~ hold fast to the Intelligence of their Time. Has ~~Expressionism~~ (Today's Theatre) fulfilled our Expectations of such an Art, which should be an Expression of our most vital Concerns?

NO! NO! NO!

~~Have/the/Expressionists~~ (Has Today's Theatre) fulfilled our Expectations of an Art that burns the Essence of Life into our Flesh?

NO! NO! NO!

Under the Pretext of ~~Turning/Inward~~ (Organizational Survival), ~~the/Expressionists/in/Literature/and/Painting~~ (we) (the New York Theatre Scene) (Theatre in America) have banded together into a Generation which is already looking forward to Honorable Mention in the Histories of Literature and Art and aspiring to the most Respectable civic distinctions. On Pretext of carrying on Propaganda for the Soul, ~~they/(we)~~ they (dramatists and avant-gardists alike) have,/~~in/their/struggle/with/Naturalism,~~ found their way back to the ~~abstract~~ ~~//pathetic~~ (illustrative, falsely naturalistic) gestures (the Authoritative Voice, empathy with) which (allows the public to) presuppose a comfortable Life free from ~~Content~~ (Ambivalence) or ~~strife~~ (Contradiction)...Hatred (contempt) of ~~the/Press~~ (Popular Culture), hatred of ~~Advertising~~ (T.V.), hatred of ~~Sensations~~ (NOISE), are typical of People who prefer their armchair to the Noise (Life) of the Street, ~~and/who/even/make/it/a/point/of/pride/to/be/swindled/by/every/smalltime/Profiteer!~~ ~~That~~ (It is a) Sentimental Resistance to the Times, which are neither Better nor Worse, neither more Reactionary nor more Revolutionary than other Times, that Weak-kneed Resistance, flirting with Prayers and Incense ...(which attempts to find in the Theatre what it has Lost in the Church.)

~~DADA/!!!!!~~

L.S.D. !!!!!

~~gathered/together/to~~ put(s) forward a New ~~Art~~ (Theatre), from which ~~they~~ (we) Expect (Pursue) the Realization of New Ideals. What then is ~~Dadaism?~~ (L.S.D.)?
~~The/word/Dada~~ (L.S.D.) symbolizes the most Primitive Relation to the Reality of the Environment; with ~~Dadaism~~ (L.S.D.) a New Reality comes into its own. Life appears as a simultaneous Muddle of Noises, Colors and Spiritual Rhythms, which is taken unmodified into ~~Dadaist/Art~~ (the Theatre), with all the sensational Screams and Fevers of its Reckless everyday Psyche and with all its brutal Reality. This is the sharp dividing line separating ~~Dadaism~~ (L.S.D.) from all ~~artistic~~ (theatrical) Directions up until now and particularly from ~~FUTURISM~~ (POST-MODERNISM) which not long ago some ~~old/dodgeheads~~ (dodos) took to be a new version of Impressionist realization. ~~Dadaism/for/the/first/time~~ (L.S.D.) has ceased to take an (Exclusive) Aesthetic Attitude toward Life, and this it accomplishes by ~~tearing~~ (exploding) all the slogans of ~~Ethics~~ (Morality), ~~Culture~~ (Politics), and ~~Inwardness~~ (Psychology), which are merely cloaks for weak Muscles, into their Components...(TO BE CONTINUED)

(Performing Garage, 1984)
212-966-3651

history as scenic elements, props and the arrangement of space repeat, echo or transform from earlier productions. The result is somewhat like a modern city built upon the foundations and monuments of succeeding generations of earlier cultures—the past is supporting the present work, emerging through the new framework to add historic resonance and significance, but the new work is still unique.

L.S.D. became the most notorious of the Wooster Group's productions because of the legal entanglement that developed with playwright Arthur Miller, whose *The Crucible* made up the 20-minute second section of the performance. (In an early version of *L.S.D.*, the entire performance consisted of a manic 50-minute condensation of the play.) Miller threatened to bring legal action against the Group if they continued to use sections of his play. Subsequent attempts to play the section in gibberish and then to use new dialog (written by Michael Kirby) within the same structure failed to appease Miller, and the production was finally forced to close in January 1985.

The Group is no stranger to controversy. Their 1977 production of *Rumstick Road* was attacked for the unauthorized use of a recording of a telephone conversation with a psychiatrist. The use of blackface and apparently stereotypic depiction of blacks in *Route 1 & 9* cost them their New York State Council on the Arts funding for a year (although little mention was made of the use of blackface again in *L.S.D.*). And many people saw their production of Jim Strahs' *North Atlantic* as sexist.

In its penultimate form (prior to the Miller-forced changes), *L.S.D.* consisted of four parts and used material from *The Crucible,* writers and poets from the "beat" generation, the debates between Timothy Leary and G. Gordon Liddy, interviews with Ann Rower (a babysitter for the Leary household), and miscellaneous interviews, biographies and writings, live and recorded music, dance and video.

Rows of metal folding chairs on the floor and on low risers face a long narrow platform about four feet above floor level behind which, and separated from it, is a steeply raked stage. Both platform and stage are nearly the width of the Performing Garage. At the front of the raked stage, a table extends nearly the entire width. Performers, for the most part, sit behind the table, speaking many of their lines into microphones. It suggests, among other things, an interrogation committee, such as the House Un-American Activities Committee that was the ostensible target of Miller's play.

Behind the table is a metal framework structure representing a house. It has appeared in one form or another in almost every Group production since it was first used in *Nayatt School* (in which it echoed certain spaces in the previous *Rumstick Road).* The arrangement of space is essentially a reversal of that for *Nayatt School,* in which the audience sat on a high bleacher looking down at a table on a high platform and on the main performing space and house on floor level.

L.S.D. is in four sections. Part I, entitled "Newton," consists of random readings by the male performers from the works of Aldous Huxley, Arthur Koestler, Timothy Leary, Alan Watts, William Burroughs, Jack Kerouac, Allen Ginsberg, John Bryan and Dr. Charles Slack (the latter two being biographical works on Leary), interspersed with material from Ann Rower, the babysitter.

Part II, "Salem," originally the excerpts from *The Crucible,* has become in the final version "scenes from *The Hearing,* a play by Michael Kirby with The Wooster Group." Part III, "Millbrook," presents a "stoned" version of *The Crucible* in rehearsal (taken from a video recording) together with live rock music and video images of Wooster Group performer Ron Vawter in Miami. The final section, entitled "Miami," is a fragment of one of the Liddy-Leary debates and a dance "impersonating 'Donna Sierra and the Del Fuegos.'"

The Performance

Part I begins with all but one of the men seated at the table facing the audience. They have microphones, although some mikes are shared. One performer (the one reading Jackie Leary) is in the "trough" between the stage and the platform. Nancy Reilly, as the Babysitter, sits at the left of the table with a boom mike and earphones. Wearing heavy black-rimmed glasses and speaking in an exaggerated nasal-toned Brooklyn-like accent, she creates the impression of a caricatured phone operator or radio announcer. (Throughout the scene, she will listen to a taped interview with Ann Rower and repeat lines from the tape as they seem appropriate in context, although it will not necessarily be clear to the audience that she is listening to or repeating anything.) Jim Clayburgh, the Group's designer and technical person, sits at the left end of the table behind a phonograph and other sound equipment. He plays a Maynard Ferguson album, and shows the jacket to the audience while reading parts of the liner notes. He will control sound levels and act as a time-keeper for the other readings.

Ron Vawter, next at the table, functions as an emcee and onstage director, as well as reading texts by Huxley and Koestler. He introduces the performers, exercises some control over the sequence and flow of readings, and enforces time limits as he wishes—according to the "rules" that he announces, each reading is to last only one minute. There is no predetermined sequence or selection of passages to be read. (In early versions, the performers frequently tried to find passages that would answer the previous one.) It is clear that these are performers reading the works of others, and there is frequent banter and commentary among them.

When *L.S.D.* was performed for a month at the Boston Shakespeare

Company, Michael Kirby, who read Watts and Burroughs, could not participate during the week. His performance was videotaped, and his place at the table was taken by a video monitor. Later, it was decided to keep the video (with the sound muted most of the time), so the audience is presented with two Kirbys, whose actions sometimes coincide, sometimes not. The Watts readings are on the video; Vawter asks the technician to turn up the sound or rewind the tape as necessary. (The cast could watch the monitor on a platform above and behind the audience.) Kirby indicates that he is Burroughs by wearing a cowboy hat.

There is a two- or three-minute break between Parts I and II as the women take their places at the table; other performers make minor costume changes and arrange props. A metal bedframe is placed under the table across the "trough" at about center stage. Rising through the bed frame, an adolescent actor dressed as a Puritan girl stands in the trough, his head on a pillow. It appears he is in bed, though no attempt is made to create an illusion. The women are all in period costume; the men are in contemporary dress. The men speak into microphones; the women do not. Kate Valk, playing Tituba, is in blackface and speaks in an Aunt Jemima accent. She also plays Mary Warren, but remains in blackface; the characters are identified by signs hung in front of her place at the table. For the most part, all lines are spoken from the actors' places at the table. Some words and phrases, all from the Miller script, are chanted loudly in chorus. The teenager (Matthew Hansell) who played Judge Danforth in *The Crucible* and is now playing the chairman of an investigating committee, walks the narrow front platform. Characters sometimes stand; during the hysteria/hallucination scenes the women run frantically in the trough, and some characters hide under the table. But it is in no way a realistic staging. Just as costumes mix with street clothes, so theatrical action mixes with the atmosphere of an interrogation or, perhaps, a staged reading. The lines are generally delivered at a frenetic clip, sometimes, especially in the case of Ron Vawter, barked out at a painfully loud volume. Yet it is strangely understated. Emotion, if present, seems to be indicated by volume and speed. Psychological realism has been undercut and eliminated. The scene ends with a dance in which three women in full skirts stand facing front at equal intervals on the narrow platform while three men, pants rolled up, sit behind them, their legs dangling off the stage. It appears, as the women move, that they have incongruous dancing legs coming out from under their long skirts.

The Crucible text consisted of "just the high points"—fragments of scenes. But the scenes were presented in order, and there was no rearranging. "I didn't just want to throw the text up in the air and have it come down on the floor and rearrange it," explained LeCompte. "It was very important to me to take full sequences of the text without changing sequences of lines. There was no reversing or adding lines to make meaning or to make the story 'work.' I wanted to make very clear that we were not destroying or dislocating the text. It was an adaptation, not a deconstruction."

As *The Hearing,* the presentation is identical. The text, however, seems to be about espionage or treason trials. Finding a needle in a poppet, for instance, becomes the discovery of a secreted roll of microfilm. The apparent analogy to the Alger Hiss trial of the '50s is, in effect, a de-historicization of Miller's play. Acting copies of *The Crucible* are placed in pockets behind chairs in the audience, and acts and scenes are announced so that the spectators can follow along in the Miller text as the Kirby/Wooster Group text is being spoken. If a performer "accidentally" slips into lines from the original, Vawter sounds a loud buzzer.

Part III appears to be an attempt to rehearse the previous scene in the midst of a party. The performers are drinking, moving about the stage, giggling, reading lines and losing their places—and their interest—in the text. Two video monitors show scenes of Miami, primarily a man (Ron Vawter) making calls from phone booths. This section is somewhat disconcerting to the audience because, unlike the previous two sections, it is not readily apparent whether it is indeterminate or fixed and to what extent the performers are acting. It also includes deadpan recreations of incidents at the Leary house as narrated by the Babysitter. For example, when she describes someone running out of the house, an actor stands and runs in place. When the narration describes people pounding on a door, several actors stand and mime knocking while unemotionally chanting, "Let us in." Toward the end of the scene, several performers take up musical instruments—electric and acoustic guitars and drums—and play fragments of old Velvet Underground songs.

In Part IV, the video monitors project a Brecht-like legend: "What is this dancing," a line from *The Crucible.* Certain of the performers, still at the table, recreate a scene from the Liddy-Leary debates (the text of which is printed in the program). It begins with an obscene poem by Liddy and goes to an attack on Leary's morality by a Vietnam vet who was blinded by a shotgun blast fired by people under the influence of LSD. Leary's reply is confused and pathetic. This is followed by a grotesque and intense dance by four performers in cartoon-style "Spanish" costumes; the men even have grease-paint mustachios. "Donna Sierra" stands on the front platform with the men on floor level on either side of her with sneakers on their hands. Donna Sierra dances to the accompaniment of pseudo-South American dance music. As she finishes a passage, the men slam the soles of the shoes onto the platform with great energy and flair. She and the men glare at each other for a moment; the action is repeated several times.

Creation of the Performance

One of the criticisms hurled at The Wooster Group following the *Route 1 & 9* controversy was, according to LeCompte, "Why don't these people just do a play?" She decided to do a whole season of American classic plays—one a week, like summer stock. *The Crucible* had been in her mind for a few years. She had never read the play; she tends to choose texts based on a visual or aural image, but she was fascinated by a line of John Proctor's dialog that Spalding Gray had once mentioned to her: "Elizabeth, your justice would freeze beer." As LeCompte recalls,

> It was such a comic strip image—it combined modern comic strip imagery with phony Puritan dialect. It was like a great meshing of two cultural languages: phony languages—both of them. By changing the tenses in lines like, "She were not . . . ," it makes it sound like really old language, but both of them are ersatz. I love the language as a mask. I don't like working with kitchen-sink realism. That is, I *do* like working with it, but as a mask, as a part, not as a whole piece. I felt we could do this play better than anyone in creation because of our particular distance. It's a distanced political play that takes its power from the situation in which it was written, not from the internal relationships. That is so often the way in which our work is conceived.
>
> I also remembered that there was a black woman in *The Crucible* and that a white author had written it with a black dialect. I considered that a similar problem to what we had faced in *Route 1 & 9*. Why was Miller not told that he could not write a black character? I thought it was an interesting irony and an injustice to us and a lack of understanding about what we had done.

LeCompte's productions have been typified by scenes of hysteria and manic activity. She enjoyed the idea that such scenes were written into Miller's script—it was Miller's hysteria, not hers.

At the same time, the Group was working on staged interpretations of records. They had recently done a piece called *Hula*. They were creating film images based on an album called *LSD*. LeCompte saw a connection between the two projects, and they eventually merged. At the first performance of excerpts of *The Crucible,* the record of *LSD* was played as a sort of curtain raiser.

Much of the show evolved out of happenstance and accident, such as the introduction of Kirby and video. In its early stages, there was a cast of 18, with the girls being played by women over 50. But the need to tour the production necessitated a smaller cast. Miller's injunction, of course, radically altered the production. "I love any kind of limitation," says LeCompte, "It's golden for me; I grab it. But it's always from the outside—practical circumstances rather than esthetic choice, though I swear it probably comes together as the same thing." When the limitations do not occur by chance, LeCompte tends to impose them, constantly undercutting easy or obvious theatricality. At one point in Part II, for example, Kirby stood up to deliver a line to the teenager playing the judge. He is very tall, angular, bald and has deep-set eyes; the mere act of standing was menacing and theatrical. LeCompte insisted that he remain almost seated: the effect was to come from elsewhere.

The Crucible is probably one of the most frequently performed plays in high schools and colleges and, as such, has a certain degree of instant recognition, as a sort of theatrical icon. LeCompte set out to stage "the perfect high school play," which to her meant giving it a certain sense of pageantry combined with "bad" acting. This image was reinforced by the presentations and tableaux she saw at Salem. Furthermore, high school productions are frequently adaptations, focusing only on the "high points," which is how the Group approached the text. The speed evolved in an attempt to get over boring sections. "Whenever I got bored," explained LeCompte, "or the actors were unable to enliven the text or make it work, I'd just say, 'Go fast and get it over quickly.'"

> It became a game structure. Whenever anyone was bored, they would go fast. Ron [Vawter] would buzz, and we'd have to get the whole thing in before he buzzed. Or they'd have to overlap so fast that they lost their place and got demerited five points. They would lose the sense of trying to make meaning out of the characters and would just get to the rhythms. This helped us when we had to switch to a new text or gibberish.

Placing the women in costume created instant historical and literary connections and recognition. The costumes have become images that, in the terms of semiotician C.S. Peirce, are "indexical signs" pointing not only to Salem but to Miller's play itself. But for LeCompte, the motivation was more sensual. She was strongly impressed by the textures and materials of the dresses of early poppets she had seen and wanted to project that soft sensuality. "Whereas, when I put men into those costumes, it hardened it into a play," she explained. She also compared it in motivation to the late work of Cezanne. "He doesn't finish a line," she notes. "He leaves the canvas showing here and there. It gives a space and an air; it doesn't solidify it into a form that's not breakable. I can't stand it when something becomes perfect, enclosed. I like to leave the system open."

The space as mentioned, was a conscious mirroring of *Nayatt School.* The use of a table was in part an intuitive decision, in part a reflection of the political nature of the repertoire of plays that had been considered (the image of a meeting hall, interrogation room, etc.), and in part an image that grew out of *Route 1 & 9.* In the latter play, there was a small table inside the frame house. LeCompte saw the long table as "growing out of this." This small table reappears in the upstage house in *L.S.D.* as a reference back to that production. But despite the tenuous political associations, the space is in no way a direct consequence of the script. It is an independent element.

The microphones referred to a hearing or investigation, but their use was purely esthetic. LeCompte wanted to play with the contrast of normal and amplified voices. The rapid juxtaposition of such voices causes information to be lost—as when eyes adjust to sudden shifts from light to dark or vice versa. LeCompte noted that "the live performer has to shout very loud and give an immense emotional output to equal a whisper on a microphone. So a lot of the performance played off huge emotional and vocal outputs against very tiny verbal outputs into the mike." Also, working against expectations, the mikes were given to the men, who are conventionally assumed to have louder voices. "The women got the costumes, the men got the mikes," says LeCompte with amusement.

The dance at the end of Part II, says LeCompte, came about simply because they felt they needed a dance there. The image was simple and childlike, resulting from the disjunctive images suggested by the levels of the set. There is also a suggestion of the disjunction of male and female, but that was not a primary impulse.

Once the connection between Leary/LSD and *The Crucible* had been made, the rest of the performance began to evolve. The opening sequence provided a cultural context for the work. The writers whose works are read are the ones in the Leary circle or ones that affected that generation. Although Miller is of the previous generation, much of his writing occurred simultaneously with Ginsberg, Kerouac, et al. LeCompte says that since she had never read any of these people ("I'm not a reader"), she used this as a chance for "self-education." The original score was taken from old television shows like "You Are There" or the Steven Allen show "Meeting of Minds" that set up round-table discussions among historical figures. But, LeCompte noted, what came up in the random selections reverberated throughout the rest of the performance on that day.

The use of chance and indeterminacy to structure the reading section was not consciously based on John Cage, but LeCompte acknowledges that through the art world, The Performance Group, and the theatre of the past two decades, she probably absorbed these ideas. "It's all there. I've just taken it. It's all recycled junk."

The babysitter in Parts I and III was equally a result of chance. Ann Rower saw an early version of *The Crucible* and wrote to LeCompte that this reminded her of certain episodes at the Leary house. LeCompte felt that the connections could form the basis of the third part. They interviewed Rower, and Nancy Reilly began working with the tapes, trying to capture Rower's tone and delivery.

Part III came about as a result of trying, in LeCompte's words, to "disintegrate" *The Crucible*. She recalled the ongoing discussion in the '60s as to whether artists could create while on acid or whether creation was a rational process. So she decided to take a section of *The Crucible* that the company already knew very well, have the actors take LSD and see what happened. She videotaped the result, although frequently she taped only closeups of the performers rather than the whole stage. The result, LeCompte felt, was the "disintegration" she had sought. The scene, therefore, is an attempt by the actors to recreate 15 minutes of this event using the videotape as text and score; they recreated their actions and dialog exactly as recorded. When the video did not show them, they tried to remember what they were doing and thinking.

The Leary anecdotes were overlaid on this scene—"etched in on top," as LeCompte says. "When it comes to that reenactment, the performers are still playing out the LSD *Crucible* underneath. They have to do both."

Part IV, of course, is derived from the Liddy-Leary debates, but the derivation of the concluding dance is less obvious. LeCompte calls it her "take" on Indian dance. When seeing certain dances in India, she was fascinated not by the technique of the dance itself or the movements of any section or raga, but by the way in which the dancer went in and out of "character" between the ragas. "To watch the dancer drop out to prepare for the next raga was the most exciting thing for me—to watch that transformation. This dance is kind of a play on that. Kate Valk picks up these idiot ragas—there's nothing to them—but the whole thing is about the change of persona. From the preparation to the execution of the dance with such incredible aplomb. That's what dancing is about! It doesn't matter what you do, it's how you do it." The dance can be disconcerting because it is humorous yet almost sinister in its intensity and persistence. This aspect of it, and the choice of this dance to conclude the play, is tied up in the themes that LeCompte finds in the piece.

Themes and Meaning

Superficially, at least, the "meanings" and messages of *L.S.D. (. . . Just the High Points. . .)* seem obvious. So much so that certain critics tended to dismiss the work as mere self indulgence. One critic commented on the oddity of taking Miller's play, which used the Brechtian technique of historification to make a contemporary point, and re-setting it in contemporary period. Certainly there are clear themes of mass hysteria, hallucination, persecution and paranoia. The latter two enter into the Group's thinking on the piece, but they form a minor component.

The attacks on previous Group works led LeCompte to feel "hounded," much the way she felt Leary was.

Q: Do you think that you are being hara ssed for your unorthodox beliefs?
LEARY: I don't use the term "harassment ," and I have no paranoid theories abou t conspiracy. The game I am involved in is set out with exquisite precision. Wh at I am doing has been done by people i n every generation in the past. It's li ke the Harvard-Yale game. It's played o

L.S.D. MANIFESTO (2)

ut every year. Now, Harvard isn't haras sing Yale. The game between those who k now that man can change and become divi ne in this lifetime and want to teach p eople how to do it completely threatens the establishment. In every generation you say, "No, it's all been done and se ttled, and just get your good lawyer-pr iest and do what we tell you to do." An d this dialogue between the establishme nt and the utopian visionaries will ine vitably exist in every historical era. It's played fairly. The fact that they want to hound me out of existence is ri ght. They should, just like the Harvard defensive team wants to throw the offen sive quarterback for a loss. I have no complaint about this; I'm perfectly goo d-humored about it. The more energy tha t is directed against me, the more ener gy that is available for me. It's the p erfect physical law of jujitsu - the mo re government and professional establis hment dynamism that is set off against what we're doing is just a sign to us t hat we're doing fine.
(TO BE CONTINUED)

The Performing Garage (1984)

I knew there was a prejudice against this way of perceiving the universe—now more than ever. The '60s were dead, and that brief flurry of "expanding consciousness," of seeing the world in a fragmented or different way, was now considered dangerous. I knew that that was a time that coincided with a kind of paranoia. There was something I identified with in *The Crucible* script because I felt hounded. So I identified with the emotional core of that. And I identified with Leary's sad desperation and his being hounded. I recognized the danger of stepping outside the system that far. It was a self-criticism that I was going through deeply. I hated Leary, I didn't identify positively with Leary, yet at the same time, I also recognized that I was in the place that Leary was in that sense. I was saying that there was another way of viewing politics that is not literal, issue-oriented—it's not attached, so to speak. My intuitive way of making theatre was being called irresponsible, and that was the main problem with Leary—he was always being attacked as irresponsible. He was working with something and not taking responsibility for the effects on people. There was some connection there, though I hated Leary. There was some criticism there that I was attracted to. I was forcing myself to look at the worst side of the way we work as a theatre company, and what art is, and what we do with it. But I tried to keep that connection tenuous. I just tried to locate an emotional center that felt right, and worked from there and watched the connections evolve.

This theme of taking responsibility for one's ideas or art became most pronounced in Part IV, in the scene in which Leary is unable to respond to the attack on his teachings. "I began to see something new in Leary," explains LeCompte.

The only thing he could say, of course, was, "I feel very sad." First of all he said, "I've never condoned violence," because this man accused him of condoning violence, just as people accused us of racism. But at the same time, he couldn't say, "That's not my fault." He could only express sadness, which is all that I could ever come to about the *Route 1 & 9* controversy. I could never get beyond that; I could never figure out what I had to do with it, or why. I always felt that it was the flip side of anything that's radical. I always identified with the women radicals who, when they bombed something and someone was killed inadvertently, didn't know what to say, how to justify the radical belief that the change must come through violence and individual violence to someone who was "innocent." I've never been able to reconcile that; I don't think anyone has or ever will be able to reconcile that. We have to recognize that there is that irreconcilable thing. And it was right there in that speech. So we finally decided that the last section in Part IV would be a question—an unanswerable one. It would have to be juxtaposed for me with my work. And my work was the dance. That is, the dance represents all the work I've ever done in the past seven years. And it is all the idiocy, all the threat, all the fun, all the violence.

The inexorable repetition of the dance movements at the end of the play became for LeCompte an equivalent to the unanswerable yet inexorable questioning. The answer to "What is this dancing," became, in essence, "My art." In a sense, then, *L.S.D.* is not about paranoia or persecution—it is about dancing.

The persecution theme, however, is clear throughout. The video images of Part III are seen by LeCompte as a sign of the future. Just as Lenny Bruce was banned from performing in New York, LeCompte fantasized about the

Wooster Group as a "troupe of ne'er-do-well drug addicts who could never perform in New York any more." Ironically, this has come true in a way because *L.S.D.* was forced to close.

> The only place we could ever perform *L.S.D.* would be in a hotel in Miami where Miller would never hear about it. So it becomes Ronnie down there casing out old hotels where the Wooster Group will eventually end up in the '80s performing. I also think of it as that we're very old, and it's an old retiree community. This was overlayed afterward. When Ronnie made the film, we didn't know that we would use it in this way, so Ken [Kobland, the photographer] just had him walking around Miami making phone calls, doing what people do. When I saw it, I said, "Oh, its Ronnie trying to find a place for us to work."

Further fantasizing on these images led to the idea of Donna Sierra and the Del Fuegos, who have cancelled their gig at the Shelbourne. The Group pretends they are Spanish and takes over. "It was just my kind of spinoff on what would happen to artists in the future, banned from their city, away from their home and wandering the backwaters of American culture, picking up whatever tidbits they could to make a living," explains LeCompte. It also ties in with Liddy and Leary, who now tour the country like old vaudeville performers, trying to cash in on some of their old glory.

One other important theme is the contrast of male and female. Part I is a clear reflection of society. The writers whose works are read are all male; the one female onstage is a babysitter. The Group wanted to include female writers from the period, but who? Burroughs' wife wrote, but there is apparently nothing readily available.

The male-versus-female theme is reinforced in Miller's play, in which women are the villains and are essentially depicted as the root of evil. As one of only four or five men who were executed for witchcraft in Salem, John Proctor, for LeCompte, is more identified as a woman. LeCompte sees Miller making this identification because Proctor lacks moral clarity. "That's one of my things about male writers of the '50s," says LeCompte, "their ability to pinpoint right and wrong. Miller is so clear about it. I can't be clear. As a woman of the '60s, '70s and '80s, I can't be clear. I don't know who the enemies are. I don't know if there are enemies." Whereas some critics have seen the ambiguity of this and other Wooster Group works as a failing, LeCompte sees it as a strength and as a necessary result of the culture and the process of their art.

Semiotics

A knowledge of these themes and ideas might help explain the process of generating the performance and enhance the understanding of text and images, but it cannot fully justify experience. Clearly, many of these themes are private, not readily accessible to a general audience. And insofar as certain motifs are comprehensible, they tend to be seen as trite. Is this merely a play about paranoia and persecution? Has The Wooster Group merely chosen to combine two symbols of persecution—Timothy Leary and the Salem witches (and, through Miller's implied analogy, current-day political dissidents)—in order to make a statement about artistic freedom? The history of the Group, with its focus on formal esthetics over sociopolitical messages makes the answer obvious. Since *Rumstick Road,* the Group's pieces have been about performance itself, which is to say, semiotics. Biographical, social and literary substance have provided the raw material upon which these explorations were founded.

In terms of the text itself, what the Group does falls into the general category of deconstruction. The group takes an existing piece of dramatic literature, in this case *The Crucible,* and through a process of segmenting the text, repetitions and stripping away theatrical and dramatic contexts, finds resonances, meanings, textures and references in the text that were either not readily apparent or were not originally intended. The new, deconstructed text becomes a commentary on the old one. The process is naive in the sense that it does not proceed from a theoretical basis; it is an instinctual response by artists to other art. Its roots may be found in John Cage's suggestion that the way to deal with past work is to quote it, not reconstruct or repeat it.

But in creating a total *mise en scène,* the process seems closer to a manipulation of theatrical signifiers and icons than to any formal deconstructive process. (Besides, just as semioticians are still grappling with ways to analyze the multilayered signals of theatrical performance, the ideas of deconstruction seem not to have moved beyond the literary field.) The Wooster Group's work seems to fall into two areas. One might be called "layering," the creation of successive layers of sign systems based upon a foundation of conventional theatrical signs. The other, a sort of reversal, is desemanticization, the conscious attempt to divorce signs from their semantic content.

A good example of these processes is the use of blackface. Tituba was written by Miller as a black character. This in itself functions as an icon. The audience immediately thinks in terms of slave or servant, the echoes of this relationship in today's society, the association of this character with voodoo, as well as a host of stereotypical images regarding personality, vocal patterns, movement, etc. By playing it in blackface, the Group is making a sociopolitical statement. Blackface is considered by many to be racist (and in many places is illegal) and conjures up images of minstrel shows and, especially in the vocal patterns adopted by the actress in this case, such popular entertainment figures as Amos and Andy. Thus, an American theatrical tradition is invoked—a tradition now viewed with some embarrassment—and the assumptions that would allow Arthur Miller to write a black slave character are called into question. At the same time, a purely theatrical sign system is being emphasized: This is an actress who, through the use of certain conventional signs (costume, makeup, physical characterization), is presenting a symbol that the audience interprets as Tituba. In terms of pure physical iconography, what she is doing is no different than what an actor playing Hamlet or Willy Loman or "Moon" (in the Mechanical's representation of "Pyramus and Thisbe" in *A Midsummer Night's Dream)* does.

But then, the sign becomes separated from its object. When the same actress appears as Mary Warren, she is still in blackface. Although the character of Mary Warren is a servant, we know, from Miller's text and from history, that she is not black. Moreover, the actress drops the other signifying elements that refer to some image of a black person. The spectator is forced to either ignore the makeup, assume that the actress is representing a black woman playing a "white" role, or that there is some sociopolitical significance to the incongruity. (In fact, the presentation is simply a result of insufficient time for the actress to remove her makeup—but the signs remain for the audience to read.) When the text changed from *The Crucible* to *The Hearing,* the Group maintained the iconography, yet it became (or could have become) totally irrelevant within the informational context.

LeCompte described the effect as being like the two images of a stereopticon coming together to create 3-D. "But here, it's two slightly different frames that mesh together and overlap each other. You have a sense of two colliding images or overlapped images that are slightly different," she says.

Although she does not use it in the strictly semiotic sense, LeCompte repeatedly refers to the Miller text and associated symbols (such as the Puritan costumes) as icons. But in the context of *L.S.D.,* these icons point not only outward—toward historic and conventional people, places and ideas—but inward, toward themselves.

Picking up on an essentially Brechtian esthetic (one that was reinforced by director Richard Schechner with the Wooster Group's predecessor, The Performance Group), LeCompte allows each theatrical element to develop independently—to "speak in its own language," as Schechner once said. Thus, the setting is clearly a theatrical creation. It is not a bare stage or empty space, yet it does not mesh iconographically with *The Crucible* or the Leary sections. "I don't ever try to make one part of the play illustrate another," she comments. "All of the elements of the piece have their own life. They are not supportive or secondary." Thus, the physical setting refers more to earlier Group productions than it does to any semantic information contained in the text.

There are many more examples of layering and separation that could be explored. Most interesting are the segments, such as the "stoned *Crucible*" sequence, in which the text and score are recreations of their own actions.

Because critics have rarely been willing to look at The Wooster Group's work as a developing and interconnected whole, and because there is an attempt to decode the works in terms of a more conventional information structure, the pieces tend to be seen only in terms of their superficial qualities. The *Village Voice* review demonstrated the critic's attempt to reunite the semantic content with the iconographic image. In Part III, the "video Kirby" aims a gun at a woman holding a glass of water on her head. There is a live gunshot, the woman puts the glass down, and another performer says, to the monitor, "Hey, Bill. Bill, you missed." The multiplicity of signifiers (performer, character, video image—which indicates a disjuncture in time as well as place—blank pistol to represent real gun, reference to circus act and William Tell, the ability to fairly realistically convey the idea of a gunshot coupled with the greater difficulty of depicting a person being shot, etc.) force the audience to interpret the moment on many realistic, theatrical and social levels. It is also funny. The *Voice* critic, however, pointed out that Burroughs shot his wife. Is this moment in the play a reference to an actual occurrence? Was Kirby "playing" Burroughs on the video? Most importantly, is the historical reference, which is obviously there, the significant aspect, or is it the layering, the multiplicity of theatrical messages? If the Wooster Group pieces can begin to be looked at in this way, their complexity and resonances, their significance in the development of a theatrical avant-garde, become clearer.

Index